HOWARD
CARTER

Also by H.V.F. Winstone

Captain Shakespear
Gertrude Bell
Leachman: 'O.C. Desert'
The Illicit Adventure
Uncovering the Ancient World
Woolley of Ur
Lady Anne Blunt

H.V.F. Winstone

HOWARD
CARTER

and the discovery of the tomb of

TUTANKHAMUN

barzan

Copyright © H.V.F. Winstone 2008

The right of H.V.F. Winstone to be identified
as the author of this Work has been asserted
by him in accordance with the
Copyright, Designs and Patents Act 1988

Published by
Barzan Publishing
Manchester and Beirut

Windrush Millennium Centre
Alexandra Road
Manchester M16 7WD

www.barzanpress.com

ISBN 1-905521-05-7

A CIP record for this book
is available from the British Library

Printed and bound by SNP Leefung Limited

Design and production: Keith Howe

In memory of Dr Roger Moorey

Late Keeper of Antiquities of the Ashmolean Museum
whose help and support was cherished
by a generation of writers and scholars

FOREWORD

By Henrietta McCall

During the decade and a half that have elapsed since the publication of the first edition of Victor Winstone's definitive biography, interest in Howard Carter and the discovery of Tutankhamun's tomb has gathered pace. Ancient Egypt is now on the national curriculum and as one of the most enthralling chapters in the rediscovery of that vanished civilisation, the boy king is enjoying something of a boom. Tutankhamun and the story of Carter's tenacious quest for his tomb can now be studied on line by visiting the website of the Griffith Institute and finding *Tutankhamun: An Anatomy of an Excavation,* where a database of 5,398 finds (including the magnificent black-and-white photographs taken by Harry Burton) can be accessed. The site also lists the most up-to-date scholarly publications on the topic.

But Tutankhamun has always had his frivolous side, originating at the time of his rediscovery which came so soon after the First World War when people were struggling just to survive. The events in the Valley of the Kings let a bright shaft of sunshine into a desperately bleak world, and together with rising hemlines, flappers, the Charleston, the early cinema, Tutmania - as it came to be called - inspired things as disparate as jewellery, face powder, furniture, sweet peas, and cigarettes, the Tutankhamun shimmy, as well as a thousand movie palaces, now mostly bingo halls. This scholarly book combines a dramatic account of the search for Tutankhamun with a forthright appreciation of the public response and the political battles that Carter fought at every stage of the quest; and it does not shy away from the social and psychological conflicts that inevitably affected the relationship between the self-taught artist digger from rural Norfolk and the distinguished academics around him. And it sits well with the Griffith Institute's on-line feast.

Such works are a welcome corrective to television's inclination to stray into the byways of conjecture. It is the period feel of the discovery that tends to surface in documentaries such as the 2005 mini-series produced by the BBC. A great deal of artistic licence is taken with the material, the characters involved in the rediscovery of the lost king, and the sequence of events; and there is the inevitable slant that political correctness forces on every aspect of our viewing. It is not appropriate to look at the events which unfolded in the Valley of the Kings in the 1920s in the light of what we consider to be the superior and enlightened hindsight of the 21st century. The past is a different country. The achievements of Carter and the support he received from the fifth Earl of Carnarvon must be looked at in the context of their time. We should indeed continue to marvel at the sheer brilliance of Carter and his bulldog determination to find what he knew he was looking for.

The 'Curse' of Tutankhamun continues to excite controversy. No serious Egyptologists give it credence but that does not prevent their deriving a great deal of amusement from any new attempt to establish its efficacy. Interesting new research suggests that the Curse was in fact invented by Victorian writers long before Tutankhamun appeared on the scene. In the USA, it was Louisa M. Alcott, the hitherto blameless author of *Little Women* who began a craze for revenge by mummies. Her short thriller, *The Lost Pyramid or, The Mummy's Curse* published in 1869, tells a tale charged with dark eroticism in which the young heroine collapses on her wedding day in a coma, from which she will never recover, brought on by smelling a beautiful but evil flower grown from red seeds stolen from the mummy of an ancient sorceress found in a pyramid. The work of later Victorian writers such as H. Rider Haggard, Bram Stoker and Sax Rohmer created a base to which could be added with a certain horrified fascination the sudden deaths of some of those involved in the discovery of Tutankhamun's tomb.

There have also been conspiracy theories, including one which suggests that papyri describing the true account of the biblical exodus of the Israelites from Egypt were found in the tomb (in fact, there were no written records in the tomb). It is argued that these alleged papyri were necessarily suppressed because they were found at a time (i.e. the 1920s) when they would have exacerbated hostility to the Balfour Declaration and the setting up of a Jewish state in Palestine; indeed, it has been suggested that like Sigmund Freud's version of the Moses story that came a few years later, identifying the monotheism of Moses with Akhenaten's apostasy, they would have cast doubt on the very foundation stone of all Western religion, Judaic, Christian and Moslem, and caused unacceptable disenchantment throughout the world.

A new appendix gives deserved acknowledgement to the role of Almina, Countess of Carnarvon, who died in her nineties in 1969. Hers was a fabulous life. The only, but illegitimate, daughter of Baron Alfred de Rothschild, she was given a massive dowry when she married the fifth Earl of Carnarvon in 1895, and it was her money which financed Carter's excavations in the Valley of the Kings. None of her subsequent vast inheritance was so fortuitously spent, nor did it yield such a massive return on its investment in intellectual, financial or artistic terms. The author gives us a miniature portrait of the Edwardian pocket Venus who played her own crucial part in the remarkable and extraordinary rediscovery of Tutankhamun's tomb.

One aspect of the life of Howard Carter which has only recently begun to be revalued (thanks to this book) is the regard in which Carter himself is held. Probably through jealousy, the Egyptological world closed ranks behind him, and although his own high-handed behaviour towards the Egyptian Antiquities Service did not help his cause or his reputation, he was undeserving of the academic contempt in which he was held by successive generations of Egyptologists. After devoting thirty years of his life to Egypt, acquiring as he did wide experience both as a field archaeologist and an expert recorder of artefacts, as well as being an accomplished painter in watercolours, he surely deserved to be ranked not only as one of their own, but the Egyptologist who made the single most sensational archaeological discovery of all time.

This biography made the first advances in putting Howard Carter's achievement into a proper context and in redressing the balance of years of grudging recognition. As the author makes clear in his introduction, he and I met some twenty years ago through my Oxford dissertation on Howard Carter. I am delighted that a new and supplemented edition of his book enables me to contribute these few words of introduction to a work with which I have been associated from the outset. I am also delighted that its sensitive, balanced and graphic description of the life of the most prodigiously successful yet most neglected of all archaeologists will be available to a new generation of readers.

Henrietta McCall
Department of the Ancient Near East
The British Museum
January 2006

But of all the learned, those who pretend to investigate remote antiquity have least to plead in their own defence when they carry their passion to a faulty excess. They are generally found to supply by conjecture the want of record, and then by perseverance are wrought up into a confidence of the truth of opinions, which even to themselves at first appeared founded only in imagination.

Oliver Goldsmith
quoted in Carter's rough notebook number 15

CONTENTS

INTRODUCTION
& ACKNOWLEDGEMENTS

In order to avoid repetition and needless explanation, I preface my original introduction with a few words about the new edition. The version that saw the light of day in 1991, published by Constable, was well received by the reading public in several countries and by reviewers world wide. It quickly passed through hard and soft back editions in the English-speaking world, and in Germany and Italy. and it had a modest book club airing in the United Kingdom. Now that my new Anglo-Arab publisher Barzan Press has embarked on a programme designed to bring all my books back into print it is promised a new and vigorous lease of life, and I thank the founder chairman of that company, Dr Mohammad AlRasheed, for the impeccable standard of book production and fidelity to his authors that have become his company's hallmark in just a few years. I would also like to acknowledge the support of Barzan directors Peter Harrigan and Richard Fye, and the company's editorial director Lionel Kelly; and of my design and production consultant Keith Howe. And I thank author Clara Semple for so willingly searching on my behalf among the photographic riches of the Griffith Institute and the V&A Museum for water-colours by Carter. In the early years of publication I received most helpful observations from several readers, including some distinguished figures in archaeology; among them Mr John R Gardiner, younger son of the late Alan Gardiner who was closely involved with the tomb discovery; also the Reverend Burton K. Janes, biographer of A. B. Mercer (1879 - 1969) who was present at the opening of the tomb, Mr Michael Jones of the American Research Center in Cairo, Dr Lawrence Keppie of the Hunterian Museum. Most specially, I must thank Mr Anthony Leadbetter, godson of Almina Countess of Carnarvon, who introduced

me to an entirely unanticipated aspect of the Carnarvon story, one that I could give only the most tardy attention within the scope of this biography. But I have included an Appendix which goes a small way towards repaying his generosity. Those acknowledgements apart, I have little to add to what I said in the writing of the book some fifteen years ago. I have tidied the text in a few places where my prose seemed to stray, and some of Carter's delightful water-colours and a few black-and-white photos have been added. Otherwise I am happy with the status quo, including the words of introduction I wrote at the outset, though I have made a few small amendments.
H.V.F. Winstone 26 January 2006

I started to research the life of Howard Carter in 1986. When I mentioned my subject's overriding achievement, the discovery of the tomb of Tutankhamun, eyes lit up and there was instant recall of the glittering treasures revealed to a new generation by the international travelling exhibitions of 1972 - 3 which marked the fiftieth anniversary of that event. But Howard Carter?

Most encyclopaedias included him, if at all, as an afterthought to the entry for his patron and collaborator, the 5th Earl of Carnarvon. Only one of the many people I approached gave me hope that Carter had not been deposited in that pit of obscurity to which England's most important sons are usually consigned in favour of the heroes of popular legend. A young woman who learnt of my intention asked pertly, 'What on earth can you tell us that we do not already know?'

I knew from the outset that I was dealing with a man for whom the English reserve the utmost desuetude, an awkward man who, to quote another writer who tried to resurrect him, 'stepped on many toes'; a man neglected to the last by fellow countrymen who, in their 'wretched lack of magnanimity', gave him not even a lowly token of Membership of the British Empire in return for the most famous discovery of all time. When I came on the scene there was no existing biography. Only obituaries written fifty years before and a censorious account of the disposal of the tomb's contents by an American writer and museum official, who had had privileged access to certain papers in the Metropolitan Museum of Art in New York, provided anything like a starting point for the would-be biographer. Yet, as soon as I had completed the basic research for the book and begun to commit my findings to paper, I became aware of a sudden and unexpected interest in Carter, centring on the forthcoming seventieth anniversary (in November 1992) of the tomb discovery. Broadcasting and television companies began to ask questions which suggested that they too were preparing to make up for three-quarters of a century of neglect by producing features of one kind or another. I am now able to proffer the first account of the life of Howard Carter.

I could not have done so without help of the most expert and generous kind. Any biography of Carter must be approached in the knowledge that his reputation rests on a single achievement. Tutankhamun was not an important monarch in terms of the New Kingdom with its magnificent royal line which began in the mid-sixteenth century BC and ended in the eleventh century with the last of the Ramesses and gave rise to ancient Egypt's golden age. He was, nevertheless, the only Egyptian king whose burial tomb survived the attentions of expert robbers in the course of three millennia. It was Carter's incomparable achievement to have anticipated the possibility of the tomb's survival and by patient method to have worked out its approximate whereabouts.

When he ascended the throne at the age of nine years at the apostate city called Akhetaten where the 'Aten' (or sun-disk or sun-globe) was worshipped, the young king bore the name Tutankhaten (Living Image of Aten). The name was given to him by his father-in-law Akhenaten ('Glory of the Aten'), the heretic king who founded the new religion in the face of priestly opposition. When he died, some nine years later, he was Tutankhamun (Living Image of Amun). The court had returned to its traditional home of Thebes, and to its traditional faith of a central sun deity within a supporting pantheon of animal and anthropomorphic gods of lesser magnitude. Almost all reference to the apostate faith had been erased. As Carter himself wrote: 'Abroad, the Empire founded in the fifteenth century by Tothmes III, and held, with difficulty it is true, but still held, by succeeding monarchs, had crumpled like a pricked balloon. At home dissatisfaction was rife. The priests of the ancient faith, who had seen their gods flouted and their very livelihood compromised, were straining at the leash, only awaiting the most convenient moment to slip it altogether...' Ever since Carter's famous discovery, scholars have argued about the precise lineage of the king and about the exact nature of the heresy to which he was heir, though, again in Carter's words, the question of royal blood is immaterial since, 'by his marriage to a king's daughter, he at once, by Egyptian law of succession, became a potential heir to the throne'.

As I say, it is a subject which any writer without a specialist background in Egyptology would be advised to view with caution, and preferably with the assistance of an expert. I was fortunate in having contact through my earlier writings with Mrs Henrietta McCall who had chosen Howard Carter as the subject of her dissertation at Oxford. Much of her academic work had focused on the Carter material in the Griffith Institute of the Ashmolean Museum. Until she examined the personal diaries and notebooks contained in that immensely important archive, they had been virtually undisturbed since they were deposited there following Carter's death in 1939. In the course of preparing her essay, Henrietta McCall visited Highclere Castle, the home of the Earls of Carnarvon, to which family Carter owed the wherewithal of his discovery, and interviewed a number of Carter's contemporaries. When she learnt of my intention to write this book she placed her dissertation, notes and collection of books and specialist papers at my disposal. I find it hard to put into words my gratitude to her for the unstinting help and assistance she has given me at every stage of my task. I must also thank her husband, Christopher McCall QC, who I suspect suffered many a disturbed and disjointed evening meal while his wife and I engaged in endless telephone conversations about Carter's character, the Eighteenth Dynasty of Egypt, or the finer points of sun-disk worship. If I am right, he did so with great good humour.

It would be impossible for anyone to attempt a biographical study of Howard Carter without recourse to the Ashmolean's Griffith Institute at Oxford. The documents and photographs in its keeping are *the* fundamental source, and I would like to express my gratitude to Dr Jaromir Malek, Keeper of the Archive, and his colleagues, for their unfailing helpfulness and courtesy in my search for evidence and requests for documents and photographs. The Institute is itself working on the mammoth task of a Topographical Bibliography of Ancient Egyptian Hieroglyphic Texts, Reliefs and Paintings in which the tomb of Tutankhamun and the work of Carter and his team will eventually find their rightful academic place. In the meantime, the *Tut'ankhamun's Tomb Series* has progressed under the general editorship of Professor J.R. Harris. Each monograph in the series is devoted to a particular group of objects from the tomb, described by an expert in the field and illustrated by the original photographs of Harry Burton, the official expedition photographer, with all the relevant entries from Carter's manuscript catalogue and copious notebooks and inventories carefully checked, and objects properly assigned to their time and place of discovery. The series has reached its ninth volume. Only when these tasks are complete will it be possible to say that full justice has been done to Carter, to his loyal Anglo-American team, and to the boy-king whom they resurrected.

There is another basic source of which I must make particular acknowledgement. Swaffham in Norfolk, home town of the Carter family, boasts a small but exceptional museum which keeps careful record of the district's most distinguished sons, among whom Carter stands high in esteem. Almost equidistant between King's Lynn and Norwich, the austere East Anglian plain on which Swaffham stands lays claim to a disparate band of heroes. It is only necessary to mention Admiral Lord Nelson, the Amhersts who hailed from London's Hackney district to establish there the finest private collection of ancient art and artefacts in Britain, Rider Haggard, the Colmans who made a household name of mustard, and Howard Carter, to make the point. There are many others represented in the delightful little museum whose curator, Mr David C. Butters, unravelled the years of my subject's youth when he lived in the family's cottage home at Swaffham in the care of two maiden aunts. I would like to thank Mr Butters and his assistants for their willing and unfailing help in providing me with background material on the Carters through several generations, as well as photographs and drawings from the museum's collection. I would also like to thank my original contact in the town, the Prebendary of the fine medieval church of Saints Peter and Paul, the Reverend Basil Jenkyns. While in East Anglia, so to speak, my grateful thanks also to Mr N.G. Stafford Allen and Miss Elizabeth Reeves for their assistance in connection with my subject's early schooling.

On the Egyptological side, my thanks are due to the Egypt Exploration Society, its Secretary Dr Patricia Spencer, and her assistant Ms Shelah Meade, for most valuable help in connection with Carter's movements in the early days at al-Bersha and Bani Hasan. I thank the Committee of the Society for allowing me access to correspondence between my subject and its officials. I am grateful also to Dr Nicholas Reeves, one of the world's leading experts on the Tutankhamun tomb discovery who was curator of the Carnarvon collection at Highclere when I wrote the first edition of this book, and to Mrs Margaret S. Drower, Petrie's biographer, whose generous help over several years has been greatly appreciated. I received most willing help from Major C.G. Harris, head of the Star and Garter Home for Disabled Soldiers, Sailors and Airmen, and from Mrs P. Moore and Mr Alured Weigall.

Again, it would be impossible to write an account of the discovery of the tomb of Tutankhamun without reference to

The Times newspaper, whose agreement with Lord Carnarvon gave its editorial staff a position of privilege unique in the annals of journalism. My thanks to the Chairman and Directors of News International PLC for access to the correspondence relating to that agreement and its consequences, and especially to Melanie Aspey, the Group Records Manager, and her assistant Emma-Jane Howell. For the loan of a most useful family collection of press cuttings kept at the time of the discovery, my thanks to Mrs Ailsa Corbett Winder.

For access to archives, libraries and papers, for help of a general kind, and for assistance in the hundreds of small but important questions which surface in any biographical exercise, my tardy but sincere thanks to: the present Lord Amherst; Dr Roger Moorey, Keeper of the Department of Antiquities, Ashmolean Museum; the Keeper of the Public Record Office; the Archivist of the Library and Records Department of the Foreign and Commonwealth Office, in particular Miss L. Baker; Mrs Judith Blacklaw of the Ministry of Defence Library; the Director and Trustees of the British Museum; the Petrie Museum, University College, London; Wandsworth Council and the Superintendent of Putney Vale Cemetery; Royal Military Police Association, Chichester; Eastern Counties Newspapers; Mr A.A.E.E. Ettinghausen; Mrs Patricia Leatham; Mr Ray Vann; Mr Peter Nahum; Dr Irving Finkel; Mr Brian Butland; Professor Luke Herrmann; Mr S.G. Roberts, Curatorial Officer of the Royal Commission on Historical Manuscripts; Miss Julia Rushbury; Mr Peter Aldersley, Secretary of the Savile Club; Mr Charles Newton, Keeper of the Collection of Prints, Drawings and Paintings in the Victoria and Albert Museum; Mr Peter Scott; Mr John Edwards; Dr Saad al-Doori; Miss A.J. Shute, County Librarian of my home territory, Devon, and in particular the librarians and their assistants at Barnstable and Bideford, Wandsworth Public Library; the Royal Geographical Society; and the Royal Commonwealth Society. As always, my family deserves praise for its forbearance.

I must also thank the present Earl of Carnarvon, though I have troubled him only through Dr Reeves, his curator. It is a thousand pities that justice has not been done, and perhaps cannot be done, to his ancestor the 5th Earl, who was not merely the financier of the Tutankhamun expedition but also the essential other half of the duo who found the tomb and showed it to the world. It is said that a bomb destroyed the entire Carnarvon archive in the Second World War. Even so, members of the family passed on papers and memories of the will-o'-the-wisp 'milord' whose adventures in small boats and motor cars in the last two decades of the nineteenth century, coupled with a devotion to beautiful women and archaeology, would surely strike a chord somewhere in the television age. He was the aristocratic patron *par excellence* with all the colourful prejudices of his class, who dined with kings and presidents, charmed the common man, adopted archaeology as a hobby, and treasured the friendship of Carter who, it has been said, was 'the hardest of men to patronize'. Surely someone will ultimately take courage and set Carnarvon's overflowing life to words, not to mention his extravagant, spoilt, beautiful, extrovert wife. For the time being Carter, the touchy, intemperate partner, must take the stage alone.

There is always a reverse side to the research coin, always an institution or body somewhere which seeks to protect its small corner of knowledge by silence or overt refusal to help. It must be said that the Carter story will never be complete until one famous institution, the Metropolitan Museum of Art in New York, behaves like the other great museums and places of learning of the world and opens up its archives freely and without reservation to serious writers and scholars. Its polite but adamant refusal to do so for this writer, despite the fact that vital documents have been referred to and published in part by one of its own sons in a partisan account of the disposal of the tomb objects, does not bode well.

I have not been unduly fussy about Egyptological niceties. This is a biography of Carter, not an account of Tutankhamun's life and times. All the same, hunter and quarry are closely bound up and I have tried to observe the academic ground rules. For example, it is strictly incorrect to use the term 'pharaoh' before it entered the vocabulary of the Egyptian court in Ramesside times, that is after the death of Tutankhamun. Many Egyptologists ignore the fact, however, and though I have generally used the terms 'king' and 'monarch' I may well have allowed a 'pharaoh' or two to slip through. I have taken one liberty which some will find less justifiable, in adopting a single spelling of Tutankhamun throughout, even in quotation. Tutankhamen is retained in the actual title of my subject's famous book on the tomb discovery, but in quotes from the text I have changed it without indication; likewise the Tutankhamon of some distinguished academics. The name appears too frequently for any other course to be taken, but I apologize all the same for traducing accepted practice. Other Egyptian names for which there is no Greek or other consistent form appear with slight variations of spelling.

Finally, the apologies demanded of anyone who deals in the languages of the ancient world, or indeed in modern Arabic, for the inconsistencies of translation which often leave the reader in a daze, wondering why a word has half a dozen different forms on a single page. In the case of ancient Egyptian names, the problem is resolved simply by using the Greek versions about which there is no dispute and no variability. Where, occasionally, I have let an Egyptian rendering through in quotation, reference to the index gives the alternative Greek form. As for Arabic words, the problem is by no means as easily solved. I am under constant pressure to accept a convention in the academic world which allows of transliteration from colloquial speech. In the case of Egyptian Arabic this is rather like offering English words and phrases within a French text with the vowel inflexions of, say, Newcastle-upon-Tyne or Glasgow: an excellent idea in a novel but somewhat Quixotic in a biography or an academic treatise. Essentially, the tendency has been to accept the spelling of archaeologists and others who have learnt to speak the language but not necessarily to write it. Thus, the Arabic word meaning hill or mound is spoken as 'tell' and is rendered thus, even though it is written *tal*. Confusion is even worse confounded by the Egyptian tendency to use 'g' or 'k' when other Arabic-speaking peoples use the soft 'j': thus, *Jamal* (camel) becomes 'gemal' or 'kemal' and so on. The Prophet's name is no exception – Mohammad, Mahommad, Muhammad, even Mehmet. The Arabic language has no capital letters, yet for some reason nouns are almost always given an initial capital in their anglicised forms. Not all academics go along with these accepted but quite indefensible habits. Some, like the American Professor Noah Kramer, insist on translating from the written form and I agree with them. The definite article as it is written is *al* not *el*. All the same, I have had to allow some inconsistencies in narrative and quotation. The argument is mainly one of principle and is of little import to most readers, but if I were to aim at genuine consistency I would have to change the spelling of almost all place names: Deir al Bahari, for example, becomes Da'ir al–Bahri. Having insisted on a principle I end up with compromise. I have used the index to give the correct and alternative versions of words that have different forms. I have also used the index to give the meanings of unusual words. Rightly or wrongly, I have assumed that the reader can make an educated guess at a foreign word's meaning when it is seen in context, and that he or she does not wish to refer to a glossary every few seconds.

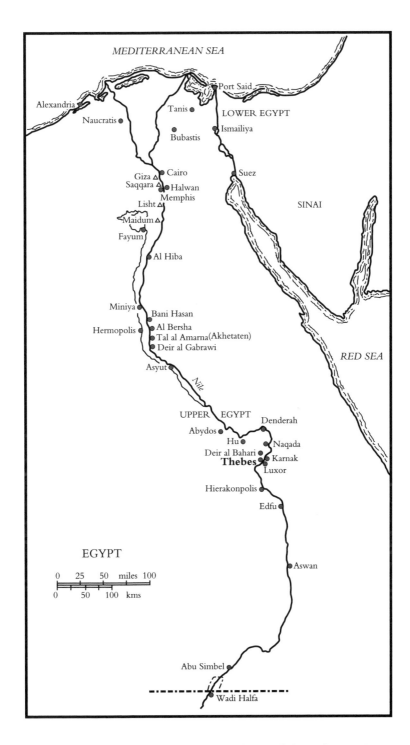

MEDITERRANEAN SEA

Port Said

Alexandria

Naucratis ●

Tanis ●

LOWER EGYPT

Ismailiya ●

Bubastis ●

Suez ●

SINAI

Giza △ ● Cairo
Saqqara △ ● Halwan
Memphis
Lisht △
Maidum △
Fayum

Al Hiba ●

Miniya ●
Bani Hasan ●
Al Bersha ●
Tal al Amarna (Akhetaten) ●
Deir al Gabrawi ●

Hermopolis ●

Asyut ●

Nile

RED SEA

UPPER EGYPT

Denderah ●

Abydos ●
Hu ●
Naqada ●
Deir al Bahari ●
Thebes ● Karnak ●
Luxor

Hierakonpolis ●
Edfu ●

Aswan ●

EGYPT

0   25   50   miles 100

0   50   100   kms

Abu Simbel ●

Wadi Halfa ●

The Nile Valley showing the chief archaeological sites and places of ancient Egypt.

ILLUSTRATIONS

HOWARD CARTER

The Valley of the Kings (Mansell Collection)
Lady Evelyn Herbert in 1923 (*Illustrated London News*)
Carter in 1922 (Mansell Collection)
Carnarvon leaving his London home for Luxor, December 1922 (Popperfoto)

Within Chapter 8, King's Messenger

Portrait of Howard Carter aged about forty-eight by William Carter (Griffith Institute)
Colour drawings by Carter (Griffith Institute)
'A pair of pelicans', water-colour by Carter (Victoria and Albert Museum)
Carter's plan drawing of the Burial Chamber, showing the outermost coffin, the sarcophagus, the shrines and other scattered objects (Griffith Institute)
Desert landscape water-colour by Carter (Griffith Institute)

Within Chapter 11, Death of a very English 'milord'

Carter arriving in the Valley of the Kings by donkey (*The Times*)
Lady Evelyn's luncheon party in the desert, following the official opening of the tomb in February 1923 (*Illustrated London News*)
Carnarvon, Lady Evelyn and Sir William Garstin aboard Carnarvon's automobile in the Valley, 1922 (*The Times*)
Sir Alan Gardiner and Professor James Breasted in the Valley, 1923 (*The Times*)
Carnarvon on Beacon Hill, Highclere, 1923 (*Illustrated London News*)
Lord and Lady Allenby with Carnarvon at the official opening of the 'sealed chamber', February 1923 (*The Times*)
Carnarvon and Carter, March 1923 (*The Times*)
Arm in arm with Lady Evelyn outside the tomb of Ramesses

VI, Carter, with Lord Carnarvon on his left, and Arthur Mace,
H.E. Winlock, 'Pecky' Callender, Alfred Lucas, and Harry
Burton (*The Times*)
Lucas at work in the laboratory tomb (*The Times*)
Harry Burton with the 'horizontal' camera used for
photographing small objects, January 1923 (*The Times*)
Crowds gather at the tomb, February 1923 (Griffith Institute)
Breasted, Burton, Lucas, Callender, Mace, Carter and Gardiner
at lunch in the canteen tomb, photographed by Carnarvon
(Griffith Institute)
Carnarvon and Lady Evelyn being welcomed at Luxor station
by Jehir Bey and Carter, 1923 (Popperfoto)
Carnarvon in the front porch of 'Castle Carter' (Griffith
Institute)
Metropolitan Museum staff, wives and visitors at the steps of
the tomb (Popperfoto)
Mace and Carter at the entrance to the burial chamber
(Mansell Collection)
Carter at the tomb, 1924 (*The Times*)
Professor and Mrs Percy Newberry at work in the tomb
(Griffith Institute)
Edward S. Harkness, Mrs Harkness and Albert M. Lythgoe (*The
Times*)
Carter at his Valley house (*The Times*)
Carter accompanying a consignment for Cairo Museum
(Griffith Institute)

Within Chapter 16, 'A mystical potency'

'Queen Hatshepsut' water-colour by Carter (Victoria and
Albert Museum)
Carnarvon, Evelyn and Carter (Griffith Institute)
Carter escorting a party of government officials to the tomb
(Griffith Institute)
The tomb entrance and Carter's surrounding excavations before

the Valley floor was reshaped (Griffith Institute)

Anubis before the doors of the golden shrine (Griffith Institute)

Carter and Callender opening the door of the inner shrine (Griffith Institute)

Unwrapping the mummy of Tutankhamun in the innermost coffin (Mansell Collection)

Carter and an assistant separating the mummy from the walls of the coffin (Griffith Institute)

The life-size guardian statues, from the north wall of the antechamber (Griffith Institute)

Ritual representations of the king emerging from their wooden coffer (Griffith Institute)

Transporting the royal coffin to Cairo Museum in 1926, photograph by Rev. E.M. Bickersteth (Bodleian Library)

Model of the king's boat from the Treasury (Griffith Institute)

Lady Evelyn, now Lady Beauchamp, and the gold mask of the king at the anniversary exhibition of 1972 at the British Museum (*The Times*)

Carter at work on the golden mask of the second coffin (Griffith Institute)

Detail from the gilt throne showing the king and his young queen, Ankhesenpaaten (Mansell Collection)

End of Chapter birds, from water-colours by Carter, (Griffith Institute)

Chapter 1

THE MAKING OF A
NORFOLK 'DUMPLING'

Howard Carter's coded telegram to his wealthy patron the 5th Earl of Carnarvon, sent from Egypt on 6 November 1922, was the prelude to revelations which would change humanity's perception of the past and its behaviour in the present. Deciphered, it read:

> AT LAST HAVE MADE WONDERFUL DISCOVERY IN VALLEY *STOP* A MAGNIFICENT TOMB WITH SEALS INTACT *STOP* RE-COVERED SAME FOR YOUR ARRIVAL *STOP* CONGRATULATIONS *ENDS*

The public pronouncement, made within three weeks of Carter's message arriving at Highclere Castle, the ancestral estate of the Carnarvons, gave the world its first auspicious glimpse of a young monarch who ruled Egypt briefly in the fourteenth century BC. Ten years of painstaking tomb clearance, angry controversy and unprecedented publicity would imprint on the minds of men and women over succeeding generations the dramatic spectacle of the gorgeously attired boy-king Tutankhamun, buried amid unimagined marvels of art and craftsmanship wrought in gold, alabaster and wood, such as the human eye had not seen before. A hundred years' contemplation of dusty remains, of headless torsos and severed heads of stone lying in the sand, gave way to a new and lovely vision of a regal journey into eternity. It was the stuff of which editors' dreams are made and within days of the announcement the world's press descended on Egypt like a locust cloud of ancient legend

1

A new word, 'Tutmania', entered the English language. Fashion, travel, architecture, the design of the automobile and household products embraced a mood which stepped lightly over three and a half thousand years. 'Wonders of the Golden Tomb', 'Crowning Triumph', 'Wonders of the Nile', declared newspaper headlines in countless languages. 'Paris reads the riddle of the Sphinx', ran the headline of a fashion magazine. 'Egypt's extreme version of the tight-across-the-hips-at-the-back silhouette', stammered yet another. The 'Tutankhamun Overblouse' was displayed in Oxford Street windows. Egyptian-style public buildings and façades came into fashion. Lady Elizabeth Bowes-Lyon, the newly-wed Duchess of York, packed an 'Egyptian' dress in her going-away trousseau. Ladies' handbags were emblazoned with the masked image of the boy-king. Mackintosh's toffees were advertised with topical if unpolished verse:

> When Tutankhamun's tomb was found
> By excavators underground
> Unearthed appeared alongside Tut
> A Tin of Mummified De Luxe.

Biscuit tins and squash bottles carried the unmistakable symbol of the king's gilded mask, General Motors designed an automobile in the shape of a pharaonic projectile, Singer sewing-machines flaunted the winged sphinx, soap and perfume makers jumped on the bandwagon and schoolchildren the world over wrote a myriad essays in tribute.

The hitherto anonymous archaeologist and the aristocratic patron at the centre of it all became instantly and unexpectedly the most famous men alive.

Carnarvon, urbane and accustomed to the public gaze, took the intrusion in his stride. Carter, a man of very different background and make-up, was resentful. For him, the discovery came as the culmination of more than twenty years of patient, unrewarding digging and many a bitter disappointment. He could only register feelings of anger and contempt for the mob of pressmen and the milling horde of tourists and notables who, at the pinnacle of his life's work, invaded his precious tomb. Phlegmatic, unsmiling, unmoved, he set his face against the government of his host country, the academic and political establishments of his native land, and the combined forces of the international press. He was not selective in his choice of enemies.

'If it is true that the whole world loves a lover, it is also true that either openly or secretly the world loves Romance,' wrote Lady Burghclere, Carnarvon's sister, in lyrical celebration of the discovery of the tomb. Composed within a year of the event, her words matched the mood of a world still open-mouthed at the splendour of the tomb furnishings – 'a story that opens like Aladdin's Cave, and ends like a Greek myth of Nemesis,' she concluded.

Fate was not even-handed when it chose Howard Carter for the long, arduous pursuit of the monarch Tutankhamun among the exhaustively searched hills and cliffs of the Valley of the Kings.

At about the time of his conception, the eleventh and last of his generation of Carter siblings, distant events, recorded in the small print of the European press, pointed obligingly to the child's future place of work. In 1873, the Khedive of Egypt rewarded the country's Director of Antiquities, the Frenchman Auguste Edouard Mariette, with the promise of a new museum at Giza designed to house his wonderful collection of artefacts from the Serapeum of Saqqara, from Tanis, Thebes, Edfu, Denderah; priceless objects which, up to then, had resided almost unnoticed in an old and leaky museum in the Cairo suburb of Bulaq. Howard Carter, born on 9 May 1874 at his parents' London home, would, fifty years later, enter the only tomb of an Egyptian monarch which had escaped the grave robber's age-old industry, and which would, in the sheer magnificence of its contents, eclipse all that had gone before in a century of intensive exploration and spectacular discovery.

A large family and a parental need to keep up appearances left little spare money at any stage of his life, certainly not enough to provide the kind of educational background or status against which society could measure him and assess his worth according to accepted standards. Without the appurtenances of the English upper middle-class life he could hardly hope to enter the ranks of archaeology, filled as they were with the classical and theological sons of Oxbridge, much less to achieve distinction as an excavator in lands where even the wealthiest American universities flinched at the cost of digging. Only patronage of the most generous kind together with inflexible determination could overcome the handicaps of birth. Tenacity and determination were Carter birthrights. A sensitive observer was to write by way of preface to Carter's own account of his work: 'He received a privilege, a blessing, a supernatural benediction, a crown of immortality – but...a blessing not unmixed with frustration and woe.'

In later years Carter described his birthplace, 10 Rich Terrace in Earls Court, as 'a quaint old house'. Its most prominent feature was a 'lovely garden with beautiful trees' and pens for animals which his artist father used for the purpose of study. The family came of hard-working stock, products for generations back of the flat, well-watered lands of East Anglia where speech and life have a distinctly leisured tread. Grandfather Samuel Isaac Carter began his working life as a farm labourer at his birthplace Great Dunham in Norfolk, though he later became gamekeeper to Robert Hamond, the squire of Manor House, Swaffham, in the same county, a job which carried with it a residence known as Keeper's Cottage. Samuel John Carter, Howard's father, was born there in March 1835.

Samuel John Carter turned out to be an artist of exceptional skill but limited imagination. Early on he lent his pencil to the representation of animals, wild and domestic, taking lessons from the Norwich artist John Sell Cotman who ran a school of drawing at Swaffham. After winning first prize in a local competition he went on to the Royal Academy Schools, winning the silver medal in his first term and leaving with a high reputation for immaculate draughtsmanship and an almost instinctive sense of animal anatomy. He returned home to Swaffham in 1858 at the age of twenty-two to marry a local girl, Martha Joyce Sands, a builder's daughter. She was a year younger than her husband.

Samuel prospered as an artist who knew his limitations and worked within them, producing animal portraiture for which his well-off clients were happy to pay a modest price. He made a respectable living from sentimental renderings of dogs and other pets. But he was more than the clever hack which such a statement suggests. He attracted expert attention. Ruskin was moved to comment that his picture *The First Taste* was 'exemplary in its choice of a moment of supreme puppy felicity as properest time for puppy portraiture'. It was, all the same, bread-and-butter art whose purpose was to provide for a large and growing family, far removed from the 'aesthetic' arguments which pervaded Victorian England – not the kind of portraiture that Wilde would have lectured American miners about, or the kind that Burne-Jones might have hung in the country house of an industrialist patron. But Samuel exhibited regularly at the Royal Academy and his work was in increasing demand. Almost all his eight surviving children (three died in infancy) inherited something of his talent. Several were capable artists. Two of the older boys, William and Verney, born in 1863 and 1864 respectively, exhibited at the Academy, as did the only surviving daughter Amy, who chiefly painted miniatures. Another son, Edgar, became a renowned clock-dial designer and painter. But none of the offspring drew more productivity than did Howard on the father's skill, and the debt was recognized. Reflecting in later years on the source of his own talent, in an essay he called 'An Account of Myself', he described his father's sureness of touch: 'Being an animal painter of no little fame …he was one of the most powerful draughtsmen I ever knew. His knowledge of comparative anatomy and memory of form was matchless. He could depict from memory, accurately, any animal in any action, foreshortened or otherwise, with the greatest ease.'

Within a short time of his marriage, Samuel was able to afford a family home and he chose a terraced cottage in Sporle Road, Swaffham, where most of the children were reared. Growing success, however, enabled him to move closer to the source of his most lucrative commissions, the Earls Court district of London, and he acquired the house in Rich Terrace where Howard was born.

Shortly after birth, Howard was despatched to the Sporle Road cottage where two maiden aunts, Samuel's elder sisters Kate and Fanny, took up residence in order to look after the infant while the parents attended to the tasks of making a living and bringing up the rest of the family. The boy was thought to be something of a weakling, and it was not until he was well past the usual starting age that he was allowed to venture to school. In fact, the only tangible illness of his childhood seems to have been a hernia which was successfully treated. He developed as a singular and secluded child, only distantly aware that he was a member of a large family, content from the earliest years with his own company and a comfortable closeness to nature, and with a rare ability to capture with brush and pen its infinity of life and mood. Notebook reminiscences recorded the passions and deprivations of youth with modest candour: 'As I was not strong, I was debarred from public school life and games... As I grew into boyhood, I developed an inclination for entomology and ornithology.'

Of his mother, Martha Joyce, Howard wrote in his notebook simply that 'she was a small kindly woman', adding that she had a taste for luxury. If that was a true description, it was written with understanding, for the son shared her weakness. He grew up with a devout love of comfort and good things, to say nothing of a keen sense of value.

Education for Howard, as with his father, depended on the patronage of the Hamond family who, in 1736, had founded a school for local children which was presided over by the vicar of the parish. Elementary learning was supplemented by drawing tuition, chiefly at the hands of his father. It is believed within the Carter family that Howard also received private tuition from a local benefactor whose wife is said to have implanted an early interest in Egyptian civilization in the boy's mind. Whoever his teachers may have been, Howard's was a modest education which began late and ended prematurely. All the same, it was the kind of early training which, if local tradition is anything to go by, had an imposing precedent. Horatio Nelson's father, Edmund, was rector of the nearby parish of Hilborough, and a governor of the Hamond School in the formative years of England's national hero. Swaffham people swear that Horatio attended their school before being transferred to the grammar school at Norwich, but there may be confusion arising from the fact that the first three Nelson children, including the first Horatio who died before he was two years old, are known to have been born in Swaffham and to have spent their early years in the town.

Swaffham town lies high on an open plain, and the region has always been regarded as healthy, which was perhaps another reason for Carter's parents sending him there while he was still in his pram. The rural charm of the market town, with its population of 3,000, was seldom ruffled by events in the outside world. It was a peaceful and largely uneventful environment for the lad to grow up in. But there were plenty of pursuits to interest a boy of serious disposition who played no games and had few friends, and who was almost always armed with notebook and sketch-pad. Neighbours to the south in the stony, heather-strewn county of Suffolk have always tended to poke good-humoured fun at the more sedate Norfolk folk. Ask them about Swaffham in particular and they are likely to say, 'Ah, thart's where they do a day's trawshing for narthing.' The rural irony may have borne a grain of truth. The broad vowel sounds would become characteristic of the young Carter's speech, but in later life he was certainly not given to the suggested willingness to do a day's threshing without promise of proper financial reward.

One of Swaffham's most familiar features, the church of SS Peter and Paul, provided an imposing introduction to early English architecture. Its perpendicular Gothic lines, perfect cruciform structure and carved wooden roof can hardly have failed to attract the attention of the visually alert youngster. And a few miles' walk to the north lie the picturesque ruins of the priory at Castle Acre, founded shortly after the Norman conquest and surrounded by earthworks which span Roman and pre-Roman periods.

Resident in the town was a distinguished traveller, the Reverend Greville Chester. That noted antiquarian was the son of William Chester who was rector of the Norfolk diocese of Denton and Walpole St Peter until 1839, and his travels in Egypt, Sinai and Palestine had been recorded in numerous books and articles. He himself was elderly by the time the young Carter was aware of him, but he was still active and a well-known local figure who returned to Swaffham every now and again from his wanderings in the 'Bible lands'.

On the rare occasions when they met, either in London or at Swaffham, the Carters, father and son, found harmony and shared purpose in art. From early observation of his father's relationships with his clients, Howard must have been acutely aware that his family belonged to the artisan rather than the professional class in a Victorian England which drew tightly the boundaries of social intercourse. By the time he reached fifteen, he was aware that he must contribute to the family purse and was ready to earn a living drawing. Norfolk has a word for its strong yeoman sons, 'dumplings', and by the time he left school Howard answered to the description. The weakling child had become a thickset youngster with broad shoulders and serious looks. Fortunately, a source of work was close at hand. Like his father, he soon became accustomed to polite welcome in large well-furnished and underheated halls to which artists, like other retainers, gained access by the 'tradesman's' entrance.

Didlington Hall, the country seat of the wealthy Tyssen-Amhersts, was situated near the village of Brandon some 10 miles from Swaffham. The estate covered more than 10,000 acres of Norfolk heath country and embraced several small townships. Mr William Tyssen-Amherst had married Margaret Susan Mitford, daughter of Admiral Robert Mitford, in 1856, and husband and father-in-law became the closest of friends through a shared devotion to Freemasonry and ancient Egypt. The Amhersts had five daughters and thus there was no male heir to the vast fortune which the family had accumulated from adroit marriage and property and business interests in and around the marshy London district of Hackney during the eighteenth century.

Samuel Carter had worked for Amherst ever since he finished his art-school training and several of his commissions graced the Hall at Didlington when Howard started to visit the Amherst home at the age of fifteen. Even while he was at school he had wandered across country during the holidays, sketching and 'watching the winning ways of insects and birds', often ending up in the Hereward-the-Wake country between his home and Brandon. It was not until he left school and decided to seek a living as an artist, however, that he began to visit the Hall at regular intervals and to make an impression on Mr and Mrs Amherst and their brood of daughters. If the social barriers between the son of a local artist of modest fame and means and the wealthy landowner were never entirely demolished, neither were they an obstacle to friendly, rewarding patronage. Amherst, devoted to books, art and Egyptology, soon recognized the boy's talent, his remarkable facility for making perfect representations of the most fleeting of images, and gave him the run of his library and galleries which displayed some of the rarest treasures of the past.

The Amherst Collection contained the most important private assembly of Egyptian art and papyri in England, and it aroused in Howard a 'longing for that country, for the purity of her blue sky, her pale aerial hills, her valleys teeming with accumulated treasures…'.

In 1881 William George Tyssen-Amherst was elected Grand Knight of the Supreme Council of the XXXIII degree in Freemasonry for England, Wales and the Dependencies of the British Crown. Egypt and Masonic affairs were the passions of this rich and intellectual squire. The two interests had a common bond. Tucked away among Amherst's personal papers was an undated press cutting from the London *Evening Standard* which quoted the *New York Herald:*

> In removing the foundations of Cleopatra's Needle, Lt Commander Gorringe, a Mason, made a discovery of the highest importance. A Masonic square was cut out of an immense block of granite. On the interior of the base he found inscribed three degrees corresponding to the three first Masonic grades. Under the square were three steps corresponding to the degrees of Apprentice, Companion and Master…

The report also spoke of references to the 'mysteries of Hiram, Osiris and Isis'. The obelisk in question is not identified but it could have been one of many which were plundered by Europeans and Americans as architectural curiosities. The first to reach Britain was a gift from the Ottoman Viceroy Mehmet Ali in 1819, and was erected on the Thames Embankment in 1878. In that year a revived Masonic Lodge was established in Swaffham at the instigation of five local gentlemen, one of whom was Howard's uncle James. Brother Amherst was proposed as the first Grand Master of the Lodge. In October 1882, the year of Britain's annexation of Egypt (delicately referred to at the time as the 'Protectorate'), and exhibition took place at Swaffham to which the eight-year-old Howard was taken with his older brothers to see some of the Egyptian treasures of the Amherst Collection displayed alongside paintings which included several of their father's works. Affinity between the Amhersts and the Hamond family strengthened the several close ties which gave Howard Carter entry to the Hall at Didlington and thus determined the direction of his life.

The Egyptian collection at Didlington Hall vied with the great public museums of the world in the importance and variety of its possessions, which stretched from the pre-dynastic Naqada period to the Ptolemaic reigns. Carter's sketchbooks began to be filled with 5,000-year-old shapes of pre-dynastic stone implements, slates, palettes and incised pottery; with hieroglyphic, Greek and Coptic inscriptions traversing 3,000 years of history; with stone figures of gods and cow-keepers, kings and queens. Among the mummy cases on view, one bore the cartouche (the royal name written within an oval outline) of the pharaoh Amenhotep I, the body still rolled in its funeral bandage. There was also the first mummy case to be brought to England (in about 1730). Another contained a body with a face of striking personality and a glass eye, believed to belong to the Ethiopian period. Another, belonging to the Roman period, came from the same district and was brought back by Amherst's daughter Mary who married Lord William Cecil in 1885 and excavated at Aswan. Lady William Cecil, heir to the Amherst fortunes by special dispensation since there was no male successor, became an accomplished amateur archaeologist who brought back many other important objects for the family museum. One in particular was destined for a niche in literature. It was a wooden *shawabti,* a little figure designed as a substitute for the dead when called upon by Osiris to work in the nether world. It inspired another of Swaffham's famous sons, Rider Haggard, to create *She.* Beside it was perhaps the most remarkable of Amherst's Egyptian works of art, a beautiful boat bearing the cartouche of Tuthmosis III, the monarch of the Eighteenth Dynasty who straddled the fifteenth and sixteenth centuries BC. Bronze and clay figures of Osiris and Neith (goddess of war), Isis and Horus and other sacred figures demonstrated some of the finest workmanship of ancient Egypt's long history. A bottle brought back by Lady William Cecil bore the inscription 'Happy New Year' in hieroglyphs. Of unexampled importance for Carter's future work, however, was the collection of papyri in the museum. Among them was a portion of the 'Book of the Dead'. The most famous, which became known simply as the Amherst Papyrus, gave a contemporary account of tomb robbery in the time of Ramesses IX, throwing a flood of light on the methods and techniques used in dynastic times to rob the burial grounds of the pharaohs, often within days of burial, and usually with the connivance of palace officials. The papyri, together with the cuneiform tablets, the ostraca and cylinder and scarab seals housed in the museum at Didlington Hall, provided a survey of language and of the written word over a period of some 3,000 years.

These sumptuous exhibits were not the only manifestations of the Amhersts' interest in Egypt. Lord Amherst was an early member and active supporter of the Egypt Exploration Fund, set up in 1882 under the dissonant joint-secretaryship of the novelist Amelia Edwards and the academic R.S. Poole. In 1887 Amherst had written to the Fund from the House of Commons to apologize for being in arrears with his subscription. He added that he had been reading of the discoveries made by the Anglo-Swiss archaeologist Edouard Naville at the Mound of the Jews at Greek Bubastis in the Nile Delta. 'I have often looked on those mounds and speculated what might be there,' he wrote. The Admiral Robert Mitford, father of Susan, Lady Amherst, was an amateur enthusiast who wrote *A Sketch of Egyptian History*. Egyptian art and history were at the heart of the family's existence and the Hall was constantly visited by prominent scholars and explorers of the time. The entire Amherst family shared the father's intense and informed interest.

In the summer of 1891, when he was seventeen, Carter, who had been paying his way as an artist for two years, working mostly at Didlington, was offered and accepted the chance of full-time employment with Amherst. An atmosphere of lively intellectual inquiry and debate infused the Hall where Carter now sat day after day, drawing, observing and listening, his serious, brooding countenance belying the facility with which he worked.

It was to be Lady Amherst who played the decisive part in consolidating the young Carter's talents and fostering his determination to find his way to Egypt.

Soon after Carter entered her husband's employment, she introduced him to another aspiring Egyptologist of the time, Percy Newberry, who had met the Amhersts through a devotion to gardening which he shared with Alicia Amherst, the youngest daughter of the family. Newberry was a graduate of King's College, London, and he entered archaeology by much the same route as Carter. He worked hard at architectural drawing techniques and became skilled as a draughtsman, but he lacked Carter's natural ability. He had been appointed Officer in Charge of the Archaeological Survey of Egypt in 1890 and before leaving for his first assignment he called on Alicia's family. Lady Amherst showed him some of Carter's water-colours and pencil drawings and he was impressed by the fine draughtsmanship displayed in the young man's work; so impressed that he invited him to help with copying tasks he was engaged on at the British Museum. Newberry needed someone to work up in ink the pencil sketches he had made of tomb scenes from Bani Hasan, some of the finest paintings of the Middle Kingdom of ancient Egypt, dating from about 2000 BC. That was not a full-time job, however, and the department for which Carter worked, under the overall direction of Sir Augustus Wollaston Frank, soon found other work for him, in particular the 'minutely accurate' copying of the manuscript drawings of Robert Hay, whose early Victorian representations of Egyptian monument inscriptions were among the finest ever executed. During his short period of apprenticeship at the British Museum, Carter was surrounded by the dignitaries and aspirants of contemporary scholarship. Alan Gardiner, an authority on Egyptian language and a man of considerable influence, took an interest in the young man's painstaking efforts. So did Frank Llewellyn Griffith, the superintendent of the Archaeological Survey, a brilliant, absent-minded expert in ancient Egyptian language who had been working with Flinders Petrie at Naucratis in the Nile Delta. In February 1891, Griffith wrote to Newberry suggesting that Carter might fill the vacancy for an artist who could trace and colour his own images. He added: 'I don't think it matters that he is not a gentleman'. In fact, Griffith thought that the young man's lack of social status would be a positive advantage. He would be less expensive than a gent.

By late 1891 Carter was ready for his first brief excursion to Egypt. He had made his mark among a new generation of archaeologists who were about to embark on the 'systematic and scientific' exploration of a territory which had suffered the best part of a century of assault by pick-and-shovel diggers and incalculable damage at the hands of tomb robbers in the course of some five millennia. As the youngest among them, without qualification of any kind and with little of the social grace or confidence of his compatriots, he viewed the prospect with remarkable self-confidence.

Carter listed the Survey team which he was about to join: 'Mr G. Willoughby Fraser for the surveying work; Mr M.W. Blackden, a painter and copyist; and my immediate chief Mr Percy E. Newberry.'

The appointment was finalized as the result of a call made by Bernard Tyne Grenfell to Bani Hasan on his way up the Nile from Aswan where he was digging for the Egypt Exploration Fund. On 5 January 1891 he wrote to Amelia Edwards to say that he had spoken to Newberry and Fraser who were doing very good work but were much in need of an artist who could colour his own tracings. Newberry knew 'a gentleman' who would subscribe £25 towards the cost while he, Grenfell, would contribute a further £25. Any additional cost could probably be met without too much difficulty. All the employees of the Fund knew only too well that matters had to be approached tactfully if they were not to founder on the rocks of secretarial dissension at headquarters. Grenfell's letter was almost certainly a contrived effort to have the young and inexperienced Carter put on the pay roll. 'I think this would be a good thing to arrange', wrote the much-respected Grenfell, 'as the colour alas! is fast fading...' Carter's appointment was confirmed within the month. Amherst paid the first £25 of his wages, which amounted in total to a little over £50 a year. Later Carter paid passing tribute to his employer. He wrote in his journal:

> Due to Lord and Lady Amherst of Hackney – to whom I owe an immense debt of gratitude for their kindness to me during my early career, – I was sent to Egypt at the age of seventeen and a half as assistant draughtsman to the branch of the Egypt Exploration Fund, called 'The Archaeological Survey of Egypt'.

Before boarding ship for Alexandria in September 1891, Carter learnt that Amherst was in negotiation with Flinders Petrie, seeking a concession in Egypt, and had suggested that Carter be apprenticed under 'the master's eagle eye'. The seventeen-year-old pupil's initial task, however, was to assist Newberry who was working on the rock tombs of the Eleventh- and Twelfth Dynasty nomarchs (governorships) of the Oryx Nome at Bani Hasan.

Chapter 2

'MY GREAT DESIRE'

THE Egypt which greeted Carter was a place of ancient conundrums and contemporary uncertainty. Ten years before he set out, the Gladstone government had sent a military force to occupy the country, casting aside the historical claims of Ottoman Turkey and the pretensions of France. Egypt was technically bankrupt. Under the old system of Anglo-French administration, the Dual Control, the country had been governed by what Lord Salisbury described as 'a combination of nonsense, objurgation and worry'. In 1883, Sir Evelyn Baring (later Lord Cromer), Britain's financial 'controller' in the last years of nominal independence, was appointed Resident and Consul-General, with powers which many a sovereign had reason to envy. He was known simply as 'the Lord'.

If some of the nonsense and much of the objurgation were eliminated by Cromer's iron rule, there remained plenty for politicians, and, for that matter archaeologists, to worry about. Tewfiq, the Khedive of Egypt (a solecism for kingship but Britain kept up appearances by insisting on 'Majesty'), was a compliant man who stood aside while Cromer and the army Sirdar, Kitchener, concerned themselves with the rising tide of nationalism, the advent of a new 'messiah' in the Sudan, and the security of the Suez Canal and the short route to India. Archaeology – under the direction of Mariette's successor, the young anglophile Frenchman Gaston Maspero – thrived for a time. But Maspero was succeeded in 1886 by the conspiratorial Eugène Grébaut, who still occupied the office of Director-General of antiquities when Carter appeared five years hence.

Carter was not politically minded. It is doubtful whether he gave so much as a passing thought to the international conflicts and nationalist ambitions which Britain's occupation both engendered and thwarted. His Egypt was a vast treasure-house of ancient art, to be unearthed, recorded, interpreted. He was a single-minded young man, and he showed early on a hazardous disdain for men of power – military or political – who might have smoothed his path and secured for him a place in the 'clubbable' world where favours are exchanged and honours disbursed.

Oblivious of all such matters, he was met at Alexandria by Newberry in September 1891 and they travelled together to Cairo where he was introduced to a man who would have a compelling influence on him, Flinders Petrie, best known of all the excavators of ancient Egypt and perhaps the most idiosyncratic. Carter found the 'Master' biding his time in search of scarab seals, 'of which there is no better Judge'.

Petrie was just over twenty years Carter's senior, born in 1853, the year in which Mariette had excavated the Serapeum at Saqqara and revealed the treasures of Memphis. But it was not until 1880, just before the British occupation, that Petrie had first visited Egypt, measuring the Giza pyramids and embarking on the first of many controversies concerning their design, structure and purpose. Mariette was still alive, though he died soon after Petrie's advent, in January 1881. His death marked the end of the first great epoch of Egyptology which began at the start of the century with the Napoleonic invasion. Yet many of the questions which fascinated and troubled earlier generations remained when Carter appeared on the scene in the last decade of the century.

An important breakthrough in the identification of some of Egypt's most prominent kingships had occurred in 1881, the year of Gaston Maspero's appointment to Mariette's post. Maspero had become aware of a black market in objects which bore the names of royal figures of the New Kingdom period, from the sixteenth to the thirteenth centuries BC. He reported the matter to the police who conducted a clandestine enquiry which resulted in the arrest of the audacious gang leader of a racket in antiquities. Others were soon arrested but would give little away to the police. One witness, however, led the investigators to an escarpment at Deir al Bahari on the west bank of the Nile just north of the Valley of the Kings and opposite Thebes, where they found a pit 6 feet wide and 32 feet deep. At the bottom of the pit they found the entrance to a corridor 76 yards long leading to a concealed room. Clambering over coffins, canopic chests and objects of every size and description, they eventually reached the room where, in the light of candles, they found objects bearing the names of Amenophis I, Tuthmosis III, Ramesses II and his queen, Nefertari. The investigators came away with hundreds of objects which they loaded on to a barge and transported to Cairo. News had spread quickly, as it always did in Egypt, and the banks of the river were lined by the citizens of modern Egypt who cheered and let off volleys of gunfire as the barge made its slow way to safety with its hoard of mummies and funerary objects aboard. It would take experts at the Bulaq Museum four years to catalogue the finds. The tomb robbers had been deprived of an illicit fortune. Yet the rescue act had merely succeeded in saving the remnants of 3,000 years of tomb robbery. Archaeologists could only contemplate the size and magnificence of the caches of gold and art they might have found had they been the first to open the tombs of some of the greatest monarchs of the ancient world.

Chronology, like the tombs of the pharaohs, was a subject which awaited systematic investigation. The ancient Egyptians and classical writers had left king lists and histories, but their records were fragmentary and many scholars inclined to think that their accounts were, in part at least, selective. After nearly a hundred years of digging and applied scholarship, the true picture of ancient Egypt was still in doubt. Such records as had survived for 2,000 years after the dissolution of ancient Greece were tragic reminders of the hazards of stewardship. The famous Turin Papyrus, compiled in the Nineteenth Dynasty, provided a list of kings, their reigns in years, months and days, going back beyond historical record to the reigns of the gods. It was almost certainly one of the documents from which the classical writers obtained their information. But by the nineteenth century AD it had been treated so carelessly that half its content had been obliterated. The Palermo Stone, originally a black basalt slab measuring some 7 feet in length and about 2 feet in height, had survived in the form of five small fragments, though Egyptologists believe that the missing pieces might yet be found in some improbable corner, perhaps in a library or museum, if only they knew where to look.

Such documents were freely available to the Greeks and Romans, and they almost certainly made use of them. Of the classical chroniclers, Herodotus had left detailed descriptions of the land he traversed extensively. But he never mastered the language of his hosts and relied heavily on hearsay. Mariette called him 'a criminal' who could have revealed much but yet conveyed 'only stupidities'. Modern scholars also had the fragmentary evidence of Manetho, a priest of Heliopolis, who wrote a history of his native land for Ptolemy II in the third century BC. Manetho's history was lost and survived only in extracts used by later writers, notably the Jew Josephus in the first century AD and the Christians Africanus and Eusebius in the fourth century.

When Carter began work, the First Dynasty had been projected by guesswork and arcane mathematical conjecture an entire millennium beyond its true limit in time, the names of the first monarchs were unknown, and most of the later kings uncertainly classified. But it was a time of exciting discovery. Men with established reputations – Quibell, de Morgan, Amélineau, Naville, and the prolific Petrie – were digging and searching along the 1,000-mile stretch of the Nile which ran from the Delta of Lower Egypt in the north, through such promising sites as Bani Hasan and Tal al Amarna in Middle Egypt, to the centres of the earliest dynasties at Abydos, Thebes, Karnak, Luxor and Edfu in Upper Egypt. New evidence of chronology, people and events was coming to light in profusion: new kings lists, the Egyptian names of rulers who were known hitherto only by their Greek appellations, and inscribed stelae and tablets relating to early contact with contemporary civilizations of the Tigris/Euphrates region.

Carter soon learnt to move confidently if not always with ease among such men, quietly assured in his exceptional ability as a draughtsman and water-colourist, unabashed by his tender age and the lack of formal education which most of those around him took for granted as a precondition of their calling. On the whole, they seem to have been impressed by him.

During the first few days in Cairo he wandered round the Giza Museum (to which the contents of the leaky Bulaq showplace had been transferred in the previous year, 1890) and the pyramids. Evenings were spent at Petrie's Cairo lodgings, listening to the conversations of men who had experienced the heat of the search and the joy of discovery, absorbed by technical, artistic and chronological disputation which brought ancient Egypt alight and reinforced his belief that, although only seventeen, he had found his *metier* by the Nile. Petrie impressed him more and more. 'The meeting of Flinders Petrie, a man of simple tastes, endowed with a discernment which gave him confidence and power to solve archaeological problems, remains one of the impressible incidents of my early life. As a son of an Artist, what perhaps interested me most, beside the extent and precision of his knowledge, was his recognition and love of fine art.' Carter resolved to find the same confidence, knowledge and discernment.

The older man took to Carter. If they were very different in manner and appearance – both dark, stocky and hirsute but Petrie immaculately bearded while Carter sprouted an embryo moustache – they had a common background of unorthodox education and upbringing. Petrie had been taught in a small neighbourly group by a strict disciplinarian of a colonel's daughter who stuffed her charges with a chaotic rigmarole of English and foreign languages. The boy was driven close to nervous breakdown and temporarily forbidden further lessons. Still, he read widely and taught himself creditably the basics of science and mathematics.

By 1891 he had already made his name as an Egyptologist and was about to publish an account of his work so far, called *Ten Year's Digging*. He had also developed something of a francophobia, particularly with regard to Mariette who had 'most rascally blasted to pieces all the fallen parts' of a granite temple, among other crimes. In that time, a furore had developed in the British press about the deterioration of Egyptian monuments, for which Whitehall was now ultimately responsible. This had led to the creation of high-powered committees and the personal intervention of the Foreign Secretary, Salisbury. As a result, the Egypt Exploration Fund had taken up one of Petrie's favourite causes, an Archaeological Survey, an ambitious plan described by the *grande dame* of the British in Egypt, Amelia Edwards, to 'map, plan, photograph and copy all the most important sites, sculptures, and paintings and inscriptions yet extant, so as to preserve at least a faithful record of those fast-perishing monuments'. It was that enterprising idea which, in 1890, brought Petrie together with the young draughtsman Percy Newberry, twenty-two at the time, and the respected field archaeologist Francis Llewellyn Griffith.

From the moment of Grébaut's appointment as Director-General of Antiquities the apportionment of sites became a matter of political clout rather than academic or exploratory competence. By 1891 Petrie was expecting to be given a most important site, Tal al Amarna, but endless committee meetings failed to clarify the question of who could have what. Saqqara, Abydos, Amarna? The argument was interminable. Cromer was called in, but even his mailed fist failed to achieve anything. Petrie and his high-powered supporters could not move the arrogant Frenchman. Petrie, it must be admitted, was not the easiest of negotiators. He had already resigned in a huff from the committee of the Egypt Exploration Fund in England, telling Amelia Edwards in October 1886 that he intended to

withdraw and adding that he 'did not wish to give his reasons'.
More than a year earlier, Stuart Poole had told Miss Edwards
that Petrie was 'working for nothing and counting on publication
for remuneration'. Chester had told Poole that Petrie was quite
willing to sleep on packing cases: 'He is silly beyond human
endurance.' Following his dispute with the Fund's Secretariat in
1886, he decided to accept financial support from a
Manchester businessman and to use some of his own limited
financial resources in order to continue digging. Now, after six
years of angry dispute with his sponsors in London and with
the French antiquities Directorate, Grébaut was proving
'impossible'. Petrie's disagreements and squabbles would prove
almost prophetic of Carter's own future in Egypt.

Griffith was put in charge of the Fund's Archaeological
survey, but he was now an employee of the British Museum
and could not carry out the work himself. He chose George
Willoughby Fraser, who had been trained by Petrie and
Newberry. Their first task would be to survey the region from
Miniya to Asgut, beginning with Bani Hasan. Carter was chosen
as the junior member of the team.

Bani Hasan, with its magnificent wall drawings and
inscriptions, offered exceptional opportunity to put Carter's
talent to the test of actual performance. Its tomb paintings
covered an estimated area of 12,000 square feet. Tracing them
would be a formidable undertaking. Petrie had already given
Newberry detailed advice on matters ranging from the need to
record the exact position of every inscription, according to a
system of decimal enumeration, to the best way of making up
a bed. One of his many hobby-horses was the inadequacy of
his contemporaries in copying the wall paintings and drawing
the artefacts and architecture of the tombs.

After a few days in Cairo, Carter accompanied Newberry to
Bani Hasan, alighting from a dusty train at Abu Qirqas, the
nearest station to their destination. They were stiff and dirty
after their long journey. The railway terminated some way from
the site of the rock tombs. Carter was about to have his first

experience of the Egyptologist's inescapable mode of transport. With the luggage and impedimenta strapped to donkeys, they rode off through cultivated fields towards the river, legs straddled, feet almost touching the ground, progress painfully slow. They crossed to the east bank of the Nile by antiquated ferry-boat and then climbed in the dark along the slope of the desert escarpment to the terrace which marked the tombs of Bani Hasan. Carter's first impressions of his baptismal archaeological site were not encouraging. 'Here, as the twilight fell swiftly and silently upon those dun-coloured cliffs, my first experience was an aspect of dreary desolation.' His first night was spent listening to bats flitting above the rock chamber where he and Newberry had made their beds, imagination calling up 'strange spirits from the ancient dead'.

A new day brought a change of mood. He looked out on a panorama such as he had never even imagined. The view was breathtaking, the Nile valley glowing softly in the sunlight, stretching far into the distance, the edge of the tawny desert contrasting amiably with the fertile plain. He began to sense the call of the Nile which had driven many a man before him to paroxysms of delight and extremes of venality. Within the tombs, he found inspiration wherever he looked. But the heady delight of his first day was tempered by a critical appraisal of what had gone before. He did not approve of the working methods employed by Newberry and his colleagues in the previous season, 1890 - 1, whether or not they were working to Petrie's precise prescription.

His first professional encounter was with the tombs of the nomarchs of the Oryx Nome (named, like the other tombs, after the name-signs of their incumbents, the viceroys or governors). In retrospect he judged that they were the most important monuments of Egypt's Middle Kingdom. 'Their historical inscriptions were of the utmost significance.' Aesthetically, the marvellous fidelity to nature of the drawings, their qualities of graceful line, balance of colour and refinement of detail, singled them out as works of the highest value in any artistic context. As for the architectural features of the tombs, they were, in a word, 'remarkable'.

The method of copying the wall decorations consisted of hanging large sheets of tracing paper on the surface, no matter whether the drawings were flat or in relief, or whether the walls themselves were smooth or granular, and working over the outlines with a soft pencil. The tracing sheets were then rolled up and sent to the British Museum where another draughtsman inked over the pencil rendering, all outlines being filled in silhouette, 'more than often … by persons without any knowledge of the original or of drawing'. Thus blackened, the tracings were reduced to a manageable scale by photography. 'From the point of view of Egyptian art,' Carter wrote, 'the results were far from being satisfactory.' He was aggrieved by the thoughtless methods used but he was not in a position to argue. 'I was young, it was my first experience, and in the struggle for existence I had to obey and carry out their extraordinary method of reproducing those beautiful Egyptian records enhanced by the romance of an immence [*sic*] antiquity.'

Fortunately, Newberry was a sensible and flexible senior colleague. Most of the essential tracing work had been completed in the previous season and to his relief Carter was allowed to devote his time to making faithful colour drawings of the more interesting details of the original murals. He had not yet reached his eighteenth birthday when he dispatched to England a notable batch of copies of some of ancient Egypt's artistic masterpieces.

By the end of November the expedition was ready to leave behind the tombs of the 'Great Chiefs of the Oryx-Province' and move off to al-Bersha, some 20 miles to the south, making the journey by river aboard a native *ghiassa,* the 'rover' of the Nile with large triangular lateen sails set to twin masts.

Cut into the sides of a ravine known as Wadi-al-Nakhla at al-Bersha were the tombs of the Hare nomarchs. 'There could be few brighter days than those we spent busily employed upon the survey of the rock-chapels excavated in steep sides of that wadi.' It was another opportunity for Carter to work not as a mere tracer or copyist but as a creative artist, rendering the originals faithfully but unslavishly, enhancing the resultant work. Indeed, it is probably true to say that Carter was the first of all the archaeological copyists to introduce an element of individuality into what was, hitherto, a purely mechanical task.

After working at al-Bersha for a few weeks he decided that some of the tombs and chapels compared favourably with those of the Oryx nomarchs. The chapel of Djehutihotpe – who lived through the Twelfth Dynasty (late second millennium) reigns of Amenemhet II and Senwosret II and III – he described as 'even finer than that at Bani Hasan'. His work in the al-Bersha tombs was perhaps the best of his apprentice period. His capture of movement, particularly with bird drawings, his brilliant command of colour and attention to detail in rendering rather than copying the wall drawings would win high praise among those who were privileged to see the beautiful reproductions of them made by the EEF a few years later. But fellow members of the expedition, accustomed to a less ambitious approach, were not altogether happy with their colleague's contemptuous dismissal of what had gone before. Even Newberry, who had first recognized the younger man's talent when introduced to his work by Alicia Amherst, was critical, though his chief complaint was directed at Carter's ponderous manner of working, and at his tendency to slope off every now and again to indulge in scenery sketching and wildlife drawing. All the same, Carter's sketches and paintings of the coloured reliefs of the chapel walls were of an exceptionally high standard when compared with anything that preceded them.

His careful observations were just as significant. Even the most experienced of Egyptologists still wondered at the logistical skills of the Egyptians in transporting the enormous stone blocks of their buildings and statues. In the chapel of Djehutihotpe, Carter noticed a scene which depicted in detail the methods used in bringing great slabs weighing as much as

45 tons each by land from the nearest quarries at Hatnub. An inscription recorded that the seated figure of the nomarch, the great chief Djehutihotpe, was 13 cubits in height and wrought from a single block of alabaster (calcite). Drawings showed how the great carved block from which the figure was hewn was bound to a wooden sledge by thick ropes which were tightened to their limit by wooden tourniquets, the sculptured surfaces protected by thick leather pads. Roads were specially prepared by gangs of workmen, each made up of forty-two 'good warriors' and a leader who carried the spare end of the hawsers attached to the front end so that the sledge could be dragged along the road. Quarrymen were organized in powerful guilds. The inscription said of the men who pulled and dragged: 'Their arms became strong, each one displayed the force of a thousand men.' Men walked alongside carrying a heavy wooden fulcrum for the purchase of levers when the sledge had to be helped over obstacles or difficult surfaces. For this statue alone, 172 gangers pulled the sledge while eighty-four 'extras' marched alongside in seven groups to relieve tired warriors. A man stood on the pedestal of the statue pouring water before the sledge to help it to slide better on the road and prevent the timbers from being burnt by friction.

The few weeks spent at al-Bersha also presented an opportunity for Carter to experience tent life. He did not like it. A well-appointed rock tomb with palm-branch bedstead was much to be preferred as a sleeping quarter, 'despite the bats'. He expanded on the theme in his notebook. 'In Egypt the tent is subject to the elements. Hot in the day, cold at night, the sides flapping with every gust of wind. You are cramped for space – practically everything has to be done on the principal piece of furniture, the camp bed.' The anti-tent lobby in general might argue that such drawbacks are not confined to camping in Egypt.

At Christmas 1891, Carter and Newberry went off in search of lost or undiscovered tombs, while Fraser and Blackden elected to share the festivities of the Egyptian Irrigation Department at Miniya along the river. On Christmas Eve they discovered the Hatnub quarries, a famous find for they had been known previously only from the calcite objects which had been rescued from them. Engraved on the quarries' banks were inscriptions which told of their having been opened in the time of the Old Kingdom in the third millennium BC. By the time they had examined the multitude of inscriptions sunset approached and they had to move on. After less than twenty-four uncomfortable hours in the wild, their food stock entirely consumed and only three blankets between them, they began to look for a comfortable haven. They were only 25 miles from al-Bersha but their Bedu guide, Shaikh Ayd of the Bani Abahda, suggested they make for the nearby village of Hagg Qandil. The Shaikh had explained to them that the village was not far from Al Amarna, a place where, he said, there was a deepening in the rock which was 'written' much like the tomb chapels of al-Bersha.

They knew that Petrie had recently started to dig at Amarna and a chance to visit his latest concession was not to be missed. They also knew that he had built a house on the outskirts of Hagg Qandil. For a small consideration Shaikh Ayd supplied them with camels and led them to their destination. Their caravan arrived at nine o'clock in the evening.

> In the east a posse of camels and men suddenly and silently descending from the desert...at night, has always an upsetting element about it, for it augurs ill, suggesting as it does Bedu bandits. Petrie stood in front of his door peering anxiously. So imagine his delight when he found that we were harmless creatures, in fact old friends, demanding only some food and a night's lodgings.

Petrie's regimes were said never to be for the fastidious or faint of heart. Some twenty years later, in 1911, T.E. Lawrence, who had been digging with Leonard Woolley at Carchemish, was sent to join Petrie at Tarkhan on the west bank of the Nile, only to find that 'tinned kidneys mingle with mummy-corpses and amulets in the soup'. Lawrence found the master 'fun' but wondered, 'why hasn't he died of ptomaine poisoning?' By then Petrie had married and his wife Hilda was famous for her chaotic housekeeping. Perhaps the great man's hospitality was better in bachelor days. Carter had no complaints, recording the 'good repast' he and Newberry had enjoyed, 'hot lentil soup, poached eggs, hot coffee, flapjack and cherry jam!'

Christmas Day was spent in exploring Amarna, where Petrie's men had begun work on 20 November. One of the first things they were shown was a recently excavated painted pavement from a chamber of the king's palace, decorated with clusters of tufted papyrus, ponds graced by wildfowl, and capering calves. It was subsequently destroyed by a local farmer in revenge for the damage done by visitors who trampled over his land in order to get to it. Looking back on that 'delightful day' some years hence, Carter could remember every detail of the pavement which was lost to posterity. And Carter recorded that in this city which was originally called Akhetaten, built by the 'heretic king' Akhenaten as 'the centre of Aten sun-worship', he had noted a boundary stela inscribed with the words: 'There shall be made for me a sepulchre in the Orient mountain; my burial shall be made therein.'

On Boxing Day Carter and Newberry returned, camel-sore, to al-Bersha. They were still full of their discovery at Hatnub and told their colleagues, who had returned from the festivities in high spirits, all about the magnificent inscriptions they had found. Fraser and the other professional member of the party, Blackden, promptly went off to Hatnub without warning and copied the inscriptions, claiming them as their own. Newberry was so incensed that he considered returning home to England. Carter never forgot the deceit, nor did he forgive it. He called his colleagues 'dirty dogs!' and spoke of 'unpleasant feeling' in the camp from then on.

The New year brought an important change to Carter's status. Hitherto his position and his relationship to the other men working for the Survey of Egypt under Petrie's ultimate control were uncertain. He was still being paid in part by Lord Amherst who in turn was negotiating with Petrie for a part interest in the concession at Amarna. For Carter, still short of his eighteenth birthday, designated artist-assistant to Newberry but somewhat loosely answerable to Petrie, the position was uncomfortably insecure. All was about to change. Before the end of the year, Petrie had been able to announce, 'I walked over the place and entered on my heritage.' His concession contract for Amarna had arrived from his arch enemy Grébaut, after weeks of Anglo-French haggling in the course of which three distinguished British representatives walked out of a meeting declaring that they would never again sit on a committee over which Grébaut presided. In consequence, Petrie was able to sell off part of the site to Amherst, thus relieving himself − and indirectly the Fund − of some of the expense while retaining in his own hands complete control of the excavation work. Amherst, having achieved his life-long ambition of a stake in Egyptian exploration, decided that if Petrie was willing, his protégé Carter should 'try his hand at excavation'.

Carter arrived by camel with Shaikh Ayd as his guide in February to begin the transition from draughtsman to excavator. He expressed 'sad misgivings' at the thought of becoming a digger. Petrie saw in him 'a good-natured lad' of seventeen, whose 'interest was entirely in painting and natural history'. There seemed little point in 'working him up as an excavator'. All the same, the master used well-rehearsed tactics in toughening up the boy and preparing him for the rough and tumble of field archaeology. He set him to building his own quarters for a start. It was not a task that Carter relished, but he went to work obediently, muttering to himself that the village bricklayer would have done the job much more expeditiously and certainly more skilfully. It was a one-room all-purpose structure made of mudbrick and unplastered. The Petrie rules, famous among archaeologists, were applied strictly; no chairs or tables; only packing cases for furniture. A month's supply of tinned food and other necessities were provided, and a small paraffin lamp, the cost to be debited to his account. 'Never throw away an empty tin,' he was told. Tins were invaluable for storing antiquities. No servants were permitted. 'I was to prepare my own bed, clean up the slops, prepare and cook my meals and wash up.'

Amarna was a place of the utmost importance in Egypt's ancient history, but its significance stretched far beyond the strict limits of Egyptian study. It was built in the fourteenth century BC by the heretic king Akhenaten to celebrate a faith unheard of in the world until then: a faith based on the notion of a single god. Akhenaten was born Amenhotep (Amenophis, according to the Greek nomenclature), becoming the fourth king of that name until he adopted the sun-disk, Aten, as his patron deity. In about 1375 BC he moved from Thebes to Amarna to establish his own city of Akhetaten, dedicated to his god, and lived there with his queen Nefertiti. After his death the heretical faith was adopted briefly by Akhenaten's successor, the boy-king Tutankhamun, before it was rejected along with the regime which had espoused it. The court went back to Thebes and Akhetaten was deserted and fell to ruin. It remained virtually untouched, a mound of rubble called in Arabic Tell (or Tal) al Amarna, for nearly 3,500 years.

The Prussian topographical artist and scholar Karl Lepsius had made a plan of the ruins as they were in the 1840s, and Petrie used his plan in order to identify the various mounds which constituted the site. He and Griffith had visited Amarna briefly in 1886. In the following year, a few tablets inscribed in the cuneiform Akkadian familiar from the tens of thousands of documents which had been discovered by Layard, Botta, Rawlinson and others in the royal palaces of Assyria, were found among the debris of the site. They represented, in academic terms, perhaps the most important find in the entire history of archaeology, opening a window on the earliest recorded diplomatic exchanges of the ancient world.

They were, in fact, a batch of letters exchanged chiefly between Akhenaten and his father, the great Amenophis III, and fellow monarchs of Western Asia, Syria, Phoenicia and Palestine, written in the Semitic Akkadian language which was the lingua franca of the time. Their discovery was attributed to a peasant woman, but their exact provenance has always been in doubt. In any case, inscribed tablets are not the stuff of which publicity and public interest are made. When Petrie and his assistants began work at Amarna, the tablets had been distributed to several universities and the manner of their discovery had been overlooked or forgotten. There had been another significant find within a year of the Amarna letters coming to light. Villagers claimed to have found several gold items 'in or about' a royal tomb, among them a signet ring incised with the cartouche of Queen Nefertiti.

The interpretation of history was a cardinal element of Petrie's approach to archaeology, one of the many grammatical linchpins he hammered into the apprentice as they made their way from the expedition quarters to the site each day, a distance of some 3 miles, Carter having to run at times to keep up with the master. On one occasion Carter murmured that a donkey would be useful. The suggestion was received 'by a dead silence'.

The strictures irritated him at first, but gradually he came to realize that Petrie's philosophy was not mere conjecture, that it embraced the practical as well as the theoretical. He faithfully recorded everything that his chief told him about the technicalities and the pitfalls of the job. Petrie was not interested in the spectacular. His approach to archaeology and the assessment of the past was based on 'unconsidered trifles', and he was often accused of pottery mania. He was known to his Arab-speaking assistants as the 'Father of Pots'. Indeed, at a time well before carbon-dating, there could be no doubt of the essential role of pottery as the instrument of chronology and cultural assessment. But Petrie's excavations gave rise to mountains of sherds that descended on unsuspecting museums and universities in such quantity that their disposal was to present a problem ever after. Nevertheless, he used his pottery finds to build up a detailed picture of the ancient world. If sherds were not exactly Carter's cup of tea, he listened and noted.

> What he made me realize most was the need of an archaeological experience. To know the objects that are usually met in an ancient civilization. The need of the all-important knowledge of history; the condition of a period, and the foreign influences affecting it. He explained that the ancient language of a country, important as it is in the study of remains, yet in its critical aspects it is not so essential during field-work. But that an excavator should at least be able to take in the sense of all written material which he finds. Lastly, a knowledge of engineering, mathematics, physics, chemistry were also required, and above all the power of observing all that can be gleaned from a discovery.

After a week spent touring the Amarna site and dutifully making notes of Petrie's observations, Carter felt ready to begin work on his own on the part of the site which Petrie had partitioned off as 'Amherst' territory. Petrie loaned him two of his older trained hands and some local workmen.

It was a small team compared to the work-force on the main site, but Carter was satisfied to be working on a small scale, even if his first efforts were 'wide of the mark and to little or no purpose'. Petrie had decided that it would take a lifetime to excavate the whole area of Amarna, which he compared in size to Brighton. He had decided to concentrate on a few typical houses, a royal palace (if he could find one), and the foundation deposits of the temples. He quickly came up with some Aegean painted ware, which he had half expected to find. He was surprised by the quantity, however. In the first season of digging he collected 1,341 fragments which, when fitted together, made 800 vessels. Petrie always counted and sorted

Howard aged eight, from a drawing by
William Carter.

Howard's father, Samuel John Carter.

Swaffham in Carter's youth, 1891.

Carter at eighteen in 1892, from a local
newspaper photograph.

Lord Amherst of Hackney as an Oxford
undergraduate, posing Oscar Wilde fashion.

Didlington Hall in 1890.

Sir William Flinders Petrie in 1923.

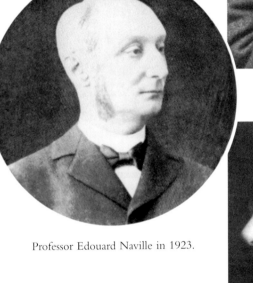

Professor Edouard Naville in 1923.

Professor F. Llewellyn Griffith.

Gaston Maspero, his deputy Emile Brugsch and Muhammad Abdal Rasul at the mouth of the shaft at Deir al Bahari in 1881.

Carter, or his brother Verney, photographed at Hatshepsut's temple, Deir al Bahari, in 1895.

Clearing debris from the vicinity of the Merneptah and Ramesses IV tombs at the
start of the 1920 season, with the assistance of the moveable 'Decauville' rail track
which Carter later used to transport objects from Tutankhamun's tomb to the Nile
five miles away.

Carnarvon painted by William Carter,
c.1920.

Carter as a young man, from a painting –
possibly by his father or one of his brothers
– found at Highclere.

Carter at his Valley house, Alwat al-Diban (Wolf's Lea).

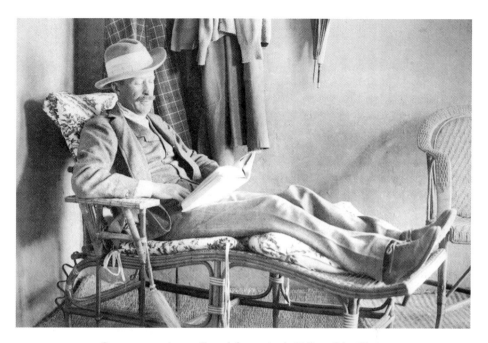

Carnarvon resting at Carter's house in the Valley of the Kings.

The Valley of the Kings with the entrance to Tutankhamun's tomb on the right in the foreground.

Lady Evelyn Herbert, Carnarvon's daughter, at the time of her engagement in 1923.

Carter photographed in 1922, just before the discovery of the tomb.

Carnarvon leaving his London home for Luxor, December 1922.

his sherds with precision. Carter was soon turning up the same kind of ware. Its significance was apparent even to the apprentice. The Amarna site could be dated from historical knowledge and from the dates found on wine jars and other objects. Petrie was able to state categorically that Amarna had been occupied for a little over twenty years at the beginning of the fourteenth century BC.

It turned out that Carter's painted pavement was only one of several examples of the same art at Amarna. Almost as soon as they began digging Petrie identified the palace area and began to reveal a pavement area of about 250 square feet. It was composed of plaster, gorgeously painted in soft colours with bouquets of lotus flowers alternating with food offerings, extending into a symphony of wildlife and aquatic scenes. This masterpiece was declared by Petrie, enthusiastically, to be the most important artistic discovery 'since the Old Kingdom statues of Mariette'. As soon as news of the find was out the inevitable caravans began to arrive bringing tourists and casual sightseers to join the archaeologists in admiration and to incense native farmers to the point of destroying some of the most valuable *in-situ* finds. Other similar pavements were uncovered in adjoining rooms, departing in their imaginative detail from the rigid formality of Egyptian art. 'The great temple of Aten, and parts of the Town were portioned off for me to investigate on behalf of Lord Amherst.' For a seventeen-year-old to be in charge of an excavation was unprecedented in modern archaeological practice. To be under the hawkish eye of Flinders Petrie was both a privilege and an irritating restraint. The master was obsessed with detail. His heart was never in social matters, only in the gritty detail of historical research. 'He taught us the ABC of archaeological research and excavation in Egypt, for which... I have a deep admiration. There were, nevertheless, times when I found him a pedant.' He was mean with money when it came to amenities and comforts for himself or his assistants, but prodigal in matters affecting the work in progress or doling out *bakhsheesh* to further the enthusiasm and honesty of workmen in handing over small finds.

Carter was soon making important discoveries, among them the remains of ancient glass factories which threw light on the methods of manufacture used in the second millennium BC. Then he found the remnants of a sculptor's experimental workshop among the rubbish beyond the boundary wall of the Great Temple of Aten which had been completely destroyed when the revolutionary faith of Aten-worship was replaced by the old and trusted deity of Amun. Seventeen fragments of heads and torsos of the deformed, effeminate King Akhenaten and his beautiful queen, Nefertiti, were rescued, though badly damaged by the zealots of 3,400 years before. They had been carved from semi-crystalline limestone, pure white and of fine workmanship, though the outlines were crude by comparison with later Amarna statuary found by Petrie in one of the private houses of the city. They showed the queen sitting on her husband's lap as they relaxed in a garden arbour while their two eldest daughters clambered over them.

When they first saw the Amarna site at Christmas time, Newberry and Carter had sensed an atmosphere of conspiracy. They learnt that there were rumours in Cairo to the effect that Akhenaten's lost tomb, somewhere in the desert behind Amarna, had been found by tribesmen some years before and plundered but that the museum authorities knew where it was. Petrie was convinced that it was another of Grébaut's unsubtle schemes and that he was keeping the secret back so that he could claim the discovery as his own. Newberry and Carter shared Petrie's anxiety that the tomb should be found, particularly when they learnt from reliable Arab tribesmen that Fraser and Blackden had made another secret journey, this time to the king's tomb, designed to pre-empt their colleagues.

Petrie was shocked to find that members of the expedition had behaved in such an 'ungentlemanly' manner. Newberry was furious, especially after the Hatnub affair, and promptly sent off his resignation to Amelia Edwards at the Fund's headquarters in London. He vowed never to return to Egypt. Petrie tried to dissuade him, but Newberry was a determined young man. Before he left Cairo news appeared in the press that Grébaut had discovered the tomb of Akhenaten. The British press picked up the story and Newberry, as soon as he arrived home, wrote a letter to the Academy accusing French officials in Cairo of having withheld the truth for two years and suggesting that Grébaut was falsely claiming credit for the discovery. The Egypt Exploration Fund, anxious not to lose favour with the French-dominated Antiquities Service, dissociated itself from the letter. Petrie threw fat on the fire, declaring in a letter to the Academy of 7 February 1892 that, 'Far from having discovered the tomb, the Director had not yet seen it.' The irate Englishman dared not to say too much since his permit forbade him to touch the tombs in question.

On 9 April, the *Daily Graphic* contained an imposing drawing of the tomb and one of the reliefs found in it, signed Howard Carter. An Italian technician named Alexandre Barsanti then claimed to have discovered the tomb on 30 December 1891, having been sent by the Cairo Museum where he was employed to equip the tombs in the cliffs with iron doors. According to Carter, the Badu who had discovered the tomb told Cairo Museum officials where it was to be found. Barsanti subsequently took Petrie and Carter to the tomb, along with Oxford's A.H. Sayce and M. Daressy of the Antiquities Service. Petrie raced on ahead so that he could at least claim that he was the first Englishman to see the tomb of Amenophis IV – Akhenaten.

Carter had not enjoyed himself so much since he arrived in Egypt. Professor Sayce was at the centre of his world, the venerable and distinguished philologist whose reminiscences went back to the past epoch of Mariette Pasha, whose diminutive stature and smiling, amiable nature caused fellow archaeologists to dub him 'Auntie'. Let it not be forgotten, wrote Carter, that he belonged to that 'distinguished class' of university men who were devoted to the truth and 'never yielded to any of the heresies' of a later generation. 'He was a kind and charming friend,' wrote the young man in tribute. Sayce kept the company amused and informed as they surveyed the abandoned sepulchre, its entrance facing east so that Aten, the sun-disk, as it rose shone into the long corridor and now-empty chambers which were cut into precipitous cliffs and hidden by masses of fallen rock and boulders.

It was clear that at some time the royal tomb had been 'raked over', perhaps by Barsanti's men. There was none of the finery which such a mausoleum should contain. 'It had been sacked by the victorious sectarians. Their base minds obviously delighted in taking revenge on the illustrious dead.' wrote Carter. Its passages were heaped with the rubbish of the ages. Only portions of its once finely engraved granite sarcophagus and fragments of funerary statues were to be found. 'Yet it still contained interesting scenes engraved upon its walls.' Most striking and most pathetic, he thought, was the picture depicting the funeral rites of the king's second daughter, Meketaten, who apparently died at the tender age of five years. The royal household lamented over the child's body. People long since gone had spoken from their hearts and recorded their feelings in the wall drawings of the king's tomb. What a contrast to look through the open doorway of the tomb and emerge into the bright sunlight, to a world that so early in its history had turned a grave into a 'bed of death'.

The king's tomb in the cliffs overlooking the Royal Valley, which Carter called the 'Darb el Melek' (Road of the Kings), left the impressionable visitor with a feeling of what might have been, a sense of awe at the magnificence which must once have surrounded the king on his journey into eternity. In a curious way, it was premonition, an insight, but for the moment it was a diversion.

Back at the site of the royal city itself, there were almost daily discoveries of glass and pottery, fine tiles and inlays from columns and walls, and plaster moulds. There were the statues and monuments, believed to be the work of Bek, son of Men, 'Chief of Sculptors of the Mighty Monuments of the King', smashed and desecrated but still conveying in their fragmentary form the artistic splendour which glowed briefly in an atmosphere of revolution. There were the painted pavements, the ruined palaces and temples, and perhaps most important of all, the remains of the office block at the eastern end of the king's house, where further discovery by Petrie of cuneiform tablet fragments and a cylinder seal proved beyond reasonable doubt the source of the famous Amarna letters of 1887.

Professor Sayce was present when the fragments were discovered and he noted that some of them were from a dictionary of the Akkadian and Sumerian languages written for the guidance of the Babylonian, and presumably Egyptian, scribes. Another important discovery was a plaster face-mask, life-sized. Carter, who understood the technicalities of mould-making and casting, pointed out that it must have been made from a dead man since the eyes were half open and there was no sign of breathing holes at nostrils or mouth. Petrie concluded that it was the death mask of Akhenaten and that Grébaut would want to keep it in the Cairo Museum. He had the forethought to make several castings before parting with it.

Such finds drew hosts of visitors. One of them, to Carter's great surprise, was the priest Greville Chester, who looked old and tired. Carter remembered him as the son of the incumbent of his parish church at Swaffham and recalled that Chester had shared a donkey with his father when they were boys. He arrived as Carter was recovering from a bout of sickness. The day after returning to Amarna from the king's tomb he had received a cablegram telling him of his father's death. Letters had warned him that a first stroke might lead to another. Petrie handed him the cable and told him with a few gentle words to go to his room to read it. Carter recalled 'a shade of inexpressible sadness' in his master's voice. On 1 May 1892, eight days before his youngest son's eighteenth birthday, Samuel John Carter had died at the age of fifty-seven at Stamford House, the new home he and Martha had moved to in the Fulham Road a year or two earlier, and where they lived with Howard's brother Verney and his sister Amy.

News of the death, the onset of the hot Egyptian summer and the hardness of Petrie's regime combined to cause Carter to sink into a state of exhaustion and acute depression. 'His body perishes,' he wrote of his father, 'but his Memory remains.' And then – 'I began to think, what in the name of common sense, had I to do with any better profession than the one my father had taught me…? Was I better digging among dusty mounds and the remains of long past ages, to be my own chambermaid, to eat tin foods and feel myself a servant?'

Such were the momentary doubts of a depressed and tired young man. By his eighteenth birthday, Howard seemed pleased with his own progress. He observed in his notebook that 'intuition, the subtle recognition of facts, develops slowly; as experience also develops, and thus the progress of true observation.' He was learning to work systematically, a skill for which he thanked Petrie and which he thought would stand him in good stead.

As the hot season arrived, Petrie and Carter were both unwell and the chief decided that 'one year of life is enough to give a single king and his works.' The order was given to start packing. Petrie's spirits should have been raised no end by the news that Grébaut had been replaced and that Jacques de Morgan, with whom Petrie had got on well at a first meeting, was to take over as Director-General. But any suggestion of rejoicing was countered by the news that, before Grébaut's departure from office, a new Khedival decree had been issued on the disposal of antiquities. In future, everything found in the course of excavation would belong to the state, but in consideration of their expenses the excavators would be allotted 'some part' of the finds. Lots would be drawn by the administration and the excavator, but the administration would have the right to buy back any article it required for the museum at a mutually agreed price. The difficulties inherent in such a scheme were obvious to Petrie and he let it be known that if the new Director-General bowed to the edict, and Britain failed to bring necessary pressure to bear on the committee, he would seriously consider taking out French and German citizenship!

Lord and Lady Waterford's *dhabiyah* had joined the fashionable river craft which brought the rich and scholarly to observe the archaeologists at work and attend the Cairo balls. A doctor travelled with them and he examined the two sick excavators. He diagnosed exhaustion and prescribed 'Valentine's meat juice, champagne and a tonic'. Carter was soon on the way to recovery but his chief's temper grew worse. Greville Chester, a benign voice in the councils of excavation in the Near East, wrote to Petrie to dissuade him from doing anything rash. So did Griffith and Flaxman Spurrell, a physician turned archaeologist who became Petrie's friend and protagonist. The master and his apprentice began to pack away the season's finds and arrange what protection they could for the beautiful painted pavements of Amarna. With Griffith's help, Petrie drew up a new chronology for the dynasty which had brought chaos to Egypt yet had given mankind outstanding treasures of art and craftsmanship during Akhenaten's short-lived reign. Akhenaten had died, it was decided, in or just after his seventeenth year, not his twelfth year as had been thought, when he was succeeded by the even younger Tutankhamun. Such debate was outside the competence or indeed the interest of Carter at that time.

Optimism returned as he went home to England in midsummer 1892: 'Due possibly to Flinders Petrie's training, it became my great desire to be an excavator. To me the calling had an extraordinary attraction.'

Chapter 3

THE PROMISED LAND

THERE was barely time to greet his family at Swaffham in the aftermath of his father's death before being called to London to assist Petrie in sorting out the Amarna artefacts which had arrived at the Millwall dock in London. An exhibition was planned for the autumn and there was urgency about labelling the thousands of items, ranging from fragmentary pots to a large stela which would form a dramatic backdrop to the display. While he and Newberry helped to arrange the exhibits in the rooms of the Archaeological Institute at Oxford Mansion, the EEF headquarters in London's Oxford Circus, Petrie himself, although oppressed by chronic illness, was experiencing the pleasure of academic recognition.

A spate of bad news awaited Petrie's team when it reached England. Petrie's benefactor Amelia Edwards had died. She had been a great power in the affairs of the Egypt Exploration Fund since she became joint honorary secretary at its foundation and without her generous support it is doubtful whether Petrie would have survived the jealousies and rivalries of the committee he so passionately despised. And Greville Chester, who had reminded the young Carter of a link with his own father's boyhood when they met by chance at al-Bersha, died aboard ship on his way home. His vast collection of books, scarabs and other artefacts, the collection of a true antiquarian with an eye for a bargain, went in large part to Petrie, to be housed at University College, London, which was already feeling the strain of an ever-growing mountain of Egyptian remains.

Of far greater significance was the gift of Miss Edwards. As a result of arrangements astutely made before her death, a chair in Egyptology in her name was to be established at University College. Her last will and testament laid down that the elected professor should not be more than forty years of age on appointment. Petrie was just thirty-eight and the obvious choice. Just as the appointment was confirmed his doctor diagnosed ulceration of the stomach with attendant haemorrhage. The physician might well have argued that his patient's famous tinned-food diet and the stark living conditions at his camps in Egypt and Palestine must have contributed to the early onset of digestive trouble. Whatever the cause, however, he spurned medical help and refused to take the matter seriously. He took a few days off in August before returning to the exhibition hall where Carter and Newberry worked feverishly with his old friend Dr Spurrell and the antiquarian dealer R.N. Riley in an attempt to sort out the pottery, scarabs, beads and so forth which continued to turn up from Egypt by the crateload, despite Grébaut's attempt to keep anything of value in Egypt.

Carter was reminded of his chief's artfulness when the objects were being loaded at the local railway station of Amarna. There were thirty-six packing cases in all, but Petrie had applied for permission to transport only thirty-five. The stationmaster refused to take the consignment since it did not comply with the documentation from the Department of Antiquities. Petrie promptly rushed to the nearest town where he purchased a few wooden planks which were cut to length and used to board up two packing cases as though they were one.

For just on ten years, staff and elected representatives of University College, the British Museum and the Egypt Exploration Fund had fought bitterly. Much of the dissention followed on the death of the first president of the Fund, Erasmus Wilson, in 1884. Removed from his calming and authoritative influence, the secretariat divided into factions. These centred largely on the mutual antipathy of the Fund's principal excavators, Petrie and Naville, the uncompromising demands of the Society of Biblical Archaeology and the

Religious Tract Society, in which Naville and Dr Samuel Birch, Keeper of the British Museum's Oriental Department, were heavily involved, and the interminable squabble between the joint secretaries, Miss Edwards and Poole.

Matters were not improved by the dictatorial powers assumed by Amelia Edwards' personal secretary, Miss Paterson, a harridan of a woman who was capable of putting the most eminent academic in his place and who became the effective power in the office after Miss Edwards' death. 'Naville's line of contemptuous silence is best,' Poole wrote to Amelia Edwards in June 1884, citing the professor's customary way of dealing with difficult people, apropos of a row that had broken out between them and the American, Cope Whitehouse, regarding the establishment of a US branch of the Fund. 'Ultimatum to Religious Tract Society'; 'Birch's impertinence'; 'Miss Edwards should do all she can…to show up B[irch] and B[udge]'; 'Only Petrie can bring him [Poole] back to reason'; 'Poole does not agree with Miss Edwards that Naville is an expensive luxury'; thus the fracas continued. At one stage Poole assured Miss Edwards that his health (and perhaps by implication his temper) had improved 'since taking the pledge'.

The correspondence of the fund reflected the friction that had dogged Petrie for the first ten years of his professional life. Warning signs were there for the impressionable Carter. By the time he came on the scene, another British Museum official, H.A. Grueber, had taken somewhat tight-fisted control of the Fund's finances, and the young man quickly learnt that he would not become rich by burning the midnight oil. While on leave from Egypt he wrote to Griffith to explain that some al-Bersha drawings had been completed by his putting in a fortnight's overtime, so as not to hinder the Bani Hasan work; 'My charge is £1,' he stated. A consequence of Amelia Edwards' warfare with Poole and other British Museum official was a further provision in her will to the effect that no one who held office in the British Museum should be eligible for the University College chair, an edict which ruled out Birch's assistant, Wallis Budge, who coveted the job.

The exhibition opened on 19 September. There happened to be an international congress of orientalists in London at the same time and Petrie, hardly able to drag himself from place to place, read a paper on 'Recent Discoveries at Tell el Amarna', visiting the exhibition between times, though he was too sick to attend the opening. A most important visitor from Carter's viewpoint was Lord Amherst. His benefactor was keen to see his colour drawings from Bani Hasan, but more to the point he wanted to talk about the treasures of Amarna, where Carter's energetic work in the rubbish tip of the Great Temple had resulted in something like a ton of plaster and stone fragments being salvaged in his lordship's name and despatched to Didlington Hall. There they remained unsorted, their artistic and historical significance unrecognised, for some thirty years.

A few of Carter's sketches of the Amarna pavements were on show. They were a small if promising contribution to the exhibition, overshadowed in his own mind by anxiety to return to Egypt and resume work on the colour facsimiles which the excavations at Amarna had interrupted. In fact, the EEF had invited two new members to join the team, Percy Newberry's architect brother, John, and the draughtsman Percy Buckman, for a further season's work at Bani Hasan. In September, Carter received a long list of questions about his work at al-Bersha from Miss Paterson, in which the secretary showed some confusion about the tomb of Tahutihotep (Djehutihotpe) and the tomb from which the scene of the colossus on the sledge was obtained. 'All the scenes that you mentioned in your list, are from the tomb of Tahutihotep at El Bersha,' she said. 'The Colossus tomb and the tomb of Tahutihotep are the same', Carter replied with brevity and a bold hand which suggested increasing self-confidence.

By the beginning of December he was on his way back to the rock tombs of Bani Hasan via the Continental Express to Naples and thence by ship to Trieste and Alexandria. This route enabled him to spend some time in Italy visiting the classical sites and art galleries, and was one he followed regularly from then on.

Petrie had remained in England to nurse his stomach disorder (having refused the doctors' entreaties to rest), to distribute the Amarna finds between Oxford, Philadelphia and University College, and consider his future as Edwards Professor of Archaeology. He did not return to Amarna, leaving the site to others, notably the Germans of the Deutsche Orient Gesellschaft in the early years of the next century.

The Newberrys joined Carter in Naples in mid-December and they arrived in Cairo on the 23rd, where Buckman awaited them. Percy Newberry had to cope with the usual administrative difficulties. Herr Brugsch was in charge of the Antiquities Department in the absence of the Director-General de Morgan who, according to Petrie, was an Englishman who had adopted French nationality and name-style. Newberry initially applied for permission to survey tombs and copy wall drawings in the cliffs east of Amarna, but he was told that no copying work could proceed until M. de Morgan had given permission, and as he was away at Aswan no permit could be expected for at least ten days. The British party therefore decided to resume work at Bani Hasan, for which a permit already existed. They arrived there by river-boat on 3 January 1893 after spending a dismal Christmas in Cairo.

> On the whole, it was a fellowship such has seldom met together; we were of all opinions, on every imaginable subject, but generally tolerant of all. In camp life the concurrence of every member of the community is peculiarly desirable. We camped as before in the uninscribed rock chamber.

The three artists worked harmoniously and argued fiercely, sharing domestic tasks with a common incompetence. High above the plain, Bani Hasan was a healthy place. 'I do not know of a healthier or more beautiful spot,' Carter wrote in his notebook. 'From the rock terrace one sees Great Nature... the view, where the land is subdued in tint, cool in contrast to the golden after-glow in the evening sky, is a veritable picture of the "Promised Land".' But he and his colleagues had not bargained for the wet season's exceptional deluge. They were soon awash in their rock-cut chamber and were forced to dam the doorway to avoid drowning. When the rains ceased, a swarm of locusts appeared like a huge cloud which took eighteen hours to pass. The insect armada moved from east to west, obscuring the sky and destroying every vestige of plant life as it went. It was a joy to move the few miles upriver to al-Bersha and the Hare Nome tombs and chapels where Carter had been working when Petrie called him to Amarna in the previous season.

Always experimenting with new and safer ways of copying the precious wall drawings, Carter devised yet another method of tracing at al-Bersha, this time using a dry squeeze, with tough white linen paper which required only slight pressure to reveal the outlines so that they could be traced with a soft pencil. Thus he was able to make accurate, life-size copies.

Just as he had perfected the new method to the point where he could work effectively, he was called to yet another of the Fund's sites, Timai al Amdid (ancient Mendes), 400 miles to the north of the Delta. Newberry had gone back to Cairo on 6 February to speak to Brugsch about the Amarna permit. There he found a letter awaiting him from Grueber in London telling him to send Carter to Cairo 'at once' to join 'a Mr Rogers'. Carter was on his way next day, joining up with Guthrie Roger, as it turned out, for the journey to the Delta and al Amdid. A large collection of scorched and carbonised Greek papyri had been found there the year before by Naville. When some of the precious rolls reached London they were 'nothing but crumbs of charcoal and ashes'. When Carter arrived a year later to examine at Petrie's suggestion the Roman area of the mound, he and the inexperienced Roger wrestled with an almost impossible task. The camp on the mound where the papyri were supposed to have been found was infested with jackals. No one knew precisely where the burnt texts were to be found. No excavation permit had been granted and telegrams to the Fund in London and the Antiquities Department in Cairo met with customary silence. Mercifully, another deluge solved their problems. After several weeks the site was under water, their tent had collapsed and Guthrie Roger – 'a strange fellow' – wept profusely. The project was abandoned after two wasted months. Carter went back to al-Bersha, joining Newberry at Cairo *en route*. Roger was never heard of again in archaeological circles.

Before going to the tombs of al-Bersha, Carter and the rest of the party had called briefly at one of the Amarna sites marked out for the attention of the Archaeological Survey, described by him as 'The Tombs of the Grandees' of Amarna, in the lower foothills just to the east of the ancient city. The hoped-for permit had not been granted by the Antiquities Department, however, and Carter was taken ill with a stomach complaint. Newberry decided to stay on at Amarna for a further week to give his assistant time to recover and to give Buckman a chance to make some sketches of the Amarna plain. Afterwards they went on to another site, Shaikh Said, and the tombs of the Sixth Dynasty nomarchs, predecessors of the 'Great Chiefs' of the Middle Kingdom buried nearby at al-Bersha.

Back at the Hare Nome tombs of al-Bersha, Carter's colleagues were still using the old tracing-paper technique: 'My bugbear – reigning with a strong upper hand,' Carter noted. Work in the tombs and temples went on until June 1893. When it was completed, hundreds of reliefs and wall paintings had been preserved with remarkable fidelity and accuracy, much of which was due to Carter's draughtsmanship and his insistence on dedication to 'truth' and infinite care in copying the art of the ancients. But when they were finally published, the overall impression created by the drawings was of their having been reduced to too small a scale. In the previous season

Petrie had told Newberry and Fraser to copy *everything* they saw. They had obeyed the injunction, as had Blackden, but much important detail was lost in reproduction. Only Carter, of his own initiative, had seen the need to copy exactly and on a same-size scale.

Recreation and drawing were as one for Carter in the rare moments of rest at al-Bersha. His notes on wildlife provided a ready reference for future drawings:

> Some scaly, a few furred like the fox and the desert hare, but mostly feathered. Several kinds of vultures, one or two falcons, a long-legged buzzard, ravens, blue rock pigeons, sand partridge and other smaller desert birds which delight in eking out a precarious existence in desolate solitude. On high eagles used to soar in the still air. And along the riverbank in the scant patches of palm were turtle doves.

Sometimes he took a shot-gun with him, hoping to obtain a wild goose for the pot, but the birds had developed a keen eye for the hunter and he was seldom able to get the better of them. On one occasion he succeeded in hitting one of the birds but it was not killed outright. As it died the creature kept its blue eyes fixed uncompromisingly on its executioner, reminiscent of Byron's eaglet which died with its eyes glued to the poet's in Italy. Like Byron, Carter was ashamed and seldom carried a gun from that moment. In any case, he preferred to draw the birds.

At al-Bersha, Shaikh Ayd reappeared to stress his devotion to the young man he had escorted in the desert during the previous season. The old Shaikh's welcome reminded him of Abraham's entertainment of the angels in Genesis 18: 'He kissed me, he hugged me, he produced water, fetched morsels of bread, cakes, butter and milk, and would have slain a sheep if I let him.' Eventually this 'Child of the Wilderness', as Carter called him, insisted on sleeping protectively outside the door of Carter's tent when they travelled together, accompanied by his

Badu followers and armed with a flintlock and a long curved sword. The Englishman had to plead with him to pitch his tent 'a little way off'. When he fell asleep the Shaikh 'made an unusual nasal proclamation of the fact'.

Newberry thought his assistant still spent too much time in commune with nature. But rough sketches of every kind of wild creature and close observation of the countryside would stand Carter in good stead should he ever again need to make his living by art alone. At nineteen, still immersed in all the varied aspects of archaeology and held in tolerably high esteem by his superiors, he was, when he thought about it, justifiably hopeful for the future. But there was forewarning of difficulties to come in his serious demeanour and often obstinate manner. Both his skill and an unbending belief in his own rightness would prove heavy crosses to carry as the years went by. For the moment, he was still gaining valuable experience and he went on to his next task brimming with confidence and optimism.

In the autumn, the fund sent him to its main expedition at Deir al Bahari, then under the direction of Edouard Naville. The new chief was a distinguished scholar and an indifferent excavator whose interests lay principally in linguistics and epigraphy. He saw archaeology as a means of illuminating the Biblical record, a view shared by many of the prominent men and women who governed the Egypt Exploration Fund and its sister body the Palestine Exploration Fund. Naville and Petrie had started their Egyptian relationship on amicable terms, and Petrie had been impressed by the older and senior academic. But ten years later they were at daggers drawn. 'What treasures we probably have lost,' bemoaned Naville of the papyri of Mendes, destroyed in a fire of Roman times. Petrie blamed Naville. In a letter to the Academy he wrote that it was essential to send a properly trained worker to rescue what had not been destroyed already 'by the finder, in cleaning the chambers of the library'. Naville was outraged. 'It is not the first time that Petrie expresses his contempt for my work.' Petrie subsequently denied using the word 'cleaning'. It was a misprint for 'clearing', he said. In a letter to Poole, Naville made his anger abundantly clear. Petrie's accusations of clumsiness and brutality were not only unjust, they were 'a miserable way of showing off his own excellence of which he is so thoroughly convinced'. The row went on, with Petrie trying to force the gentlemanly Naville to resign from the Fund. To dismiss him would, he thought, be 'unthinkable'.

The dispute had been the reason for the Fund's decision to send Carter to Mendes in March 1893 to rescue the papyri. By the time the committee was ready to consider the acrimonious correspondence between Naville and Petrie, the former was on his way back to Egypt to report to de Morgan and start work at Deir al Bahari. The committee sent a telegram which caught up with him at Aswan, asking him to defer his application for Deir al Bahari and suggesting that he ask de Morgan for Karnak. The elderly and respected Naville was understandably furious. 'If my work is of so little value, not to say none, as Petrie thinks, I shall not impose myself any longer on the Society, and it is far better that I should go.' Having vented his anger he ignored the telegram and agreed with the director that he should start work at Deir al Bahari. Even so, Petrie convinced the committee that Naville would almost certainly cause irreparable harm to the delicate reliefs of 'the beautiful cliff temple'.

Count d'Hulst, the French aristocrat who was working with Naville, was another of Petrie's *bêtes noires*. He had gone so far as to recommend *'wet* paper' for copying the priceless graffito of Maidum. De Morgan was another black sheep, 'a mere businessman'. As for the other Frenchman, Amélineau, his work was 'scandalous'. Fortunately for the committee, d'Hulst by his own action solved the problem of dismissal. He insulted de Morgan and was sent packing so that the committee was spared the need to insist on Naville getting rid of him. As for the rest, Naville was told that Carter, 'or some other trained excavator', should accompany him to ensure that small finds were not ignored. It was Naville's lack of interest in 'small finds' that particularly incensed Petrie. At any rate, the insistence of the EEF committee on Carter's credentials as a 'trained excavator' in its dealings with one of the world's senior academic figures was a feather in the cap of the Englishman as he approached his twentieth birthday and joined Professor Naville at Deir al Bahari where the mortuary temple of Queen Hatshepsut was being cleared.

Chapter 4

'DIDLINGTON UP THE NILE'

IN the three-month interval between finishing work at al-Bersha and taking up his next appointment at Deir al Bahari, Carter spent much of his time laboriously inking in drawings for Griffith at a wage of £1 a week, assisted by his brother Verney. Unexpected hot weather and high winds in the previous season at al-Bersha had made it difficult to work to plan and he found it impossible to use the 'rubbing' (or squeeze) technique in copying a large frieze representing the transport of a colossal statue. Instead, he had to trace it painstakingly. 'It is an awful job' he wrote to Newberry on 17 January 1893. 'I have been a week at it now & it is not done yet. I think a week or ten days now will finish all. I have painted all the most important scenes and also 98 examples of hieroglyphs, and there are yet about 20 more to do.'

He had received a letter from Grueber at the British Museum asking him to stay on so that he could revise colour plates for a forthcoming publication on the spot, but another letter arrived at almost the same time from Miss Paterson explaining that the committee did not wish him to stay on after finishing at al-Bersha. While the Fund dithered, Carter had suggested that Verney, who was very experienced in such matters, might help with the plates and he was sent out hurriedly. A postscript to the letter to Newberry suggested the perennial difficulty. 'I should be very much obliged if you could let my brother have £20 of my salary, as the bad weather of this last winter having destroyed his plates has put him so far behind… I am sorry to bother you but you know how awkward money matters are.'

Carter's role at Deir al Bahari, where he arrived in October 1893 with another young draughtsman, Percy Brown, was to copy the wall sculptures, paintings and historical inscriptions of the mortuary temple. The task was to occupy him for six contented years. Naville gave him a free hand and he decided there and then to abandon tracing paper for ever and to devise his own approach to the difficult and delicate work of 'facsimile-copying'. When it came to the point, he changed not only the approach but the definition too.

The procedure, set out in the instructions issued by the Fund and hammered home by Petrie, Griffith, Newberry and all the experienced men he had worked with, was unequivocal: 'Mechanical exactitude of facsimile-copying is required rather than freehand or purely artistic work.' Carter copied the injunction in his notebook. He also recorded his objections. It was a misguided attitude, just as wrong as if a tracing were made of a good portrait, 'mechanically accurate perhaps but lacking the essence of what made it a good portrait'. The same was true in the case of ancient art: 'When reproducing an ancient [work of] art, let us by all means be accurate, and employ every kind of mechanical aid to obtain that objective; but let that mechanical aid be our assistant, not our master.'

He set out his own ethos: 'to first observe the fundamental laws of Egyptian Art; how it eliminates the inessentials; to copy that art accurately and intelligently with honest work, a free hand, a good pencil and suitable paper.' He quoted Ruskin's dictum in support of his cause: 'In true art, the hand, the head and the heart of man go together.' And he compared the existing approach to the copying of ancient art with a schoolchild 'carefully tracing a map (about the making of which the child knows nothing) for a lesson in geography'.

Some of his colleagues, and most of the elders of the Fund, saw his theories as a naïve attempt by a twenty-year-old beginner to elevate copying to an undeserved significance. It was a process which most practitioners and observers looked on as a purely technical procedure having nothing to do with creativity

or art. But the apprentice was right. He was the first to see the
shortcomings of the old method and he instituted a new, more
imaginative and, essentially, more vital approach. At the time,
however, his assertive, confident thesis met with half-hearted
acceptance by a few of his fellow workers, and downright
condemnation by others.

Some thought his work 'soulless'. That collective view was
expressed many years later by the American Thomas Hoving of
New York's Metropolitan Museum of Art, who steeped himself
in Carter's legacy and who was to write the self proclaimed
'inside story' of his ultimate achievement. He spoke for many
in the related worlds of art and archaeology when he described
the young man's patient recording of the paintings, reliefs and
inscriptions at Deir al Bahari:

> Howard Carter was the perfect man for the job. Quiet,
> retiring, awkward in the presence of anyone who seemed to
> have been blessed with greater privileges in life, he was a
> loner, and an utterly dedicated worker. The very fact that his
> water-colours gave no hint of inner spirit, or demonstrated
> any sort of creative spark, made them perfect for the task at
> hand. He made his eyes and his fingers totally subservient to
> the process of recording the precise shape and outline,
> and the exact colors, of his subject matter. A number of
> water-colours by Howard Carter are on exhibit in the
> Egyptian Department of the Metropolitan Museum. They
> display punctiliousness, verisimilitude and no life at all.

It is not necessary to pursue the argument. The contrary
evidence is partly in New York's Metropolitan Museum. Much
more is contained in the six volumes of work from Deir al
Bahari, faithfully reproduced by the most painstaking of printing
processes, collotype, and published by the Egypt Exploration
Fund under Naville's editorship. Each eye that sees can make
its own judgement. Some of his representations of Egyptian
wildlife paintings must rank alongside accepted masterpieces of

specialist 'nature' drawing such as the Audubon studies of American birds or Kaendler's masterly sketches of the Elector of Saxony's zoological collection for Meissen porcelain decoration and modelling. Theirs, like Carter's, was functional art, but art none the less. Carter was reviving the work of 4,000 years before with fidelity and affection. In doing so he produced works of stunning beauty which preserved the spirit of the prototypes, executed necessarily in accordance with the need to reproduce them by a modern printing process. They show feeling for subject and material and fine draughtsmanship.

Within a month of arriving at Deir al Bahari for the second season, on Friday 30 November 1894, Naville wrote a progress report to the Fund telling them that David Hogarth, Sir Arthur Evans' deputy as Keeper of the Ashmolean Museum, had turned up from Crete at the beginning of December along with his wife. Hogarth had attended a Fund committee meeting with Naville in October at which Naville explained that no important discoveries were to be expected in the forthcoming season. The initial task was to finish the clearing of the temple which he had begun the year before.

There was great economic distress locally due to a fall in the price of the corn grown on the fertile plain of the Nile. All the men flocked to the temple of Deir al Bahari when they heard of Naville's presence. He took on 112 workmen on the first day to help build and operate a railway extension to the site which was originally intended to serve the French expedition under Daressy nearby at Madinat Habu. On the following day he took on an additional hundred men to excavate the vast rubbish heap which covered the middle part of the temple site. Another crew set to work on the Hathor shrine of the temple, while others looked for undiscovered chambers. 'It is no easy thing to engage one's workmen this year,' he wrote. Although he had been able to give modest employment to well over 200 men, many more were left without work or food for their families. Fighting broke out when he selected a hundred men from the six or seven hundred who sought jobs. While Naville dealt with the disorder, Carter and Hogarth went off to spend a day or two with Petrie at the predynastic site of Naqada.

Naville was confident that the temple would be cleared that winter. But rebuilding the temple according to plan would take much longer. The task was one which an experienced architect or engineer would require more than a year to complete, 'especially when one has to work with natives and native implements'. Doubtless Petrie would have completed the task in 'half the time'. The gentlemanly Naville was not always willing to use silence to counter the attacks of his arch rival.

By 30 December, Naville was able to report to Miss Paterson that Carter had dispatched the last batch of drawings for the first stage of the work on the temple at Deir al Bahari. In January 1895, Hogarth reported the final clearance of the great rubbish mounds from the north court of the temple, down to its pavement. 'At the smallest computation, over 42,000 cubic metres of rubbish have been removed from this court alone.' The temple of Hatshepsut could now be seen in all its glory from across the river at Luxor. There was a postscript to Hogarth's report:

I reopen this letter to record the discovery (due to Mr H. Carter) of several blocks belonging to the ruined south wall of the Punt scene. We have recovered now the last king of Punt and much of the scenery of his land; this find in view of the admitted excellence of these particular reliefs and the unusual interest attaching to pictures of marsh-dwellings in tropical Africa, may rank among the best results of our work here.

Another report from Naville, dated 18 March 1895, informed the committee in London that Carter and Brown would be leaving Deir al Bahari for England in April and taking with them a set of thirty-two colour plates, 'collated and ready to be started for publication'. A separate note to Miss Paterson reminded the secretary that, as he was leaving for Switzerland at the end of the season, he had left some money with Carter, 'but he will require more when he leaves for England'. He 'must be empowered to draw it at Cook's when he wants it.' When Naville arrived at his Swiss home, a letter awaited him announcing that the committee was so pleased with results so far at Deir al Bahari that it wondered if the time had come for an exhibition. 'I very much hope the committee will decide to have one,' Naville replied. There was plenty of material and more to come, as they would see when Carter turned up. 'Petrie would make one for much less' (he meant, presumably, with much less material), 'but it was worth waiting for Carter's paintings.' 'Do you know anything about Carter's return?' he asked. The committee knew no more than Naville.

On 9 May Naville had word that Carter had gone off to Bani Hasan to do some work for Griffith. 'He expects to be there for three weeks,' he informed Miss Paterson, who had reluctantly agreed to Carter's drawing funds from Cook's Tours for the journey home. On 10 June, Naville told his employers that he was delighted to hear that they had decided to go ahead with an exhibition at the beginning of July. The time suited him and Hogarth perfectly. As for Howard Carter, he 'must be back by that time'. Apart from bringing the paintings with him, he would be very useful, particularly for mending some of the objects from the temple.

Carter had been caught up in a social diversion as well as archaeological asides. The Amherst family and their in-laws the Mitfords had decided to invade Egypt *en masse* for an extended holiday which stretched from December 1894 to June 1895. Alicia, the youngest daughter, kept a diary which she headed 'Didlington up the Nile', with reference to a remark made by her great-uncle Charles Fountaine when her father asked him if he would like to accompany himself and his wife on a Nile excursion in 1860.

They were at Port Said on 20 December 1894, to find Arabs 'yelling and praying'. At Ismailiya they were met by the embassy dragoman Selim Pietro, 'simply charmingly Eastern'. They found the local Arabs 'nice…not the awful mixture of races at Port Said'. 'Sketching mania very strong.' Alicia noted, filling her journal with attractive line and tone drawings of classical Roman themes before she arrived in Egypt. From then on, hieroglyphs, at which she exhibited an expert hand, occupied the margins. Percy Newberry, reinforcing his long-standing friendship, and his wife Essie were guides and companions for much of the journey, while Carter, whom Alicia remembered from childhood visits to Didlington with his father, flitted in and out of her memoir.

Altogether, she recorded an accurate picture of an aristocratic journey through the two Egypts, vastly rich and extravagantly poor, existing uncomfortably side by side; a picture which archaeologists seldom paused to record though it was to be seen in stark reality alongside most of their digs. After leaving Lord Amherst's calling cards with General and Lady Walker, the Sirdar (General Kitchener) and Lord and Lady Cromer, they set out on a pre-Christmas spree at the Cairo races (where Alicia's pet dog Ducker, left in the care of one of Lady Walker's servants, disappeared never to be seen again). On Christmas Eve, the Newberrys took them round the Giza Museum, 'Kings Ramses, Tothmes, Seti lying in cases'. The display she thought 'sad, unplanned', the jewellery 'lovely'. Christmas Day 1894 was spent with the Newberrys and 'Wiffy' Bramly, keeper of the Giza zoo and later on military governor of Sinai.

The New Year saw them aboard their *dhabiyah* as they made their way from one archaeological site to another, towed by the tug *Ptab*. At Saqqara, where they saw Mariette's old house near the Step-Pyramid, Alicia noted cartouches of the Twenty-Second Dynasty kings on the temple stones. Bebbeh, Biba al Fashan, al-Hiba… As they proceeded ashore each day, Alicia's husband-to-be, Lord Rockley, shot every creature in sight in the grand manner of the time. A kestrel and a hooded chat came tumbling from the sky. 'The latter is rather rare,' observed the young lady, 'and I skinned him after.' Villagers tried to sell them a mummy case but they thought it too expensive at £5. As they approached Bani Hasan, Coptic monks came down to the river bank to beg alms. 'One swam after us. He was only given an empty bottle.' Newberry showed them the rock-cut tombs at Bani Hasan. 'Charming,' was the verdict. They were told they must not touch the sacred mummified cats of the feline necropolis, but two were smuggled out for the Amherst collection.

By 10 January they were at Tal al Amarna. They found Akhenaten's tomb to the north badly desecrated and full of bats, as Petrie and Carter had found it four years before. Of the reliefs which Carter had copied, they were most impressed by the wall representations of 'women weeping and wailing and worshipping the "Aten" sun's rays, some of them really well drawn'. The river journey took them to Asyut where Newberry showed them round the tomb of Khety and told them that he proposed to revise some of Griffith's past work there. They saluted Professor Sayce's river-boat *Ishtar* on the way to Gezira al Dum where they arrived on 16 January, noting the point on the river bank where 'old Shaikh Salem, lately died, sat naked…for 53 years'.

On and on at leisurely pace past Abydos to Denderah and thence Naqada where Petrie was digging up the pre-dynastic past with two of the Fund's men, Price and Grenfell. The master's latest site, associated in archaic times with Libyan occupation, reminded Alicia of a passage from the father of history: 'Heroditus [*sic*] mentions a Libyan race who used to kill their parents at a certain age and eat them to prevent their growing too old.' By 20 January they were at Thebes and Deir al Bahari where Carter emerged from the temple of Hatshepsut. 'After lunch the Egertons of Tatton came on board – also Howard Carter who is working with Mr Naville clearing out the temple at Der al Bahrah' (the spelling was as good as any). They sat together and watched the sun set over Luxor.

There was no further reference to Carter until a month

later, 23 February, when they returned from the long journey via Aswan and the island of Elephantine to Abu Simbel and Wadi Halfa and the cataracts of the Nile. Back in Middle Egypt, they went up to Deir al Bahari, 'saw H. Carter and M. Naville and had a short look around the temple, rode on to see Mr Newberry's tomb.' Next day the Newberrys, Carter and Naville dined with the visitors. 'He [Naville] is one of the nicest excavators we have met. H. Carter slept aboard.' Alicia always referred to the young man she had known since her own girlhood as 'H. Carter'. Everyone else was 'Mr' and 'Monsieur'. They were invited to M. Naville's 'cool house' at Qurna above the Valley where Naville's team was at work. 'We looked at H. Carter's drawings after lunch and then saw the temple. H. Carter came back to sleep on board.' Carter dined and slept aboard their river-boat every night during the week they were at anchor off Luxor.

Alicia Amherst's observations were always matter of fact. Unlike the Newberrys and Navilles, and the various tourists and bounty-hunters they met on the way, Carter was received into their midst with unadorned yet warm hospitality. At Karnak they found Maggie Benson, youngest daughter of the Archbishop, digging at the Temple of Mut. A classical scholar just down from Lady Margaret Hall, she was about to join the Sisterhood of the Epiphany. There were several evening parties but Carter seems to have been at none of them. 'Dr May and Newberrys and Crossley for evening party... Lord Compton sang to us most beautifully.' It was the last evening of their grand tour. They left by river on 1 March for the long journey home and Alicia's marriage to Baron Rockley.

Carter turned up in England in late June 1895, just in time for his paintings to go on show at the Fund's exhibition in London. Entitled 'Guide to the Temple of Deir al Bahari', it attracted the faithful to Oxford House and enhanced Carter's reputation among those devotees and experts for whom Egyptian mural art had a particular appeal. But the public at large was only marginally aware of the great discoveries being made year by year in Egypt. In 1893 there had been exhibitions in London and Manchester of facsimile water-colours of scenes from the tombs of Bani Hasan, al-Bersha and Deir al Gabrawi. They were described in the official catalogue as having been 'made for the Egypt Exploration Fund by Mr M.W. Blackden, Mr Howard Carter, and Mr Percy Buckman, under the superintendence of Mr Percy E. Newberry, directed by Mr F.Ll. Griffith'.

It was much the same cast list at the latest London show. The catalogue went on to explain to visitors who by and large still knew little of ancient Egyptian art that the women were painted in yellow tones, the men red 'because their skins were generally tanned by greater exposure to the sun'. The presence or suggestion of water was 'indicated by parallel waved or zigzag lines, as well as colour'. Chemical tests had shown that the red pigment used was essentially of ferric oxide; yellow was derived from iron ochres; shades of blue and green generally came from oxides of copper and iron in ground frits, or glassy pastes. Their white was obtained from lime, their black from lamp-black. In fact, colouring materials for the painter, and indeed the potter, had changed little if at all in 4,000 years.

After the London exhibition, Carter went home to Swaffham and at the end of August took up Lord Amherst's invitation to go over to Didlington Hall to help sort out the Amarna objects. It was a hopeless task but he stayed at the Hall for a week trying to make sense of the great heap of fragmentary material that had arrived from Egypt in the aftermath of Petrie's excavation. While he was there, the family forwarded a postcard from Miss Paterson asking Carter in her emphatic way when he would be available. He replied on Amherst's notepaper in the abrupt manner he had come to use in dealing with that formidable lady: 'Your postcard was forwarded to me. I shall be returning by the end of the week.'

He was back with Naville in Egypt in November, having sent on two insured packing cases, one containing drawing and photographic materials, the other personal belongings including an expensive leather saddle. He was determined to solve the painful problem of travel by horse and donkey among the rocks and dunes of his workplace.

By January 1896 Naville was able to report to Grueber in his rather halting English that his assistant had added a financial coup to his other excellent work:

> We had yesterday Mr Horniman's visit, he had luncheon with us. Carter took him over the temple, and he was so much interested and struck by the beauty and the size of the work that he said at once he would give us one day's profit, £100, and an annual subscription of £5. He immediately took out his cheque book, and wrote out the enclosed cheque... I am bound to say that it is to Carter that the Society is indebted for that gift. It was he who made Mr Horniman acquainted with the Fund, and who took him over the temple yesterday.

Horniman, who was head of the wealthy tea family, was Member of Parliament for Falmouth.

After describing Carter's current work, which involved the superintending of repair work on the temple, Naville went on to explain that he had been compelled to suspend work on copying the wall paintings. He also gave some idea of Carter's progress in the six years he had now spent in Egypt.

> As I said, Mr Carter has done the work admirably. He has a very quick eye for finding the places where the stones belong to; besides, as he has a thorough command of Arabic, he can direct and superintend the men or rather teach them what they can do. It would be absolutely impossible for him to do any drawings at the same time.

Naville suggested that someone else should be sent out to look after the building work. 'I agree with Mr Carter that it would be a pity if he was prevented from drawing because he had to

61

work after those ceilings.'

Home visits between seasons in 1896 and 1897 were marked by weddings which provided rare opportunities for the family to come together. In June 1896, Carter's sister Amy Joyce married a publisher from south London, John Walker, and in the following June his thirty-six-year-old brother Samuel married Mary Brown, a farmer's daughter. Ten years earlier, his elder brother William had married another Walker, Julia Mary of Swaffham, who was the daughter of the Returning Officer for Norwich.

In the 1896 – 7 season Carter was able to return to his drawing work; he refused to call it copying. The fund appointed Margeritis A. Crissocopolu, an experienced Cypriot who had worked for Hogarth, for 'superintending the works of preservation and repair at the Temple of Deir al Bahari'. The contract was dated 12 December 1897 and covered the completion of 'certain walls', the building of columns with architraves, and covering the work with brick vaults. The specification was precise. The work would be done partly in masonry, partly in burnt brick and partly in crude brick, surfaces to be plastered and whitewashed. The work was to be 'directed and approved by Mr Howard Carter, Inspector for the Service of Antiquities', acting on behalf of the committee of the Egypt Exploration Fund.

Carter's duties were even more exhaustively defined. His responsibilities included the dismissal of incompetent workmen, approving the disposition of the headman's tent, removal of scaffolding, paying the work-force, keeping track of building materials and the ordering of any additional materials, and approving the work on completion. For taking on the extra burden he would be paid the sum of £9. The superintendent's pay was not specified in the contract. By 27 February, Naville was able to tell the committee: 'It is certainly quite remarkable how well that difficult work of rebuilding is done.' If he was not making himself rich in the process, Carter was in the ascendant professionally and his future in Egypt seemed assured.

There was another season at Deir al Bahari, marked by storm damage to the temple which had been so carefully restored. Dr Somers Clarke, a distinguished committee member, saw the damage in November 1898 and wrote to a colleague, Hilton Price, who was about to leave for Egypt, 'When you come to Luxor please give particular attention to the condition of the wall surfaces at Deir al Bahari... The colour had begun to run. The surfaces are scaling off... Carter will point out to you the sad results... We must set about roofing over the most valuable part as soon as possible.' Price wrote to Grueber from Cairo with a copy of Clarke's letter: 'I have just seen this from Clark [sic] – it reads most disastrous. What can be done? I am now off up the Nile. Carriage is waiting to take me to boat.'

At the end of December Carter wrote to Grueber to tell him that at least £300 would be required to cover the palace area with a protective roof with column supports. The work would take at least four or five months and all the best men had been attracted to Aswan and the Sudan where they were offered better pay by the Americans digging there. He had already written to Miss Paterson telling her that he wished to go down to Aswan for a week and asking her to put his request before the committee. He hoped that major construction tasks could be held over until the following season so that he could complete the drawing work in the chambers. He did not seem to think the damage was as great as Somers Clarke and Price made out, nor did he think the remedial work so urgent. 'Might I ask if the committee wishes me to do this work?' Indeed, he wondered whether the committee would require his services at all when work finished at Deir al Bahari in 1899.

The drawings and building work were completed in the following season. Some stones removed from the palace walls years before had found their way to the Marquess of Northampton's private collection and he presented them to the EEF so that Carter could return them to their original places. Carter had worked side by side with Naville for six years at Deir al Bahari and he had nothing but good to say of the gentle, intensely religious Swiss whom Petrie so openly despised. His new chief had left him at liberty for the first time in his life to work in his own way, at his own pace, on the restoration of some of the finest decorative art of the ancient world.

He was never entirely satisfied, however. Isolated in the bare mud-brick house which Naville had built as a makeshift home for himself and his assistants at the head of the valley – except for giving sanctuary to the occasional visitor (Petrie stayed with him in 1896 while preparing quarters for his team at the back of the Ramesseum at Thebes) – he spent most of his spare time drawing and exploring the surrounding countryside. He wandered a great deal along the cliffs and among the craggy hills which housed the royal mortuary temples and beyond to the Valley of the Tombs, or to be precise, the adjacent valleys which housed the kings' tombs to the north and the queens' to the south, cut off from the Nile by the cultivated flood plain. Already his notebooks began to reflect an obsessive interest in the tombs and to anticipate a later reflection, that had he not been an archaeologist he would have made a good detective. Loneliness did not seem to bother him even at an age when most young men seek companionship and shared adventure, not least with the opposite sex.

In fact, the sickly youth of school days had become a strong, contemplative man who could happily endure his own company for months or even years on end in the remote necropolis of the Valley of the Kings. But many of the diggers and scholars who trod the same paths sought him out. One was the German epigraphist Wilhelm Spielberg who was working at Thebes. Petrie's wife Hilda was pleased with the hospitality he and Newberry, together with Spielberg, were able to offer her soon after her marriage in 1898. Carter conceded that the Fund's principal site of Deir al Bahari had 'a certain charm', but he found it unbearably hot except in mid-winter.

He had enjoyed the work Naville set him. He had copied elaborate wall pictures chiefly of mercantile scenes such as the transport by ship of great monoliths of granite from the quarries at Aswan to Karnak, and a naval expedition to the land of Punt in search of frankincense and myrrh, ivory, apes, bustards, precious metals and scented woods. There were also portrayals of the 'divine birth' of Queen Hatshepsut, and many hieroglyphic inscriptions which he rendered with a confident hand and read with increasing ease. He pieced together the history of ancient Egypt as he copied the paintings of the mortuary temple. Aromatic gum trees depicted in transport, probably brought to Egypt from South Arabia, were planted in the sanctuary in honour of the national deity, Amun. Notebook asides had a parochial quality. 'As a matter of fact the commodities brought by this expedition, are very similar to the precious materials conveyed by King Solomon's ships from Tarshish, and they also call in mind the custom of the King's Epiphany gifts of gold, frankincense and myrrh, that are offered annually in the Chapel Royal at St James's.' The delicately sculptured reliefs he had so lovingly and imaginatively preserved were, he noted, 'a permanent feast for the mind'. Later in life he wrote, 'In those six years, although full of hard work, I learnt more of Egyptian Art, its serene simplicity, than in any other time or place.' Perhaps there was unconscious significance in his always writing the word 'art' with a capital 'A'. He still regarded himself as an artist first and foremost and an archaeologist by chance circumstance.

All the same, there was modesty in his self-assessment. Time and again in his notebooks he acknowledges that it was the austere Petrie more than anyone else who taught him to be an excavator. And at the end of the long Deir al Bahari adventure he paid handsome tribute to the young man who worked alongside him: 'I have several colleagues to help me; there were tragedies, professional jealousies, and often amusing comedies; but I was lucky. For several years I had the great fortune of having Percy Brown's good help – a sincere and admirable draughtsman who help[ed] me to earn my wages.'

His last skirmish with the Fund as a member of its excavation staff was on the familiar ground of salary. In March 1899 he wrote to Miss Paterson concerning missing stores which the Fund claimed as its own. 'I should think they must belong to Mons. Naville,' Carter told the secretary. He took the opportunity to remind her that his second quarter salary was about due. In the light of past experience he sent her a receipt in advance of payment, for £68 15s.

As work at Deir al Bahari came to an end in 1899, Maspero entered into his second period of office as Director-General of Antiquities in succession to de Morgan. The 'English', the denomination of all Britons in the East, were back in favour. Unlike the majority of his fellow countrymen, Maspero had always worked in the friendliest way with his British counterparts and with Cromer's administration. He remembered the boy Carter whom he had met briefly when he appeared in Egypt at the age of seventeen. Eight years on, the Frenchman offered the dedicated, taciturn adult from Professor Naville's expedition an important post in the Antiquities Service – Inspector of Monuments for Upper Egypt and Nubia. His headquarters would be at Luxor. Carter accepted the offer without hesitation.

Chapter 5

ARCHAEOLOGISTS AND VANDALS

THE new century heralded the dawn of a promising era for Howard Carter. Fortune had rescued him from anonymity as a member of a large and often quarrelsome archaeological team and given him power and freedom under an energetic chief for whom he had the very highest regard. It was an ideal dispensation and he was prepared to make the most of it. The new appointment took effect from 1 January 1900. His first task was to prepare a preliminary report on the Theban necropolis and its monuments with a view to organizing a system for their future protection.

His excursions during the Naville years had made him familiar with the vast graveyard which stretched across the silent no man's land beyond the lush pastures of the river's west bank, a desolate wasteland which rises relentlessly until it reaches its craggy summit in the cliff which marks Deir al Bahari. At its base is the Valley of the Tombs of the Kings, a rendering of the Arabic Wadi al Biban al Maluk. Carter already knew, more than most men, about the tortuous paths which led from one ledge to another, from one derelict and empty tomb to another, marking out the routes of countless thieves and robbers who had visited the place in the course of 5,000 years and made off with greater riches than Croesus can ever have imagined.

Initial tasks were mainly practical and long overdue. If exact duties had yet to be defined by Maspero and the limits of the inspectorate laid down, Carter was happy to occupy the fringes of any administrative plan which might emerge. He began by arranging for an electric light supply to six known royal tombs of the Valley, no small project since it involved about 3,000 feet of cable, fed underground where possible so as not to mar the prospect. When illumination was provided, he arranged for the tombs to be tidied up and made as secure and waterproof as possible. The tombs themselves were widened and shelters for donkeys, 'sadly wanted', were erected. Iron gates were fitted to the tombs themselves. He was glamourizing the stable and changing the door locks several millennia after most of the horses had bolted, but it was all part of the new policy of attracting tourists. He arranged for electricity to be taken far to the south, to the great Nubian temple at Abu Simbel. And he played his part in what, for him, was the most unattractive of roles, taking sightseers round the tombs and temples.

He expressed his own feelings about the place in the aftermath of breathtaking events some twenty years later, but his words belong to ardent youth and to the anticipation of a drama just beginning to unfold:

> The Valley of the Tombs of the Kings – the very name is full of romance, and of all Egypt's wonders there is none, I suppose, that makes a more instant appeal to the imagination. Here, in this lonely valley-head, remote from every sound of life, with the 'Horn', the highest peak in the Theban hills, standing sentinel like a natural pyramid above them, lay thirty or more kings, among them the greatest Egypt ever knew. Now, probably, but two remain – Amenhotep [Amenophis] II – whose mummy may be seen by the curious lying in his sarcophagus – and Tut.ankh.Amen, who still remains intact beneath his golden shrine.

He had learnt much of the history which Petrie had commended as an essential tool of his work when he first arrived in Egypt, and he gave visitors a graphic description of the plunder which had left the 'God-forsaken' valley devoid even of its dead. In the early part of the Eighteenth Dynasty, in the sixteenth century BC, Tuthmosis I decided to build a cavern in the cliffs opposite Thebes for his last resting place, thus inaugurating the royal necropolis of the Valley. No tomb of note in the whole of Egypt had yet escaped the attentions of the robbers who began their vile profession in the days of the first pyramids, in the archaic period of about 3000 BC.

Carter explained the importance of Tuthmosis's 'unostentatious' tomb, so 'easily overlooked and rarely visited' and 'notable as an experiment in a new theory of tomb design'. That inviolability which earlier kings had sought was achieved by erecting over their bodies 'a very mountain of stone'. Well-being in the netherworld involved a lavish use of gold and treasures to enhance the prestige of the traveller. 'The result', he explained, 'was obvious enough.' Gold and treasures are irresistible and within a few generations at most the mummy would be disturbed and all its accompanying treasures plundered. The kings – indeed, the queens too, and the nobles buried nearby – tried to keep the intruder at bay. Passages were plugged with huge granite boulders, false passages and secret doors were tried; hundreds of false scents were laid. But in every case the robber could outwit the tomb builder. The monarch of that day, as of more modern times, was at the mercy of those who served him, the mason and architect, the goldsmith and carpenter. 'Careless workmanship could leave a danger point in the best planned defences, and, in private tombs at any rate, we know that an ingress for plunderers was sometimes contrived by the officials who planned the work.' Efforts to guard the royal tombs – nearly always built close to their mortuary temples – were 'equally unavailing', however large the endowments left behind for the purpose.

Strange sights The Valley must have seen, and desperate the ventures that took place in it. One can imagine the plotting for days beforehand, the secret rendezvous on the cliff by night, the bribing or drugging of the cemetery guards, and then the desperate burrowing in the dark, the scramble through a small hole built into the burial-chamber, the hectic search by a glimmering light for treasure that was portable, and the return home at dawn laden with booty…

It was Amenophis I who first thought of a secret tomb as a means of outwitting the robber. He built his resting place some distance from his funerary temple, hidden beneath a boulder on the top of a low hill. But Tuthmosis I took the device further. He broke completely from tradition by opting for a small, inconspicuous tomb at the head of the valley. There was to be no monument over the tomb and it was to be situated a good mile away from the funerary temple on the other side of the hill. Tuthmosis entrusted the task to his chief architect, Ineni, who inscribed on the wall of the funerary chapel a testament to his work: 'I superintended the excavation of the cliff tomb of His Majesty, alone, no one seeing, no one hearing.' As Carter told visitors, Ineni failed to reveal anything of the workmen he employed or of how their silence was assured. His own theory was that the work was carried out by prisoners of war who were slaughtered on its completion. But in any case, the secret was probably not kept for long. 'What secret was ever kept in Egypt?'

When Tuthmosis's tomb was discovered in 1899, little but the plain stone sarcophagus remained. The body had been removed and placed alongside that of his daughter Hatshepsut in her tomb, and later hidden with other royal mummies at Deir al Bahari. The fashion had been set, however, and all the remaining kings of the Eighteenth Dynasty, and the two succeeding dynasties, covering a period of some 400 years, were buried in the Valley of the Tombs of the Kings. As Carter remarked, for a few generations under the powerful kings of the Eighteenth and Nineteenth Dynasties, the tombs must have been reasonably safe. Strong rulers meant discipline among populace and officials. It was a different story under the weaklings who reigned for parts of those dynasties, and for the whole of the Twelfth Dynasty. Indeed, from the sixteenth regnal year of Ramesses IX onwards, well-preserved papyri have come down to the modern world which deal with the very subject of tomb robbery. 'We get from them, in addition to very valuable information about the tombs, something which Egyptian documents as a rule singularly lack, a story with a real human element in it, and we are able to see right into the minds of a group of officials who lived in Thebes three thousand years ago.'

The story concerned a conflict between Khemwese, the overseer of Thebes, and Paser and Pewero, mayoral bigwigs respectively of the city's eastern and western banks, during the Twentieth Dynasty. In their rivalry and servility to the overseer, the local officials caused an investigation into the state of the royal tombs. Of the ten royal tombs in the Valley, one had been broken into and attempts made to enter two others. Of the priestesses' tombs, two had been pillaged and two were intact. The private tombs had all been plundered. 'To people of our class what do the tombs of private individuals matter?' wrote one mayor to the other. In the ensuing row over the accuracy of officials' stories, the unfortunate Paser announced that he intended to bypass the overseer and go straight to the king, whereupon the offended overseer ordered a court of inquiry at which the unhappy Paser, a judge of that same court, was tried for perjury and found guilty. It became clear from the evidence that both the overseer and local officials were guilty of living off the proceeds of tomb robbery.

Soon the trail of evidence led to other robbers. The American scholar James Breasted translated the papyri, recalling in one part the confession of a prisoner who had been a member of a gang which tunnelled through rock to a burial chamber and found a king and queen together in their sarcophagi. Before giving evidence the prisoner was beaten with a double rod and his feet and hands smitten, the customary way of assisting the memory:

We found the august mummy of this king... There was a numerous list of amulets and ornaments at its throat; its head had a mask of gold upon it; the august mummy of this king was overlaid with gold throughout. Its coverings were wrought with gold and silver, within and without; inlaid with every costly stone. We stripped off the gold which we found on the august mummy of this god, and its amulets and ornaments which were at its throat, and the covering wherein it rested. We found the king's wife likewise; we stripped off all that we found on her likewise. We set fire to their coverings. We stole their furniture, which we found with them, being vases of gold, silver and bronze. We divided, and made the gold which we found on these two gods, on their mummies, and the amulets, ornaments and coverings, into eight parts.

Virtually all the royal tombs of the Eighteenth and Nineteenth Dynasties had, it seemed, been broken into. The tombs of such great kings as Amenophis III, Seti I, and Ramesses II are specifically mentioned in court records as having been pillaged. Eventually the court began to move the royal mummies from one sepulchre to another in a desperate bid to head off the robbers. Ramesses III was buried three times at least. Others were known to have been transferred to other graves. Ramesses the Great was shown to have been moved to the tomb of Osiris, King Menmaatre (Seti I), on the 'day of bringing Osiris' in year 17 of the new calendar. Later, another record tells of father and son, Seti I (Sethos of the Greeks) and Ramesses II, being moved together to the tomb of the long-forgotten Queen Inhapi in the distaff necropolis of the royals. Then it is learnt that Ramesses I was removed from the tomb of Seti II and placed in Inhapi's burial chamber. Could any of the tombs have survived intact, even in their own time? Could such riches, even the riches of a single tomb, have survived the avarice of thirty centuries since?

Carter cannot have been optimistic. He gathered detailed information on all the burial sites of Upper Egypt for his inspectorate report, completed and submitted to Maspero in 1903. And by extensive reading he reinforced the depressing picture of ancient depredation with knowledgeable accounts of what had happened in the nineteen centuries of the Christian era. There was, for example, the graphic account left by Dr Richard Pococke in his *A Description of the East,* published in 1743, with its illustration of Ozymandias (Ramesses II) of whose headless torso rising out of the sand of Thebes to greet a legion of travellers Diodorus Siculus wrote 2,000 years before Shelley. Carter found Pococke 'extraordinarily accurate' in his description of the Valley and 'the Sepulchres of the Kings of Thebes'. The eighteenth-century traveller gave entire plans of five tombs – including those of Ramesses IV, VI, XI and Seti II – and part-plans of others. Some he could not enter, since they were 'stopped up'. But the Valley was not a place to linger in and Pococke happily left it to the bandit horde that by then occupied the hills around Qurna. Other travellers described the bandits living in 'their grottoes' and 'the holes of the mountains'. As he read the tales of earlier witnesses, and surveyed for the Antiquities Service the centuries of turmoil and pillage, Carter painted a woeful picture: 'Nor did even the magic of Napoleon's name suffice to curb the arrogance of these Theban bandits, for the members of his scientific commission who visited Thebes in the last days of the century were molested, and even fired upon.' All the same, the Emperor's savants were able to make a complete survey of all the tombs known at that time and even carried out small excavations.

'Let us pass now to 1815, and make the acquaintance of one of the most remarkable men in the whole history of Egyptology.' Carter referred to Giovanni Belzoni, the Italian giant who, before he went to Egypt, made a living in England, using his enormous strength to entertain circus crowds. Belzoni had been intended for the priesthood but studied engineering instead, and he went to Egypt in the hope of making his fortune by introducing that backward country to the hydraulic wheel. He met the turncoat Ottoman Viceroy, Muhammad Ali, whose descendants still reigned after a fashion under the British occupation. He saw richer pickings, however, on the fringes of archaeology. He spent five years, much of the time in the service of the British Consul Henry Salt, dragging the great monuments of Egypt from their resting places to barges on the Nile, whence they were shipped to the museums and gentlemen's gardens of England. In competition with a rival Italian-born collector, Drovetti, representing France at the time, he performed near miracles of brute force in lifting and conveying the massive sculptures of the ancients.

In his own account of his Goliath tasks he told hilarious stories of mishap and adventure, of how on one occasion he dropped an obelisk weighing several tons in the Nile and fished it out again. It was he who used muscle and impudence to bring an obelisk from the island of Philae, with Greek and hieroglyphic writing which helped significantly in the eventual decipherment of the ancient Egyptian script. He removed the great head of Ramesses II from the Ramesseum at Thebes, which Salt and the Anglo-Swiss scholar Burckhardt presented to the British Museum in 1817. He carried out the first large-scale excavation of the Valley of the Kings and cleared some notable tombs, though all had been robbed of their most precious treasures, including those of Ramesses I and Seti I, finding in the latter a magnificent alabaster sarcophagus which was acquired by the Soane Museum in London.

Carter was full of praise for the way in which Belzoni had carried out his excavations in the Valley, though he had reservations about the Italian's method of dealing with sealed doors by means of a battering ram. He did not commit himself, on the other hand, with regard to Belzoni's opinion that 'In the Valley of Beban el Malook, there are no more [tombs] than are now known, in consequence of my late discoveries.' Carter recorded the exhibition of the Italian's treasures in the Egyptian Hall, Piccadilly, following his return to England in 1820. The giant had died a few years later on an expedition to Timbuctoo, he recalled.

The list of those who followed Belzoni and Drovetti was

impressive: Salt, Jean-François Champollion, James Burton, Hay, Niccolo Rosellini, Wilkinson 'who numbered the tombs', Sir Henry Rawlinson, Alexander Rhind. Then came the Prussian expedition under Richard Lepsius who made a complete survey of the Valley, cleared the tomb of Ramesses II and part of the tomb of his son, Merenptah. The Prussian expedition was supposed to have exhausted all further possibilities in the Valley of the Kings. Nothing more happened in that desolate region until the end of the century. But just outside the Valley, on the cliff-top at Deir al Bahari, there was evidence of a discovery made in 1881 by Maspero. Carter told the full story of the detective work which had led to the discovery of a pit containing some of the most important monarchs in all Egypt's long history, huddled together in exactly the positions they had been left by the priests who rescued and hid them from sight more than 3,000 years before.

The official report showed that it was the family of Abdal Rasul from Qurna, where Carter had lived for several years while working for Naville, in the hills above the Valley, who discovered the pit in 1875. They sent to market a few pickings at a time so as not to alert the authorities, thus adding discreetly to the wealth of a dynasty of tomb robbers that had plied its trade since the thirteenth century BC. In 1881, the Cairo secret police got on to the trail and Maspero, through his museum curator Emile Brugsch, effected the rescue of the kings and such accoutrements as had survived several removal operations. Abdal Rasul himself was arrested and interrogated but the entire village of Qurna turned out to give evidence on his behalf, proclaiming him the most honest of men, and he was released for want of evidence. But a member of his family made a full confession to the authorities and on 5 July 1881 the great rescue act took place.

It was seventeen years later, in 1898, as Carter worked high above in Hatshepsut's temple, that Victor Loret made what was believed to be the final discovery in the Valley. Loret was Director-General of the Antiquities Service between de Morgan and Maspero, from 1897 to 1899, and in that time he found the thirteen royal mummies which, as Carter had noted from the papyrus records translated by Breasted, found sanctuary in the tomb of Amenophis II during the Twenty-first Dynasty. Only the mummies remained. All their finery had gone, probably before they were taken to Amenophis's burial chamber, but they had been spared the last indignity. The body of Amenophis II, however, lay within its own sarcophagus, and the Khedive, after consulting Sir William Garstin the British adviser to the Public Works Ministry, decided that it should remain where it was. Within a few months the tomb was broken into by practised modern robbers and the mummy removed from its sarcophagus. The thieves did not get away with much, and they were tracked down and tried, but released by a native court.

A moral was to be drawn from that and other such episodes, Carter thought. 'Those who called archaeologists "vandals" for removing objects from tombs should think again. By removing antiquities to museums they were ensuring their safety and survival.'

Chapter 6

THRESHOLD OF
MAGNIFICENT DISCOVERY

IN 1902 the American millionaire Theodore M. Davis was granted a concession to excavate in the Valley of the Kings 'under Government supervision'. Maspero invited Carter to oversee the wealthy amateur who was well known to Egyptologists for his annual excursions aboard his *dhabiyah,* the generic name for luxury vessels of the Nile, named after that elegant creature of the wild the female gazelle.

By now Carter too was a familiar figure among the multi-national excavators working along a 1,000-mile stretch of the Nile, from the Delta in the north to the Nubian sites beyond the cataracts at the far south. His knowledge of the history and the arts of ancient Egypt was already considerable. He could speak Arabic well, with colloquial grasp of the guttural Egyptian consonant. Working with the kindly and brilliant Maspero, he had become less abrasive, on the surface at least, than in his days with Petrie at Amarna and Naville at Deir al Bahari. He spoke of the 'new chief' with genuine affection. 'A more distinguished savant, a more charming gentleman, or kinder master could not be found.' Page after page of the notebook for this period underlined the tribute. 'Maspero's single-hearted devotion to Egyptology, and his encouragement and consideration for others occupied in its search – irrespective of nationality – were but one manifestation of his noble and generous nature.'

Even so, there was a need for new challenges. His devotion to the Valley had become absolute. The hot summer months which he had become accustomed to spending in London or

Norfolk (sometimes travelling overland through Europe and spending many happy hours imbibing the visual delights of Venice, Sienna and Florence on the way home), had always ended with a longing to return to the bleak necropolis where he found a 'religious feeling' so profound 'that it appears almost imbued with a life of its own'.

He found Davis an enlightened and tenacious man to work with. There was, as one informed commentator put it, conspicuously more to him than was found in most of those millionaire diggers 'bored with life's mild adventures... dallying with relics in the hope of finding some thrill to stimulate their sluggard imaginations'. The American was quite willing to allow Carter to nominate the sites worthy of investigation, and to supervise the digging. He was soon rewarded with the discovery of the Eighteenth Dynasty tomb of Tuthmosis IV. Inevitably, it had been plundered. 'The whole aspect of the hypogeum resembled more the scene of a riot rather than a hallowed shrine of the illustrious dead,' Carter wrote. The sarcophagus was empty, as was expected, but they found the magnificent remains of a chariot and, nearby, the king's gauntlet. But it was an alabaster saucer discovered in the foundation deposit, and a small blue scarab seal in the entrance to the tomb, which pointed to a more important discovery. Both items bore the cartouche of Queen Hatshepsut. At least Carter believed that he was on the trail of the actual tomb of one of Egypt's most fascinating personalities, the queen who usurped the male prerogative and pronounced herself king, insisting that court sculptors represent her with all the accoutrements of kingship, including false beard. Davis was delighted. Hatshepsut was one of his 'particular favourites', Carter observed. At the beginning of February 1903 he discovered a foundation deposit bearing cartouches of the sovereign immediately in front of an explored tomb, number 20 according to Carter's list, and some 65 yards north of the tomb of Tuthmosis IV.

It took several months for them to reach the burial chamber. They had to remove heaps of rubbish from four chambers and

Carter's drawings from decorated panels of the war chariot of King Tuthmosis IV. *Top:* right side, exterior, showing the king using a bow; *bottom:* left side, interior, showing the king as a human-headed lion trampling his foes underfoot.

passages, together with debris from the cliffs which had been cemented by the attrition of centuries of rain. Foul air drove them back time after time. As they advanced to the burial chamber, broken vases suggested the old story of vandalism.

When they entered the chamber they found that the roof had collapsed. The entire space was choked with rubbish. Clearing away the mess took a month, 'one of the most irksome pieces of work I ever supervised'. Eventually, Carter led Davis to Hatshepsut's sarcophagus. Alongside was the queen's canopic box and the sarcophagus of Tuthmosis I. Both sarcophagi were made of red sandstone. Both were empty.

Davis gathered confidence and went on to other tombs, recording his finds in a book entitled *Description and Excavation of the Tomb of Hatshopsitu*. No royal corpses rewarded his efforts, but he found some tomb furniture and a few commoners' mummies.

A vault was thought to have contained the body of Akhenaten after its removal from the heretical city of Akhetaten, modern Amarna. There were mummies galore, one mistakenly thought by Davis to be that of Akhenaten himself. Fragments of wood were believed to belong to the shrine of the king's mother, Tiye.

The American was admittedly more interested in the discovery of works of art than in the kind of minutiae which made up Petrie's mountains of sherds, scarabs and fragmentary tablets. But he was not alone in that, as Petrie's constant complaint about Naville's indifference to 'small things' attested. Even the greatest archaeologists, by and large, preferred gold, paintings and jewels to pottery sherds. Most had a healthy publicity sense and were well aware of the journalist's preference for articles of tangible value and photographic appeal. Davis did not complain at the haul of the first year. The world was not noticeably enchanted, but the finds were impressive enough to encourage a businessman whose intentions were good even though his approach was 'wholly unsystematic', and who was finding his way in archaeology. They might have been even better had he and Carter remained together, but that was not to be.

Carter's devotion to the Valley and its community was to bring about his downfall towards the end of a year spent profitably in the service of Davis. In a series of sketches contained within his notebooks, number V was called 'Summer Life and a Tale from the Coffee Hearth'. It was in that sketch that he told of the discoveries made while working for Davis. In twenty close-written pages he told also the embarrassing story of the discovery of the tomb of Nebhepetre Mentuhotpe, the first King of the Eleventh Dynasty (2061 - 2040 BC).

It was a story with a strong warning for Carter and all the archaeologists who sought that greatest of all prizes in Egypt, an unviolated tomb, and it caused another rift with the EEF soon after he joined the Antiquities Department, with the Fund's approval, as one of its principal inspectors. The story had its origin in an accident back in 1898 when Carter returned home to the house that Naville built at Qurna. His pony stumbled in a hole and horse and rider were thrown to the ground. Carter investigated the hole and just beneath the surface found traces of masonry of 'dry-rustic' appearance. It turned out to be the top edge of a buried retaining wall. 'I conjectured that it was probably an opening in the valley bed leading to some subterranean vault or tomb.'

He consulted Naville who uncharacteristically poured scorn on the young man's enthusiastic belief that he had found an important royal burial site. 'All that I received for my pains was a somewhat splenetic remark, that had a taint of ridicule.' Maspero's response two years later was very different. He offered Carter funds from the Service coffers to carry out a full-scale excavation. By the second week of March 1900 Carter had discovered a doorway cut in the rock at the western end of a vast underground chamber, 55 feet below the surface. Hundreds of workmen were engaged in the dig which involved the removal of some 3,000 cubic yards of rubbish.

The structure was built of crude sun-baked bricks. There were no inscriptions suggesting royal occupation. Yet Carter felt instinctively that it was a tomb of an Eleventh Dynasty monarch. Maspero had warned him not to be 'too optimistic', but surely a bricked-up doorway in so large a chamber, dating probably to 2000 BC or beyond, could not 'lack a dramatic element'. After all, he wrote, 'Consider the circumstances,' proceeding to describe a young excavator, alone 'save for his staff or workmen', on the threshold of 'magnificent discovery'. He needed all his will-power, he wrote, to resist the temptation to knock down the wall, more than 12 feet in thickness, to find out there and then what lay behind it. He paused for a day before making an all-out assault on the hypogeum or underground chamber which lay 300 feet beneath the surface, at the foot of a vertical shaft which his foreman discovered.

Carter's description of the month-long search, of clambering over stalagmite growths of salt which formed out of the rocks into celery-like sticks, was graphic. When he eventually reached the end of a passage 157 yards in length, he found himself in a lofty chamber with no furnishings but an empty coffin, suitable only for an ordinary citizen, and a royal statue elaborately wrapped in linen, about 5 feet in height and unidentified by any inscription. There were also some meagre offerings on crude pottery dishes. But the tomb at the bottom of the shaft seemed to be intact. The doorways were sealed and Carter thought that at last he had found a virgin sepulchre. An official opening of the last sealed door to the tomb was arranged. Lord Cromer, the Prime Minister Mustafa Pasha, Sir Eldon Gorst (Cromer's successor), and a few friends were invited by Maspero to witness the opening of the inner sanctum. 'The size and great length of the hypogeum augured a rich harvest,' but Carter could not imagine how he was going to transport his important guests to the bottom of the shaft. In the end he devised a cradle which would safely accommodate them two at a time. In the event, it was not needed. He wrote in his notebook:

> I had everything prepared. The long wished for moment had arrived. We were ready to penetrate the mystery behind the masonry. The foreman and I descended, and with his aid I removed the heavy limestone slabs, block by block. The door was at last open. It led directly into a small room

which was partially filled with rock chips, just as the Egyptian masons had left it, but it was otherwise empty save for some pottery water jars and some pieces of wood. At first glance I felt that there must be another doorway leading to another chamber, but a cursory examination proved that there was nothing of the sort. I was filled with dismay.

His embarrassment was complete. Fortunately, the sensitive Maspero was there as the contrite archaeologist stepped into the daylight to face his country's present and future Consuls General. 'I cannot now remember', Carter wrote many years after the event, 'all the kind and eloquent words that came from Maspero, but his kindness during this awful moment made one realize that he was really a worthy and true friend.' The statue found in the upper chamber, before they dug down to the bogus chamber 300 feet below, was one of the most remarkable *ka* figures – the heavenly *alter egos* of the deceased – ever found in Egypt.

There was another discovery which was to prove of value to Carter in attributing the tomb to Mentuhotpe. Through a small hole in the long passage leading to the upper chamber they spotted an aperture containing a miniature coffin, similar in design to the empty one in the chamber itself. It included the royal title 'Son of Re, Mentuhetpe'. Carter was reminded of a famous papyrus document which dealt with tomb robberies during the Twentieth Dynasty. That document, which would prove of great value to Carter in the detective work he had begun to pursue in the Valley of the Kings, mentioned an inspection of 'the graves of the kings of old and the tombs and resting-places of the blessed ones of days gone by'. Among the tombs listed as having been inspected in the valley of 'Western Thebes', there was reference to the tomb of 'King Nebhepetre. Re, son of Re. Mentuhetpe', 'which is in Zeser'.

There was a sequel to the costly enterprise in the shadow of Deir al Bahari. Carter's star was rising in Egyptological circles. The spectacular set of volumes entitled *The Temple of Deir al Bahri,* under the imprint of the Egypt Exploration Fund and edited by Naville, had been coming off the press since 1895. Carter's colour plates of Egyptian scenes, and especially the wildlife studies taken from the wall paintings, together with his brother Verney's and Percy Brown's contributions, had won deserved praise among the world's *cognoscenti.* Naville, in his introductions, had been unstinting in his praise for Carter's artistic skill. By June 1900, at the height of his new-found fame, Carter's services were being sought by the Fund, by Naville and Maspero.

The digging at Qurna had, by unfortunate chance, come close enough to the Fund's site house, in which Naville and Carter had been living, to cause the kitchen to collapse. Thus alerted to Carter's activity and convinced that any finds in the vicinity of the house should belong to the EEF, Grueber wrote from the British Museum to Miss Paterson asking her to call a meeting of the committee to discuss 'the circumstances under which Mr Carter carried out his examination of the underground passage and funeral (?) chamber at Deir al Bahari'. The question mark was Grueber's. He enclosed a copy of a letter he had written to Carter asking for an explanation.

On 30 June Carter replied in a long letter to the treasurer, with a copy to Miss Paterson, acknowledging a cheque for the last of his work on the Deir al Bahari plates, and denying Grueber's charge of double-dealing. 'To start with may I say that in no way should I think of depriving the EEF from any find that they have a right to. As it happened, the tomb was some distance from the boundaries of the permit granted to the Fund by the S. des A... otherwise I should have informed the Committee at once'. He explained that his duty was to M. Maspero and that after informing his chief he had officially opened the tomb on 20 January 1900. During the work, he admitted, 'a private person did subscribe a sum towards its cost, but without any right to the results whatever.' He went on to explain how he stumbled on the tomb in 1898 and how he had confided in Naville when the latter was at Deir al Bahari. In giving Grueber details of the interior and the few discoveries made, he stressed that he did so in the strictest confidence.

Surprisingly, he stressed that he had stopped work on the tomb only 'for the time being', because of faults in the rock. He had dug to 250 feet and there was still no end. 'I think good results await at the bottom,' he assured his old employers, perhaps in the hope that they would finance further work should Maspero approve; but he knew perfectly well that there was nothing in the bottom chamber. He would not be going home that summer, he told Grueber, but hoped to do so the following year, thus bringing to an end a decade of work for the Fund with a slightly strained impression of goodwill. Dissimulation, of which he would be accused as time went on, seems to have found a fertile start in the conspiratorial backwater of Deir al Bahari.

The notebook sketch also related how his journeys to Europe and England had lapsed for three years after he had taken on the inspectorate under Maspero: 'The prosecution of my new duties would not allow of this luxury, in fact I would be lucky if I were able to get permission for three months' summer vacation in two years.' The hot months spent in Egypt had compensations. Soon after abandoning the 'Tomb of Mentuhotpe' and leaving Naville to join Maspero, he moved into a new house provided by the Service at Madinat Habu, just outside Luxor. Life was spent almost totally out of doors. He even slept on the roof of the house. The first glimmer of dawn came at 4.30 a.m. when the sleeper awoke. Then, suddenly, 'the sun–disk, beloved of the House of Akhenaten', appeared above the horizon and everything was bathed in golden light. Summer days seemed to vie with a fleeting vision of the future in Carter's journal.

After a light breakfast of coffee and yoghurt, the early morning freshness sharpened the mind and enlivened the muscles, but before noon the intense heat made it necessary to seek refuge in a darkened room. Lunch was followed by a nap.

Then tea and a bath, and a walk, preferably in the desert. Darkness fell by 6 p.m. and dinner was eaten under the stars. Carter was still very much a lone wolf, unable or unwilling to make friendships, to enter into anything more than the most casual or businesslike relationship, unmoved by the opposite sex and the preoccupations of most young men. But in his new job, spent mostly in the Valley, there was no option, and even he sometimes longed for passing company. The wearisome sameness of each passing day, the companionless months, provoked admission of loneliness 'that can at times become almost intolerable'. Without some mental occupation, he would, he believed, 'become suicidal'.

Luckily, Carter found plenty to occupy his mind. There were thousands of different birds to draw, especially during the periodic inundation. He had a small boat made by local craftsmen so that he could sail on the newly filled basins and observe and draw the wildlife. Camouflaged with straw and lying motionless in the bottom of the boat, he could watch flocks of pelican fishing and feeding.

There was another way of passing the time in the towns and villages around the Valley. The universal Arab meeting place, the *kahawah* or coffee hearth, drew Carter to its endless cups of rich black Turkish coffee, its interminable inquiries as to the health of the visitor and every member of his family, and its enlightening chatter about local affairs. It was at such gatherings that he polished his Arabic, until he could eventually pass muster as a native in conversation. It was in the *kahawah* too that he gained his unique insight into tomb burglary, past and present. European officials did not share his liking for the coffee hearth. By and large, they took the view that to mix with the natives was to encourage a dangerous sense of importance and independence. 'I must admit, however, that this practice was liable to serious criticism: some colleagues in the Government Service frowned upon it as a bad habit: they thought it degrading.'

By the early years of the twentieth century Carter was confident of his professional ability and quite willing to take physical retribution on wrongdoers when his quick temper was aroused. Familiarity with the local population and a determination to put an end to tomb robbery combined to put his mental and physical resources to a dangerous test.

It was the tomb of Amenophis II, where the famous thirteen royal mummies had been found by Loret in 1898, which caused the first major outburst since Carter's appointment as inspector. When, despite the presence of a permanent guard, the mummified body of the king was removed from its sarcophagus, Carter promptly dismissed the chief guard although he had not been on duty at the time of the robbery. It was Carter, too, who rounded up the other suspects, several of whom he knew well, and sent them for trial at Luxor. After the court had found them not guilty, the locals who had been deprived of their expected share of the proceeds by Carter's action made him the target of their wrath. In order to keep the peace, Maspero was forced to transfer Carter to the inspectorate of Lower and Middle Egypt, with headquarters at Saqqara. Newberry interceded with the Director-General to secure the new post for Carter, otherwise Maspero might have been compelled to dismiss him from the service altogether to prevent an uprising in the Valley. Carter was grateful, writing to his old friend and colleague on 28 December 1903 to thank him for 'your kindness in recommending me for this work which I am certainly very pleased with'. Charles Breasted, son of Professor James Henry Breasted, the distinguished translator of the records of the ancient world, told the story of Carter's close involvement in the Amenophis II affair.

It was Newberry who told of the more serious sequel, a year later. Carter, in his published version of events, skipped lightly over it. At Saqqara, the vast necropolis high above Memphis, the foremost treasures were in the great complex of the Serapeum where almost exactly fifty years earlier Mariette had found the tombs of the sacred Apis bulls. A mummified bull had held centre stage for 4,000 years. The *mastaba* tombs, forerunners of the pyramids, were believed to be the resting places of Egypt's very earliest pharaohs. A remarkable store of jewellery was revealed to the world. While Carter was working in Upper Egypt, Petrie had applied for the third time for concessions at Saqqara but each time he had been refused on the grounds that Saqqara, like Thebes, was reserved solely for the Cairo Museum's own excavations. Carter was now in charge of perhaps the most valuable and sought-after site in all Egypt, and he protected the place as if it were his own.

One afternoon, according to Newberry, the *rais* or chief of the guard of the necropolis reported to him that a party of Frenchmen, mostly the worse for drink, were demanding entrance to the Serapeum even though they did not have the necessary tickets. One of the visitors struck a guard, which led to fisticuffs. It was not long before Carter was on the scene, exchanging angry remarks with the French visitors. He ordered the guards to protect themselves and one of the Frenchmen was knocked to the ground. The party returned to Cairo to make a formal complaint about Carter's treatment of them to the French Consul-General. The Consul demanded that Carter make an apology. Newberry waited until the end of Carter's life before telling the rest of the story.

> Carter refused to give it [the apology], saying that he had only done his duty and as a result of his refusal he had to resign his post. Maspero was greatly distressed about this affair and wrote to several of Carter's friends saying that he did not know what the Antiquities Department would do without him, and begged us to persuade him to return to the Department. Carter, however, was adamant in his refusal to apologize and preferred to return to private life.

The documented story of Carter's first major dispute with the Egyptian authorities was held back until fifty-one years after his death. Carter, in a rare moment of self-examination, wrote subsequently of his 'hot temper' and of what his enemies called 'un mauvais caractère', which he insisted, 'I can't help!' Events at Saqqara bore out his inability to curb his explosive nature and were indicative of many a heated argument to come.

On 8 January 1905, Carter wired the Resident, the Earl of Cromer:

> My Lord, I am exceedingly sorry to inform you that a bad affray has occurred today here at Mariette's house Saqqara 5 p.m. with 15 French tourists who were here in a drunken state. The cause of the affray was started by their rough handling of both my inspector and gaffirs. As both sides have been cut and knocked about I feel it is my duty to inform your lordship immediately and will report the matter to you personally tomorrow morning. *Carter, Service des Antiquités*

Next day an anxious Carter cabled 'The Lord' again, explaining that police inquiries prevented his leaving for Cairo as promised. By then, accusations and counter accusations were being exchanged between Maspero and his assistants, the chief accountant of the company responsible for issuing tickets to visitors to the Serapeum and other monuments on the Grand Tour, the British and French Residencies, and Carter's private force of gaffirs, or tomb policemen.

On 10 January Carter sent a 'summary report' to the Director-General in response to a request from Maspero's deputy, Emile Brugsch. In Carter's words, it was the 'case against a party of visitors at Saqqara on the previous Sunday'.

He proceeded to give a minute account of the French party's rowdy conduct and how, after behaving in an offensive manner at Petrie's camp nearby, they finished up at the Saqqara rest house known as Mariette Pasha's House. Some of the Frenchmen apparently refused to buy tickets, others refused to pay for the tickets they had acquired. When they eventually reached the Serapeum, the party demanded candles which the gaffirs (or 'bedouin') accompanying them explained they could not supply. The French visitors demanded their money back. A fight ensued and the ticket inspector was threatened and his tarbush knocked from his head and trampled on.

Up to this time, Carter was some distance away with his fellow archaeologist Arthur Weigall and 'the misses' Kingsford and Hansard (two young women who were to marry distinguished men in the world of antiquities, Sydney Cockerell and Cecil Firth). Hearing from his *rais* or foreman of what had been going on, Carter went to the house where he found the Frenchmen in occupation and the gaffirs locked out, while the unfortunate ticket inspector had been set upon and told to hand over money. Asked for an explanation, one of the party spoke up in English. 'He spoke to me in an exceedingly rough way,' Carter reported. Carter remonstrated with the visitors and asked them to leave the house, which they refused to do. The party refused to give him their names. One of them turned on a gaffir and punched him in the face, and on Carter's interfering, 'the same man raised his hand and threatened to strike me.' Carter, who was at this stage in his life extremely strong and fit, went on: 'I arrested his stroking arm and warned him.' The *rais* Khalifa and the gaffirs were told by Carter to summon aid. As some of them went to leave the room, the Frenchmen attacked them with chairs and any missiles which came to hand. Carter then ordered a counter attack. 'In the affray', wrote Carter, 'some of the party were hit, one of them being knocked down.' The rest ran for cover. One Frenchman returned to give Carter his visiting card. Others hurled stones at Carter and his men. Eventually the police arrived and made notes which covered thirty-five sheets of foolscap. 'I wish to commend the gaffirs on their behaviour during the whole affray,' the report concluded.

It transpired that after Carter gave the order, his men used their 'nabouts' (truncheons) on the offending Frenchmen. By the 19th, Maspero, who all along took Carter's side, was becoming concerned. 'I think your case is good: there would be nothing to say against us, and the issue would be certainly in our favour, if your men had not used their nabouts.' The sagacious Director-General made a universal point. 'That is the bad part of the business: policemen may be beaten, they are not allowed to beat except under extremities.' The matter had become front-page news in Egypt, and a tribunal had been ordered in the native Court of Appeal. The court sat to take evidence not to give judgement. 'I was not at all pleased at the general atmosphere, though I feel sure that they thought I was in the right,' Carter afterwards told Sir William Garstin, the British adviser to the Egyptian Ministry of Public Works.

The report in *L'Egypte* on 12 January gave a rather different account. It told of the unprovoked attack by Carter's 'bedouins', of the hurried attempt by the French to protect the 'ladies and children' from danger, and of the men on the terrace being attacked by men with their nabouts, while boulders and pieces of rock were thrown at them. The chief accountant of the gas company had his head broken and he fell to the ground covered in blood. Monsieur Baudry, decorator at one of the royal palaces, was felled by a nabout blow to his back. It was not until several hours after the attack that a doctor was called, according to the press version.

At the inquiry held on 25 January, five of the Frenchmen made statements affirming their injuries and insisted that all the adults had taken tickets, only the children neglecting to do so, at their parents' instigation. They could not produce all the tickets when requested to do so, however. Carter noted that several of the visitors understood and spoke Arabic, a clear indication that they were not the greenhorns they pretended to be.

On 3 February, Maspero wrote a long letter to Carter telling him that he had met with Cromer and Garstin and that they had decided that 'you are to come with me tomorrow between nine and ten and pay a call on M. de la Boulinière there to express our regrets that the order you gave brought so strong consequences.' Maspero pleaded with Carter not to take offence, or to resist the course which had been agreed at the highest level. The French consular official in charge of the matter, de la Boulinière, was well disposed and friendly. A quiet meeting would settle the matter. He, Maspero, would share the blame with Carter. Carter's response was a refusal to attend the meeting or to make any kind of apology unless the Frenchmen apologized first to Maspero. Even at that late hour, Cromer, Garstin and Maspero made up for Carter's intransigence, making excuses to the French official on their joint behalf and promising to 'reprimand' Carter. Maspero tried to avoid further embarrassment by telling his English friend that quite apart from the Saqqara business he had intended to rearrange the Inspectorate anyway, giving Quibell the Giza district with residence at Saqqara, while he, Carter, would take his office to Tanta in the Delta, thus taking on a role subsidiary to Quibell's. 'I hope you will take the proposal in the spirit in which I make it,' wrote Maspero on 17 February, more in hope than conviction. 'You know that I, for one, will not esteem you less nor be your friend less than I have been up to the present time.' Carter wrote back to his old and dear friend, the man about whom he had written a paean of praise so recently:

> Sir
>
> In reply to your letter of the 17th Feb 1905, deposing me for my late conduct regarding the Saqqara affair, I beg to be allowed before taking any course in the matter that I may have a copy of the findings of the inquiry which was held upon the above matter and which up to the present time has not been shown me. Believe me, Yours Howard Carter.

Forced into a corner, Carter decided to ask for three-and-a-half months' leave from 14 March 1905. Maspero granted his request, and meanwhile Carter found himself temporary accommodation at Tanta, 'suitable for office and house for the Inspector-in-Chief for Lower Egypt'. The 'humiliation' which he said Maspero's decision had caused him was concealed for the moment by a self-determined rise in rank and status. The pretence did not last long. Carter was not happy in the new appointment and his threatened resignation soon took effect.

When Carter was first appointed to the inspectorate, his fellow countryman James Quibell, with whom he shared the advantage of an apprenticeship with Petrie, was already working for the Antiquities Department as Inspector-General. The two men proceeded to play a game of musical chairs. When Carter was appointed to the northern and middle regions, Quibell became inspector in the south. When Carter turned his back on the Antiquities Department and effectively cut himself off from the mainstream of Egyptian exploration, Quibell was working with Theodore Davis in the Valley. Quibell had much in common with Carter, not least a physical power which enabled him to dispense summary justice to thieves who invaded his excavations.

Davis was to hold the Valley concession for another nine years, up until the outbreak of the First World War, and to make a number of important finds under Quibell's guidance. But he regretted the enforced exile of Carter who, for the first three of those years, until 1905, was in the wilderness, paying the penalty for his stubborn refusal to help Maspero out of the Gallic mess into which he had delivered his chief.

Carter moved back to Luxor where, according to Charles Breasted, he was offered hospitality by none other than the chief guard he had held responsible for the robbery of the tomb of Amenophis II and subsequently dismissed. The guard still held Carter in high respect and despite the treatment meted out to him provided accommodation and meals for his unemployed ex-chief. Thus he enabled Carter to take up painting as a livelihood. For three years Carter worked the same vein as his father before him, observing people and animals and representing them in water-colours which he offered for sale to rich tourists in the Winter Palace Hotel at Luxor. Many of the pictures of the time combine the decorative art of his excavation sites with natural subjects, such as a brightly coloured hoopoe bird emerging from a crack in an inscribed and decorated wall. It was a precarious way of making a living but Carter was adaptable as well as intractable. He had no apparent regrets. Old friends of the Egypt Exploration Fund did not forget him. Petrie gave him several commissions for drawings for use in exhibition catalogues. But it was not an altogether happy time. There was inevitably a bitter taste in the offer of work by Davis who wanted him to be his freelance draughtsman.

It was under Quibell's guidance, in February 1906, that Theodore Davis made a most spectacular and unexpected discovery in the Valley. British and American magazines were full of it. In England, the *Illustrated London News* ran a special supplement under the banner: 'Egypt's Richest Treasure Trove: Wonderful Discoveries in the Valley of the Kings'.

> The excavation… revealed early in February a flight of rock-hewn steps half hidden by debris from the neighbouring tombs of Ramesses III and Ramesses XI. By the afternoon of the twelfth the overhanging hillside was so far cleared away that one could go safely down the steps to a wall closing the entrance of a corridor leading to an unknown tomb

By nine the next morning Davis had arrived aboard his *dhabiyah,* but Maspero and Quibell were delayed. Eventually, Maspero joined Davis in making the formal entry.

> Squeezing their way between the wall and the rock ceiling, M. Maspero and Mr Davis were soon in the midst of such a medley of tomb furniture that, in the glare of their lighted candles, the first effect was one of bewilderment. Gradually, however, one object after another detached itself from the shimmering mass, shining through the cool air, dust-free and golden.

In the confident language of the reporter, working on material supplied by Davis, they had penetrated the tomb of Yuya and Tuya, parents of Tiye, the mother of Akhenaten the heretical king of the Eighteenth Dynasty, great grandparents of the girl who would become queen to the boy-king Tutankhamun. The furniture found by Davis was ornate and 'almost in the style of Louis XVI', though some had an 'Empire' look to it. 'Yet alabaster and gold leaf – cloth, too, and veiling – were almost absolutely uninjured. The graceful alabaster, three beds, three chairs, the mummy cases, came glowing flashing and glittering into the day.' There were canopic jars of alabaster containing the viscera of the dead, little sentry boxes each holding a *shawabti* figure (an image of a servant of the dead), mummies of ducks, legs of mutton, seventy-two sealed jars of fruit. As a pitcher was examined a wasp buzzed into view to sip the honey that had been poured into it more than 3,000 years before to satisfy the cravings in eternity of Yuya and Tuya. It was the most spectacular find so far in the Valley of the Kings and Queens. Yet these were no sovereign rulers. Merely the parents of a queen. What wonders might have disappeared forever from the Valley? What riches might still reward patient and tenacious research? For Carter, such questions had an as yet unsuspected significance.

In September 1907, Carter was working for Davis again, in the capacity of draughtsman. He wrote to Newberry saying, 'Davis had behaved like a bear to me of late…'

By then, he had been introduced to a nobleman who would change the course of his life.

Chapter 7

A 'TRUE ETONIAN' AT THEBES

IT was his lordship's eldest sister Winifred, Lady Burghclere, who offered up an unblushing hymn of praise in her posthumous sketch of 'Porchy', the 5th Earl of Carnarvon: 'A private school and Eton are the successive steps which automatically prepare a boy in Porchester's position for a future career. His private school was not happily chosen. It subsisted on its former reputation, and neither diet nor instruction was up to the mark.'

Eton was another matter:

> To the end Eton retained in his eyes that glamour which marks the true Etonian, and his tutor, Mr Marindin, shared in that affection. Yet it was something of a misfortune that school did nothing for the formation of methodical habits in a boy endowed with an exceptionally fine memory and unusual quickness. It would, for instance, have been a blessing if an expensive education had taught him to answer his letters.

George Edward Molyneux Stanhope Herbert, Lord Porchester, was born in 1866, and was thus eight years older than Carter. Age apart, it is almost impossible to imagine two more conflicting personalities. Yet they were to form the perfect partnership. 'For the next sixteen years the two men worked together with varying fortune, yet ever united not more by their common aim than by their mutual regard and affection,' to quote Winifred once more.

Porchy, as he was always known to his friends, was the eldest son of the 4th Earl by his first wife, Lady Evelyn Stanhope, a daughter of the 6th Earl of Chesterfield. His father was an outstanding classical scholar who, before going to Eton, was reading Homer, Virgil, Horace and Herodotus, and writing precociously to his father, 'I do four different kinds of verse, Elegiacs, Sapphics, Alcaics, and Iambics, of which Sapphics are my favourite.' He took a first in Greats at Oxford and served as Colonial Secretary in both the Derby and Disraeli governments, resigning on both occasions on matters of principle. He subsequently served as Viceroy of Ireland under Salisbury's premiership, befriended Parnell, won the hearts of the Irish people, and resigned when the Conservative Cabinet rejected his conciliatory policy.

Little of the father's serious and scholarly approach to life rubbed off on the son. The English Dictionary of National Biography describes the 5th Earl of Carnarvon as an 'Egyptologist'. He certainly was not that. At Cambridge he was more often at the races than at lectures. At the age of twenty-one he sailed round the world. His handsome features and rather diffident manner – he was sometimes thought to be a prototype of Wodehouse's Bertie Wooster – made him popular with all classes of people wherever he went. To some extent he was the victim of parental disenchantment. His father took little interest in him, preferring his half-brother Aubrey Herbert, born of a second marriage to a cousin, Elsie Howard. Porchy inherited the earldom in 1889 at the age of twenty-three. On his twenty-ninth birthday he married Almina Victoria Maria Wombwell. As it happened, Lady Carnarvon's father was not Sir Frederick Wombwell but the Baron Alfred de Rothschild who settled £250,000 (about $1 million at the time) on the couple as a wedding gift. The 5th Earl was a keen gambler and it was his gambler's instinct that took him to Egypt.

His generosity to friends, relatives and servants alike was legendary. If he had led the life of an aristocratic playboy before and after his marriage, children and a road accident intervened to change his life-style. His only son, Henry Lord Porchester, was born in 1898. A daughter, Lady Evelyn Leonora Almina

Herbert, followed in 1901. She was the apple of his eye. Horse racing was the chief of his many and catholic enthusiasms, and he eventually built up a famous stud farm and became a member of the Jockey Club. He also became an accomplished photographer and 'scratch' golfer. He travelled a good deal with friends such as Prince Victor Duleep Singh, became a pioneer motorist, owning cars in France before they were permitted in England, and enjoyed a growing reputation for recklessness.

There was a streak of seriousness in his make-up, however. At Cambridge he had collected 'blue-and-white' in the Oscar Wilde tradition, and he often toyed with the idea of digging for ancient treasures. It was, ironically, a motoring journey in Germany that decided his future. In 1903, he and his chauffeur Edward Trotman, who had been at his side for twenty-eight years, were travelling at breakneck speed along a forest road towards Schwalbach, where Lady Carnarvon was waiting for them. A sudden dip in the road prevented their seeing two bullock carts drawn up ahead. Carnarvon was driving. He took the car on to the grass verge, hit a pile of stones, two tyres burst, and the open car somersaulted, landing on its driver and throwing Trotman clear. Trotman extricated his master and splashed cold water in his face to revive the heart that had stopped beating. The physical effects of the accident would follow him for the rest of his life. There was a lengthy convalescence and the doctors advised that he should winter out of England. It was for that reason that he went to Egypt in the winter of 1903.

According to his own testimony, in a uncompleted article written just before his death, he was instantly fascinated by digging. 'It had always been my wish and intention even as far back as 1889 to start excavating, but for one reason or another I had never been able to begin,' he wrote. In fact, it was not until 1906 that the opportunity presented itself. The able and influential British adviser to the Public Works Ministry, Sir William Garstin, had a word with Maspero and Carnarvon was given permission to dig at Thebes.

It was a brave decision. A man of Carnarvon's disposition might well have been attracted by Cromer's Cairo, with its weekly balls at the Residency and smart hotels, the opera, polo and shooting parties. Such familiar activities were cast aside by Porchy in the excitement of a newfound enthusiasm. He went off to Luxor for the winter season of 1907 brimming with the confidence of the novice: 'I may say that at this period I knew nothing whatever about excavating, so I suppose with the idea of keeping me out of mischief, as well as keeping me employed, I was allotted a site at the top of Sheikh Abdul Gurna.' That site was the plateau above the valley where Carter had lived while he worked for Naville nearby at Deir al Bahari, and where he was now planning to build a new residence with bricks supplied from Carnarvon's own kiln in England. 'I had scarcely been operating for 24 hours when we struck what seemed to be an untouched burial pit,' wrote Carnarvon.

> This gave rise to much excitement in the Antiquities Department, which soon simmered down when the pit was found to be unfinished. There, for six weeks, enveloped in clouds of dust, I stuck to it day in and day out. Beyond finding a large mummified cat in its case, which now graces the Cairo Museum, nothing whatsoever rewarded my strenuous and very dusty endeavours. This utter failure, however, instead of disheartening me had the effect of making me keener than ever.

The honest self-appraisal must have mirrored Maspero's alarm. After taking a look at the English nobleman's methods, the Frenchman thought it prudent that he should seek the services of an expert excavator. The Director-General suggested Carter. After his long ostracism, there could have been no better outcome for the still youthful and ambitious archaeologist. He had found the patron, and the friend, he so patently needed.

Davis still had his concession in the Valley. Maspero, anxious to avoid a conflict of interests, suggested to Carnarvon the west

Theban sites close to Deir al Bahari. Porchy recorded his first efforts under Carter's supervision in his notebook. The first success was the discovery of the tomb of an Eighteenth Dynasty prince, Tetaky. It consisted of two painted chambers with a few objects, including *shawabti* figures in model coffins and wooden sarcophagi. Such figures represented the *shabti,* servants in the afterlife. Sometimes they appeared in groups, representing military formations, kitchen staff, brewers, craftsmen, and were usually made in earthenware or faience, sometimes in stone or wood.

They quickly moved on to Deir al Bahari itself. The first find there was an unmarked Seventeenth Dynasty tomb. Carnarvon wrote: 'After perhaps ten days' work at Deir al Bahari we came upon what proved to be an untouched tomb. I shall never forget the first sight of it.' Carter, familiar with such minor discoveries, was matter of fact in his journal. His patron was excited by the age and freshness of the find: 'There was something extraordinarily modern about it. Several coffins were in the tomb, but the first that arrested our attention was a white brilliantly painted coffin with a pall loosely thrown over it, and a bouquet of flowers lying just at its foot. There these coffins had remained untouched and forgotten for 2,500 years.' In fact, the tomb was at least 3,500 years old. But the absence of funerary furnishings suggested that the owners were poor people. The family had put all its collective resources into a communal tomb, most of the money going on ornamental coffins. Carnarvon presented one of them to the Newberry Museum in England.

Some 400 yards from the temple at Deir al Bahari they found what appeared to be another unmarked tomb. 'In the morning, I rode out, and no sooner did I see Carter's face than I knew something unpleasant and unforeseen had occurred,' wrote Carnarvon. 'Alas! What looked promising the day before turned out to be merely a walled-up sort of stable where the ancient Egyptian foreman had tethered his donkey and kept his accounts.' Carnarvon was philosophical. Disillusion was, he observed, a common occurrence in Egypt. In excavation, he said, 'it is generally the unexpected that happens and the unexpected is nearly always unpleasant.'

With a work-force often reaching a strength of 270 men, they continued digging along the cliff-tops beyond the left bank of the river, between 1907 and 1912. Mariette, Petrie, Naville and others had worked the same area tirelessly before them, and there was little left for the newcomers. All the same, they came up with one important find – a tablet – bearing an ink inscription which referred to one of the seminal events in Egyptian history, the expulsion by Kamose of the hated Hyksos, Semitic rulers of Egypt from the Fifteenth to the Eighteenth Dynasty (between 1640 and 1532 BC). It came to be known as the 'Carnarvon Tablet', marking the first real achievement of the partnership.

Under Carter's guidance, Carnarvon began in 1907 to assemble his great Egyptian collection. 'My chief aim was then, and is now, not merely to buy because a thing is rare, but rather to consider the beauty of an object than its pure historic value. Of course when the two, beauty and historic interest, are blended in a single object the interest and delight of possession are more than doubled.' Much of the credit for Carnarvon's fine collection, and for his enlightened attitude to the artefacts of the ancient world, belonged to Carter who, in the years of his isolation in and around Luxor, had ensured his survival by getting to know the thieves and vagabonds and recognized dealers who seemed between them to have an inexhaustible supply of artefacts, and to assess their market value. By the time Carnarvon came on the scene, his assistant–adviser had become a proficient dealer, respected as much by the distinguished archaeologists who passed his way as by the shadowy figures of the *suq*. But the world's attention turned naturally to the noble member of the duo. Sir Wallis Budge, Birch's successor as head of the Oriental Department of the British Museum, which at that time embraced Egypt and Western Asia, paid his own tribute to Carnarvon:

He only cared for the best, and nothing but the best would satisfy him, and having obtained the best he persisted in believing that there must be somewhere something better than the best. His quest for the beautiful in Egyptian design, form and colour became the cult of his life in recent years. His taste was faultless and his instinct for the true and genuine was unrivalled. When compared with a beautiful 'antica' money had no value for him, and he was wont to say with Sir Henry Rawlinson, 'It is easier to get money than anticas.'

Already, the fame and credit redounded to the patron. Carter was not yet a man for the limelight, and he had little sense of the importance of publicity to his work. For the moment at any rate he was happy to live in the shadow of the wealthy and charming accomplice whom he had met by chance, and with whose support he embarked on the most productive period of his life.

Their first five years of endeavour were not encouraging. Carnarvon was to write despairingly of 'open and half-filled mummy pits, heaps of rubbish, great mounds of rock debris with, here and there, fragments of coffins and shreds of linen mummy wrappings protruding from the sand'.

While the two men dug with unspectacular results at several spots along the 5-mile stretch of the necropolis of Thebes, Carter's ex-patron Davis worked on in the Valley below them. He soon added to the already significant finds made under the inspectorates of both Carter and Quibell. In 1906 he discovered a small, beautifully shaped cup of light-blue faience under a large rock. It bore a cartouche with the hieroglyphs of Nebkheprure, the coronation name of Tutankhamun. There were other significant finds relating to that Eighteenth Dynasty monarch of whom so little was known. In the 1907 – 8 season there were unmistakable signs of a tomb which had been flooded. In a room filled almost to the ceiling-height with dried mud they found a broken box containing gold leaf stamped with names of the same king and his wife, Ankhesenpaaten (or Ankhesenamun as she became when the religion of her husband's predecessor was revoked forever and the court reverted to Thebes). When the gold foil was pieced together it revealed Tutankhamun hunting from his chariot in one scene, slaughtering a prisoner of war in another, the queen urging him on. Accompanying hieroglyphs read, 'All protection of life is behind him, like the sun.'

Shortly after that find, Davis discovered an unmarked pit just above the explored tomb of Seti II, and 100 yards or so from the tomb of Ramesses VI. Beneath the accumulated rubbish of the centuries he found many rude pottery jars filled with linen, clay utensils, animal bones, floral wreaths, two small brooms, bags containing a powdered substance, and in another jar a miniature funerary mask decorated with bright yellow paint. Another jar had been broken open and rewrapped in a cloth bearing the name Tutankhamun. Davis attached no particular significance to the finds. Indeed, he though them 'disappointing'.

The partnership of the disparate Englishmen who dug along the cliff-tops above Davis's anonymous burial pit was very nearly brought to an abrupt end in the summer of 1909 by another of Carnarvon's motoring accidents. He had decided to travel home through Europe by way of Constantinople and by 26 August had reached southern Germany when he skidded off the road and hit a tree. He spent a week in hospital before discharging himself and making for Highclere where he rested before returning to Egypt for the winter season.

Supposing that Carter had been left high and dry by his lordship's latest accident, the Egypt Exploration Fund decided to offer him employment at Abydos, an important site about 100 miles north of Thebes, which Petrie had abandoned three years earlier. Grueber wrote to him on 25 September, offering him his first major excavation site. Still smarting from the accusations of double-dealing at the Deir al Bahari excavation in 1900, and mindful of the way in which he had been left to his own devices in 1903 when he was dismissed by the Antiquities Department, Carter was less than grateful. On 7 October 1909 he replied to Grueber from Luxor:

> Re – your request whether I could carry on the excavations at Abydos on behalf of the E.E.F. – I regret I have to tell you that I could not possibly undertake such work, my professional work not permitting it. Furthermore the fees I should be obliged to ask would be too exorbitant and prohibit it. Believe me, etc. Howard Carter

Carnarvon returned before the year was out and while he continued to dig along the stony escarpment near Deir al Bahari in the winter of 1909 - 10, Davis was visited by a most arresting American from the Metropolitan Museum of Art in New York, Herbert E. Winlock. He was described piquantly by Thomas Hoving: 'Short in stature, slightly roly-poly in physique, with short legs and splayed-out feet, Winlock gave the impression of a balding, mature Kewpie doll.' Despite those unprepossessing features, the visitor was universally popular, respected for his broad intellect and sparkling wit, and for his kind and benevolent attitude to his fellow men. All the same, he could be vitriolic. He once castigated the most distinguished of American field archaeologists, George Reisner, who ignored the glorious possibilities of the Valley in favour of the dismal graves of Giza, calling him 'the finder of those Ethiopian heroes, Asphalta and Concreta!' Winlock went off to explore the rocky cliff area where Carnarvon and Carter had worked among the Valley mortuary temples but with as little success as the English pair. Then after calling on his millionaire fellow countryman, Davis, he met up with Carnarvon and Carter who had just unearthed the foundation deposits of the Valley Temple of Hatshepsut. He and Carter were attracted to each other with the force of opposite poles of magnetism. They began to visit each other's sites and to develop a mutual respect which was both unpredictable and genuine. In later years the reticent Carter would say, even after they quarrelled, that the voluble American was his 'only true friend'.

In these early years of excavation, Carnarvon was accompanied occasionally by the very attractive and very determined Almina, known to family and friends as the 'Pocket Venus', who made her own lasting image among the workmen of the Valley and staff and guests of Egypt's best hotels. Carnarvon himself was sensitive to practically all the ills of the desert, and especially to its flies, and in very hot and infested conditions he liked to inhabit a protective fine-mesh cage from which he would look out at the workmen, his wife sitting nearby. She has been described as 'dressed for a garden party rather than the desert', always wearing the most expensive and becoming patent leather, high-heeled shoes, adorned with much jewellery which flashed brilliantly in the sunlight. They must have been a rare anachronism in that part of the world.

In 1911, Carnarvon and Carter discovered the colonnade and foundation deposit of the Valley Temple of Ramesses IV. It was close to Hatshepsut's temple, a fact which may have explained why the queen's temple had been so thoroughly demolished. The ancient kings of Egypt were among the most culpable of tomb and temple wreckers, always prepared to ransack a predecessor's monument in order to obtain building blocks for their own. But beneath Hatshepsut's temple they found rock-cut tombs dating from the Twelfth Dynasty (1991 - 1783 BC) to the Second Intermediate Period (1640 - 1532 BC). All the tombs had been plundered in antiquity but Carter recorded their remaining contents, though they were of small value, with his usual meticulous care.

It was time for a home visit. For five years Carter had borne the brunt of continual work and vigilance in the extremes of the Egyptian climate. Carnarvon, with heavy responsibilities at Highclere, had inevitably to return home between seasons, sometimes leaving Carter to cope alone in mid-season, during those months – usually from about October to March – when the weather is most benign and most work is done.

The relationship forged between Carnarvon and his hard-working assistant had become solid enough in five years of great anticipation and modest harvest. But his lordship had almost certainly expected more. Perhaps that was one reason why, when he returned home in the summer of 1911, he contacted Hogarth, the fount of all eastern scholarship at Oxford, to see if there were any other young Egyptologists who might like to work with him. Whether he had in mind a substitute for Carter, or simply someone to work with Carter and perhaps lead him along more fruitful paths, it is impossible to say. It was almost certainly Hogarth who suggested Leonard Woolley, a thirty-year-old archaeologist who had until recently been working with the Anglo-American MacIver among the sites of the Sudan and Ethiopia, and was shortly to take charge of Hogarth's site at Carchemish in Syria, with T.E. Lawrence as his assistant. Woolley had been working meanwhile for the Central Asian explorer Aurel Stein, making an inventory of his finds in the British Museum, and in June he wrote to Stein to say that he had finished the work he had undertaken and was proposing to go into hospital for a minor operation and would be staying at Highclere afterwards at the invitation of Lord Carnarvon. Stein greatly admired Woolley's work and wanted him to become his assistant. So, it seemed, did Carnarvon. On 20 July Stein wrote 'with reference to what you recently told me of your plans', and went on to ask if he, Woolley, could possibly help him prepare some photographs of objects – 'with your special experience I should find your help very useful'. He added: 'Hope that you will have an enjoyable and profitable time at Highclere.'

On 23 July Woolley replied that he would like to help, the 'only uncertainty' being the 'possibility of doing work with Lord Carnarvon in August'. He thought it unlikely that he would come to terms with Carnarvon but it was something he must bear in mind when undertaking other duties. Three days later, Stein wrote to say that he had 'sounded out the India Office', presumably about the possibility of Woolley joining him in Turkestan where he was currently working, and he thought there would be no serious difficulty, 'in case your work with Lord Carnarvon does not keep you occupied beyond the expected period'. By the end of August, Woolley had left Highclere in good health and on good terms with Carnarvon, but having accepted an offer from Hogarth to take charge of the British Museum's Carchemish excavation. Carnarvon returned to Egypt where Carter awaited him.

In 1912, it was Carter's turn for a holiday. It was the year of the publication of *Five Year's Exploration,* the joint work which told the archaeological world of their endeavours on the fringes of the Valley, and in May while they were on their way to England, the *Times Literary Supplement* carried the only substantial review of the work, probably contributed by Newberry, drawing attention to the fact that Lord Carnarvon had perhaps profited 'by peculiar information which must have come Mr Carter's way during his residence at Luxor as Inspector of Monuments for Upper Egypt'. The author also remarked that, 'without knowing something of what is known, as a rule, to the Gournah [Qurna] *fellahin* and, by exception, to the police, ninety-nine diggers out of a hundred would waste their time and their money there.' But Lord Carnarvon was not digging altogether in the dark.

'Lordy', as the American fraternity in Egypt dubbed the Earl in preference to the universal English nickname of Porchy, suggested that after visiting his family, Carter should accompany him on a tour of Europe. In August the two men set off together for Paris, Turin and Florence. Although their friendship grew to be a true one, they were always to be far apart in manner and background, and Carter seems to have been content with the role of the knowledgeable shadow, ready to advise and intervene where his expertise, his knowledge of ancient Egyptian history and convictions about art and architecture were called for. Generally he trailed along quietly while his urbane patron-companion captivated every section of society with discreet largesse and that easy amiability which Lady

Burghclere would doubtless have attributed in good part to Eton. As in the days when he travelled alone through the Continent on his rare home visits, Carter was happiest when quietly admiring and absorbing the countryside or the artistic treasures of the region. He was awkward in company and never became accustomed to the herd activities of his more clubbable fellow countrymen.

After the grand tour, Carnarvon decided to dig in the Nile Delta. Maspero readily gave him permission to excavate at Sakha, Carter recalling that the Director-General had himself found a Roman inscription there in the early 1880s which identified it as ancient Xois, once the capital city of the Hyksos kings. Unfortunately, there was no documented history to speak of. Petrie had investigated the site in 1884 but did not dig there. Perhaps he was deterred by the same thing as Carnarvon and Carter—a plague of cobras. At any rate, the sight of the swarming giant snakes was too much for the latest excavators. They left after a fortnight and Carter persuaded his chief to apply once more for the Valley.

Davis had become disillusioned. The rewards for his great expenditure of energy and money had, he thought, been small, and he decided to relinquish the concession just before Carnarvon reapplied for it in November, soon after the start of the 1913 - 14 season. The concession was finally granted early in 1914 for ten years from the 1914 - 15 season. It was not in fact signed until 1915 by the acting Director-General George Daressy, standing in for Maspero. The latter proudly wearing the insignia of knighthood conferred on him in 1909 at the instigation of Eldon Gorst, Cromer's successor, told Carter that he did not consider the effort of further digging in the Valley 'worth the candle'. The finds they were likely to make would hardly repay the cost of the excavations.

Before the matter could be put to the test, war was declared between the Entente and the Central Powers. Carnarvon rushed home to shoulder the obligations of his estate and many dependents. Ill health prevented him from taking an active part in the conflict, much to his dismay. For Carter, fit and just forty years old, it was another matter. He returned to Egypt in September 1913 in the knowledge that Aunt Fanny, who along with Aunt Kate had brought him up at the family cottage in Sporle Road, was dying.

Four years earlier, at the beginning of 1909, another death – that of Lord Amherst – had signalled the end of the era of youth, a break with the years of financial dependence which had left their inevitable mark. Amherst and his wife had been good to the Carter family, and particularly to Howard who would never have reached Egypt and gained a footing in that jealously guarded academic territory without their help and encouragement. But the loss of a knowledgeable and enlightened collector, a much admired antiquarian, was lamented more by Newberry and Griffith, who were genuine friends on a social parity, than by Carter who exhibited the common resentment of whose who depend on patronage. The subsequent break-up of the Amherst estate and the dispersal of the magnificent library and collections of Didlington Hall, which resulted from poor legal advice in the drawing up of the will, was a tragedy shared by scholars the world over.

When Carter returned to Egypt in 1913, he was still dependent on aristocratic patronage, but no more so than if he were working for one of the universities or museums which sponsored the great digs of the Middle East. His skills as a dealer in antiquities and adviser to Carnarvon and other rich prospectors had given him a considerable measure of financial independence and social standing, but the bitter sense of class 'difference' which had followed Carter from birth to Egypt, the conceit of many of the more privileged young men with whom he had worked, made a deep impression. Almost inevitably, an unconscious sense of grievance was embedded in the adult Carter. By the time news of Aunt Fanny's death reached Egypt in December he was, nevertheless, hard at work in the Valley of the Kings and more or less at one with the world.

The various artefacts which Davis had shown to Winlock in 1909 were given to the Metropolitan Museum by their finder, but they were of no more interest to Winlock and the museum than to Davis, though the latter subsequently decided that the chamber in which he had found the cache of gold foil bearing its royal name was the tomb of Tutankhamun. Carter thought the idea 'ludicrous'. The pit was too small and insignificant for such a royal mummy. All the same, he was convinced that the Valley was not exhausted; that somewhere among the royal tombs there was one that had remained inviolate. He faced four years of enforced idleness in which to contemplate the matter.

Chapter 8

KING'S MESSENGER

THE declaration of war in Europe in August 1914 made little immediate impact on British controlled Egypt. Field Marshal Lord Kitchener, who took over from Sir Eldon Gorst as Resident and Consul-General in 1911, had wanted to stay on, but Prime Minister Asquith insisted on his joining the Cabinet as Secretary of State for War. The Young Turks had promised their allegiance to the Kaiser's Germany, despite reservations about fighting alongside the old enemy, the Austro-Hungarian Empire. But for the time being the East remained passive, waiting for the Ottoman power to make up its mind. Two battle cruisers of the German Navy, *Goeben and Breslau,* trapped in the Mediterranean at the onset of war, played hide-and-seek with the Royal Navy and made a monkey of their powerful adversary, breaking through the Dardanelles and entering the Sea of Marmara on 10 August 1914. The scene was thus set for the Turkish bombardment of Odessa and the Allies' declaration of war on 4 November.

While those events captured headlines around the world, Britain at last made a positive move with regard to its crypto-dominion Egypt and annexed the country, though the Foreign Secretary, Sir Edward Grey, spoke of a 'Protectorate'. At the same time, the Khedive Abbas Hilmi, who had ruled since 1892 under the firman of the Sultan of Turkey which made his family hereditary viceroys, was told that he must abdicate and accept exile, and that his uncle Husain Kamil would take his place on the throne, be given the title of Sultan and addressed as 'Your Majesty'. It was to be understood, however, that the Khedival princes would henceforth make the first call on

Britain's diplomatic emissaries. Husain Kamil's lips trembled when the acting Resident, Sir Milne Cheetham, conveyed the news.

With Maspero at home in France – tired and ailing and reported to have returned to Paris to die – Britain's Residency, in the temporary charge of Cheetham and Ronald Storrs, took over responsibility for archaeology and much else.

Carter was able to view the evolving drama from the comfortable setting of the Grand Continental Hotel. Whenever he could justify an overnight stay in Cairo, he made for Shepheard's, but with the comings and goings of businessmen, soldiers and diplomatic emissaries that famous establishment was full. Carnarvon's favourite hotel, the 'Continental', always had a place for members of his entourage. Carter was quite capable of enduring the rough-and-tumble of camp life, or the lonely austerity of a mud-brick village house, but he made no pretence of liking either. The love of luxury which he acknowledged as a maternal inheritance was allied to fastidious concern for dress and appearance which owed much to Carnarvon's example. He affected Porchy's 'style', even down to the half-cigarette held in an elegant holder, the bow-ties, and the trilby hat, in his case a rather staid homburg, worn incongruously in the desert. His fashionable clothes and acquired mannerisms were unremarkable in the Luxor and Cairo hotels where he often stayed with the Carnarvons and their entourage, but they lent a strange air of tweedy respectability to the village coffee table at Qurna.

Taking stock in the months of military stalemate, he must have been struck by the fact of his lack of progress in his profession and his relative obscurity in the world at large. Among fellow Egyptologists he was, admittedly, respected as a most thorough and diligent excavator, as well as being by general consent the finest artist-draughtsman in the business. He was also seen as a difficult, uncommunicative fellow whose withdrawn manner did nothing to raise the spirits of his co-workers in lonely and often hostile habitats. He had been at work in Egypt now for twenty-three years, digging and copying in the most prodigious of ancient treasure houses. Yet in a world where the old-guard archaeologists bestrode the stage like prima donnas, unveiling the wonders of Egypt and Mesopotamia, of Mycenaean and Minoan Greece, he had won neither renown nor recognition outside the ranks of fellow diggers.

While he had prospected in the Nile Valley under the auspices of Amherst, Davis and Carnarvon, seeking the breakthrough which always eluded him, German teams under Koldewey at Babylon and Andrae at Assur had uncovered whole cities, magnificent artefacts and great libraries, elucidating historical periods and events stretching from Hammurabi's law-giving empire of the early second millennium BC to the Babylonian captivity of the Israelites and the Persian conquests of the sixth century BC. Carter's contemporary, Leonard Woolley, had joined up with his young Oxford contemporary T.E. Lawrence at Carchemish, taking over from Hogarth after turning down Carnarvon's offer of employment in Egypt. He had captured the popular imagination with articles in the press which, if they indicated no major discoveries, at least conveyed the spirit of Hittite domination of northern Syria and Anatolia, and of famous battles fought in the vicinity by Egypt, Assyria, Babylon and Persia. In Greece and Crete, Evans and Hogarth, Frederico Halbherr of Rome University, and the Bostonian Harriet Boyd had attracted world-wide attention in the first decade of the twentieth century, as had Aurel Stein in Chinese Turkestan. Nearer home, excavations at Glastonbury in England had temporarily obliterated even Egypt, Babylon and Greece from the public gaze. And as war came, the tombs of the Scythian kings in Russia, described in all their gorgeous splendour by Herodotus, gave up their treasures of gold, silver, bronze and wood to Professor Wesselowsky's team. Most signally from Carter's point of view, German archaeologists working under Ludwig Borchardt at Amarna between 1907 and 1914 had uncovered a complex of houses and studio workshops belonging to the 'king's favourite', the sculptor Djehutimose, where they found plaster casts and partly finished busts which, at a glance, cast a new, exalted light on Egyptian art. Among the finds was a life-size painted wooden bust of Akhenaten's queen, Nefertiti, made by the court sculptor as a guide to lesser artists, a remarkable rendering of a head of astonishing beauty.

In truth, however, competition and the fame won by others did not cause Carter real concern. He did not seek personal aggrandisement. Others contributed regularly to the columns of the heavier newspapers and magazines, but his words were so far hidden away in his notebooks. He was a writer of demonstrable skill. His writing had always had a natural simplicity although the earlier notebooks often betrayed a lack of elementary discipline: an eccentric use of the capital initial was evident, and he sometimes used the wrong word with disconcerting effect. His occasionally naïve, often touching phrases gave poignancy to observations which were meant only for his own consumption. But the same notebooks, with their careful and detailed observations on every known tomb and discovery, on the whereabouts of every royal or notable whose mummy or resting place had ever been traced, showed that ambition was not lacking, and that the treasure he most coveted lay in the region he knew like the back of his hand, the Valley of the Tombs of the Kings.

While the rest of the world concentrated on the terrible first battles of the main war fronts, Carter returned to the Valley in October 1914 as though preparing for the start of a perfectly normal season. He reported to the authorities in Cairo but neither the military nor the civil power seemed interested in his services, though he was one of the few Englishmen in Egypt who spoke Arabic with native fluency. The military nucleus which had taken over the Savoy Hotel as staff HQ, while finding a luxurious billet in the Grand Continental next door, might have seen a rare usefulness in his ability to speak several Arabic dialects and to converse with the Arabs of the desert, as though he was one of them. But for the moment the Egyptian War Office was paralysed by last-ditch efforts to neutralize the Turkish Empire. Nobody quite knew if, when or where an eastern battleground might materialise. Carter was used by the army command in an *ad hoc* way to round up young men around Qurna and Cairo for service with the Egyptian levies, but in the main he was pointedly ignored by the authorities and encouraged to go on digging.

With a few workmen taken on with funds left in his care by Carnarvon he quickly found a tomb which he believed to be that of Amenophis I. The Amherst Papyrus, Carter recalled, contained details from the reign of Ramesses XI, who came to the throne 400 years after Amenophis I, of an inspection of the tomb of that latter king in 'Year 13, third month of *ahet*, day 18'. Respecting the 'eternal horizon' of the king, it said: 'Inspected on the day; it was found uninjured by thieves.' Fifty years after that inspection, however, thieves had entered the tomb and as a result the burial was 'renewed'. Another thirty years passed before robbers again broke in. Then, sometime shortly after the turn of the millennium in about 980 BC, the mummy was removed by royal decree to a safer place. In 1881 it was found in the famous royal cache which Maspero and the police traced to Deir al Bahari.

What Carter had discovered was an empty tomb consisting of two galleries and a burial chamber, with connecting passages and entrance pit. Others, including Winlock, agreed with Carter that it was the tomb of Amenophis I, but later opinion held that it was probably the burial chamber of the king's mother, Ahmose-Nofretari. It was, as so often before, a find of promise rather than manifest riches.

Carter was to tell in the economical, often haunting prose which marked a later literary masterpiece, of the decline and eventual obscurity of the Valley, and of the Egyptian civilization that had lasted for three millennia, of 'cavernous galleries plundered and empty', home to the desert fox, the owl and to great colonies of bats, though many of the tombs were subsequently used, in the reign of Osorkon I (about 900 BC), for the burial of priestesses:

> One final picture, before the mist of the Middle Ages settles
> down upon the Valley, and hides it from our view. There is
> something about the atmosphere of Egypt – most people
> experience it I think – that attunes one's mind to solitude,
> and that is probably one of the reasons why, after the
> conversion of the country to Christianity, so many of its
> inhabitants turned with enthusiasm to the Hermit's life.
> The country itself, with its equable climate, its narrow strip
> of cultivable land, and its desert hills on either side,
> honeycombed with natural and artificial caverns, was well
> adapted to such a purpose... In the early centuries of the
> Christian era there must have been thousands who forsook
> the world and adopted the contemplative life, and in the
> rock-cut sepulchres upon the desert hills we find their
> traces everywhere... and in the II—IV centuries AD we
> find a colony of Anchorites in full possession, the open
> tombs in use as cells, and one transformed into a church...
> Magnificence and royal pride have been replaced by humble
> poverty. The 'precious habitation' of the king has narrowed
> to a hermit's cell.

So far as Carter could see, that was how the Valley stood, a
deserted honeycomb of hermit cells, as he left yet another
empty tomb and returned to Cairo in time for Christmas in a
war-torn world.

The administration that awaited him in Cairo was a ragtag
ensemble, enjoying the creature comforts of a city as yet
unaffected by war, uncertain of its role and still with no proper
staff organization despite the entry of Turkey into the conflict.
But as far as Carter was concerned it had the merit of being
under the command of a man who was keen on archaeology,
one of the early members of the Egypt Exploration Fund,
General Sir John Maxwell. Just as fortunate was the appearance
at the end of the year of the General's senior staff officer,

Colonel Neill Malcolm, whose campaigns stretched from the North-West Frontier to South Africa, and whose record of bravery in countless engagements was matched by a good and sympathetic mind which encompassed a particular liking for archaeology and the practitioners of that discipline.

Several of Carter's contemporaries sat comfortably at table with the army chiefs and engaged in earnest conversation about the prosecution of the war, the need to divide the Arabs from their Turkish masters, and their own exploits in unravelling the skein of ancient history. But not Carter. Solitary and taciturn as ever, he kept very much to himself as the Dardanelles adventure took shape and Australian troops began to pour into Cairo by the trainload.

Among the brilliant, argumentative band of British academics that arrived in Cairo at about the same time as Carter, mostly at the behest of Captain 'Blinker' Hall, the Admiralty intelligence chief, perhaps the most voluble were Lieutenants T.E. Lawrence and Aubrey Herbert, Carnarvon's half-brother. The former came with Woolley, his chief at Carchemish, with whom he had served his apprenticeship in both archaeology and intelligence work. Early in 1914 the two men had completed a 'dummy run' through Sinai and along the Hijaz railroad under the watchful command of Lieutenant-Colonel Stewart Newcombe.

Aubrey Herbert, the favourite son of the 4th Earl of Carnarvon, was myopic, clever and wonderfully eccentric. He was often mistaken for a vagabond when travelling on public transport and on one occasion was ordered from his first-class seat until he was able to produce his tattered ticket. Carter had met him at Highclere when visiting Carnarvon in 1911. Lawrence and Herbert, each in his idiosyncratic way, would chart the course of events in Egypt which led to the creation of a secret service organization called the Arab Bureau. This was formed primarily to carry out the plan of Kitchener to make an alliance between Britain and the Arabs through negotiation with Husain bin Ali, the Sharif of Mecca, keeper of the Islamic holy places under the Caliphate of the Sultan of Turkey.

Lieutenant-Colonel 'Bertie' Clayton had been chief of civil and military intelligence under Kitchener's pre-war regime, and he remained in day-to-day charge of the 'wild men', as Lawrence was to dub them, at the Savoy Hotel, though Ronald Storrs was, in terms of Foreign Office seniority, the 'first' among them. Others, like Gertrude Bell, George Lloyd, Mark Sykes and Hogarth 'our father confessor', arrived later. Lawrence was to describe them all famously – 'Skinface' Newcombe, Herbert – 'a joke but a very nice one', Kitchener's nephew, Colonel Parker, Graves, Robert and Philip (*The Times'* man in Cairo pre-war) – 'all of the creed'.

Aubrey Herbert, who travelled out with Lloyd, Woolley, Edwin Lutyens and William Nicholson in a 'simmering revel', supplemented Lawrence's famous description. He detested Newcombe, the immediate chief. 'Newcombe, captain and head, a vain ambitious inarticulate man; Leonard Woolley, a good sort, archaeologist.' Lawrence he described as 'an odd gnome, half cad – with a touch of genius'. Clayton was 'fatherly and shrewd'. Herbert found Maxwell 'a good man, and strong', none the weaker for his liking for port and pâté de foie gras. In that garrulous gathering, nobody, it seems, spoke to Carter or he to them, neither was he beckoned to join them at the bar of an establishment which Herbert likened to an oriental railway station. Few of the newcomers acknowledged his existence. Theirs was an Oxbridge fraternity almost to the last man, and Carnarvon's assistant was not by any stretch of the imagination one of them.

The universal patriotism brought on by war was a demanding force in archaeology as much as any other walk of life. Miss Paterson had made the point as trenchantly as could be in a characteristic letter to a young man named Louis Olza who applied for a job with the Fund in October 1915: 'I am instructed to inform you that the Egypt Exploration Fund had no place on its staff for a young man of 23 who knows several languages, can manage men, and obviously, if he can "rough it" on excavations, is fit for military service.'

Miss Paterson would almost certainly not have approved of Carter in the early months of danger, digging at Thebes and buying and selling *antikas,* even though he had the same excuse as many able-bodied men of the time, including no doubt the unfortunate Mr Olza, that nobody showed the slightest interest in their services. In fact, despite approaches to both military and civil authorities, Carter had to wait until March 1915 before being given a war job of any kind. In the meantime, he went on digging.

In February 1915, he went to the western edge of the Valley of the Kings to clear the tomb of Amenophis III, one of the greatest of ancient monarchs. It was a gesture of impatience, but an important one archaeologically as it turned out. Members of Napoleon's expedition had explored the tomb superficially in 1798, and many fine pieces went to the Louvre. Other notable artefacts remained, however, including some calcite fragments of *shawabti* figures containing part of the king's beautifully modelled face, and a cartouche prenomen, Nebmaatre. The interest of Carter and his patron had been aroused earlier by the purchase in Luxor of three beautiful bracelet inlays of cornelian which Carter believed had adorned the mummy of King Amenophis III.

At the entrance to the tomb, six foundation deposits were uncovered, most with intact implements, vessels and food offerings. Inside, the tomb was almost bare, having been invaded by robbers during or soon after the reign of Ramesses II (1304 - 1237 BC), and the body having been removed more than a century later to the tomb of Amenophis II, along with other royal sarcophagi.

After little more than a month of fruitful work in the Valley he was called back to Cairo by Kitchener's successor, Sir Henry McMahon, a kindly man who, until he arrived in Cairo as High Commissioner for the 'Protectorate', had been Foreign Secretary to the government of India. McMahon's first task was to take up the secret negotiations with Arab politicians which Kitchener had begun before the war and which were intended to bring the Sharif of Mecca, and through him, the Moslem communities of the world, over to the Allied side in the event of conflict. It was an impossible policy, but like McMahon himself, Carter was expected to play his part with loyalty if not with relish.

When asked about his war work, Carter always replied that he served as a King's Messenger. In a sense, that was true. He carried secret dispatches for Sir Henry McMahon in the vitally important year of 1915 under the seal of the Foreign Office, and he carried verbal messages and acted as translator in the course of clandestine exchanges between British and French officials and their Arab contacts. He was not a secret agent or an officer of the intelligence service, though he was inevitably involved with the intelligence arm of the General Staff. He could not properly claim, either, that he was a bona fide member of the elite band known as King's Messengers, whose badge is the royal coat of arms with silver greyhound pendant, and whose origins lay with the Civil War and the famous 'Forty' of the Great Chamber in Ordinary. Strictly speaking, Carter was a messenger *extraordinary,* but his work was vitally important all the same. The appellation King's Messenger would come to have a more appropriate, and as yet unsuspected, significance.

Carter, like many others of the British community who had served in Cairo since the British occupation, had come to know about the Royal Corps of Messengers through one of its most distinguished servants, Lieutenant Harry King 'Bimbashi' Stewart of the Gordon Highlanders. Stewart was a legend in the British Army, having served with distinction in the campaign of 1882 and two years later with Redvers Buller in the Sudan. He was the first British officer to be given the rank of Bimbashi or Major in the Egyptian Army but injury and consequent bad health forced his retirement. He was a prominent figure in Cairo, and, in 1895, Lord Salisbury as Foreign Secretary made him a Queen's Messenger. It was a title and role that the forty-year-old Carter would have been proud to take on in wartime Cairo, even though it took him away from the Valley of the Kings. But before the Dardanelles campaign had drawn to its close and a British army in Mesopotamia had fallen into a well-laid trap at Kut al Amara, he was back in the Valley having fallen foul of the army and the High Commission in Cairo.

Precisely what happened was never revealed by Carter or the official record, but it is probable that his abrasive manner and unsubtle approach to authority made enemies among his civil and military superiors. As well as carrying important messages to and from Arab revolutionaries and deserters from the Turkish army, he acted as interpreter to military and naval officers who interrogated Arab 'recruits'. Perhaps he objected to the entire plan of the Arab Bureau under direction of the High Commissioner Sir Henry McMahon, which was based largely on Kitchener's belief that the Caliphate should be transferred from Constantinople to Mecca in order to prevent its control falling to the Russian allies. If so, he was in good company, for much of the British Cabinet, the Viceroy and most of the Imperial General Staff objected too. Whatever the actual cause of disagreement, Carter as always stood his ground, asserted that everyone else, from McMahon to the merest secretary, was wrong and he right, and he was dismissed from the service of the Crown in October 1915. The authorities might have saved their breath. Carter was already at Thebes planning the excavation which would lead to the cliff tomb of Queen Hatshepsut.

The part of messenger to the wartime administration of Egypt in a jejune political scheme had been no more than an inconvenient interruption to his chief purpose. His every waking thought was for the Valley, and what he believed still to be the real possibility of a single intact royal tomb, so cleverly concealed that it had survived the attentions of the most skilled thieves.

In the winter of 1915 - 16, in the aftermath of the Dardanelles disaster and the siege of Kut al Amara, with rumour and intrigue rife in every hotel bar in Cairo, Carter went once more to

Luxor, ostensibly for a 'few days' rest. 'I found myself involved quite unexpectedly in another piece of work,' he wrote. In the absence of officials who had all gone off to war, the region had reverted to rival gangs of robbers. Prospecting parties were everywhere at work. Carter had taken up his Qurna village residence, armed with a large-scale map of the Valley carefully constructed during his exile in Cairo and designed to make certain that he had not neglected an inch of the rocky slopes where a royal burial might be concealed.

One afternoon a breathless villager arrived to tell him that a find had been made in an unfrequented area on the west side of the slopes above the Valley. Before Carter could prepare himself to meet the challenge of the unauthorized excavation, a rival party of well-armed diggers turned up and a lively battle ensued. The original party was driven off to lick its wounds and plot revenge. Carter was asked to intervene to prevent further bloodshed. He hastily collected a gang of workmen who had escaped conscription into the Egyptian Army levies and made his way to the scene of action, climbing the hills above Qurna to a height of some 1,800 feet by moonlight, and then down the other side to a cliff-top.

It was midnight when he arrived and a guide pointed out to him a rope which dangled over the sheer face. Standing at the cliff edge, he could hear the robbers at work. He severed the rope, thus cutting off their means of escape, and then secured a rope of his own and lowered himself down, in his own words' 'shinning down a rope at midnight, into a nestful of industrious tomb robbers'. He added with notable understatement that such a pastime 'at least does not lack excitement'. Eight men were at work and they were sufficiently impressed by the Englishman's miraculous appearance to make their exit by way of his rope.

The rest of the night was spent in uncomfortable, sleepless preparation for the dawn light. At daybreak he was able to make a thorough examination. The entrance, he discovered, was in the bottom of a natural cleft, worn away by the age-long attrition of wind and water, 130 feet from the cliff-top from which he had lowered himself, 220 feet from the valley bed. The cavity faced west and the rising sun was just bright enough to illuminate the inconspicuous opening, so cunningly concealed that 'neither from the top nor the bottom could the slightest trace of it be seen'. A passage ran laterally for 55 feet into the face of the cliff, and proceeded at right angles. The short passage running inwards into the cliff became a sharp slope with a passage leading down into a chamber about 18 feet square. The place was full of rubbish but the first party of robbers had succeeded in burrowing a tunnel 90 feet long leading from the chamber, which Carter was just able to crawl through. Having ascertained the layout of the tomb he called his workmen down and for twenty-eight days and nights they laboured in shifts to clear the rubbish. At first they shinned up and down the rope to gain access and return after their arduous stints of work. After a few days, however, a running tackle was put in place so that they could let themselves down to the foot of the valley or pull themselves up as they wished. Carter had a net constructed so that he could be let down from the cliff-top in relative safety.

The great excitement of the find led quickly to anti-climax. Surely such a well-concealed tomb must contain wonderful treasure. The thought was dispelled by ghostly emptiness. The tomb had neither been finished nor occupied. It did, however, contain a large sandstone sarcophagus, itself unfinished, with an inscription which showed it to be yet another grave intended for Queen Hatshepsut. Presumably, said Carter, that 'masterful' lady had arranged for the tomb to be constructed for her as the wife of Tuthmosis II. When she later seized the throne and ruled as king, it was vital that she should have a tomb in the Valley itself (the tomb which Carter himself had discovered in 1903). The grave at the cliff-top had been abandoned and, like those of all the other kings, her Valley tomb had suffered the discourtesy of violation after death. As Carter said, she would have been better advised to have stuck to her original plan: 'In this secret spot her mummy would have had a reasonable chance of avoiding disturbance: in the Valley it had none. A king she would be, a king's fate she shared.'

Having drawn yet another blank, Carter spent Christmas of 1916 at Luxor. When he returned to Cairo at the turn of the year, much had changed. The general who had taken joint command with Maxwell early in 1916, Archibald Murray, who had been Chief of the Imperial General Staff, was preparing a final push along the old Roman coast road of Sinai in a bid to take Jerusalem. Woolley had gone to sea from Port Said on an espionage mission aboard Lord Rosebery's requisitioned yacht, and been taken prisoner by the Turks. Lawrence had gone off to the bourn of his desire, the desert heartland of Islam, where he joined the camp of the Sharif's son Faisal. The Turks remained entrenched in Sinai and at the Prophet's city of Madina. Malcolm was still Chief of Staff. Hogarth was running the Arab Bureau. Clayton had been replaced as director of military intelligence by Major Holdich.

The personnel of the Savoy Hotel had changed face almost entirely. The war was not going well and Carter felt in honour bound to volunteer his services, but there was little that he could usefully contribute to the chaotic allied effort. He was still the solitary dreamer, a man apart, uncommunicative, doodling in hieroglyphs, drawing tomb layouts remembered from the Amherst and other papyri, or studying his large, heavily pencilled map of the Valley of the Tombs of the Kings, the place which everyone of authority, including Maspero himself, had written off as an empty, exhausted and worthless necropolis.

Nine months of earth-shaking events in the world at large followed, and to all appearances left him unmoved. In March 1917, as Murray at GHQ Ismailiya marched his army from Arish to Gaza, the first stage of his compliance with the order from London to adopt a more offensive role and to 'Capture Jerusalem', his opposite number in Mesopotamia (Iraq), Sir Stanley Maude, entered Baghdad and proclaimed the country's future independence. The Reuter wire capped that news with the story that Kerensky's provisional regime had taken control of Petrograd and the Czar had abdicated. On 20 April, Murray's advance on Gaza faltered and was abandoned. Without sufficient troops, two more divisions at least, the British GOC thought the task impossible. In May, Murray was told that he was to be replaced by General Sir Edmund Allenby, 'the Bull', fresh from an indecisive campaign at Arras on the Western front. Lloyd George had wanted Jan Smuts to take the job but he refused. The decision to send Allenby was another of the strokes of fate which seem to have visited Carter at critical moments throughout his life. He would see much of the new army commander in later years. For the moment, Allenby took a sympathetic view of Carter's predicament: he had nothing to do and a reputation for being virtually unemployable. He had, after all, been dismissed at the end of 1915. In September 1917, he was told that he could take indefinite leave and, as it were, carry on digging to his heart's content.

'In the autumn of 1917,' wrote Carter, 'our real campaign in The Valley opened.' He added: 'The difficulty was to know where to begin.' Rubbish thrown out by previous excavators covered the entire Valley, and Carter observed that 'no record had ever been kept as to which areas had been properly excavated and which had not.' That was the truth of the matter, but the American writer Thomas Hoving, among others, would call it a 'curious statement', claiming that unspecified notes on file in New York's Metropolitan Museum 'indicate strongly that Carter had made a careful study of where the earlier explorers had gone and had a fairly good idea where he would find virgin territory'. That also was true, but hardly reprehensible. A subsequent curator of that famous American museum's Near East department, Charles Wilkinson, went further: 'Carter never wanted anyone to know his techniques; for, you see, he was always planning... to go after the legendary tomb of Alexander the Great, and, I suppose, wished to keep to himself all his methods, even those based on the logical results of deduction – and at that he was brilliant.' He could, said Wilkinson, read directions in the random stones of the Valley, 'laid out in a language no one else could even recognize'. Whatever the truth of such conjecture – and it must be allowed that if Carter spoke to Wilkinson of digging in Egypt for Alexander's 'tomb', up to that time at least, he mentioned it to nobody else, neither did he confide such a curious ambition to his diaries – the avowed focus of his attention was never far removed from the Valley of the Kings from the moment he set foot in Egypt.

At the end of 1917, he wrote to Carnarvon to suggest that he should take as a starting point the triangle of ground 'defined by the tombs of Ramesses II, Merneptah and Ramesses VI'. There was no secret about his plan or his belief that this was the area 'in which we hoped the tomb of Tutankhamun might be found'.

If Carter's detailed notes told him exactly what had been investigated and what had not in a century and a half of systematic digging and millennia of pillage, the knowledge had availed him nothing in the past. And it would avail him little in the months that followed.

Convinced that the heaps of rubbish surrounding the tombs concealed virgin ground, he began his new campaign in the sure belief that he would find a tomb. In the first season's work, from November 1917 to March 1918, a vast accumulation of rubbish was removed and the foundations of the tomb of Ramesses VI reached. A sentence of prophetic importance was thrown off in his recollected account of that dig. 'Here we came on a series of workmen's huts, built over masses of flint boulders, the latter usually indicating in The Valley the near proximity of a tomb.' He decided that to enlarge the clearing he would cut off all access to the Ramesses tomb, a popular resort of visitors. The season's work, in the end, produced no more than a few *ostraca* (sherds of pottery and limestone flakes used in ancient times for writing and sketching). 'Interesting but not exciting,' he wrote. The final battles of the Great War raged as he closed the Valley site and returned to Cairo to endure a last hot summer of inactivity.

His had been an inglorious war. Many an archaeological colleague collected his DSO or his Croix de Guerre on the recommendation of Allenby or British and French politicians, and went on his way. Allenby himself returned to Cairo to take over the High Commission, while the unfortunate McMahon was blamed for the political consequences of the Sharifian adventure, and Lawrence went home to bask in the temporary glow of the same events made glorious by the exaggerated accounts of professional propagandists.

Carter, obsessed by the Valley that had become his home, untouched to the last by a war which had left Europe and much of Asia Minor mutilated, did not bother to return home at the armistice, even though there was news of the serious illness of his brother Verney who was a victim of the immediate post-war influenza epidemic. Verney and his wife Audrey had moved from the family home in the Fulham Road to Bowerdean Street in neighbouring Chelsea, and it was there that Verney, whose superb engraving work had complemented Carter's art in Naville's 1895 volume of the copying work at Deir al Bahari, died of the so-called Asian 'flu.

Carnarvon was enthusiastic to resume the work that had come to an abrupt end in 1914, and wrote that he would be back in Egypt, with Lady Carnarvon, towards the end of the spring season of 1919. The financial resources necessary to employ a large work-force in order to make a thorough survey of his 'triangle' were guaranteed for the moment. Carter went back to the Valley in October 1918, determined to clear the whole of the triangle marked out on his large grid-map of the entire royal necropolis.

The first task was to clear an area close to the excavations which could be used as a rubbish dump. It was in the course of clearing the chosen ground, close to the tomb of Ramesses IV, that he found a few fragments which could be dated to that king's reign. He had worked for nearly six months, clearing the ground with a work-force of more than fifty men, when the Carnarvons duly arrived in March 1919. They were just in time to witness the discovery of a small cache of thirteen alabaster jars bearing the names of Ramesses II and his son Merneptah. Carter thought they were probably from the tomb of the latter. 'As this was the nearest approach to a real find that we had yet made in The Valley, we were naturally somewhat excited, and Lady Carnarvon, I remember, insisted on digging out these jars – beautiful specimens they were – with her own hands,' he commented.

Carter, though he would not admit it, particularly in the presence of his patron, was coming close to despair. He studied his grid-map frequently, pored over it night after night, and convinced himself that somewhere within the triangle in which he had chosen to dig there was an undiscovered tomb. His evidence was circumstantial but persuasive. He summed up the situation: 'With the exception of the ground covered by the workmen's huts, we had now exhausted the whole of our triangular area, and had found no tomb. I was still hopeful, but we decided to leave this particular section until, by making a very early start in the autumn, we could accomplish it without causing inconvenience to visitors.' Carter was not keen on visitors. As far as he was concerned they were one of the necessary evils of Egypt, but they provided a useful excuse when he was forced to admit defeat in one area and go on to another.

By the onset of the autumn season in 1919 they furnished a good enough reason for moving to the small lateral valley where the empty tomb of Tuthmosis III was located, found by Loret in 1898. At the bottom of the cliff which had once housed the sarcophagus of Tuthmosis, they discovered the foundation deposits of an uncompleted tomb, probably designed for the same king.

The Carnarvons went home, disappointed but with a residue of hope. Porchy still shared Carter's admittedly 'superstitious' belief that in the corner of the Valley to which they had turned their attention a missing king would one day be found. They returned for the following two seasons, which yielded nothing but an interesting *ostracon* depicting a red jungle fowl which

Portrait of Howard Carter aged about forty-eight, painted by his brother William.

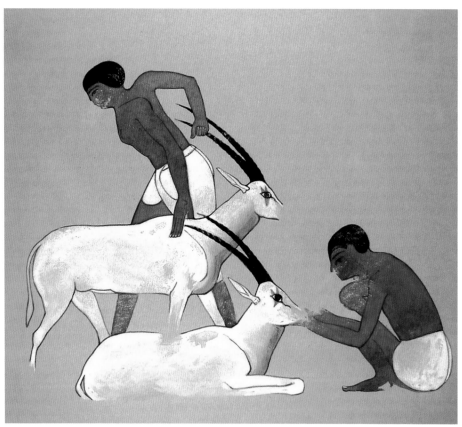

Colour drawings by Carter.

Right:
'A pair of pelicans' copied by Carter
from wall paintings at Bani Hasan.

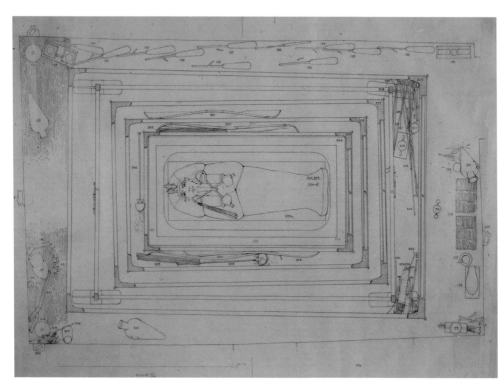

Carter's plan drawing of the Burial Chamber, showing the outermost coffin, the sarcophagus, the shrines and other scattered objects.

Desert landscape water-colour by Carter.

Carter believed to be the earliest known drawing of the domestic cockerel. It was found between the tomb of Ramesses IX and an unidentified tomb chamber of the Eighteenth Dynasty. Carter concluded that it must date between 1425 and 1123 BC, and that it depicted the genus if not the actual fowl referred to in the annals of Tuthmosis III, as part of the tribute brought to that great king by Syrian and Babylonian vassals. It was a significant find, archaeologically speaking, but it hardly compensated Carnarvon for the expenditure of £50,000 (a sum equal to the best part of £2 million or, say, $3 million in the late 20th century) in the course of fifteen years' digging in and around the Valley.

The fruitless search continued into the 1920 - 1 season. In the winter of that year, Mrs Carter, eighty-four years old and degenerating rapidly, was stricken with bronchitis at the home of her son Samuel in Fulham Road. Howard, as often happened in moments of family crisis, was digging in the Valley when news came of her death, certified as the outcome of senile decay. Howard does not seem to have been unduly affected by the news. He had never been particularly close to his mother and, in any case, she had had a long and reasonably contented life.

If he was to retain an interest in Egypt he must find better argument for doing so than he had been able to produce so far. There remained the area of flint boulders and ancient workmen's huts within the triangle, at the foot of the tomb of Ramesses VI. Though Carnarvon and Carter came close in 1919, it had not been investigated. Carter thought the stratification of the debris in that region gave hope of a tomb somewhere underneath, but they dug there without success in the autumn of 1921. Carnarvon was by now inured to Carter's optimistic belief that amid the desolation of the Valley there remained an inviolate tomb, but his patience and his resources were close to exhaustion. The rich man and his assistant finally left for England to reconsider their future plans in April 1922.

Chapter 9

'TOMB OF THE BIRD'

CARNARVON'S vast estate of some 36,000 acres on the borders of the southern English counties of Hampshire and Berkshire, entailed responsibilities and burdens which he carried amiably through the thirty or so years since he inherited the title from his father. Even by his standards, however, the post-war commercial decline suggested a need for caution. Rising inflation and reduced income from the estate were worrying developments. Egypt, the other part of a depressing equation, had become the cause of financial haemorrhage. He was in no mood for more pie-in-the-sky theories about the Valley of the Kings when Carter arrived at Highclere in June 1922, anxious to find an opportunity to unroll his grid-map and take his lordship once more through the sea of 'hatched' areas where so much money and effort had been spent to so little avail.

The assertion of all other experts, including the late Gaston Maspero, that the Valley was exhausted, now rang decidedly true for Carnarvon. The host was disinclined to discuss the matter further. He had made up his mind to finish with Egypt. To do otherwise would be to throw good money after bad. True to form, he invited his guest to join him and his daughter Lady Evelyn Herbert at the races during Newbury Week. It must have taken all Carter's not inconsiderable acting ability to pretend that he enjoyed spending day after day among the rich and the improvident as they shed money with abandon while he sought just one more chance to present his lordly patron with the trophy of all time. He had never willingly attended a sporting event of any kind and would rather a thousand times

have ridden a donkey in his beloved Valley than a Derby winner
at Epsom. All the same, he waited patiently for the ferment of
the race course to die down. Despite his preoccupation, even
the relatively stuffy Carter must surely have been affected by
the generosity of his host and hostess and the magnificence of
Highclere, the work of Sir Charles Barry with gardens fashioned
by Capability Brown, widely regarded as the finest Victorian
house in Britain. Whatever his impressions he never recorded
them in a surviving document.

When the moment of decision came, Carter showed himself
to be an adept negotiator. He unravelled his map and pointed
to the relatively small area that had yet to be properly
investigated close to the Ramesses VI tomb with its workers'
huts above the boulders. Carnarvon was aware that Carter had
dug there in 1917 before closing the tomb because of 'visitors'
to 'await another opportunity', and that after his own arrival in
1919 further excavation had revealed nothing of significance.
He was unimpressed. The time had come to call a halt.
Then, perhaps seizing on his host's renowned weakness for an
on-the-nose bet, Carter declared that he was determined to
make a last effort to find the tomb he believed to be still intact
and that if necessary he would finance the search himself. The
offer took Carnarvon by surprise. He knew that Carter made
money as a skilled dealer in Egyptian *antikas* and that collectors,
including himself, had sought and paid for his advice (the
current year's diary entries speak of the sale of gold rings,
pottery and a bronze head for several hundred pounds and the
purchase of similar articles; and there was a note of shareholdings
totalling some £4,000), but his fees and savings could not
begin to finance a full-scale excavation in Egypt. Perhaps the
Metropolitan Museum in New York would be willing to take
over the concession. Herbert Winlock at the museum had
recently had occasion to examine the jugs, cups, and linen
wraps which Theodore Davis had allowed him to take back
to America in 1909. And Winlock had written to Carter to
tell him of his belated discovery – that the clay items carried

not only the seal of Tutankhamun but also that of the royal necropolis, thus proving beyond question that the young king was buried among the honoured dead and not, like his predecessor and putative father-in-law Akhenaten, in a heretic's grave.

Winlock, it seems, deduced more. Thomas Hoving, the official of the Metropolitan Museum who was able to interview many of the men who knew both Carter and Winlock when they were alive, and who made a detailed study of the Metropolitan Museum correspondence for his own controversial account of the matter, wrote:

But Winlock deduced much more than that from the evidence. Eventually he was able to show that some of the material pertained to the actual ceremony of the mummification of Tutankhamun. Others were implements used in the final, ritual funerary banquet held within the tomb just before it was sealed for the last time. Winlock had deduced that the dried-out substance in the linen bags was natron, a material used in embalming. And by piecing together all the evidence he deduced not only the nature of the ritual banquet but its menu, the number of guests and some of the clothes they had worn. Eight individuals, wearing floral and leaf wreaths and linen headbands, one inscribed with the last known date of Tutankhamun – the sixth year of his reign – had partaken of five ducks, a couple of plovers, and haunch of mutton, washed down with beer and wine, and had reverently, carefully swept up after themselves with two small brooms. At the end of the ceremony the eight priests or necropolis officials – for it is not known exactly who they were – gathered up their dishes, cups and pottery jars, stuffed the latter with leftovers, and buried them all in a pit dug for that purpose. To have left those remnants in a tomb symbolizing the purest manifestations of the afterlife would have rendered it unclean.

To have inferred so much from the remains of a few jars and cups and pieces of linen more than 3,000 years old was no small achievement. Hoving, suspicious of Carter's motives, said that he 'dealt inaccurately with Winlock's discovery', believing that the American had assessed the real significance of the contents of the pit as soon as he saw them in the courtyard at Davis's headquarters. In fact, Carter's account in his book *The Tomb of Tut.ankh.Amen* summarized Winlock's conclusions accurately: 'the whole representing, apparently, the material which had been used during the funeral ceremonies of Tutankhamun, and afterwards gathered together and stacked away within the jars'. He made it clear that, because Davis refused to take an interest in the jars, Winlock, who 'immediately recognized their importance', sought Davis's permission to have them sent to the Metropolitan. If Carter did not state Winlock's version of the funeral feast in so many words it may have been because he was not entirely convinced of its veracity in scientific terms. Be that as it may, Winlock's reading of the story as it stood in 1922, just fifteen years after the jars and other items were rescued, came at a fortunate time for Carter.

Carter was by now heavily committed to the purchase of antiquities for wealthy clients. In fact, he had been appointed on a commission basis as the joint negotiator for the Metropolitan and for Carnarvon. Most of the treasures of the Davis and Carnarvon excavations, and much of the bounty bought by Carter in the market place, ended up in New York, the British Museum having been elbowed out of the contest by the financial stringency of the post-war period. Carter's experience of dealing with the Luxor traders was unrivalled and his services were widely sought. But the Metropolitan connection had a more vital significance for him than was suggested by his role as a source of *antikas,* for there is an implicit suggestion in his correspondence with Winlock that the Museum had expressed an interest in taking over Carnarvon's contract.

Did Carter mention that possibility to Carnarvon at their

meeting? And if so, did he put it forward as a veiled threat or simply as a statement of fact? There is no proof that Carter put the matter to his patron at all. But there is no reason why the subject should not have come up for discussion. There were, in any event, other equally persuasive arguments for continuing for a further year, not the least of them the pronouncement of the new Director-General Lacau that he proposed to change the rules relating to compensation for 'foreign excavators' so that the time to strike, financially speaking, was now. Whatever the substance of the discussion, Carter won a temporary reprieve. Carnarvon agreed to one more season.

There is other contemporary evidence of Carter's determination to persevere with the Valley, despite the overriding air of pessimism. In the 1920 - 1 season, after Carnarvon had seen with his own eyes the enthusiastic work of Carter and his gangs as they hauled their moveable railway – 'Decauville track' as it was called – from one part of that critical triangle to another and uncovered the cache of alabaster vases above Merneptah's tomb, the archaeologist Gertrude Caton Thompson turned up. She found Carter determinedly digging alongside the tomb of Ramesses IX and contemplating what he believed to be the earliest drawing of a domesticated cockerel. Carter, who suspected that he was on the verge of vital discovery, told her 'dejectedly that this was the last year of the fruitless search and that Lord Carnarvon, for whom he worked with some 80 workmen, could not continue much longer'.

In the light of subsequent events, and of the varying interpretations put on those events, it is important to appreciate the unique understanding that had come about between Carnarvon and Carter. It is unlikely that Carter kept any significant detail of his talks and correspondence with Winlock from his employer. The two men enjoyed an unusually honest and direct rapport considering their very different backgrounds and personalities. Carter had spent many a weekend at Highclere in the intervals of digging before the war, and he and Carnarvon were able to talk easily and without inhibition of their shared aim. For both men, ambition transcended financial reward or fame; the discovery of that tomb among all the royal tombs of the Valley, one – just one – tomb, had become an obsession.

Carnarvon may not have been the archaeological scholar that his family protagonists liked to picture, but he was no fool either. He was generous and quick-witted. Even the matter-of-fact Carter was capable of reeling off amusing anecdotes when he and Carnarvon strolled together in the beautiful Highclere grounds or lounged comfortably in one of the castle's several drawing-rooms. He had come to know Lady Carnarvon in the same informal, relaxed way, and he doubtless knew, as did many of his fellow archaeologists, that it was the vast fortune settled on her by her natural father, Sir Alfred de Rothschild, that enabled her husband even to contemplate, year after year, the continually rising cost of maintaining his vast estates and of digging in Egypt. And Carter took pleasure in the attention of his patron's attractive and flirtatious daughter, Lady Evelyn Herbert. His diary revealed a closeness which certainly suggested more than a formal but friendly relationship. Soon after arriving in Egypt at the beginning of the 1922 season he had spent a few days in Cairo, in which time he had two meetings with Lord Northcliffe, the owner of *The Times,* and showed him round the Cairo Museum, before retiring to his house at Qurna to prepare for the arrival of 'Evelyn', on 17 February.

Carter subsequently told James and Charles Breasted of his meeting at Highclere. James Breasted went to Oxford in October 1922 to receive an honorary doctorate. Within a month or so he was to offer his uniquely valuable services as one of the world's leading epigraphists to Carter. The professor's story recounted how Carnarvon had expressed his appreciation of Carter but regretted that he would have to give up the barren undertaking:

He [Carter] therefore wished to propose that Carnarvon grant him permission to undertake one more season's work at his – Carter's – own expense, using Carnarvon's concession, and the same workmen and equipment he had employed for years; and if at the end of this final season he had found nothing, he would of course, and with a good conscience, agree that they should abandon The Valley. But if on the other hand he should make a discovery, it should belong to Carnarvon exactly as under their long-standing agreement.

It was, according to Breasted, that eminently fair proposal which touched Carnarvon's sporting instinct and led him to change his mind – 'at his own, not Carter's expense'. On 5 October 1922, Carter left London for Marseilles where be boarded the *ss China*. By 28 October he was back at Luxor.

Before leaving London, where he had taken up residence at a new and expensive flat at 11 King Street, St James's, he had spent some time with Newberry and Quibell. He told them that he was tired of living alone in Egypt and sought a companion. It occurred to them that he must, at long last, have met a woman and intended to marry her. The two men met the Breasteds in London, on their way to Egypt, and told them about the impending 'happy event', confided to them by Carter. But the Americans, when they arrived at Luxor a week or two later, learnt that Carter was talking not about a wife but a canary. The little yellow companion accompanied Carter from England in its cage and its merry singing outside the Qurna house soon attracted natives from far and wide. Their countryside has no indigenous songbirds and they had heard nothing like it before. 'The bird will bring good fortune,' they said after listening to its musical trills.

With a work-force of nearly a hundred men and three foremen, Carter began work on 1 November, concentrating on the small segment of ground which he had earmarked for his final bid, just to the north-east of the tomb of Ramesses VI. In the background, the sheer black cliffs and rising hills frowned on the proceedings and seemed to reduce the excavated tombs of the Valley to puny insignificance. Carter began to trench southwards. In order to clear the way his labourers had to lay bare the workmen's huts which had been erected in the twelfth century BC, at about the time of the Exodus, for the labourers who worked on the Ramesses tomb. They turned out to be part of a workers' estate, stretching south in the direction of Carter's intended trench, joining up eventually with another group of huts on the other side of the Valley, discovered by Davis a decade before when he was working on the Akhenaten vault. By the evening of 3 November, they had cleared enough of the huts to dig away the soil that lay beneath them to a depth of 3 feet.

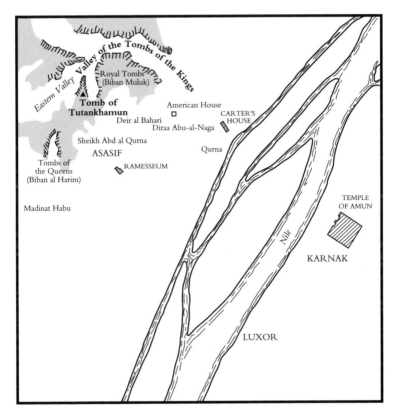

Valley of the Tombs of the Kings showing Carter's House and the American House and area of the Tombs of the Queens.

It is important to follow Carter's movements as he recorded them. When he arrived at the site that Saturday morning there was an uncommon air of silence. Carter felt instinctively that something out of the ordinary had happened. A foreman announced that a step cut in rock had been discovered underneath the first of the huts they had demolished. It seemed too good to be true. Carter ordered his men to go on digging. Extra clearing soon revealed that they were actually within a tomb entrance created by a step cut in the rock, about 13 feet below the entrance to the Ramesses tomb and slightly to the right as the onlooker faced the tomb entrances. It was, to Carter, a familiar form of cutting indicating, almost always in the Valley, a sunken stairway entrance. 'I almost dared to hope that we had found our tomb at last,' he was to write in reflective calm. There was no calm at the moment of discovery.

Several years later, while on a lecture tour of the United States, Carter was to relate a slightly different version of the discovery to the president of the bureau which handled his engagement bookings, explaining that it was the industrious water boy, emulating his elders by digging with a stick in the sand, who first hit the hard surface of a stone step, and who then ran 'as fast as his legs would carry him' to deliver the sensational news. Carter also explained that the discovery by the 'most insignificant member of the team' was made *not* under the hut as stated in his book, 'but a bit outside the area' that Carter had instructed his foremen to begin upon the evening before.

Whichever version was the more accurate, that limestone step was to prove the most redolent chance discovery in the entire history of archaeology. Carter was neither the first nor the last archaeologist to change his story in the press or in the course of a lecture tour in order to lend a little extra glamour to his achievement. It is worth recalling that at the moment of Carter's cynosure, Leonard Woolley – with whom he had rubbed shoulders in Cairo in 1915 and who had recently excavated the workers' city at Petrie's old site at Amarna – was currently digging up Ur of the Chaldees in Mesopotamia (modern Iraq), where he would proudly point to ancient dwellings and inform his enchanted visitors, 'That is where Abraham and his family lived.'

Work went on at fever pitch, Carter exhorting his men to the utmost effort through the morning of 5 November. In the afternoon, the last of the rubbish covering the rock-passage was removed. The upper edges of a stairway could be delineated on all its four sides. 'It was clear by now beyond any question that we had before us the entrance to a tomb, but doubts, born of previous disappointments, persisted in creeping in.' Could it be another false alarm? Was this another of the tombs like that of Tuthmosis III, he asked, unfinished and unoccupied? Even if it had been completed, was it likely that this tomb alone had been spared by the plunderer?

As workmen cleared the steps one by one, doubt mingled with excitement. The cutting receded at its western edge under the slope of the rock until it became a roofed-in passage, 10 feet high, 6 feet wide. At the level of the twelfth step the upper part of a doorway came into view. It was blocked with boulders, plastered over, and sealed. With excitement at fever pitch Carter examined the seal impressions on the door, hoping to find the identity of the occupant. But he could find no name. Only the familiar necropolis seals could be deciphered, with their impression of Anubis, the sacred jackal, and nine slaves. That at least proved royal association. But was it, all the same, another royal 'spoof' tomb, or simply that of a noble buried there by royal consent, or could it be the resting place of the king whom he had pursued for so many years? The questions tumbled forth. Even if it was the tomb of the king whose name he hardly dared to speak, it was, after all, a minor sovereign, in all probability a mere commoner by birth whose claim to the throne was almost certainly based on marriage to a daughter of the despised Akhenaten. If his most optimistic hope was realized, would the contents of the tomb justify the effort and expense incurred so far?

139

It took all his powers of self-control not to have the door broken down. Anything, literally anything, might lie beyond. He made a small peephole, just large enough to insert a battery torch and leave a crack to view through. He could see only stones and rubble, packing the passage beyond from floor to ceiling. Once more he looked for a seal but in vain. Had he but known, a few inches under the rubbish which remained, the door exhibited a perfectly clear impression of the seal of Tutankhamun. But it was late and the light was fading. He covered in the peephole, selected his most trustworthy workmen to keep watch through the night, and rode home by moonlight. Never in all his life had he felt such a sense of elation.

The canary chirped merrily as Carter made his way to the Luxor office of Eastern Telegraph on the morning of 6 November to send his famous telegram to Carnarvon. Afterwards he returned to the tomb which his workmen, never neglectful of a talisman, had named the 'Tomb of the Bird'. He ordered the men to refill the entrance with stones and rubbish to surface level, and to cover it with the flint boulders which were there before. The tomb vanished from sight. 'I found it hard to persuade myself at times that the whole episode had not been a dream,' he wrote.

Chapter 10

'YES, WONDERFUL THINGS'

F OR nearly three weeks there was relative calm, and then the flood gates opened. Before he resumed work on 1 November, Carter had realized that he could not proceed with his task single-handed and he contacted a man he had worked with in his early days with the Egypt Exploration Fund, Arthur 'Pecky' Callender, asking him if he could leave whatever he was doing and make his way to the Valley. Callender approved of Carter's careful, systematic approach to his work. He travelled to Luxor with Carter next day from the site he was working on at Armant. Phlegmatic, unshakeable, and remarkably versatile, he was to become Carter's most devoted assistant.

Carter's meticulous financial records for the period since his arrival from England showed that he was not so preoccupied with the thought of penetrating the new-found tomb as to neglect business matters. He noted 'salaries to date £9' (for some seventy workmen), the sale of items such as a faience hedgehog for £45, purchases of bronze figures and a glass bottle for £60, and investments in bonds and ordinary shares totalling £6,145.

Accounts of the sequence of events in the critical days which followed Callender's arrival, recorded in Carter's diary and in his later work, *The Tomb of Tut.ankh.Amen,* show inconsistencies. But differences are not as significant, and certainly not as sinister, as subsequent conspiratorial essays have suggested.

The 'rough' personal diary is sparing in its detail, but its record of events is vitally important in view of all that was to follow.

141

In the first volume of *The Tomb of Tut.ankh.Amen,* Carter stated that he received two messages from Lord Carnarvon in answer to his cable, the first of which read 'Possibly come soon', and the other 'Propose arrive Alexandria 20th'. Thus, according to that version, Carter went to Cairo on 18 November for three days, to pick up some supplies and to meet his chief. He added: 'On the 23rd Lord Carnarvon arrived at Luxor with his daughter, Lady Evelyn Herbert, his devoted companion in all his Egyptian work, and everything was in hand for the beginning of the second chapter in the discovery of the tomb.' Callender had been at work all that day, the 23rd, clearing the upper layer of rubbish. The diary, on the other hand, recorded that Lady Evelyn arrived at Luxor on the 24th together with Engelbach, an Englishman who was Chief Inspector of Monuments for Upper Egypt.

Progress was rapid. 'By the afternoon of the 24th the whole staircase was clear, sixteen steps in all, and we were able to make a proper examination of the sealed doorway.' Seal impressions on the lower part of the doorway were well defined, and several bore the name 'Tutankhamun'. Carter was certain that he was about to enter the tomb of that 'shadowy monarch, whose tenure of the throne coincided with one of the most interesting periods in the whole of Egyptian history'. Yet there were clear signs of past mischief which might reduce to nothing the expectations of the present. The door betrayed several openings and closings and the seals he had found at first depicting the jackal god and nine captives had been applied to the reclosed section, while the seals bearing the name of the young king covered the untouched part of the doorway and were surely those which originally secured the tomb. The tomb had been entered at some time in the past, 'not later than the reign of Ramesses VI'. Hope, though, resided in the resealing of the doorway. The thieves could not have rifled the interior completely.

There was an even more upsetting discovery as they cleared the last of the rubbish from the entrance stairway. Potsherds and boxes bore the names of several kings – Akhenaten, Smenkhkare, Tuthmosis III and Amenophis III – as well as Tutankhamun. Why this mixture of names? asked Carter. Were they about to discover another of those graveyard miscellanies of Eighteenth Dynasty objects, familiar from other graves in and around the Valley, brought from Tal al Amarna perhaps and deposited here for safety?

The evidence was disquieting. Carter's retrospective account suggested growing concern. 'So matters stood on the evening of the 24th,' he wrote. In his book, he said nothing of sleeping in the tomb that night. He concluded his diary entry for the 24th, 'Slept night in tomb.'

Eighteen days or thereabouts after Carter dispatched his telegram in promise of 'wonderful discovery', Carnarvon and his daughter had arrived at the Valley of the Kings, and on 25 November they, Carter, Callender, and an official of the Egyptian inspectorate stood at the threshold of discovery, before them the first and only intact tomb of a king of ancient Egypt.

On that day, the seal impressions in the plaster of the stone door had been photographed and the doorway removed. Callender had set carpenters to work to make a wooden grille to replace the door. As the final clearing of the rubbish was proceeding, Engelbach announced that he had been instructed by Pierre Lacau (the Jesuit who in 1913 succeeded Maspero as Director-General in the Department of Antiquities) to remain on site while preliminary inspection was made. He could see the passage filled with boulders and rubble which Carter had espied three weeks before through the hole he made in the outer door. There were confirmatory signs of earlier infill of an irregular hole in the original blocking stone which 'coincided with re-openings and successive re-closings found in the sealed doorway'. By nightfall they had cleared much of the passage but as yet could find no second doorway or chamber. There were more scattered fragments, waterskins, smashed alabaster jars and painted vases, suggesting to Carter's experienced eye that they belonged to 'some disturbed burial'.

Callender was staying with Carter in the Qurna site house which had become the latter's permanent home in Egypt and was known far and wide as Kasr Carter (Carter's Castle). They went home together on the night of the 25th to prepare for the grand entrance into the holy-of-holies, in which they would be joined, of course, by Carnarvon and Lady Evelyn. It was not, Carter said, until 'about the middle of the afternoon' of Sunday 26th that a second door was eventually traced. Workmen had cleared the camouflage infill of the entrance and Carter and his companions passed through the first wooden door and cleared the rubble-filled passage which led to a second door. 'The entrance and passage both in plan and in style resembled... the tomb containing the cache of Akhenaten discovered by Davis in the very near vicinity; which seemed to substantiate our first conjecture that we had found a cache.' That end-of-November day was to prove 'the day of days, the most wonderful that I have ever lived through, and certainly the one whose like I can never hope to see again'.

It is necessary to go back to the notebooks for a precise record, and to capture the spirit of the moment.

Sunday 26 November
Feverishly we cleared away the remaining last scraps of rubbish on the floor of the passage before the doorway... in which, after making preliminary notes, we made a tiny breach in the top left hand corner... Darkness and the iron testing-rod told us there was an empty space ...Candles were procured... I widened the breach and...looked in... It was sometime before one could see; the hot air escaping caused the candle to flicker, but as soon as one's eyes became accustomed to the glimmer of light, the interior of the chamber gradually loomed...with its strange and wonderful medley of extraordinary and beautiful objects. Lord Carnarvon said to me 'Can you see anything?'. I replied to him, 'Yes, it is wonderful'. I then with precaution made the

hole sufficiently large for both of us to see. With the light of
an electric torch as well as an additional candle, we looked
in. Our sensations and astonishment are difficult to
describe... The first impressions suggested the property-
room of an opera of a vanished civilization... We closed the
hole, locked the wooden grill which had been placed upon
the first doorway; we mounted our donkeys and returned
home contemplating what we had seen.

The later version of the finding of the tomb portrays Carter's
ability to reconstruct the event in prose of astonishing and
perfect harmony.

> Details of the room within emerged slowly from the mist,
> strange animals, statues, and gold – everywhere the glint of
> gold. For the moment – an eternity it must have seemed to
> the others standing by – I was struck dumb with amazement,
> and when Lord Carnarvon, unable to stand the suspense
> any longer, inquired anxiously 'Can you see anything? It
> was all I could do to get out the words, 'Yes, wonderful
> things'. Then, widening the hole a little further, so that we
> could both see, we inserted an electric torch.

Engelbach, it seems, was not present when the Carnarvon
party first glimpsed the treasures of the tomb. Carter does not
record the exact comings and goings of officials. There is no
timetable of events, only the note that the inspector was
'advised'. The exact words of the diary were: 'Advised the
Chief Inspector of the Antiquities Department, who was with
us at the commencement of the opening of the first doorway,
and asked him to come as soon as possible, preferably in
the following afternoon, to enable us to prepare an electrical
installation for careful inspection of this extraordinary and
pleasing discovery.' Thus, although there was no independent
witness to the event, which was not at all unusual, Carter had
done all that was bureaucratically necessary at the critical

moment. Few archaeological discoveries in history have been better or more precisely recorded than Carter's, despite its inevitable gaps. The excavator is seldom sure what lies round the next corner and hardly ever invites officialdom to the scene until he or she is sure.

In subsequent accounts, Carter expanded on his notebook entry for 26 November. Two years after the event he wrote with feeling and candour of his first reactions:

> Three thousand, four thousand years maybe, have passed and gone since human feet last trod the floor on which you stand, and yet, as you note the signs of recent life around you – the half-filled bowl of mortar for the door, the blackened lamp, the finger-mark upon the freshly painted surface, the farewell garland dropped upon the threshold – you feel it might have been but yesterday... Time is annihilated by little intimate details such as these, and you feel an intruder.

There followed admissions of emotions such as Carter had never before acknowledged in letters of diaries, made in simple, direct prose which does not allow of insincerity: of remembered sensations – 'the exhilaration of discovery, the fever of suspense, the almost over-mastering impulse, born of curiosity, to break down the seals and lift the lids of boxes, the thought – pure joy to the investigator – that you are about to add a page to history, or to solve some problems of research, the strained expectancy – why not confess it? – of the treasure seeker.' Did such thoughts actually pass through their minds? Or had Carter imagined them? His questions were rhetorical. 'I cannot tell.' His memory, he said, was a blank. All the same, writing in retrospect, he was able to describe the contents of the first chamber of the tomb before, as he said, they went to bed and 'slept but little, all of us, that night'.

According to the evidence of one of his professional assistants, who came after the event, he neglected to say that following the return of Carnarvon and his party to Luxor on their donkeys that night to enjoy the luxury of sleep, they refreshed themselves and returned, surreptitiously, to the tomb.

In his book, Carter described the scene as though observed by torchlight through the small hole in the door, the detail recalled from the remarkable summary contained in the diary entry for the 26th.

Uncanny beasts enough to look upon at any time: seen as we saw them, their brilliant gilded surfaces picked out of the darkness by our electric torch, as though by limelight, their heads throwing grotesque distorted shadows on the wall behind them, they were almost terrifying. Next, on the right, two statues caught and held our attention; two life-size figures of a king in black, facing each other like sentinels, gold kilted, gold sandaled, armed with mace and staff, the protective sacred cobra upon their foreheads.

He describes the countless vases, strange black shrines, one with a gilt snake peeping out, bouquets and bedsteads, a gold-inlaid throne, a heap of white oviform boxes, a lotiform cup of translucent alabaster, a confused pile of overturned chariots, a portrait of a king; but most of all the sentinel figures, keeping guard it seemed at either side of a third door which took up almost the whole of the north end of the antechamber. The black varnished *ka* statues were life-size, bearing the name 'the royal *ka* of Harakhti, the Osiris-Tutankhamun'. But there was no king, no coffin, no trace of a mummy.

The truth dawned on Carter. They were only at the threshold of discovery. 'What we saw was merely an antechamber.' He was sure, now, that behind the guarded door, beyond the sentries of the nether world, lay other chambers, just as in the Amherst Papyrus, 'possibly a succession of them, [where] beyond any shadow of doubt, in all his magnificent panoply of death, we should find the Pharaoh lying'.

The suggestion of a secret re-entry of the tomb was first

made by a member of Carter's team, Alfred Lucas, in an unsensational aside written in 1942, twenty years after the event. In an article in a learned journal he wrote: 'Lord Carnarvon, his daughter and Mr Carter certainly entered the burial chamber and also entered the store chamber, which latter had no door, before the formal opening.'

The American Thomas Hoving, sometime Director of the Metropolitan Museum of New York, in a later expostulatory account, was to put the worst possible interpretation on the events of that night – the presumption of theft. An unpublished article by Carnarvon, found among the undocumented records of the Metropolitan, described how Carter made an opening in the inner doorway of the passage, large enough for the party to gain access, 'with difficulty', to the antechamber and how, in the still of night, they went on a jamboree of discovery in other chambers as yet unrecorded in official documents and unnotified to the Egyptian authorities. Hoving, dramatising Lucas's sober article and Carnarvon's admission, described how Lady Evelyn, the smallest member of the party, went first. 'As she flashed the light around her, she was transfixed by a forest of creamy white alabaster vases standing upright. Soon the others followed.' Lucas did not mention that 'Pecky' Callender was present. Carnarvon's article and Hoving's researches in the Metropolitan Museum files suggest that he was. Pages of description set out the contents of the antechamber and the responses of the Carnarvon party as it went about its nocturnal invasion. The scene described by Hoving is that which Carter recalled as greeting him on the next day, the 27th (the date would, of course, have been the same whether the inspection took place in the small hours or in daytime):

> After the depressing years of 'barren labour', to have happened upon the most magnificent and extraordinary discovery in the entire history of Egyptian archaeology brought on euphoria... One can imagine the scene. A tiny chamber, dark, haunting... Hundreds and hundreds of

objects, each single one worth a whole season – seven full months – of digging… a treasure house of magnificent objects, furniture and works of art… The near-embarrassment of being intruders themselves haunted the party… An aeon had passed since another human being had stood where they were standing. Yet it seemed but yesterday…

Carter's description of the treasures of the antechamber has the advantage of first-hand commentary. Next morning (27th), he wrote, they were at the site early, despite lack of sleep. The resourceful Callender laid down wires and connected up with Carter's Valley lighting system. Carnarvon, a keen and experienced photographer, took pictures of the new door (the door that they had allegedly penetrated during the night) as he had the first, while Carter examined the seal impressions. The plaster-covered stone door-blocking was then removed. By noon everything was ready. In response to the note of the previous day, Engelbach, who was apparently away on business, sent his local inspector, Ibrahim Effendi, in his stead. Armed with a temporary electric light unit, Ibrahim joined Carnarvon's party for the 'official entry' to the antechamber. But Carter was already worried about the other chamber beyond the north wall, espied between the life-size statues the day before. His account is as follows: 'By the aid of our powerful electric lamps many things that had been obscure to us on the previous day became clear, and we were able to make a more accurate estimate of the extent of our discovery. Our first objective was naturally the sealed door between the statues, and here a disappointment awaited us.'

Hurried observation the day before had suggested an intact blocking to the door. On examination it was found to have a hole near its base just sufficient to admit a small boy. 'We were not then to be the first.' Carter's worst fears of having been anticipated by the thieves of antiquity seemed about to be realized. He resisted a natural impulse to break down the door and find out the facts as quickly as he could. Reluctantly, he decided to leave the opening of the inner sealed door until the antechamber was cleared, which would ensure that nothing was damaged during the 'ticklish' operation of removing the door blocking.

Hoving, fifty-six years on, from the evidence of Carnarvon's unpublished 'news account', suggests that Carter already knew what lay beyond the inner door, that the night before he had removed some of the irregular blocks of stone which marked the break-in of earlier intruders and entered feet first, followed by other members of the party.

Carter's description of the lesser room beyond the antechamber, entered in his notebooks and recalled soon after in his book, has the virtue of immediacy:

The state of this inner room (afterwards called the Annexe) simply defies description. In the Antechamber there had been some sort of an attempt to tidy up the plunderers' visit, but here everything was in confusion, just as they had left it... Not a single inch of floor space remains vacant, and it will be a matter of considerable difficulty, when the time for clearing comes, to know how to begin. So far we have not made any attempt to enter the chamber, but have contented ourselves with taking stock from outside... Beautiful things it contains, too, smaller than those in the Antechamber for the most part, but many of them of exquisite workmanship... I think the discovery of this second chamber, with its crowded contents, had a somewhat sobering effect upon us. Excitement had gripped us hitherto, and given us no pause for thought, but now for the first time we began to realize what a prodigious task we had in front of us, and what a responsibility it entailed... moreover, the extent of our discovery had taken us by surprise, and we were wholly unprepared to deal with the multitude of objects that lay before us... Clearly, the first thing to be done was to render the tomb safe against robbery... We had our wooden grille at the entrance to the

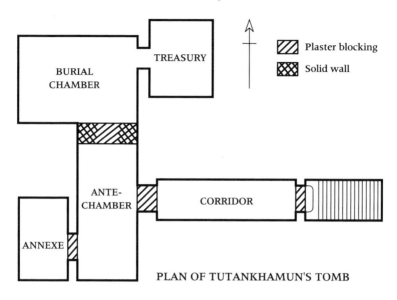

PLAN OF TUTANKHAMUN'S TOMB

passage…we must go to the labour of filling in the tomb once more.

According to Hoving, Carter in the 'long night' of intrusion as he called it had known perfectly well that he was 'invading' not just the annexe with its easy access but the burial chamber itself, beyond the massive walled door at the northern end of the antechamber. Callender, thickly built, could not get through the hole which Carter had made by prying loose a stone, and so the three more willowy members of the party who could squeeze through made a breathless penetration of the sacred precinct. Making liberal use of Carter's subsequent prose, Hoving described how, in an atmosphere charged with conspiracy, the ebony bolts of the great walled door were released to reveal the doors of an inner shrine beyond a 'gossamer' screen of linen, 'so diaphanous that it seemed to be made of the very motes in the air'. Golden flowers decorated the linen screen and one fell into Carter's hand. The door to the inner shrine was magnificently gilded and covered with hieroglyphs. At the centre of the shrine

151

was a coiled and braided rope, stamped with the seal of the royal necropolis. Carter is pictured *in flagrante delicto,* observing to his companions 'in a hushed voice' that the king had not been disturbed. Between the shrines stood a box-like object, which Carter found to be of solid gold, decorated with images of a squatting Tutankhamun, inlaid with lapis lazuli, cornelian and obsidian, each figure with a lock of lustrous black hair falling down the side of its head. Carter thought it 'unique in Egyptian art'. He is said to have put it in his pocket to study it at leisure. The intruders went on, northward, along what Carter believed to be a corridor. Looking to his right he alighted on a startling sight, nine wooden oars, arranged to assist the king on his voyage into eternity. On the walls of the chamber, rows of paintings portrayed the rituals for the preparation of the mummy, including a traditional 'weighing of the heart' in final affirmation to the gods of the king's true worth in earthly guise. But Carter, in his own later version, was disappointed with the tomb paintings, their 'banality' pointing to an 'uncommon' construction, contrasting unhappily with the 'great shining halls of majesty' hewn out of the rocks of the Valley for such great monarchs as Seti I and Ramesses the Great.

At the north-east corner of the burial chamber, facing east, was an open, unsealed door. He flashed his light inside, to find another room, almost square. He would later call it the 'treasury' or store-room. At its centre was a large wood sculpture of Anubis, the jackal god, on an elevated pedestal, 'almost shocking in its beauty'. Carter thought it one of the most impressive works of art he 'had seen in his life'. Carnarvon and daughter followed behind. Callender, who remained silent about those first two days of discovery, presumably remained in the antechamber. There was more to follow in what must have been one of the most astonishing adventures in the history of archaeology. There was a life-size head of a cow, the goddess Hathor, complete with golden horns. Behind that, they came to an object which made Carter 'cry out with wonder and admiration'. It was a chest about 8 feet high, overlaid with gold and surmounted by a cornice carved with cobra images. Surrounding it were free-standing statues of four goddesses, each about 3 feet high. The figures at front and back gazed firmly towards the shrine-like chest, two others looked over their shoulders, towards the entrance, as though keeping watch. Carter was to write of the discovery at a later date and was not ashamed to say that it brought a lump to his throat. It was the canopic chest, one of the most famous of the tomb's contents.

According to Hoving, they proceeded in the night of the 26th (it must be supposed that the clock had by now passed midnight and that they were into the next day) to find two more golden chariots; thirty caskets, only two of which had been opened by the thieves; heaps of golden jewellery including a magnificent 'vulture' necklace; golden statuettes of Tutankhamun standing on the backs of black leopards, wrapped in linen sheets.

At the conclusion of that extraordinary night, on the threshold of the antechamber as they turned to make their way out of the tomb, Carter is said to have looked down on an alabaster cup of remarkable thinness, with a hieroglyphic inscription which he translated as 'wishing the king millions of years happily enjoying the cool breezes from the north and his eyes beholding felicity'. He is said to have pocketed the cup, reclosed the hole in the door, and returned with the others down the Valley, 'strangely silent and subdued'.

It was not until three months later, on 17th February 1923, that Carter officially recorded the pulling down of the walled door between the antechamber and the burial chamber.

There was, however, another retrospective account of that eventful day, provided by a man who claimed to be present from the start of the excavation. According to the uncorroborated story of the man himself, Carnarvon appointed a military policeman, Sergeant Richard Adamson, as his own tomb guard. Adamson had been present at the execution of one of the Egyptian members of the Wafd Party found guilty of attempting to murder the Sirdar of the Army, Lee Stack, and was sent to

Carnarvon to keep him out of the public eye. At the end of 1922, Adamson claimed to be in charge of the tomb at night although, until early in 1923, he 'slept in a tent' just beyond the tomb rather than within its chambers. He told his story fifty years later to the author of a book published in 1972, describing the events of the 26th much as Carter told them in his book. In 1981, taken back to the tomb he is said to have guarded by a journalist working for an oil company magazine, Adamson, by then in his eighties, was asked to comment on the question of the break-in. He replied: 'Impossible. They could not have spent the whole night in the tomb without me knowing it. I slept at the top of the steps all night. Anybody going in or out would have had to have stepped right over me.' As for entering the burial chamber: '...they could never have reached it without first removing hundreds of objects crammed into the antechamber. You couldn't move a step in there.'

As the Carnarvon party left the Valley on the 26th, Carter is said to have turned to Adamson and said, 'Richard, this is only the beginning. You will have to remain on guard again tonight. Tomorrow I will arrange for police protection.'

Adamson's evidence has all the appearance of clear and truthful recollection. He told his story to packed audiences up and down Britain and is said to have given Prince Charles a private account of his Egyptian adventure. But his story must not be allowed to anticipate Carter's. It remains uncorroborated and must be re-examined further on, in the light of subsequent evidence of the disposal of articles from the tomb.

Allegations made so long after the discovery of the tomb proved, in any event, something of a storm in a teacup. Within a few weeks of the so-called 'invasion', on 11 December, *The Times* published an article in which Lord Carnarvon admitted that the 'peephole' in the second doorway had been enlarged on the 26th so that Carter, followed by Lady Evelyn and himself, could clamber into the antechamber, but added that they resisted the urge to break down the 'tantalizing wall' leading to the burial chamber.

The 29th was the day chosen for the official opening. It was a bad moment for the British High Commissioner. Lord Allenby was dealing with a wave of murders of British citizens which followed the unilateral Declaration of Independence made in February, the proclamation of Fuad's kingship in the following month, and the subsequent imposition of martial law and exile by Britain of the vain, charismatic nationalist leader Saad Zaghlul Pasha. The High Commissioner had been so busy during the year that he was unable to return home for the funeral of his own ninety-two-year-old mother. Allenby's biographer, Lord Wavell, believed that his subject 'was one of the privileged few who were present at the opening of the tomb and thus one of the first to see the wonderful store of treasure in it'. In fact, Lady Allenby had to go alone to Luxor to join the Carnarvon's for the great occasion.

Invitations had also gone out from Carnarvon to Lacau at the Antiquities Department, to the Provincial Governor and the district police chief, to the British Adviser to the Ministry of Works, and to the correspondent of *The Times*. In the event, it was a low-key celebration. On the Egyptian side, only the Governor, Abdal Aziz Bey Yahia, and the police chief, Muhammad Bey Fahmy, turned up, along with the *Times* man Arthur Merton, to join Lady Allenby, Carnarvon and his daughter, and a few local notables for Carter's conducted tour. After the official ceremony, Lady Evelyn was hostess at a lunch in the open by the tomb of Ramesses VI. Lacau and his British assistant, Paul Tottenham, arrived the next day to make their inspection.

Together with the invitation to Merton of *The Times,* Carter had had the good sense to enclose a hand-written account of the discovery and a general background to Tutankhamun and the Eighteenth Dynasty. It was vital to ensure that *the* newspaper made the most of the story. The lessons of other archaeologists in need of funds and official recognition had not escaped Carter's notice in his Egyptian enclave.

On 30 November *The Times* fired the first salvo in what was to prove the longest-running news saga of modern times, outshining any recorded event in war or peace in the longevity of its public appeal, and outdoing most in controversy. 'An Egyptian treasure: great find at Thebes: Lord Carnarvon's long quest', ran the headings. The report from 'Our Special Correspondent' was datelined Valley of the Kings (by runner to Luxor), 29 November, and was spread over two pages:

> This afternoon Lord Carnarvon and Mr Howard Carter revealed to a large company what promised to be the most sensational Egyptological discovery of the century. The find consists of, among other objects, the funeral paraphernalia of the Egyptian King Tutankhamun, one of the famous heretic kings of the Eighteenth Dynasty, who reverted to Amun worship. Little is known of the later kings, including Tutankhamun, and the discovery should add invaluably to our knowledge of this period and of the great city of Tal al Amarna, which was founded in the fifteenth century BC by Amenhotep IV [Akhenaten], the first of the heretic kings.

A sketchy account of the Amarna episode in Egyptian history was followed by the story of the 'diligent' sixteen-year search by Carnarvon and Carter in the Valley up to the historic moment when Carter, 'by dogged perseverance, his thoroughness, above all his *flair'*, was rewarded by the discovery directly below the tomb of Ramesses VI. 'Mr Carter covered up the site, and telegraphed to Lord Carnarvon who at once came out from England.'

Then came a catalogue of treasures, listed during the three days of hurried investigation:

> ...magnificent State couches, all gilt with exquisite carving...beds, beautifully carved, gilt, inlaid with ivory and semi-precious stones... innumerable boxes of exquisite workmanship [one]...inlaid with ebony and ivory, with gilt inscriptions; another contained emblems of the underworld:

in a third, which contained Royal robes, handsomely embroidered, precious stones, and golden sandals... Beneath one of the couches was the State throne of King Tutankhamun, probably one of the most beautiful objects of art ever discovered... There was also a heavily gilt chair with portraits of the King and Queen, the whole encrusted with turquoise, cornelian, lapis, and other semi-precious stones.

Throughout the report, there is evidence of the correspondent's reliance on Carter's written testimony and on what he was told as he and the others were led through the hastily cleared passage, antechamber and annexe. Merton, unfamiliar with the objects or the history of the dynasty, can have had little idea of the significance of the things he was shown. The Luxor 'runner' must have taken with him what was substantially Carter's press release. Even so, it was enough to stimulate to fever pitch the interest of readers of *The Times,* and to cause proprietors and editors of the rest of the world's press to send their best writers and photographers to cover a story that was clearly of major importance.

Carter had spent many hours with Merton, who had been among his nodding acquaintances since the aspiring journalist arrived in Cairo in 1902 as an employee of the Bank of Egypt, and their joint essay provided the newspaper's readers with impressive background:

The sealing and blocking of the doors and passages which have so far been opened suggest that metal robbers had attacked these chambers and that inspectors of Ramesses IX had reason to enter and to re-close them. From the famous Abbott and other papyri it is known that these Royal tombs suffered at the hand of robbers. But whatever the chambers may have contained originally, their contents to-day are sufficient cause for sensation in the Egyptological world.

An historical pointer of importance to archaeologists was

contained in the report. Among the aspects of Eighteenth Dynasty rule which were still obscure was the relationship between Akhenaten, Tutankhamun's supposed father-in-law, and his likely co-regent Smenkhkare. Sepulchral objects found in the tomb, the report said, bore the names of both monarchs, suggesting that Smenkhkare may have died or ceded the throne simultaneously with Akhenaten. The article concluded:

> What adds interest to the discovery is that there is still yet a third sealed chamber, which, significantly, the two figures of the king discovered are guarding, and which may possibly turn out to be the tomb of King Tutankhamun, with members of the heretic's family buried with him. Until the vast amount of material in the other chambers has been completely removed it will be impossible to ascertain the contents of this third chamber.

There followed a long appreciation by Petrie:

> Professor Flinders Petrie, the well-known Egyptologist, with whom Mr Howard Carter first went out to Egypt in connexion with exploration work in 1892, was informed of the discovery in the Valley of the Kings last night by a representative of *The Times,* and expressed himself as highly gratified at the success which had attended Mr Carter's efforts.

'Nothing like it had ever been found before,' said Petrie, who went on to tell once more the story of the Amarna heresy, and to predict momentous things to follow. Some time later, in a letter to Newberry, Petrie proclaimed his good fortune at 'not having to have been involved in the unseemly quarrels and petty jealousies that hindered the work of clearance in the months that followed'.

By the beginning of December, the great men of archaeology were queuing up to contribute their mites to the rapidly unfolding drama. On the 1st, Sir Wallis Budge, Keeper of

Egyptian and Assyrian Antiquities at the British Museum, gave the readers of *The Times* a potted survey of Egyptian discovery, from the pioneers like Wilkinson, Salt, Belzoni, Maspero, Grébaut and Davis, to the pertinacious Howard Carter.

Reuters and the Egyptian newspapers carried their own version of the story. The popular press took heed and suddenly hundreds of reporters and photographers were on their way to Egypt in ships crowded with wealthy sightseers, antiquarians, would-be film makers, and commercial adventures of every kind.

On 3 December, faced with the onslaught of visiting VIPs and journalists and the spread of rumour – 'extraordinary and fanciful reports' – Carter took the kind of peremptory action for which he was already famous in the Valley. He boarded up the entrance to the tomb with heavy timber, filled it with rubble to surface level, and paid off his men. Operations were suspended. Carnarvon left the next day for Cairo, on his way back to England, pursued by the world's press. Lady Evelyn remained at Luxor for two days.

On 6 December, Carter noted that he had loaned 'Eve' £4 on account. Lady Evelyn accompanied him to Cairo where she joined her father. Carter went shopping. His chief purchase was a steel gate as protection for the tomb entrance. Armed with Carnarvon's promissory note he also ordered a Ford automobile, photographic materials, chemicals needed for cleaning and preservation work on the objects, thirty-two bales of calico, more than a mile of wadding, and about the same expanse of surgical bandages. That was but a small part of the shopping list entailed by the work he and Carnarvon had agreed upon. There was the need for skilled assistance, too. But where was the necessary scientific and technical expertise to be found?

Fortunately, at about the time he departed for Cairo, he received a telegram of congratulations from the Curator of the Egyptian Department of the Metropolitan Museum in New York, Albert Lythgoe, whose teams were working at Lisht and Deir al Bahari, close to the Carnarvon excavation though separated by a range of hills. Carter responded immediately: 'Thanks message. Discovery colossal and need every assistance. Could you consider a loan of Burton in recording in time being. Costs to us. Immediate reply would oblige. Every regards, Carter.' Lythgoe replied: 'Only too delighted to assist in every possible way. Please call upon Burton and any other members of our staff. Am cabling Burton to that effect.'

That reply, Carter suggested, should go on record as an example of 'disinterested scientific co-operation'. Lythgoe's generous response gave birth to co-operation between Carnarvon and his assistant and the distinguished American museum which was to last for many years and make the Metropolitan the main centre outside Egypt of records and objects associated with the tomb of Tutankhamun.

Carter's original contact with the Metropolitan Museum, Herbert Winlock, the man who was indirectly responsible for the continued excavations which gave rise to the discovery of the tomb, was the principal loser under the new dispensation, for as the director of the American excavation he was denuded of senior assistants who went off to help Carter with the full approval of the trustees and directors of the Metropolitan Museum. Soon Lindsley Hall and Walter Hauser, experienced draughtsmen, joined Burton at Carter's camp. Then Arthur C. Mace, the quiet Englishman who was in charge of the museum's excavations at Lisht, offered his services. The American team lived in their own site house (a much more palatial establishment than the one Carter had constructed on the site of the EES house) which was built in 1912 when work began at the Metropolitan Museum's site in the Valley, known as the Asasif. Most moved in with their wives, who proved a constant source of friction and entertainment. Mace moved into the American House, south-west of Kasr Carter and east of Deir al Bahari, in early December 1923. Soon after, his wife Winifred and daughter Margaret arrived, the former's grand piano hauled in her wake, strapped to a camel's wilting back.

Before Carter left Cairo, he met Alfred Lucas, director of the chemical section of the Egyptian Public Works Department, the man who many years later would raise the question of the excavator's 'unauthorized' tomb entry. Lucas was about to embark on three months' leave prior to retirement and offered to help with the delicate and complex tasks of preserving some of the most precious objects in the world. Dr Alan Gardiner and Professor Breasted were on hand to help with decipherment of inscriptions and seal impressions. Callender, the man for all seasons, was still at the tomb, in charge in Carter's absence. A most imposing team was assembled and Carter returned light-heartedly to Luxor on 13 December 1922, complete with his steel gate, refreshed by a few days of luxurious living at Shepheard's. He had seen Carnarvon and his daughter off from Alexandria on the 11th.

He returned to reopen the tomb temporarily, for the benefit of the world's journalists, to familiarize his new staff with progress made so far and to set up storage and laboratory facilities.

Carnarvon had by this time spent something like £50,000 during fifteen years' work, an enormous sum at the time, and had received nothing in return. His expenditure would undoubtedly increase still further. It is against that background that accusations of theft and deception, levelled against both Carnarvon and Carter long after their deaths, must be examined.

Hoving saw perfidy even in the choice of date for the official opening of the tomb. 'To quell the disturbing rumours that the excavators had broken in and stolen some treasures, Lord Carnarvon and Carter staged an official opening of the tomb on November 29, without asking the Antiquities Service for permission. On their own they issued invitations.' It may have seemed odd to Mr Hoving some decades later, but it was not common practice to have an official ceremony at all. Few excavations in the past had merited celebration, and Carter, on the one occasion he had felt a formal 'opening' to be necessary, had been embarrassed by the revelation of a 'spoof' chamber.

Fanciful rumours there were indeed. Hoving cites several,

including one that three aeroplanes had landed in the Valley and taken off again loaded with treasure. News, as Carter observed, 'spreads like wildfire in Egypt'. So did rumour.

The tomb of Tutankhamun was, and remains, a unique discovery. Hitherto, of the forty-odd tombs found in the Valley, all had been broken into and, apart from their wall paintings and intrinsic features, none called for official sanction or for more than cursory inspection. There was no known precedent for the Antiquities Department being consulted about matters such as the opening of a tomb. Even with surface discoveries, such as the decorated pavements of Amarna or the wall paintings at Deir al Bahari, it was customary for the director to be invited only after the event, and then as a courtesy rather than an obligation. It is very unlikely that Petrie ever invited an official to his sites unless and until he felt that an inspection was necessary. Of course, it was a matter of form to invite the director to an official opening such as Carnarvon and Carter deemed necessary. Hoving was wrong. Lacau was invited at the same time as the other guests but chose to turn up on the following day.

Lacau was perfectly capable of laying down the law. The Jesuit director was clever and autocratic; not a man to trifle with. He would almost certainly have complained if he thought he had been slighted, but there is no evidence that he did so. He chose to attend at his own convenience, and there the matter rested. That Carnarvon's party went back to the tomb at night, unable to contain their curiosity, is possible, and understandable, but it is not actually attested or admitted. The suggestion that he and his companions necessarily returned out of cupidity on the night of 26 – 7 November cannot be proved. Lucas, whose passing reference to the matter in a learned paper brought the matter to notice, was not present at the material time and the memories of those from whom he obtained his information could easily have been at fault. Nevertheless, he was a responsible observer, not given to sensationalism or invention, and it is possible that Carter himself related the facts of the 'long night'. Equally, it is possible that the 'intrusion' was common knowledge among Carter's assistants. Among workers at an archaeological site, the event would not have been regarded as at all remarkable. It would have been easier and more intelligible in public renderings of the story to telescope the discoveries made in the inner chambers in the early hours of the 27th with the record of events for the 'next morning'. Since Carter did not state the hour, merely that 'We were early on the field,' he did not stretch the truth unduly. The failure to record in his diary an account of exactly what happened on the following day, the 27th, is another matter. Indeed, the detailed record of this vital period ends in his 'rough diary' with the long entry for 26 November. Next day he reverts to the truncated entries of earlier fallow periods. But such practices and omissions are so commonplace in archaeology that a conspiracy theory would indict almost everyone who ever conducted a dig. Indeed, another possibility has been overlooked by Carter's accusers. Had he set out to secrete a few small, choice items for his patron, and perhaps for himself, might he not have found them in the entrance passageway, along with many other salvaged pieces, on the night of the 24th, when, by his own admission, he slept alone in the tomb?

Changes in the antiquities laws had been promulgated by Lacau and the Egyptian Ministry of Works just six weeks before Carter discovered the tomb. In place of the arrangement agreed in 1912, that excavators could keep 'half the value' of their finds, it was now proposed that the excavator must be content with academic renown. Cairo Museum, Lacau announced, would take everything. A Foreign Office note observed that it was 'a terrible blow to excavators, societies and museums', and asked the Joint Archaeological Committee under the chairmanship of Frederic Kenyon of the British Museum to prepare a memo on the changes, with its own counter-proposals, for presentation to Allenby and the Egyptian Council of Ministers. The Society of Antiquaries in London complained directly to Lacau. The British Association

asked the Foreign Office to take action. Whitehall had enough
problems with Egypt at the time, however. It was compelled to
remind everyone concerned, including Lord Carnarvon, that
Egypt was now an independent sovereign state in law, the
'Protectorate' having been officially abandoned 'on 28
February last', as Carnarvon's team neared the climax of its
discovery.

There is no conclusive proof that Carnarvon or Carter
helped themselves to any of the artefacts directly – though
there is inescapable evidence that they came into possession
of valuable items which subsequently found their way into
museum collections – but whatever sins they may have been
guilty of were committed against the background of Lacau's
arrogant and intransigent attitude. As the question of excavators'
rights came to the fore, Egyptian newspapers, egged on by
Lacau, began to demand the return by Berlin Museum of the
famous 'head' of Nefertiti.

In the light of the past example, Carnarvon and Carter
could not at that stage have been accused of acting improperly
had they helped themselves to 'half the value' of their find.
After all, French, American and German museums groaned
under the weight of Egyptian, Babylonian, Hittite and Assyrian
antiquities which were simply taken from the sites where they
were found. Admittedly, it was common practice after 1918
to consult the host nation and divide the spoils in a fair and
civilized manner. But there were few rules or even conventions.

Leonard Woolley's discoveries at Ur in Mesopotamia, which
competed for the headlines with Tutankhamun in 1922 - 3 and
would continue to do so for the following eight years, provide
an interesting parallel. Not even the formidable Gertrude Bell,
Iraq's Director of Antiquities, dared to tell Woolley when he
should or should not enter a tomb, or whom he might invite
to official functions along with the kings and queens, the
millionaires and famous writers and artists who flocked to see
the supposed birthplace of the patriarch Abraham. The great
death pit in the royal necropolis, where so much sensational

material was found confirming the Sumerian rite of human sacrifice, was excavated and entered entirely at Woolley's discretion. No officials were informed and no special notes of time or method of entry were made. Woolley wrote many differing accounts of his work, and he was often accused of 'inventing' tales of Abraham's life at Ur in order to attract publicity. Many a visitor to Ur went away with a small keepsake. Woolley's Anglo-American regime was admired by fellow archaeologists and visitors alike and it was never thought to be deceptive or questionable.

In historical perspective, the charges against Carnarvon and Carter are trivial. If they are to be accused of deception in going back to the tomb they had discovered after so many disappointments and false alarms and of telescoping the night's events with those of the morrow in a single day's report, what must be said, for example, of Schliemann's famous excavation of Troy? Without a word of consultation with anyone, and in almost total disregard of Ottoman law, Schliemann went into the Troad and Mycenae like a half-crazed building contractor, moving hundreds of tons of earth without noting the levels at which he was digging, so that a century later scholars were arguing bitterly over the actual places and levels at which the 'jewels of Priam' and other treasures were discovered. Pictures of Sophia Schliemann wearing the famous jewels as if they were her own were published in journals throughout the world. The Schliemann home in Athens was piled high with treasures indiscriminately dug up in Greece and Turkey. At Mycenae, the German digger who before Carter could lay claim to the richest find in history was said to have treated the distinguished Greek Overseer of Excavations as 'a mere government clerk'. In such a context, the alleged transgressions at the tomb of Tutankhamun hardly deserve comment.

Some small but artistically delightful treasures said to have come from the tomb eventually reached the Metropolitan and other museums, most through later acquisition from undisclosed sources. If their provenance should eventually lead to Carter or his patron, many would argue that it was fortunate for America that they anticipated Lacau's autocratic decision to 'take whatever he wished, without discussion', for retention by Egypt. Another note on the Foreign Office file in London remarked: 'Independent Egypt will probably not be liberal to its Antiquities Department.' Higher standards and more money for the Antiquities Inspectorate and for Cairo Museum had been called for by Lord Milner when his commission reported on Egypt in 1921. David Hogarth of the Ashmolean Museum had followed up Milner by recommending that a Briton should be appointed to the post of Director-General of Antiquities. Lacau was determined to stamp his – and France's – authority on the job. Carnarvon and Carter were caught in the ensuing cross-fire; and in the snare of their own conflicting personalities.

Chapter 11

DEATH OF A VERY ENGLISH 'MILORD'

Lord Carnarvon, the latest conqueror from the East, the now world-renowned discoverer of King Tutankhamun's place of sepulchre, has landed at Marseilles on his way home from Egypt. There is no reason why such acclaim as is commonly accorded to conquerors, should not be given to Lord Carnarvon, for he sets foot on French soil as incontestably the greatest, or the greatest for many years, of a long line of English *milords* famous for their antiquarian proclivities and artistic connoisseurship... The romance of Lord Carnarvon's story grows with every fresh detail that is made known.
The Times, **18 December 1922**

Arthur Sidney Merton, correspondent of *The Times* in Cairo, was in a privileged position in reporting the discovery of the tomb and the breathtaking aftermath. His newspaper was trusted as no other by archaeologists for its proven commitment to their diverse causes.

Ever since the Napoleonic invasion of Egypt which gave the first real push to the scientific investigation of the past, *The Times* had opened its columns to news reports and feature articles through which the informed public had been able to follow every movement of the great men of the profession and admire in words and pictures the record of their achievements in the remotest corners of the world. The roll of honour stretched across the academic world. The names of every notable digger and the story of every significant discovery from Greece to Central Asia and South America, had been recorded in the pages of the 'Thunderer' for well over a century by the time Carter informed his chief of the latest discovery and took Merton into his confidence. Yet Carter himself had not featured among the good and the great in the newspaper's august columns. Carnarvon, of course, had been tracked from Highclere to Luxor and back again whenever he went to Egypt. But that had more to do with the fact that he was the colourful 5th Earl of Carnarvon than with the nature of his work in the Valley. Until the moment of revelation, Carter's anonymity was assured by the lonely, unglamorous role he had chosen among the derelict ruins of the royal graveyards of Thebes. When fame ensued, he was nonplussed. Suddenly faced with hordes of reporters and photographers, hanging on his every word, waiting round corners to question him, to trap him into sensational admission, seeking deals for 'exclusive' pictures, bombarding him with requests and propositions, he turned to Merton for help.

Merton, forty years of age, was a controversial figure in Egypt. As a young man fresh from studies in France and Germany he obtained his first reporting job with the *Pall Mall Gazette.* Promise of a career in journalism was countered by broader ambition, however, and he applied for entry into the Egyptian Civil Service, serving with the Bank of Egypt and then the Ministry of Agriculture in Cairo. While working for those institutions he took on freelance assignments for the *Observer* and *Daily Telegraph,* and in 1912 Lord Northcliffe appointed him to the staff of *The Times* on the advice of Ronald Storrs, Kitchener's Oriental Secretary. In 1918, Reuter's man in Cairo complained to the editor of *The Times,* Dawson, that Merton, while acting for *The Times,* remained an official of the Egyptian government, an anomaly which placed other correspondents at a distinct disadvantage. Dawson referred the matter to the Foreign Office, stating that he hoped some day to find 'a bigger man for the job'. Merton explained to Reginald Wingate, Allenby's predecessor at the High Commission, that his appointment in 1912 had been 'political'.

Ten years later, as Cairo correspondent of the same newspaper, under its new owner Colonel J.J. Astor, and with Dawson still in the editorial chair, Merton took on the role of adviser to Carnarvon and Carter in addition to his journalistic task. The anomaly of his position doesn't seem to have worried him at the outset of what was to prove one of the longest-running and most sensational stories in his or any other journalist's career. It was not a role that the opposition press was likely to look on with equanimity.

On 1 December, a *Times* leading article asked:

What matters it to any save Egyptologists and archaeologists that LORD CARNARVON and MR HOWARD CARTER should have discovered in Egypt the tomb of KING TUTANKHAMUN, who reigned and died more than thirteen centuries before our era? What avails this new proof that, in days so distant, the silver cord was loosed, the golden bowl broken, or the pitcher shattered at the fountain?

And it answered its own question with an evocation to the world to follow the example of Carnarvon and Carter.

Admiration for men who have done actively or suffered passively great things is addressed even more to their effort than to its result. The true answer to those who would have us eat and drink, for tomorrow we die, is, 'Let us join hands and work, for we are alive together'... Dead kings in their tombs, past civilizations and their records, however much they may enlighten us upon the history of mankind, are in themselves of less import than the activity that leads to their discovery.

Pictures and reports 'exclusive to *The Times*' could thus take their place in the newspaper as the story unfolded. For the time being, it was the only newspaper with pictures, and they were chiefly Carnarvon's, taken outside the tomb. Photography, even with magnesium flares, had proved impossible within.

On 2 December came news of 'a warm message of appreciation' from King Fuad, the country's newly crowned monarch. Carter had been inundated with letters and telegrams of congratulation as well as visitors. Looking back, he wrote:

> One must suppose that at the time the discovery was made the general public was in a state of profound boredom with news of reparations, conferences and mandates, and craved for some new topic... The idea of buried treasure, too, is one that appeals to most of us. Whatever the reason, or combination of reasons, it is quite certain that, once the initial *Times* dispatch had been published, no power on earth could shelter us from the light of publicity... We were helpless, and had to make the best of it.

Confronted with the influx of people and messages, and the need to preserve the precious objects of the tomb, Carter had suspended all operations until proper arrangements could be made for their protection.

On 4 December, Alan Gardiner treated readers to an historical summary of the Amarna heresy and on its back page the newspaper carried the first picture of the tomb entrance, flanked by photographs of Carnarvon and Carter. Familiar to readers of the society and 'quality' press, with his crinkled hair, long cigarette holder and film-star good looks, the former was already a household figure. Carter, with dark penetrating eyes, thick black moustache and neatly knotted bow-tie, was something of a revelation. It was the first time his image had appeared in a national journal and he seemed to carry his forty-nine years with aplomb: mature-looking, strong in build and character, a man of the world.

While Carnarvon was on his way home and Carter shopped in Cairo and the press corps of Europe and America advanced on Egypt, *The Times* kept an impatient world informed. When Merton had visited Carter and Carnarvon at the former's 'picturesque mosque-like' house in the Valley a few days after the discovery, Carter had told him about the construction of the tombs exemplified in the Turin papyrus of Ramesses IV, and about the robbers' confessions in the reign of Ramesses IX contained in the Abbott, Meyer and Amherst papyri. The 'King's funerary' was 'most magnificent', he was able to assure readers. On 11 and 12 December there were more pictures, this time showing guests at the official opening and at Lady Evelyn's luncheon party, concluding with the walling up of the entrance to the 'Treasure House' preparatory to the installation of Carter's steel gate. A note announced that the pictures had been taken by 'our Cairo correspondent★'. The asterisk indicated that he was the only journalist authorized to take pictures. For a few days all was quiet.

Shortly before Carnarvon's arrival in England, on 19 December, Percy Newberry gave a talk to the Egypt Exploration Society (the 'Fund' became 'Society' in 1917) at the Royal Society's headquarters in Burlington House. He proudly read out a letter from Carnarvon, a member of the EES council, stressing that the discovery of Tutankhamun's tomb was but a continuation of the drama of the Amarna experiment and the revolutionary art which accompanied it, discovered by Petrie, with Carter's assistance, in 1892. 'My dear Newberry... It is so wonderful that one can only regret that our lack of funds has prevented the continuation of the Amarna excavations.' Newberry told his audience that he had responded to his lordship: 'Thebes surpasses anything that archaeologists had hoped for.' Next day *The Times* carried alongside its report of Newberry's meeting a letter from Sir John Maxwell, now President of the EES, appealing for funds. Passive interest in archaeology had become active and money began to pour into the Society's London office.

December 22nd was an important day for Carter in Egypt and for Carnarvon in London. When Carter arrived back at Luxor the press corps had gathered in strength and he was bombarded with requests to open up the tomb. He responded to the clamour by agreeing to a guided press tour. He took the opportunity to invite 'a certain number of native notables of Luxor, who had been disappointed at not receiving an invitation to the official opening'. Merton was there for *The Times* and was able to report with barely concealed satisfaction that the rest of the international press was able, 'by kind permission of Mr Howard Carter', to see for the first time those treasures which his newspaper had revealed to the world on 30 November. The same correspondent also spoke, in a separate article, of a 'vernacular press campaign', inspired by a press release from the Ministry of Works, which cast doubt on the ability of the excavators to protect and preserve Egypt's heritage. The hostility of the Egyptian and American press was almost guaranteed by their exclusion from the tomb for three weeks while Merton made the most of his privileged position. The *Daily News* tried to upstage its rival newspaper by announcing that its correspondent 'will remain in King Tutankhamun's tomb... while the work of removing the treasure is proceeding'. When it came to it, the correspondent had to admit that with other journalists he was 'compelled to be content with a brief view from the barrier placed at the entrance chamber'. Carter, utterly inexperienced in such matters, failed to see the danger inherent in his policy of favouring a single newspaper, however powerful and academically acceptable it might be.

While the tomb lights were temporarily switched on and Carter took astonished reporters and local dignitaries into the splendidly decorated antechamber and annexe and introduced them to the treasures, Carnarvon was at Buckingham Palace. Above the daily report brought by 'runner to Luxor', *The Times* recorded the royal audience:

The King received Lord Carnarvon... and listened with great interest to a description of the important discoveries made recently by him and Mr Howard Carter as the culmination of the excavations which they have carried on for nearly sixteen years. Lord Carnarvon assured the King of his confident expectation that still further objects of great importance would be found when the third sealed chamber, believed to be the actual tomb of King Tutankhamun, is opened.

The arrival of Arthur Mace to join the team on Christmas Day 1922 enabled Carter to plan his campaign for removing and preserving the tomb treasures. Arthur Cruttenden Mace, assistant curator of Egyptian art in the Metropolitan Museum, was a Tasmanian by birth. An exact contemporary of Carter's, he spent much of his youth in the care of clerical relatives in London's Hackney and Bethnal Green parishes, before embarking on a high-church education at St Edward's School and Keble College, Oxford. There was a close family tie with the Oxford Movement and the Church was seen as Arthur's obvious path to a career. However, the young Mace went to work for his cousin Flinders Petrie, the starting point for just about every aspiring Egyptologist of the day. He went on to join Reisner at Giza and the early dynastic necropolis at Nag'ed Der, and then, in 1906, joined the staff of the Metropolitan Museum and went to dig at Lisht with Herbert Winlock. By the time he was ready to join Carter at Lythgoe's invitation, he was a fine all-round archaeologist, a retiring man and in particular an expert in the treatment of fragile materials. He and Alfred Lucas, the Egyptian government chemist, were responsible for setting up a makeshift laboratory in the nearby derelict tomb of Seti II which Engelbach had reluctantly agreed to let Carter use as a rehabilitation centre. Winlock was to observe that 'the Bank of England was not better protected – or more time-consuming to enter'. Two days later, on 27 December, the first objects were photographed by Harry Burton and gently transported to their barred, bolted and padlocked shelter.

Immediately upon his return from Cairo to Luxor before Christmas Carter had called to see the Breasteds who were living on their family yacht on the Nile. The Americans had just missed the official opening ceremony in November, having sailed down to Aswan at the foot of the first cataract, where James Breasted found a note from Carnarvon awaiting him, expressing regret that a messenger sent to him on the 26th of that month had just failed to intercept him at Luxor. The professor and his son had returned from a visit to the tomb when Carter caught up with them on 15 December. Charles Breasted described the journey:

On the day before Carter's return we visited the Valley of the Kings… approaching it by the usual road which enters it from the river flood plain. As we neared the mouth of The Valley, we passed on our right the one-storey house in which Carter had lived all through the years of his fruitless quest. I thought back to my boyhood visits to this strange burial place of ancient kings, and to my first meeting with him on the day when Davis's workmen had uncovered another royal tomb which like all the rest had been robbed in antiquity. But now at last Carter had apparently earned his reward. Immediately below and slightly to the right of the entrance to the tomb of Ramses VI, we came upon a freshly-excavated pit which had been walled on three sides with newly laid, unmortared rubble. In the middle of this pit was a pile of debris topped by a crude slab of limestone upon which had been hastily drawn with black paint the arms of the house of Carnarvon. Guarding this pile of debris sat a Mr Callender, one of Carter's assistants, a loaded rifle across his knee. Three trusted native carpenters were busily constructing a small shack for housing watchmen, protecting equipment and the like; while at intervals along the rubble-retaining walls stood native soldiers, also guarding the place with loaded rifles. An occasional passing tourist would peer perfunctorily into the pit and in the gleaming hot sun would note chiefly huge beads of perspiration upon Mr Callender's uncovered and balding head.

In a description at once more colourful and precise than anything Merton or other newspaper men had been able to contrive from a brief tour of the tomb of Tutankhamun, Breasted conveyed perfectly the flavour of what he called a 'particular moment of calm before an unparalleled deluge of world-wide publicity'. And at that 'particular moment', James and Charles Breasted found the scene of Carter's discovery 'singularly unimpressive'.

When Carter called on them in their Nile houseboat, the Breasteds listened with bated breath to his story, told in two hours 'which flew like as many minutes'. Afterwards, Breasted concluded that from what he had been told Carter had found not a funerary tomb but another cache, a place where the king's treasure was hastily hidden in politically troublesome times, and that the burial might have taken place elsewhere. Carter invited his hosts to join him three days hence, on 18 December, just before the press visit. They should avoid prying eyes. 'On the third day from to-day, please cross the river as if on a routine visit to the Theban temples, climb the mountain as if for the view – and then drop down into the Valley.' They should aim to reach him at 3 p.m. and should bring a change of clothing, the temperature in the tomb being such that after only a brief stay the visitor came out dripping with perspiration. The new and, to Breasted, familiar team lined up to receive him. Carter, Callender, Mace, Burton, Winlock – and the latter's wife and daughter. A great deal had changed in the few days since their last visit. 'Everything wore a purposeful, businesslike air... the men took off their coats,' Breasted wrote. 'Carter now stepped to the head of the stairway and said, "Are we ready? Come, please!" – then turned and began the short descent.'

Charles Breasted, the devoted son, described the scene as if his father was speaking:

> ...an incredible vision, an impossible scene from a fairy tale, an enchanted property-room from the opera house of some great composer's dreams... the heaped-up riches of a

Pharaoh who had died some three thousand two hundred and fifty years ago – before Crete had passed her zenith, before Greece had been born or Rome conceived, or more than half of the history of civilization had taken place. In the brilliant sunlight, against the white limestone wall, the colours of all these things were vibrant yet soft – a medley of brown, yellow, blue, amber, gold, russet and black.

They were only in the entrance passage. Carter unlocked four large Yale locks and swung open the barred steel gate. The others waited hesitantly. 'Will you not enter?' asked Carter. The men all had tears in their eyes. Words failed them all. Again, Charles Breasted wrote down the words of his father, most distinguished of Egyptologists:

I could only utter one exclamation of amazement after another, and then turn again and shake Carter's hand... Emotion struggled with the habit of years to observe and to understand, a struggle in which my critical faculties were for the moment completely routed. All about us lay a totally new revelation of ancient life, transcending anything we had known before. Here was the magnificence which only the wealth and splendour of the Imperial Age in Egypt in the fourteenth century before Christ could have wrought or conceived – and as it at first seemed, with everything still standing as it was placed there when the tomb was last closed. Never was anything so dramatic in the whole range of archaeological discovery as this first view of what must surely be Tutankhamun's tomb... Not vulgar and ostentatious magnificence, but the richness of matured and refined art, formed the daily environment of these great rulers of the Nile... I aimlessly fingered notebook and pencil. Of what use were notes made in such a state of mind, with myriad details and whirling thoughts crowding to be recorded all at once?

The Breasteds now examined the glistening treasures: alabaster vases, 'no one had seen such vases before'; a casket of jewellery; a courtier's magnificent baton with handle of gleaming gold, its filigree work and chevrons backed by a sheet of solid gold; the regal furniture of the annexe. The visitors entered inch by inch, their way lighted by Carter's electric torch, afraid to touch a single item for fear of damaging it. Then the statues of the king, roses and batons and staffs, sumptuously gilded. The heat of the tomb forced them back, but they soon returned, 'unaware of being utterly wilted'. James Breasted examined the seal impressions in the plaster which had covered the first two doors to the tomb, providing Carter's evidence of the robbers' entry in the reign of Ramesses IX.

During the course of the next few days, Breasted copied 150 seal impressions, while all the time he could hear creaking noises from the objects within, warning him that the incursion of air was causing physical and chemical changes in the tomb chambers. It was imperative that they moved fast in rescuing and treating the precious objects of the tomb. But too much haste had to be avoided. Each article must be drawn or photographed *in situ,* numbered or lettered, and then carefully removed to the laboratory (tomb 15, the empty burial site of Seti II), where it could be treated and made ready for the journey to the Cairo Museum. Carter described it as 'like playing a gigantic game of spillikins'.

Breasted, in a final assessment of the break-in question, thought it 'inconceivable that the robbers of that notorious period would have left so much treasure behind'. Carter replied that there were no known robberies in the royal cemetery before 'the close of the Empire', the period commonly referred to as the New Kingdom which began with the Eighteenth Dynasty in about 1540 BC and ended with the last of the Ramesside kings in 1070 BC. Breasted pointed out that the seal which Carter had read as that of Ramesses IX (of the Twentieth Dynasty) was actually the seal of Tutankhamun. Both the sealed doorways were covered with impressions bearing the name of Tutankhamun and the administrators of the cemetery, and no other. Breasted also reminded Carter that the tomb of Tuthmosis IV which he, Carter, had excavated, had been restored by Tutankhamun's almost immediate successor Haremhab who left on the wall of the tomb a record of his pious deed. 'If another royal burial had suffered robbery soon after Tutankhamun's death,' said Breasted, 'might not the same robbers have entered *his* tomb?'

'My God, I never thought of that!' Carter exclaimed. Breasted reminded Carter that the huts of the workmen who built the tomb of Ramesses VI had concealed the mouth of Tutankhamun's tomb long before the reign of Ramesses IX and the robbers of the latter's time. 'My God,' Carter repeated, 'I never thought of *that.*' The theory of the invasion of the tomb published by *The Times* on 5 December, after Merton's first interview, was already in doubt. But academic questions of chronology and antique robbery were about to give way to events of more universal appeal.

As Breasted sat making copies of the seals in the plaster skin of the door he glanced sidelong at one of the statues of the king guarding the door to the annexe. It winked at him. The alarmed epigraphist soon realized that a tiny flake of dark pigment used in the colouring of the statues had caught the light coming from the open entrance, suggesting a wink. It was a small matter, the kind of false impression easily received, and just as easily exaggerated by the receiver, in the piercing light of Egypt, where movement is sharpened in a way unknown to those who spend their lives under cloudy skies. Yet it reminded Breasted of an incident a few days before, when Carter sent an assistant on an errand to his house. As the man neared Carter's home he thought he heard a 'faint, almost human cry'. On reaching the house he looked at the bird cage hanging in the entrance. Coiled up within it was a cobra, the symbol of Egyptian monarchy, Carter's canary dead in it mouth. News of the discovery soon spread to Luxor and through the Valley. The dead king's cobra had vented his anger at the betrayal of its master's tomb. 'Now something terrible will happen' they said.

Events which would lead to the fantasy of the 'curse of the pharaohs' had begun to take hold of Egyptian peasants and soon infused a superstitious world with forebodings of disaster. There were other native reactions. A Cairo wit, Dr Athanasius, wrote to the newspaper *Al Mukattum* demanding that nothing be removed from the tomb since he proposed to make legal application for the contents as a 'lineal descendant of Tutankhamun'.

Breasted concluded that whatever early robbery might have taken place, it was not later than the Nineteenth Dynasty which lasted into the early twelfth century BC. In any case: 'The hole made by the robbers at the bottom of this doorway was obviously much too small to have permitted the removal of anything but quite small objects.' Therefore, he concluded, 'The body of the only Pharaoh of the Empire which may have escaped the destruction of post-Empire disorder and lawlessness, lay behind this doorway.'

After making the pronouncement which finally destroyed Carter's carefully reasoned theory of a Twentieth Dynasty break-in, Breasted went off to the Cairo Museum to work on texts already removed from the tomb. He went about his scholarly task in the long sky-lighted gallery for two weeks before another summons arrived, this time from Carnarvon, to return to the tomb. The antechamber had been cleared and by 15 February 1923, the day after the American's arrival, Carter was ready to open the burial chamber.

While in London, Carnarvon concluded the *de facto* arrangements with *The Times*. The agreement was signed by William Lint Smith, the manager of the newspaper, and Lord Carnarvon, and announced on 10 January 1923, 'with the cordial concurrence of Mr Howard Carter.' In future, all material would be distributed to the rest of the world's press from *The Times'* office in Printing House Square. A week later the newspaper declared that it would 'not allow any extracts from this news service to be published except by previous arrangement'. The response of the rest of the world's press was to tell its correspondents in Egypt to use any means, fair or foul, to obtain details and photographs in order to break *The Times'* stranglehold. Both Carter and Carnarvon had promised Merton in the course of discussions at Luxor that neither would sign a contract with any other news service until a settlement had been reached with *The Times.* There can be little doubt, though documentary evidence is flimsy, that they also agreed between themselves that the unexpected bonus of international press interest would contribute to excavation funds and help to reimburse Carnarvon for his immense outlay over the past sixteen years.

Carter veered between enthusiasm for a deal with his friend Merton, a man he trusted to report a serious archaeological discovery with decorum, and concern for the interests of his patron. Negotiations were complicated by a simultaneous offer to Carter from Goldwyn Limited in America for the right to make a motion picture of the tomb furnishings as they were removed and prepared for shipment. Carter was also worried about his own right to use photographs once an exclusive arrangement was struck with Merton's employers.

In a letter to Carter written from Highclere on 24 December 1922, Carnarvon suggested that they should employ a press agent. At the same time, he explained that he had seen Geoffrey Dawson (editor of *The Times*) on the previous day and had asked him to 'make an offer', though in fact he had told Dawson that he could not give his newspaper priority under the terms suggested. Dawson went away to consider his position and in the mean time Carnarvon consulted Alan Gardiner. The eminent Gardiner thought the *Times* arrangements satisfactory from every point of view and, in particular, because it would ensure accurate reporting.

In his letter of the 24th, Carnarvon also told Carter that Pathe and other film people had applied for the 'rights', and that he had asked for definite financial offers. Porchy was always at home with film moguls and publicity schemes, though he had little acumen in business dealings and was often given to recrimination in the course of negotiations. The idea of a film appealed to him greatly and he set out, for his assistant's benefit, his ideas for a film covering all their joint work in the Valley, beginning with a panorama of the haunting Theban scene and ending with a 'strong and uplifting' finale. Further discussion ranged over books and the rights to use their own photographs, the possibility of a four-volume account of the tomb and its treasures, with a popular edition, and a run of 20,000 copies, to be written by Carter and Gardiner. 'The two of you can muddle it out,' said Carnarvon. Thinking of Carter's financial welfare, he suggested that the best object from the tomb should be reserved for a colour painting. It ought to produce 'a lot of money'.

Before deciding on *The Times'* offer, Carnarvon went to the Royal Geographical Society in London to learn how it handled press matters in connection with its Mount Everest expedition. He was told that the Society had sold the rights to *The Times* for £1,000 for fifteen cables. The arrangement apparently gave rise to 'much grumbling'. But events in the Valley were forcing Carnarvon to make up his mind. While he talked and bargained, and found time to shoot 1,700 head, 'mostly rabbits', in a single day, the *Daily Telegraph* reported scenes of chaos which awakened 'memories of Derby Day'. The road leading to the tomb was packed with vehicles, animals and pedestrians of every description.

Carter meanwhile expressed his agreement with Gardiner's view and the contract was finally signed with *The Times*. It provided for a cash payment of £5,000 plus 75 per cent of all profits from the syndication of articles to other newspapers and magazines. 'I am afraid you have had a very poor time with the press,' Porchy told Carter. 'I could have settled earlier, but I wanted to consult you.' He also remarked that he did not much care for Geoffrey Dawson, the editor they would be dealing with from now on, but he was, after all, 'a straight gentleman'. In the event, the signing of the contract held problems in store for Carter which far exceeded the inconveniences of delay.

Within days of the signing of the agreement, Geoffrey Davis was telling Lint Smith, 'Merton should not be regarded as the principal channel of information under the new agreement.' He also told the manager that Carnarvon should make it clear to the Egyptian government that *The Times* would be responsible for the distribution of material to the 'entire world press including Egypt'. On 12 February, the Exchange Telegraph reported a government ultimatum demanding strict impartiality'. Either 'all or no' correspondents would be allowed into the tomb. Lacau, meanwhile, abided by the agreement to Carter's surprise and refused to give interviews, insisting, 'It's Carnarvon's affair.'

Carter, on whose shoulders the 'exclusive' arrangement rested, was having troubles of his own in the Valley. Tourists appeared from every quarter. When, on 12 January, he let it be known that there was evidence of a royal cache in the third, unopened chamber, the dam burst. 'Carter denies widely rumoured intention of excluding public,' reported *The Times* on the 13th. On the 17th pictures were released of Nile steamers bringing more crowds to Luxor. One ship was said to be carrying three ex-ministers of the Egyptian government with 'their families and ladies'. After Carter had showed them around the tomb, all were said to be 'enraptured'. Like it or not, the rest of the press was compelled to use *The Times'* photographs showing ever-growing crowds of sightseers, Carter removing more and more 'wonderful treasures', the Model-T Ford ordered by Carter being pushed by willing helpers up the Nile embankment with the trilby-hatted archaeologist taking charge from the majestic heights of his donkey.

There were popular touches, as when Merton described the daily journey to the tomb at the sugar-cane season: 'On the way we linger and watch fellahin cutting the canes.' But day after day the front pages were filled with more of the marvels of discovery: another chair with fittings and braces of gold, the pharaoh's chariot wheels, Tutankhamun's glove 'of finest fabric', the royal couch, the 'magnificent' bedstead, and always 'great crowds of spectators', with Carter at the centre of it all. Another Merton communiqué read:

> Every one was astir this morning, as it was known that Mr Howard Carter was ready to remove some of the larger articles... There was a short pause and then the sound of muffled orders and dragging footsteps, as if something heavy or difficult were being moved... Presently there appeared glittering in the sunlight a magnificent 'Hathor' head surmounted by high horns and the sun's disc, and with long legs and body.

Suddenly, everyone could recognize 'Hathor', and what was more everyone knew who Howard Carter was – he and his aristocratic patron had become the most famous men in the world. When Carter left Luxor on 26 January to meet Carnarvon at Cairo, the event was trumpeted by the world's press. When Newberry lectured on the discovery of the tomb at the Victoria and Albert Museum at the end of the month, a limit had to be placed on the number of tickets made available to the public to prevent disorder.

The *Illustrated London News,* under the editorship of Bruce Ingram, an avuncular man and avid collector who was to form a close attachment to Carter, struck a bargain with Carnarvon whereby it shared the 'exclusive' reports sent to *The Times* by Carter (not those of the paper's own correspondent), while it enjoyed 'national exclusivity' in respect of colour illustrations. In consequence, as a spin-off of the infectious craze which came to be known as 'Tutmania', Ingram's magazine became a national institution, achieving the remarkable feat of establishing a large popular readership for archaeology and a status for archaeologists which often approached that of the film star in terms of popular esteem. Henceforth, articles by distinguished academics bore titles such as 'The *Egypt* of American Antiquity' (a description of Maya ruins) and 'Mycenae in Tutankhamun's Time (Alan Wace's account of work on the Citadel Palace of Mycenae).

The ink was hardly dry on Carnarvon's contract with *The Times* when the seething anger of the newspaper opposition exploded. Carter's immediate response to the arrangement had been to invite Merton to join the staff of the expedition. Merton – who was officially one of a team of *Times* journalists hurriedly gathered together under the direction of the journal's chief foreign correspondent Sir Harry Perry Robinson – accepted the offer with alacrity. He confirmed that he would represent Carter's interests in the Valley in 'all publicity matters connected with the work at the tomb of Tutankhamun'. With regard to all news and data he would be guided entirely by his principal's wishes.

Lythgoe at the Metropolitan Museum, by now deeply involved in the enterprise, having placed his most expert staff at Carter's disposal, wrote to the museum's director Edward Robinson informing him of Carnarvon's contract with *The Times* and warning against any statements by the Americans which might reach the press. 'Although we are doing the lion's share of the work in the tomb, the tomb is Carnarvon's and Carter's and the right to speak publicly of it in any *definite* way is solely theirs – at least for the present.'

Reuters' correspondent Valentine Williams sent his wife to the Valley, artfully asking Merton to escort her home while he, Williams, tried to gain access to the tomb. The *Daily Express* in London, irked by the Carnarvon-*Times* conspiracy, sent the distinguished travel writer H.V. Morton to Luxor to begin a bitter campaign on behalf of the Egyptians, advising them to keep their kings and treasures at home. Such observations in the British press were grist to the mill of Lacau, who had less and less time for Carter and who had been seeking since his appointment a decade before to increase the Cairo Museum's share of archaeological finds.

A.H. Bradstreet, the choleric correspondent of the *New York*

Times and the English *Morning Post,* decided to take the bull by the horns. He had been enraged from the outset by the favouritism shown to Merton and his journal, and within a few days of the announcement of the 'exclusive' agreement he went to Lacau for information. The director, surprisingly in view of the friction between him and Carter, refused to break the vow of silence. In any case he and his inspector knew only what Carter had told or shown them. Bradstreet wrote a dispatch asserting that Lacau would give nothing away even if ordered to do so directly by the Egyptian government; an 'illuminating sidelight whereby a French official in the Egyptian government is willing to and can disregard an order from the government'. The opposition met in Morton's Luxor hotel apartment to form an anti-*Times* group in which Mrs Williams was prominent, acting as hostess at champagne parties from which Merton was pointedly excluded, and bombarding Lacau with protests.

Valentine Williams had been assigned to Egypt by his Editor-in-Chief in London, who happened to be his brother, Douglas Williams, as soon as the first *Times* report appeared. He was the ideal man for the task, having served in the Irish Guards with Porchy's half-brother Aubrey, knowing the other half-brother Mervyn well, and having many close associations with the Herbert family, even though he had not met the Earl himself. On hearing that Carnarvon was on his way to Egypt aboard the *ss Adriatic* in January 1923, Williams demonstrated his journalistic sense by travelling to Monte Carlo with his wife and boarding the ship there. By the time they arrived at Alexandria in January, he was on first-name terms with Carnarvon and on the friendliest terms with Lady Evelyn.

'The proposal was that I should go to Luxor and do what I could to provide a news service independent of *The Times.* I would not be alone: the *Morning Post,* the *Daily Mail* and the *Daily Express* were also standing out against the monopoly...' Everyone was Egypt-bound, 'for King Tut had put Luxor right on the map'. Conversation aboard ship was easy and relaxed. Carnarvon was 'the very reincarnation of a certain type of eighteenth-century peer'. Unaffected in manner and simple in his mode of life, he had, nevertheless, 'all the arrogance of his class in his approach to his fellow-man, particularly the Egyptians, whom he frankly despised and was at no great pains to conceal it'. Williams found him 'highly cultured', with 'the inquiring mind of the dilettante'. The journalist noted his lordship's profound interest in spiritualism. As he sat with Porchy and Lady Evelyn in the smoke-room of the *Adriatic,* Williams noted that his host at dinner wore an old brown cardigan over his evening waistcoat as a precaution against draughts, and he noted the 'tender friendship' between father and daughter, a friendship 'delightful to watch'. Despite their rapport, Carnarvon told Reuters' man he was wasting his time. He did not intend to be bothered by the press. 'The Times would get the news – if other newspapers wanted it, they could take it from *The Times.'*

While the press battle raged, Carter worked feverishly at the tomb. The first interior pictures taken by Harry Burton on his return from London and published in the press 'by arrangement' on 30 January had startled the world with their detail of the ceremonial couches with their 'lion' and 'hathor' supports, the life-size *ka* or 'guardian' figures at the entrance to the inner sanctum, the alabaster unguent vases and boxes with desiccated food, decorated with the royal cartouches, inlaid and gold encrusted. But that was merely the paraphernalia of the antechamber.

As work proceeded, political dispute broke out in several of the world's capital cities. In London, the Foreign Office pondered a telegram dated 9 February to the Senior Under-Secretary Sir William Tyrrell from Williams at Luxor. Reuters' correspondent also knew the FO intimately and he had no hesitation in going to the administrative fountain head. He asked that 'endeavours should be made to secure for correspondents other than the *Times* representative, proper facilities for getting immediate news when Tutankhamun's tomb is opened'. He meant the sarcophagus or coffin, to which he had been alerted by astute questioning of an official of the antiquities inspectorate.

Tyrrell noted in the FO diary: 'I don't see we can interfere between Lord Carnarvon and *The Times* as Mr Williams desires.' He felt the matter could safely be left to Lord Allenby. An Assistant Under-Secretary wrote, 'No action.' Another A/US wrote: 'The political aspect is important.' The eminent Sir Eyre Crowe noted, 'I would certainly not interfere.' Another, initialled note observed that the opening of the inner chamber was not to be announced in advance 'so that *The Times* can get a good start'. And then, significantly: 'The money consideration is said to be so huge that I hesitate to repeat the figure – I don't blame Lord Carnarvon. The job has caused him vast expense, and he doubtless feels uncertain as to how much he will get in the way of antiquities.' Eyre Crowe, enigmatically: 'I do.'

On 10 February a message came from Allenby. 'Lord Carnarvon is quite willing to grant all reasonable facilities consistent with his contract with *The Times*.'

James Breasted resumed his work re-examining the seal impressions on the antechamber doors as soon as he returned to the tomb on 14 February 1923. The 16th was to witness the opening of the king's burial chamber in the presence of Lacau and several officials of the government along with their British 'advisers'. Two days later, on the 18th, an official opening was to take place in the presence of the Queen of the Belgians, the High Commissioner, and a host of princes, politicians, diplomats and academics, at the request of the new Minister of Public Works, Abdal Hamid Sulaiman Pasha. Finally, from the 19th to the 25th of the month the tomb would be open to press and public. Carter hoped fervently that so generous and extended an exercise in public relations would satisfy the curious once and for all and enable him to concentrate on the formidable tasks that awaited him.

Breasted, who had been contributing 'special' articles to journals in Britain and America before Carnarvon signed the *Times* agreement, described the first event in an interview which he and the Belgian archaeologist, Professor Jean Capart, gave for syndication by *The Times*. The *Manchester Guardian* gave it particular prominence on the 23rd:

> The next afternoon, February 16, in the presence of Lord Carnarvon and Lady Evelyn Herbert, several high officials from the Egyptian Government and various notable representatives of England, France and the United States, Carter with the assistance of Mr Mace broke open the last sealed doorway. For three hours the little group sat utterly enthralled while the men methodically removed stone after stone, until they had revealed a great catafalque or shrine built of wood covered with sheet gold and inset with plaques of blue faience – the outermost of a series of shrines within the last of which the King lies buried.

There was immediate confirmation of Breasted's theory that thieves had never infiltrated the holy of holies. The seal on the door to the next inner shrine was unbroken. The evidence of the outer door seals was corroborated, 'I carry with me an imperishable vision... At last a great civilization in a land which was the earliest home of refined culture ever brought forth by man is adequately revealed to us in works of supreme beauty and power,' wrote Carter in his notes. He also wrote of 'a number of other wonderful things in the chamber', though he found it hard to take them in at the time.

Press comment and academic description were equally unrestrained. *The Times,* whence all others were now supposed to obtain their stories, seasoned by the eye-witness accounts of correspondents who could observe only from a distance, set the tone. 'Secrets to be revealed', announced on Thursday 15 February, were duly paraded on the Friday and reported in Saturday's newspapers. But it was not until Monday the 19th that full descriptions of the objects could be given, communicated to Merton by Carter but attributed to Carnarvon. This was following the visit of the Belgian Queen, the High Commissioner and other VIPs.

On the 18th, the Queen of the Belgians had arrived at precisely 2.15 p.m. by special train from Alexandria, accompanied by the Mudir, the Governor of the province. The Queen had travelled incognito with Leopold – as the Count and Countess de Rethy – and then they had made their way separately from Cairo to Luxor. On 'a day of glorious sunshine', she and the Allenbys, the princes and politicians and governors, were taken by motorcade along the 6-mile route from the river to the Valley, guarded the entire way by blue-uniformed gaffirs, spaced at intervals of 40 yards and sporting fezzes 'made gorgeous with stripes of red, green and magenta, and a glistening brass plate in front'. As each notable went past, in file behind the Queen, the watchmen saluted smartly with their nabouts. The spaces between were filled by policemen on horses, donkeys and mules, while the road itself was patrolled by the famous desert Camel Corps.

Escorted by Lord Carnarvon, Carter and Lacau, the royal visitor, said *The Times,* went straight into the tomb, and, just as she did so, 'Prince Leopold, accompanied by Dr Kepart, arrived and went in, as did Lord and Lady Allenby, and following them M. Gaillard and the Comte C. de Lalaing of the Belgian Legation.' At 3 p.m. the Queen emerged, and by then the lesser guests had formed a queue 'in readiness to descend'. At the Winter Palace Hotel afterwards the Queen told the press of her 'profound emotion'.

Carter was to write in recollection: 'At a quarter past two we had filed down into the tomb, and when, three hours later, hot, dusty and dishevelled, we came out once more into the light of day, the very Valley seemed to have changed for us and taken on a more personal aspect. We had been given the Freedom.'

From a distance, America was reported to be 'obsessed': *'(From our own correspondent.) New York, Feb. 18.* In private houses, hotels, subways, suburban trains, theatres and in Wall Street, everywhere one goes one hears constantly of the great Pharaoh and his treasures and the light which is about to be thrown upon a historical mystery.'

The historical mystery about to unfold, adding to all the diversions of superstition and uninformed comment which caused Carter to explode in anger and frustration, was that the pharaoh sleeping in the last chamber of all was none other than 'the Pharaoh whose armies perished in the Red Sea, when pursuing the Israelites'. The king's body had yet to emerge, however. Carter and his team laboured on, methodically and carefully, while the world admired each new artefact and conjectured. The crowds surrounding the tomb and lining the route to and from work each day became oppressive. Carter had not been spared the attentions of hundreds of visitors, many of them waving letters of introduction from government ministers, or of pressmen supposed to be barred by the arrangement with *The Times*. Merton tried to deal with the pushing, shouting crowds, the amateur and professional photographers occupying every vantage point. But nobody could cope with the VIPs, often appearing unexpectedly, bringing letters of introduction to Carter, and interrupting the busy work schedule. Carter's temper, easily roused, became dangerously frayed.

The internecine press war combined with anti-British sentiment in Egypt at large to spread rumour and conflict. Within days of the formal opening of the tomb and the revealing of the king's sepulchral chamber, a crisis brewed in the Valley of the Kings which would ultimately lead to the law courts and to international dispute.

On 23 February Merton sent an essay to London which clearly indicated the temperature at Luxor.

NO REMOVAL OF KING'S BODY
The unscrupulous methods of those who, from interested motives, are seeking to discredit Lord Carnarvon's agreement with *The Times* are excellently illustrated by the attempts which are being made to inflame feeling against him because of his supposed intention of carrying

Tutankhamun's body to England or elsewhere... It would be ridiculous if it were not being used to arouse anti-British sentiment among Mahomedans [sic]. It is being especially used to work on the passions of the Turks in the matter of the Gallipoli graves. It is an absurd thing that no one seems to have thought it worthwhile to ask Lord Carnarvon what his own real views or intentions are... He hopes that Tutankhamun's body will be treated with the utmost reverence and left lying in the sarcophagus unmoved from the spot where it has lain for three-thousand years.

Carnarvon and his assistant had alienated the world press – a very dangerous thing to do. A letter from Carnarvon in the same issue of *The Times* confirmed his lordship's view that the body must remain in Egypt. But rumour of perfidy did not stop there. Carter's anguish at the diversions which had begun to dog the greatest archaeological find of all time began to manifest itself in angry exchanges with his aristocratic benefactor and friend. His mood was not improved either by reports coming through from Mesopotamia that Woolley's excavations at Ur of the Chaldees were stealing the limelight from the tomb of Tutankhamun. In the very edition of *The Times* which detailed the disputes raging in Cairo and Luxor, the newspaper gave pride of place to a report from Baghdad under the headline 'Ancient Temples of Ur. Brick Walls Built in 3600 BC. Nebuchadnezzar's Jewels Found,' The story was given piquancy by the improbable theory of Professor Flinders Petrie that the treasures found in the tomb of Tutankhamun 'were possibly transferred to Egypt from the Euphrates'.

On 19 February the *Morning Post* published a dispatch from Bradstreet who, according to Hoving, had told friends that he would 'drive C. and C. out of their minds for having sold a piece of the world's ancient history to the London Times'. Bradstreet's article contained the words:

There is going to be bitter complaint back in America, for

a collection of energetic correspondents have been telling these Americans that while the Met's staff have been loaned to Carnarvon in the interests of archaeology, Carnarvon is capitalizing on the brains of these experts in London, where he has sold information and pictures related to the tomb to be distributed thence to buyers around the world.

On 25 February, A.C. Mace retorted in a letter to the editor of the *Morning Post* that the staff of the Metropolitan Museum were not in any way concerned with the sending of information to American journals and that 'Our relations with Lord Carnarvon and Mr Carter are extremely cordial in every way.' Furthermore, he and his colleagues deeply resented their 'exploitation' by 'irresponsible mischief-makers'. The *Morning Post* refused to publish the letter. On 14 March it appeared in full in *The Times,* as from the staff of the Metropolitan Museum of Art, Egyptian Expedition, and signed by Mace as 'Associate Curator' of the museum, along with a stern editorial lecture arising from new complaints about the secrecy of Carter's laboratory assistants working under Lucas's and Mace's direction in the tomb of Seti II:

> The public should learn to curb its curiosity until the excavator sees fit to announce, at the time and in the manner he may choose, the result of his investigation... Let us leave Mr Howard Carter and his assistants in peace to execute the task of preserving for us all these wonders, and let us respect their choice of the manner in which they choose to communicate to the public the result of their discoveries. We do not say that it is their legitimate reward; it is their incontestable right.

Protestation came too late. On 22 February the world's newspapers had carried the latest of Carnarvon's 'special articles', ghost-written by Merton, in which he portrayed the 'amazing sight' of the inner chamber of the royal tomb – 'For

Dressed in a Homburg and tweed suit, Carter arrives in the Valley by donkey.

Lady Evelyn's luncheon party in the desert, following the official opening in February 1923.

Lord Carnarvon's automobile leaving its tomb garage, Sir William Garstin, Carnarvon and Lady Evelyn aboard, 1922.

Left: Sir Alan Gardiner (*left*) and Professor James Breasted in the Valley, 1923.
Right: Carnarvon on Beacon Hill, Highclere in 1923, on the spot chosen as his burial place.

Lord and Lady Allenby
with Carnarvon at the
official opening of the
'sealed chamber',
February 1923.

Carnarvon and Carter
before their quarrel and
the fatal insect bite,
March 1923.

Arm in arm with Lady Evelyn outside the tomb of Ramesses VI, Carter, with Lord Carnarvon on his left, and Arthur Mace, H.E. Winlock, 'Pecky' Callender, Alfred Lucas, and Harry Burton.

Left: Lucas at work in the laboratory tomb. *Right:* Harry Burton at the tomb entrance with the 'horizontal' camera used for photographing small objects, January 1923.

Crowds gather at the tomb, February 1923.

Lunch in the canteen tomb (Ramesses XI), photographed by Lord Carnarvon. (*From left to right*): Breasted, Burton, Lucas, Callender (at the head of table), Mace, Carter and Gardiner.

Carnarvon and his daughter at Luxor railway station, 1923, welcomed by the governor of the province Jehir Bey, and Carter.

Left: Carnarvon poses at the front of 'Castle Carter'.
Right: Metropolitan Museum staff, wives and visitors at the steps of the tomb.

Left: Carter in the burial chamber during the removal of the partition wall, with Mace on the right. *Right:* Carter, immaculate, with 'Carnarvon' style cigarette holder, 1924.

Professor and Mrs Percy Newberry at work in the tomb.

Left: Edward S. Harkness, Chairman of the Trustees of the Metropolitan Museum, Mrs Harkness and Albert M. Lythgoe. *Right:* Carter relaxing at his Valley house.

Carter in his sun helmet accompanying a consignment for Cairo Museum.

a surety I never dreamed I should gaze upon the amazing sight which met my eyes.'

On 26 February Carter closed the tomb, following a blazing row with Carnarvon. Merton wrote a valedictory notice as Carter personally attended the blocking of the doorway. 'It is impossible not to be moved on paying a farewell visit to the tomb.' On the 28th he reported that the door would remain sealed 'for several months'. In fact, it was a false alarm, though the contretemps with Carnarvon was real enough. Carter resumed work a week later, but unsuspected tragedy was to cause him to close it again after a few days.

James Breasted – whom Carnarvon had asked 'to do all the historical work involved in the discovery' – was closer to the parties concerned in the dispute than anyone, and his balanced and sympathetic account of what happened in February and March 1923 must, for the most part, be taken as authentic.

The fame which the discovery conferred on Carter and Carnarvon 'almost overnight' brought with it, he said, 'a host of unaccustomed and extraordinarily harassing problems'. Carter, faced with a task the like of which was unknown to archaeology, and with an inundation of visitors such as Egypt had not experienced 'since the Persian invasion', kept a tight hold on the tomb but he began to lose control of himself:

> The seasonal volume of mail at the Luxor post office was doubled and trebled. The telegraph office at the station was completely buried under a deluge of newspaper dispatches. Tourist shops quickly sold out their stocks of cameras and films, and of books on the history of Egypt. The two leading hotels of Luxor set up tents in their gardens, where many guests were fortunate to be accommodated for a single night on army cots. Each day, the hordes of visitors swarmed across the river and into The Valley, where they gathered around the pit at the opening of Tutankhamun's tomb and lined the path along which, once the work of removal had begun, the contents were carried to an incompleted tomb

set aside as a workshop and preparatorial laboratory.

Breasted spent many a day and night in Carter's house and observed the comings and goings of the famous and mighty as they called on the great man. He observed Carter's 'nervous and high-strung' nature under pressure. Guests, many of them artists whose company Carter would normally have enjoyed, were ordered summarily from the house. Carnarvon, whose urbane manner and effortless 'upper-class' mannerisms Carter sought to emulate, was comfortably removed from day-to-day tribulations and work, as the financiers of enterprises usually are. Irritation gave rise to open antagonism. Breasted perceived that, 'In their effort to ameliorate a situation unique in their experience, both men committed errors of judgement, the consequences of which were to extend far beyond the discovery itself.'

The problems were created by the agreement Carnarvon had reached with *The Times*. That agreement had been welcomed equivocally by Carter, who saw and advocated the advantages of dealing with only one journalist but who also saw useful profits for himself and the expedition being put at risk. Breasted said that Carter 'flatly disagreed' with Carnarvon over the *Times* deal. That was not true. Carter questioned the merits of the scheme but it was he, through his contact with Merton, who gave *The Times* priority from the outset. The more immediate cause of dispute between these two men who had enjoyed so close and mutually advantageous a relationship was the question of the disposal of the tomb's artefacts.

Attempts to update the concession agreements were bedevilled by the political climate in Egypt. The agreements under which Carter and other archaeologists were, for the moment, operating under specified that all mummies of kings, princes and high officials of antiquity were the property of the state, and that tombs discovered intact and all their objects must by handed over to the Cairo Museum without division. There were, however, riders to these stipulations. In the case of tombs which had already been 'searched' (a word which presumably implied 'robbed in antiquity') the above regulations would still apply and all objects of 'capital importance' would be the property of the state, but the remainder would be shared with the 'permittee'. There was also a clause which stated that 'the permittee's share will sufficiently recompense him for the pains and labour of the undertaking'.

As with all such contracts, interpretation depended very much on viewpoint. Carnarvon's view was that the Antiquities Department was bound by the contract to share with him a large portion of the tomb's artefacts. Again, Breasted asserted that Carter was unequivocal in his belief that his patron should 'unreservedly renounce any rights or claims whatsoever'. In fact, Carter had had many disputes with Pierre Lacau as well as Carnarvon about the rights of excavators, not least himself, to a fair share of their finds, and evidence was to emerge over the years that Carter had taken matters into his own hands in respect of certain items from the tomb.

There was an unmistakable atmosphere of bitterness which amounted almost to rivalry by mid-February and on the 21st of that month Carnarvon called at Carter's home to try to resolve their differences. Far from achieving that objective, tempers were inflamed to the point where there was an almost complete rupture in their relationship. Carnarvon, by now looking worn and ill as a result of the problems which stemmed from the heady achievement of so few months before, tried to make amends. On 23 February he wrote a letter to Carter which suggested an immediate cause of conflict and made handsome apology.

My dear Carter, I have been feeling very unhappy today… I did not know what to think or to do and when I saw Eve she told me everything. I have no doubt that I have done many foolish things and I am very sorry… but there is only one thing I want to say to you which I hope you will always remember – whatever your feelings are or will be for me in the future my affection for you will never change.

It was a touching note. Carter's reply, if there was one, is not recorded. Subsequent suggestions that Carnarvon's words showed the dispute to have been caused primarily by Carter's encouragement of Evelyn's advances are by no means proven. There is no intrinsic evidence that the daughter's revelation concerned a personal relationship, though if it were so the letter would be even more poignant in its implication of a beloved daughter's unrequited affection than in its uncharacteristic self-depreciation. Carnarvon continued: 'I am a man with few friends and whatever happens nothing will alter my feelings for you. There is always so much noise and lack of quiet and privacy in the Valley that I felt I should never see you alone although I should like to very much and have a good talk. Because of that I could not rest until I had written to you.'

It is possible of course that Evelyn, half Carter's age, felt an attraction, perhaps even a girlish infatuation, for the older man. It is more likely that she was acting merely as peacemaker in the unfortunate quarrel between her beloved father and the archaeologist of whom she was in some awe. Carter may well have been flattered by the attention and approbation of a young woman of signal beauty and noble birth, coming on top of the world's praise and after so many years of unrewarded and unsung service; but he was not a man to allow a complicated or time-consuming relationship to keep him from his work. Romance stopped short at art and archaeology. By report in later years, there were a few perfunctory and purely sexual encounters while he was on leave in London, but he had never shown more than a passing interest in any woman. From the time he first arrived in Egypt as an inexperienced young man, he had been virtually celibate.

If Lady Evelyn had given him any indication of her feelings beyond a light-hearted flirtation, Carter could have been relied on to brush them aside. He was polite to her, charming even, but it is most unlikely that he gave her the slightest encouragement.

The assumption that her father remonstrated with Carter in the belief that there was an insurmountable 'barrier of birth' between him and Eve is, equally, unsubstantiated. Carnarvon is unlikely to have welcomed the prospect of his only daughter forming a liaison with Carter, but if the inescapable class barriers between English people of divergent backgrounds intervened, they surely did so with the discreet silence which in English society marries prejudice to the deed. In any case, his deep regard for Carter which his letter reveals would surely not have permitted the ultimate insult of rejection. He knew how easily Carter's sensitivity was scathed.

As personal wounds chafed, differences with the Antiquities Department over the disposal of finds grew more intense. Carnarvon went to Aswan with Mace to talk to the Americans there about ways and means of dealing with the Frenchman, and then to Cairo to appease Lacau, but the Frenchman had influenza and could not see him. Alan Gardiner and Breasted spoke to Carnarvon and Carter, together and separately, and tried to pour oil on troubled waters. In doing so, they incurred Carter's wrath. When Porchy returned with Evelyn to Luxor in the first week of March he called on Carter again. More bitter words were exchanged and Carter ordered his erstwhile chief and friend from the house, telling him never to return.

Perhaps the envy of the years, certainly the intense frustration of the moment, caused Carter to utter words and to commit deeds at this time which were so lacking in sensitivity that the memory of them would follow him to the grave. Breasted was forgiving. He wrote in his diary on 12 March: 'A complete break seems inevitable.' He added: 'The man is by no means wholly to blame. What he has gone through has broken him down.'

Carter and his chief had been unnerved by the experience of past weeks. Neither acted with much discretion or nobility, but it was Carnarvon who seemed to suffer the most distress, mentally and physically. While Porchy was seeking the aid of the Americans and Lacau in putting the excavation on a more tenable and friendly footing, Carter was busily negotiating the purchase of a papyrus on behalf of the Metropolitan, lunching with some of his dealer cronies, entertaining the Maxwells, and having tea with the Queen of the Belgians and Lady Evelyn.

Just after their final blazing row at Qurna, on 6 March, Carnarvon was bitten on the face by an insect, probably a mosquito. While shaving in his suite at the Winter Palace Hotel in Luxor he scraped the small pimple which formed. Instead of applying disinfectant, he allowed the wound to bleed and, according to Breasted, a fly – an 'unspeakably filthy' Egyptian fly – settled on the seeping spot and infected it further. A doctor was called and Carnarvon was ordered to bed, as much for his tired and strained demeanour as for the infected bite.

On 18 March, Evelyn wrote to Carter – she had been in regular correspondence with him ever since the dispute with Carnarvon began – to tell him that her father was confined to bed and that he was almost unable to move. He had a high temperature and swollen neck glands. Doctors had prescribed a strict diet and had forbidden alcohol but the patient brushed aside their advice imperiously, ordering for dinner a bottle of wine which had been sent out from the cellars of Highclere. On 20 March, Lythgoe wrote to Carter from Cairo, where Carnarvon had been taken for the less oppressive air. Carter had relented before his old friend's departure and called at his hotel. They shook hands and were reconciled. Now Lythgoe wrote to tell Carter what 'an anxious time it was for everyone'. Lady Evelyn did not feel that the danger had passed by any means. And, he continued, 'I wanted to send you some word as to how his condition stands. Lady Evelyn has been carrying the strain wonderfully, but she has certainly had a heavy burden of anxiety the past two days.' On 26 March a letter from Richard Bethell, son of Lord Westbury, who had been acting as Carnarvon's secretary, brought an even more anxious report: 'I am sorry to tell you that Lord C. is seriously ill. Eve does not want it known how bad he is, but that poisoned bite has spread all over him and he has got blood poisoning... Eve has telegraphed to Lady C. So I suppose she will get out next week.'

On the day he sustained the bite, 6 March, Porchy had written to his half-brother Aubrey Herbert from Luxor, drawing attention to the chaotic state of Egypt under Allenby's faltering tutelage:

> I have had a somewhat unpleasant time out here. The papers have been quite poisonous but that I don't mind. What at present is fussing me is the state of Egypt. The whole business has been allowed to drift and the only thing to do is to get rid of Allenby. That is the first step… He is very weak, is badly advised, and I am sorry to say drinks. The last statement is confidential, but one day is sure to come out… I am very sorry for him, he is very straight, but slow and rather stupid. Nothing good will happen until King Fuad has been definitely told that he must behave or go and Allenby cannot do this.

It was a magnificent final blast from the aristocratic milord who could not look lightly on the trampling of the Union flag, or on the lack of support he had received from Allenby's officials in his negotiations with Egyptians determined to assert their national sovereignty. Within a month of writing that letter, Porchy told a friend, 'I have heard the call. I am preparing.' He lived long enough to hear that the Ministry of Public Works and the Antiquities Department had shelved any changes in the antiquities law until at least 1924. The argument about ownership and recompense would go on.

General Sir John Maxwell, as President of the EES, wrote a spirited defence of Carnarvon in *The Times* of 20 March, scorning continued press attacks which claimed that he was defying the orders of the Egyptian government, 'prostituting science to commercialism', and acting in a manner 'derogatory to his position and to archaeology'. Such attacks emanated largely from Bradstreet, writing in the *New York Times* and *Morning Post,* but the *Daily Express, Daily Mail* and other important newspapers took them up with glee. Maxwell described the charges and activities of pressmen in Egypt as 'importunate' and accused them of using the anti-British vernacular press to drum up feeling against Carnarvon. Relations between Carnarvon and Lacau, of which some newspapers painted lurid pictures, were in fact fairly amiable, though visitors to the Winter Palace Hotel were astonished by the 'ridiculous situation created by these bickerings'. Carter went to Cairo on the 20th to be at his chief's bedside. They had discussed the week before the completion of the season's work.

On 22 March a telegram arrived for Carnarvon from the King wishing him well, and news came from London that Carter had been awarded honorary membership of the Egypt Exploration Society for 'services to Egyptology'. Lady Carnarvon arrived at the bedside on 26 March. On the 30th *The Times* reported from Cairo that Lord Carnarvon was suffering from lobar pneumonia and that there was cause for anxiety. His condition was described as 'very serious'. It was the time of the death of Sarah Bernhardt and the execution of Catholic bishops in the Soviet Union, but it was of Carnarvon's fate that the world waited most anxiously to hear. On 5 April *The Times* reported from Cairo: 'Lord Carnarvon died peacefully this morning at 2 o'clock. He was conscious almost to the end – Reuter.'

Carter's diary noted simply: 'Lord Carnarvon dies, 2 a.m.' below a record of the receipt of £973 from the Metropolitan Museum for the purchase of 'the papyrus from Mr Nahman', £200 of which was his commission.

The rest of the world press, still smarting over his 'exclusivity' deal, gave Porchy grudging obituary notices. The gloss had been rubbed from the wonders of the discovery which his money, and his willingness to back Carter when no one else would have done so, made possible.

There were a few more pictures and details of the season's work to follow, such as the painstaking removal of the king's robe with its 20,000 beads and a parcel of the young sovereign's gold rings wrapped in linen. The expedition collapsed for the time being in a hail of recrimination and the public was left to admire Woolley's achievements at Ur and Amundsen's polar expedition, and to contemplate the deeds of the Belvoir hunt and the death throes of Lenin.

Chapter 12

'RAPE OF THE LOCKS'

LORD Carnarvon's death at the Continental Hotel in Cairo, watched over by Almina, Evelyn, and his son Lord Porchester, who had been called from army service in India, brought forth reports of strange events.

As he passed peacefully away in the early hours of the morning of 5 April, all Cairo's lights are said to have gone out. A thousand miles away at Highclere, the family's three-legged terrier Susie (she had lost a leg in a motoring accident in Berkeley Square) is reputed to have howled inconsolably and died within minutes of the Earl. Neither event is scientifically attested, but both were confirmed at the time by people of presumed sanity. Lord Allenby himself confirmed the Cairo black-out. He is said to have asked the engineer in charge of the electricity supply for an explanation, but none was forthcoming.

The legend of the snake and the canary was, it seemed, but an early warning of mysteries lurking in the depths of the royal necropolis. 'The Curse of the Pharaoh' and 'The Curse of King Tut' were about to become the new, repetitive headlines. Myth and superstition joined the more tangible woes of Carter's 'game of spillikins'.

He was alone now to confront the consequences of his erstwhile patron's tendency to generous deeds and foolish commitments. Carnarvon's last will and testament was dated 29 October 1919, with a codicil of the same date, and it said nothing of his concession which, at the time the will was written, was valueless. He wanted 'no mourning' and asked that he be buried at Beacon Hill overlooking Highclere, 'if possible, and if it does not cost more than fifty-pounds'.

Evelyn and her brother, the 6th Earl of Carnarvon, left by
P. & O. on 9 April; Lady Carnarvon went home by the same
route on the 14th, 'with Lord C's remains and Johnnie
Blumenthal', having promised Carter that she would maintain
the Valley concession in memory of her husband. The interment,
a family affair, took place at 11 a.m. on the 28th, at the vantage
point of his choice, whence he could keep an eternal eye on
his stud farms, his gardens and farms, lakes and lawns, reaching
as far as the eye could see in one of England's greenest and best
manicured corners. The purchase of his simple grave was
charged to the Carnarvon estate, for it was on his own property,
and did not exceed fifty pounds.

There were bequests to his sisters, and he left £500 to
Carter without comment. Dr Alan Gardiner was bequeathed
£100 'to buy a souvenir of me'. His entire Egyptian collection,
of which no inventory had been made, was left to Almina,
though she was asked to give one object to the British
Museum and one to the Ashmolean. He also requested that
his wife should donate a 'Tothmes III' cup of blue glass to the
Metropolitan Museum. If his wife was forced to sell the collection,
in part or whole, Mr Carter should have charge of negotiations
and should be the sole arbiter of price. Should she decide to
keep the collection, or part of it, for her son, she should consult
Dr Gardiner and Mr Carter. To his son, Lord Porchester, 'my
watch, chain and cigarette case.' To his faithful butler Alfred
Streathfield, his valet George Fearnside, and his head keeper
Henry Maber, he left £100 each. 'To any eight old men and
women of Highclere, a good thick blue coat with red cotton,
each.' When probate was granted to his executors, headed by
General Sir John Maxwell, the record shows that his effects
were valued at £416, 554 18s 6d., the estate passing directly to
his son and heir. The will, like the man, was compounded of
thoughtfulness and hubris.

Within days of Carnarvon's death and his quiet burial,
Carter was noting the prosaic matters of the archaeologist
closing down his site at the end of the season. There were more

deals: scarabs, a Turcoman 'compound bow of horn, wood and ligament', a Damascene inlaid box. There was a social and business visit to Cairo, a return to Luxor on 16 April to pay off his workmen and settle Callender's salary and expenses, followed by farewells to Lucas and Burton in early May. On 14 May he noted the dispatch in 'cars' of thirty-four cases, containing eighty-nine boxes of treated artefacts from the tomb, bound for the Cairo Museum. In fact, the 'cars' were improvised rail carriages, used in an extraordinary transport exercise. Because automobiles could not cope with the 6-mile stretch of sand between the tombs and the Nile, the military-style railway was again used by Carter's workmen, the track being put down in the sand, wagons pushed to the end, and then the expended rails at the rear taken up and reused at the front. The removal began at sunrise and was completed by 6 p.m. In the last week of the month there was a numbered 'good housekeeping' list, reminding himself to garage the car with the Ford agency in Cairo, send a papyrus destined for New York to England for mounting, place the concession in a bank safe, draw money, cable Maxwell and Lady Carnarvon.

He left for Cairo on 24 May and boarded the *ss Vienna* at Alexandria on the evening of the 25th. He took his usual sea route to Trieste and thence Venice and the Transcontinental Express to Boulogne. He reached London on the last day of the month and noted on arrival, 'Saw Lady Evelyn.' The next day he called on Lady Carnarvon. He spent much of the summer of 1923 in London, though he paid several visits to Almina at Highclere.

The fame which descended in a torrent of press and public interest, even adulation, a year before had mostly devolved on Carnarvon. The alienation of the entire press, save for *The Times,* had tarnished both his and Carter's image. By the middle of 1923 it was common for newspapers and magazines to speak of the tomb of Tutankhamun without mentioning Carter or his late patron. *The Times* and the *Illustrated London News* kept faith, however, and his diary soon filled with callers to the St

James's flat, and appointments with journalists, dealers and colleagues from Egypt. Mace was in town. Callender lived fairly close to Carter in London and was a frequent companion. There were few grand invitations such as he might have expected from city guilds, learned institutions or university caucuses, but there was one which must have brought a twinkle to the eye of the country lad made good, from Buckingham Palace, bidding him to the garden party on 26 July at 4 p.m. The Royal Scottish Geographical Society asked him to deliver a talk. And some of London's less frivolous hostesses were 'At Home' during the holiday months.

In the first fortnight there was lunch with Maxwell and the solicitor Molony at the latter's Lancaster Gate office; several meetings with Percy White, his old Cairo acquaintance who gave him valuable advice on dealing with the press; a lunch in his honour at the Author's Club in Whitehall Court; a visit to the editorial offices of the *Evening Standard;* dinner with Gardiner, just back from Syria, at the Travellers'; lunch again with the Maxwells at their house in Cadogan Square; and on 12 June a meeting with Dawson at the *Times* offices to discuss the terms of a new agreement now that the chief signatory to the first arrangement was dead. Sir William Garstin, a man held in the highest regard on all sides in Egypt in his years as adviser to the Public Works Department, was concerned about Carter's deplorable relationship with Lacau, the man with power of life and death over the tomb excavation. He called at St James's for lunch and a heart to heart chat, and invited his host to lunch at Brooks's, before he returned to Egypt. Gulbenkian and the Marquess of Northampton were among the many enthusiasts and collectors, mostly Porchy's friends, who turned to him for advice and invited him to White's and the Turf, the Savile and Reform. It was a busy homecoming and one which embraced a social circuit entirely novel to him.

Not until the third week of June was he able to find time for a few days at Highclere. He turned up there late on the 16th, having lunched *en route* with Gulbenkian and sold him an Egyptian cat for £350. Maxwell joined him for discussions with Lady Carnarvon about the future of the excavation. Almina, anxious to do the best she could in memory of her late husband, did not need much persuasion, even though she would now have to grapple alone with matters which were likely to involve her in international problems and disputes and which she knew little about. In any case, she needed Carter's help and advice in disposing of her husband's collection. She agreed to renew the concession with the Egyptian Antiquities Department for a further year, until 1 November 1924.

Lady Evelyn was present during most of his stay at the Castle. The diary offers no suggestion of particular attention on Carter's part. By now he was certainly on the most familiar terms with Carnarvons' vivacious daughter. But the down-to-earth 'rough' diary notes, recording meetings in Cairo, Luxor and England, give rise to no cause for believing that the relationship was anything more than an agreeable friendship between a dutiful daughter engrossed in her father's most famous achievement, and the confirmed bachelor who was the instrument of that achievement. Germane to the question of romance, though apparently unnoticed by later commentators devoted to fringe theories about Carter and the Carnarvons, is the fact that soon after arriving home from Egypt she married Brograve Campbell Beauchamp, the twenty-six-year-old son of Sir Edward Beauchamp, Chairman of Lloyds and Liberal Member of Parliament. Within two years of the marriage Brograve succeeded to the title and Eve became Lady Evelyn Beauchamp. Her mother-in-law, Betty Campbell Beauchamp, was the daughter of a wealthy American, Archibald Woods. Carter was a frequent caller at their Prince's Gate home.

As he strode from place to place, elegantly 'got up' in Savile Row suit and homburg, brandishing a cane in the manner of his cinema idol Charlie Chaplin, and a cigarette-holder in the manner of Carnarvon, he radiated a confidence which amounted almost to affability. But neither fame nor achievement provides automatic entry to the halls of that guarded institution, the English establishment. Carter remained on the periphery of the social and academic worlds, like brothers William and Verney before him a member of the Burlington Fine Arts Club and a recognizable figure in the 'arts' community, but with no claim to tangible honour or recognition. It was the press, trying to circumvent the *Times* arrangement, which provided most of his free meals.

Robert Emmet Sherwood, about to take over the editorship of *Life* magazine, came over from America in the hope of a spectacular photo-feature, and there were several meetings at his Park Lane apartment. Bruce Ingram, the owner-editor of the *Illustrated London News,* protected by his private agreement with *The Times,* kept up a close rapport with Carter which bore fruit a few months later with the publication of the first colour pictures taken by Harry Burton of the interior furnishings. Hitherto readers of the magazine, avid as the editor wrote 'for something better than Carnarvon's *Dantesque* photos', had been treated to the colour drawings and reconstructions of the Anglo-Egyptian artist Hamzeh Carr, the landscapes of Charles Whymper, and the familiar work of Amedeo Forestier who had been drawing archaeological sites since the first decade of the century. Back in January, Ingram had been so anxious to illustrate the chariots of Tutankhamun that he asked Newberry if he could provide notes and drawings on the subject. Newberry supplied him with Carter' drawings of chariots from other tomb decorations, notably those of Tuthmosis IV, to accompany Burton's photo of the dismembered vehicle found in the antechamber of Tutankhamun's tomb. Forestier's first reconstruction drawings of the tomb were based on material supplied by Flinders Petrie.

Now the reader could feast on the state chariot and throne, the former with wonderful gold-plated panelling, showing the young king as sphinx, trampling on his enemies, and as husband, being ministered to by his attentive Queen Ankhesenamun, the latter of almost indescribably brilliant workmanship in its interplay of materials. In an article due to appear in November,

Carter wrote:

The panel is overlaid with heavy sheet gold and richly adorned with glass, faience, and coloured stone inlay. It is the chief glory of the throne, and there can be no hesitation in claiming it to be the most beautiful tableau that has ever been found in Egypt. The scene depicts one of the halls of the palace, a room decorated with flower-garlanded pillars, a frieze of royal cobras, and a dado of conventional 'recessed' panelling. Through a hole in the roof, the sun shoots down his life-giving protective rays. The King himself sits in an unconventional attitude upon a cushioned throne, his arm carelessly across its back. Before him stand the girlish figure of the Queen, putting, apparently, the last touches to his toilet. In one hand she holds a small jar of ointment, and with the other she gently anoints his shoulder, or adds a touch of perfume to his collar.

It was a titillating promise of things to come. Business and pleasure vied for attention as the summer months fled. The austere days of Petrie's stale tinned meat must have seemed a long way off. 'Maxwell 11 a.m. Gardiner 1.30. Robinsons, Berkeley 7.15. Theatre. P. & O. Office', ran one day's diary entry. Edward Robinson, Director of the Metropolitan, who had finalized the informal arrangement with Carnarvon the year before by which the American museum became a partner in the tomb exploration, was in London with his family, and Carter dined with them twice in one week at the Berkeley, discussing among other matters the prospect of a lucrative US lecture tour. It was the other Robinson, though, Sir Harry Perry of *The Times,* who with Merton and Allan Sinclair, recently arrived from the *Glasgow Herald,* and the editor himself, took up most of his time in their determination to maintain their stranglehold on news and pictures. In July, Professor Breasted's son Charles reinforced the American contingent.

As Carter made his was round London's club and restaurant

circuit he still showed tell-tale signs of the homely East Anglian upbringing which knows little of such things, and of the years of social isolation which followed. He still spelt Savile with two ls, whether referring to the Club or the Row, and he often mistook the names of hostesses who were almost as intriguing to him as he to them.

The Palace garden party came and went with no more than a laconic diary entry in late July. The King, who had listened intently to Carnarvon's first-hand account, asked Carter about the burial chamber. Audience was long enough for George V to tell Carter that he did not think the mummy should be removed from the tomb. James Breasted had been to the Palace on the 20th. He had attended the Lord Mayor's reception at Mansion House the day before, where Lord Chalmers, President of the Royal Asiatic Society, drew him to a corner and said, 'You are to be taken to the King tomorrow.' Breasted drew up at Buckingham Palace just as the guard changed, accompanied by Emile Senart, President of the Société Asiatique of France, Sten Konow the Norwegian Orientalist, and an old friend, A.V. Williams Jackson. He described his visit: 'Lord Chalmers met us at the door of the Palace, led us across the great court and through the entrance of the King's apartments, past the grand staircase up which the lucky ones go to make their curtsies at Court.' King George V engaged his guests 'with much animation and interest'. When the professor's turn came, the King 'asked at once about Carnarvon and said that he wished there were time for us to talk at length about the tomb of Tutankhamun'.

Excited by all the publishing and film offers coming his way, Carter took on the services of a literary agent in August, the American Curtis Brown. Before he or his agent could sell his services effectively, however, several more meetings with *Times* officials were necessary to regularize his own position and the future contribution of Merton and his assistants to tomb publicity. He was anxious that, when work resumed, he should be spared the disasters of the previous year's press and public invasions. Carnarvon's agreement with *The Times* had caused dissension in Printing House Square as well as Fleet Street generally, to say nothing of the squabbles in Carter's camp. The accounts of *The Times'* chief correspondent, Perry Robinson, showed frequent payments to members of Carter's staff and to experts like Jean Capart and Arthur Weigall, the popular young archaeologist working for the *Daily Mail,* who were on the sidelines. Efforts to bring the Egyptian press to heel and prevent attacks on *The Times* featured in correspondence between the management in London, Gresham House (the address of the paper's Cairo office), and Luxor, where Robinson and two other reporters, Moyne and Warhurst, had taken up residence in the 'digging' season. There were threats of withdrawing the news service from the native press if it continued to bite the hand that fed it. National animosities were not smoothed by the *Saturday Review* which in March, when Carnarvon had been under attack, introduced its defence of the British expedition with Pliny's description of the Egyptians, *'ventosa et insolens natio'* ('a windy and insolent people'). Merton, who followed Carter to London for talks at *The Times,* had telegraphed his manager, Lint Smith, in May after a long meeting at Carter's home in the Valley: 'Visit Carter satisfactoriest'.

All the same, Carter was far-seeing enough to make contingency plans by getting to know other proprietors and editors. In July he had accepted an invitation to lunch at the Carlton with William Berry, heir to the Camrose fortune and editor-in-chief of the *Daily Telegraph.* For the moment he was happy to advise Lady Carnarvon to stand by the existing arrangement, even though Dawson was proving difficult about financial terms. He took advice from Maxwell, White and Newberry before telling Richard Bethell to tell Lady Carnarvon to continue the 'exclusivity' agreement. Just before he left for Egypt, Ingram took him to the Ivy restaurant to sign up a series of articles, via *The Times,* for the next few months. Then Gulbenkian wanted to lunch him at the Carlton. And

Sybil Amherst wanted him to go on from Highclere to Foulden Hall in Norfolk, the latest seat of the family close to the Didlington estate which was lost through the faulty wording of the first Lord Amherst's will. Sybil had taken charge of the family fortunes at the death of her sister Mary (Lady William Cecil) in 1919, though the latter's grandchild William, then seven years old, inherited the title.

Two lectures booked for his return to England were enormously successful. Carter was still thought of, even by the closest of his professional acquaintances, as somewhat gauche; not at all the gentlemanly, urbane type represented by fellow archaeologists such as Newberry and Griffith, or the magisterial Petrie or Breasted. His appeal, though he was not conscious of the fact and would probably have denied it, was to the common man. His performance before a crowded audience in the Usher Hall, Edinburgh, on 10 September, demonstrated that appeal and showed that there was a vast public interest in Tutankhamun and in the popular presentation of archaeology. Carter, perhaps unconsciously, used some of the stage tricks of the man he had studied so intently in Cairo and London picture houses, Charlie Chaplin, and the effect was startling. The Scottish audience, gathered at the invitation of the Geographical Society, responded as if it was witnessing a music hall act to the carefully delivered shafts of humour which laced his commentary on Harry Burton's slides. It was the same two weeks later at the New Oxford Theatre in London's Oxford Street, this time addressing an audience assembled by the Egypt Exploration Society. Again it was a sell-out and an enormous success. Still with the broad vowels of Norfolk speech evident beneath his polished diction (a broadcast which he made a few years later suggested a carefully contrived 'Oxford' accent), and delivering the humour with solemn face and theatrical gesticulation, Carter proved himself to be one of the best and most colourful lecturers in the business, and by the consent of his peers among the most knowledgeable of Egyptologists. But the academic world was not comfortable with his kind.

Remarkably, no place of learning in Britain would seek to make use of his rare gifts.

In the last few days before his departure for Egypt he stayed overnight with the Newberrys at their home near Godalming, and lunched with Percy at the Burlington. He still relied a good deal on the advice of the man who had first commended him to Amherst and Egypt some thirty years before, and there were signs that he was nervous of the new nationalist regime in Egypt which he would now have to face alone, not as the executive arm of the rich and powerful Carnarvon but as a principal, the protector rather than the shadow of the lady he now represented. There were also last-minute meetings with Garstin and with Lady Burghclere who did not share her niece's fine opinion of him but who wanted to be sure that her late brother's proudest achievement was in good hands. And there was the mandatory call at Fortnum's to order a regular supply of hampers. Fame and sound investment had brought about a change in living standards at Qurna. He had purchased the estate which he and Carnarvon had taken over from the Egypt Exploration Society, and he gave it a new name, Alwat al-Diban, Wolf's Lea in translation.

Carter left London for Trieste on 3 October 1923, and was in Cairo on the 8th. He spent two days there talking to Quibell, Lacau's chief assistant, about his campaign for the forthcoming season and then went off to Alexandria to discuss his plans with Abdal Hamid, the Minister of Works, and Prime Minister Zaghlul Pasha. He had taken Garstin's – and Breasted's and Gardiner's – pleas to heart and was determined this time to keep on the right side of authority. On 11 October, three days after his arrival, Carter went to a meeting of the Antiquities Department and negotiated a renewal of the excavation contract in Lady Carnarvon's name. Quibell referred felicitously to the 'skill and punctiliousness' with which the work had been carried out so far and said that he was honoured to be asked to grant a renewal. Carter suggested that from now on his work should be described officially as 'clearing' rather than 'excavating' the tomb.

There were other matters to be resolved, however, which tested Quibell's calm and courteous approach. Carter insisted on the continued exclusion of all newsmen other than Merton of *The Times,* and on 'generously' supplying the Egyptian press with daily bulletins which would give local journalists advance news before it reached even *The Times.* As for the public, including members of the High Commission and other notables, they should be allowed into the tomb only when the major work of removing furniture and shrines had been completed and any necessary preservation work carried out. Carter, who had all along regarded Merton as his publicity agent, revealed to Quibell an agreement which he had made with *The Times'* man while they were both in London, that he would be henceforth a member of the archaeological staff. On 1 October Merton had written from his London hotel accepting the 'offer of a staff appointment as publicity agent', saying that he would be in Trieste on the 26th and would report to Carter as soon as he arrived at Luxor. It was not an adroit act on the part of a senior correspondent on the staff of a national newspaper. Quibell described the arrangement as 'unwise'. The press at large would not take kindly to it.

As for the public, many of those who pestered the Antiquities Department for permission to visit the tomb were important Egyptians who regarded the matter as entirely their affair and nothing to do with the British. How could Lacau, or he, Quibell, a British archaeologist and an official of the Cairo Museum, simply brush them aside? When the parties went to Alexandria to ratify the agreement, Quibell was anxious about the details and asked for time to consider certain points. Finalization was held over for another four days when they would meet at the museum in Cairo. There and then the Antiquities Department accepted Carter's unequivocal and unbending demands about press and public exclusion. Quibell did not mention that Lacau had opposed Carter's proposals as had most of the politicians involved, but Carter's case was supported by a well-known anglophile in the Cabinet, the Minister of Works, Abdal Hamid Suleiman Pasha. The minister had refused to listen to prolonged arguments and announced that Carter should be allowed to proceed in his own way. Unfortunately for Carter, by the time the Egyptian Civil Service was ready to wreak revenge, the minister's office would be occupied by a renowned anglophobe.

Carter arrived at Luxor on 16 October. He told Quibell that he expected to complete the task of clearing the tomb in about a month. Callender was waiting for him. Operations resumed in mid-November, after a work-force of eighty Egyptian labourers had spent a fortnight in removing the 1,700 tons of rock with which Carter had filled the entrance eight months before.

The Breasteds arrived soon after work was resumed on the burial chamber. At the onset of the Egyptian summer of 1923, James Breasted had returned to the Oriental Institute of Chicago University which he had help to found and to turn into the foremost academic institution of its kind in the world, to work on the coffin texts and prepare an essay on the Egyptian New Kingdom period for the Cambridge Ancient History.

Charles Breasted had used the privileges which followed from his father's official work in the tomb to take on a journalist's role in the new season. He accepted an appointment as correspondent in Egypt of the *Chicago Daily News* and the *Christian Science Monitor,* thus placing himself in a unique position to contravene the Carnarvon-*Times* agreement. When Carter met him in London he was working for those journals under the assumed name George Waller Mecham, and everyone wondered who that knowledgeable commentator could be since none could remember meeting him in the flesh. Charles said that he had adopted the pseudonym to protect his father. 'We were all agreed', he said, 'that Carnarvon's contract with *The Times* was eminently unfair to, and not legally binding upon, the rest of the Press.' All the same, he informed Carter immediately of his journalistic appointments. Carter replied that any such arrangements were his own affair and that he, Carter, would forget what he had been told. By November, Carter was much more interested in the father than the son. He ceased work on the tomb while he drew James Breasted aside to 'go over the situation' in the tomb with him.

There had been other meetings with the Ministry of Works in Cairo while workmen removed Carter's immense blocking stones and preliminary clearing work was undertaken within the tomb. In discussion with Lacau's office there was mention of the possibility of the concession being transferred to him, Carter, 'in the name of the Society' (presumably the EES). He and Merton were together for much of the time, and they went to the royal palace on 3 November to sign the visitor's book. At the Ministry next day, Lacau sat opposite him at the conference table, flanked by his British assistants Paul Tottenham (Ministry of Works adviser) and Quibell. The meeting, which started at 10.30 a.m., had been called to discuss press visits and the surveillance of work in the tomb. By noon they had reached agreement on the limiting of press and public access and the access to be given to Lacau's men. At 12.30 the Minister, Abdal Hamid Pasha, took the chair and the proposals formulated by the committee of three were set before him. He agreed the document, with one small amendment respecting press invitations. Carter dined at Shepheard's that evening with Tottenham. Administrative arrangements seemed to be running smoothly. There was much coming and going between Cairo and Luxor in the following two weeks, with meetings with Lord Allenby and Egyptian officials, ending with a call to the High Commission on the 15th at which Carter told Allenby that he had come to total agreement with the government on proposals for continuing the tomb excavation. Afterwards he told Tottenham of his desire to resume work on amicable terms. In the mean time, Richard Bethell, former secretary to Carnarvon, arrived to work as a general factotum on Carter's staff while representing Lady Carnarvon's interests.

At Highclere in the last days of September, just before Carter left England, he and Sir John Maxwell had finalized the arrangements with Almina whereby she agreed to take over the concession and to finance it, partly with the aid of royalties accruing from *The Times* which, in the first year, paid an advance of £5,000 and 75 per cent of all revenues to the estate, diminishing to £2,500 and 50 per cent in subsequent years. The 'exclusive' agreement was renewed and Maxwell underscored Carter's insistence on 'full rights' and freedom from 'harassments or interruptions'.

In Carter's absence in August, Gertrude Bell, 'The Lady' of the Arab lands (and Director of Antiquities in the new Iraq administration), visited Cairo. At the time, she was busily setting up her own museum in Baghdad to house the rapidly growing collections of Sumerian discoveries from Ur, Nippur, Kish and other sites: finds which in many cases pre-dated the tomb of Tutankhamun by 1,000 years and more. The temperature in Cairo was about 110 degrees in the shade, but the intrepid Miss Bell found it 'not a bit hot', wondering to herself whether the Egyptians and their American and European guests knew 'what real heat is like'. After receiving most of the ministers of the Egyptian government who trooped to see her at Shepheard's, she went off to the Cairo Museum to meet Quibell and James Breasted, writing to her father on 30 August in an informative if casual vein. 'I went to the museum and spent a delightful hour with dear Mr Quibell.' They talked about the Iraq Antiquities Department and of how she should frame the new laws which would govern the activities of Leonard Woolley, Stephen Langdon, Max Mallowan, Henry Frankfort and others, at ancient sites such as Ur, Kish, Uruk, Khorsabad and Nineveh. 'Mr Quibell's long experience makes his advice most valuable.' She continued:

After which we went to see the Tutankhamun things – there are a few already on exhibition, one of the boxes, two sentries [?], some alabaster jars, and one or two small objects

– among them the famous mannequin on which they tried the Pharaoh's clothes; from the look of it I didn't think they would fit him for it was worn perfectly 'frontal'… i.e. quite flat back and sides, Mr Q was very interesting about it all. There's nothing that they haven't got from other tombs, nothing in the furniture and trappings of which we heard ad nauseam, only they never got so complete a collection from any other tomb. One of the much described gold engraved thrones is no better than a previously acquired specimen, though it's in better condition; in quite splendid condition in fact. Another, a much simpler piece of work, wood and gold, is really lovely. Mr Q said he thought it the best bit of furniture in the tomb and I thought it the best thing of its kind I had ever seen. The alabaster jars were frankly hideous, extraordinarily elaborate so far as the craftsmanship in a simple bit of stone went, and far too elaborate for beauty… Mr Q said that Mr Carter is going to do his utmost to ward off the newspaper people this year, but doesn't think he'll succeed. As you may imagine they're a horrid nuisance, but it pays to give one paper carte blanche (*The Times* has it), as it may help to bar out the multitude… Lady Carnarvon is paying for the completion of the work on the tomb which will cost her a pretty penny. There are three chambers full of things none of which has yet been touched, including the great shrine which they think contains the mummy. There are, you know, probably 5 shrines, one inside the other – they've only opened the outermost one – with a coffin in the centre. A stone sarcophagus they think it will be, & they expect to find it untouched, in which case they ought to find some splendid jewel on its breast. In another little room there is the shrine which contains the Canopic vases &… the four [?] guardian figures… which Professor Breasted told me were masterpieces of art… Mr Q said they were certainly very fine but marred by their thick covering of gold leaf. How like kings and courtiers, isn't it, to think that gilding improves the lily.

Breasted, it seems, was able to pass on information in August about matters which were not, officially, settled until Carter' reappearance in Cairo two months later.

'He is still far from the point where he can open the sarcophagus,' Breasted observed as clearing work began in October. Pressmen and tourists arrived in ever-increasing numbers. The Egyptian press, outraged by Carter's refusal to interrupt his work in order to allow even the most important of the country's citizens a sight of their own heritage, renewed its vitriolic anti-British campaign. Local newspapers found powerful allies in the British and American press. 'By making an exclusive secret of the contents of the inner tomb he has ranged against him the majority of the world's most influential newspapers', The *Daily Express* had written in an editorial back in February, referring to Carnarvon's original arrangement with *The Times*.

Carter's journal recording the season's work noted the most important and delicate tasks so far undertaken, amid the confusion caused by the massive publicity which still attended every move in the Valley, and by a world press determined to break *The Times'* monopoly. First, the team had to remove the sentinel statues which had stood guard for 3,500 years. Then they had to remove the whole of the north wall which divided the antechamber from the burial chamber. Wall paintings must be removed, treated and replaced at a later date. Wood scaffolding had to be erected. When the ebony bolts of the first shrine were drawn and its doors swung open, the second shrine was revealed, with similar bolted doors but with the seal of Tutankhamun intact. Between the first and second shrines a broad space was filled with a heavy wooden frame, covered with gold, which supported a pall of black linen studded with gold rosettes. Breasted likened it to 'a night sky spangled with stars'. Before it could be transported to the laboratory, the linen had to treated with a chlorinated rubber compound to strengthen it enough to be gathered on a wooden roller. When the bolted doors of the second shrine were released, the third shrine was revealed with an identical unbroken seal. Finally, Carter drew the bolts on the third shrine to reveal the last, innermost structure, 'even more brilliant in workmanship'.

Work on the inner sanctum began on 19 November, with Burton making photographic records and experimenting with a cine-camera loaned by Goldwyn, while Mace helped in the careful removal of objects from around the shrine. The ground outside tomb 15 had been levelled off and made ready for building an open-air studio and carpenter's shop. Then came the task of dismantling the four shrines, numbered in ascending order from the outside inward, fitted together like a vast nest of Fabergé eggs. The 'tongued' roofs of the three outer shrines were removed. When they came to the roof of the fourth, innermost, shrine it was found to consist of a single piece of heavy wood, five inches thick at its broadest section, and weighing several tons.

Breasted reconstructed the events of more than 3,000 years before as the king's body, 'sumptuously encased in a close-fitting coffin', was lowered into the sarcophagus. When the ceremonies were concluded, the craftsmen and engineers took over, moving deftly amid the 'gorgeous array of glittering golden shrine sections', marshalling an army of assistants – 'slaves', Breasted called them, but it was an inaccurate label, for slave labour as such was never used in ancient Egypt, though prisoners of war were used without scruple for civil engineering enterprises. In the time-honoured ritual of their trade, foremen would scratch identification marks on each piece, writing with black ink such catchwords as 'front', 'back', 'north', 'south', 'middle', 'end'. The marks were as legible to Carter as on the day they were written. Confused alignments showed that even in the great Amarna period of craftsmanship and its immediate aftermath, elementary mistakes could be made which were more easily glossed over than righted. A section at the north end of the inner shrines was marked 'south'. The engineers who lowered the parts into the burial chamber had done so in the wrong order. To right the mistake they would have had to lift the great assembly out, realign it and drop it into position again. To the accompaniment of cabinet-makers' remarks which can only be imagined, the parts were left as they were, the wrong way round.

There was confusion too between sections of the second and third shrines. The woodwork at the corners of the third shrine was, said Breasted, 'barbarously hammered together by clumsy mechanics'. But such human frailty could not diminish the glory of the moment.

When Carter and I opened the doors of the third and fourth shrines and beheld the massive stone sarcophagus within, I felt for the first time the majesty of the dead Pharaoh's actual presence. As we explored with a flashlight the space between the still standing side walls of the second and third shrines, we found lying there exactly as they were left on the day of his burial, several of the King's bows with a supply of arrows, and beside them a long object which we did not at first recognize. The last proved to be one of the Pharaoh's large ostrich plume fans which his slaves bore on his either hand when he went abroad in his palanquin or sat in state on a high throne.

The once lengthy plumes had crumbled to grey-brown dust which lay in little heaps, suggesting faded scenes of what Breasted called 'Oriental splendour'.

Mace charted with minute precision the dismantling of the shrines through November and December, adding technical detail to Breasted's almost poetic descriptions. By 12 December, Carter was exhausted and ill. When Lacau visited the tomb on that day he was shown round by Callender and Mace. On the 13th Lacau called on Carter to discuss recent demands by the Egyptians that they be shown the names of employees 'for approval'. Edward Harkness, chairman of the Metropolitan's board of governors, and Lythgoe came over from the American House to hear Carter tell the French chief that there would be 'no more concessions'. Lacau, angered by Carter's adamant refusal even to discuss the matter, left the house with his head in the air, inwardly shaking but determined to maintain a dignified presence. Lacau told the Americans before he left that the government was arranging for fifteen 'native ladies' to visit the tomb. On 15 December a telegram arrived from the Ministry of Public Works summoning Carter to Cairo. Meetings with the Minister and Allenby did nothing to solve the growing difference between Carter and the authorities. Mace worked away at the chariots rescued from the tomb, lovingly restoring and waxing the wooden parts, and waiting for Carter's return. On the 21st the Englishman arrived and without a word about his dispute with the Minister in Cairo, he resumed work on the shrines.

There was to be no let up in work over the Christmas period, or respite from the tourist invasion. Only a visit from the classical scholar Sir John Marshall provided a moment of composure, of leisurely conversation over lunch. Marshall's fame in unveiling the Indus Valley civilizations had vied with Evans in Crete and preceded Carter in Egypt and Woolley at Ur of the Chaldees, but he had not had to endure the twentieth century publicity onslaught and he sympathized with Carter.

The task of dismantling the shrines which Carter had allowed a month to complete took four months in the event. As work proceeded to Christmas 1923 and beyond into the next year, James Breasted was taken ill with a recurrence of an old feverish complaint and ordered to bed at the Winter Palace Hotel. Carter often needed him for urgent consultation at the tomb, however, and he was taken to the Valley on such occasions in an open carriage, which had to be ferried across the river, a linen mask protecting mouth and nostrils from sand and dust. Between times, he planned an expedition to Sinai, continued his work on the coffin texts and the famous Edwin Smith surgical papyrus, and created the 'Luxor Epigraphic Expedition' at the Chicago Oriental Institute. Busy and sick as he was, Breasted shared Carter's growing concern at the crowds of sightseers and pressmen who were bringing work in the

Valley almost to a standstill. Carter built up an army of lacerated enemies who would not readily forgive him when the moment of reckoning came.

By February 1924, when the world waited in suppressed wonderment to see the shrines, Carter was in a stage of almost constant distemper. Even his closest colleagues gave him plenty of elbow room. A special viewing was arranged for 12 February, when selected Egyptian officials and eminent archaeologists would witness the opening of the king's sarcophagus. Of course *The Times* would be there in the shape of Arthur Merton. The hundreds of correspondents gathered at Luxor would have to take their chance as usual, looking to rumour or overheard conversation to supplement the syndicated reports sent to their editors. Charles Breasted went each night to the telegraph office at the railway station to file his reports. His pen-name, as much as his articles, still intrigued the world press. Who was George Waller Mecham? Where did he obtain his authentic-sounding information? Editors wired their correspondents constantly to ask how it came about that Mecham's articles were better informed than those of *The Times* itself. Even Valentine Williams who knew everyone and nearly everything, was at a loss. The *Chicago Daily News* man retained his anonymity even though he brushed shoulders with most of the bona fide correspondents as they passed in and out of the telegraph office.

Just before Carter's moment of glory, the opening of the sarcophagus, another visit reinforced the air of mystery that surrounded the tomb. A French-Canadian professor of English literature named La Fleur appeared at Luxor. He was a pleasant man, tall and slim, with a pointed beard and quick sense of humour. Carter took to him and invited him to the tomb, by which time the guest was in bed with a mild attack of influenza. He could not resist the invitation, however, and Carter showed him round. He returned to his hotel coughing and spluttering. The English doctor called to attend him said he was 'very ill'. He died in the early hours of the following morning. Even

Charles Breasted and the doctor were beginning to take the 'curse' seriously. On hearing of La Fleur's death they persuaded Breasted senior not to go on a proposed survey of Sinai.

The great day finally arrived. On 12 February a party which included the Under-Secretary of the Ministry of Works, Muhammad Zaghlul Pasha, Pierre Lacau and a group of archaeologists made up chiefly of Carter's mentors, Breasted, Gardiner and Newberry, stood in silence at the doorway which led from the antechamber to the burial chamber. Lifting tackle was in position. So, to the surprise of the guests, was a movie camera, operated by Harry Burton.

Carter gave the word. 'Amid intense silence,' Carter wrote afterwards, 'the huge slab… weighing over a ton and a quarter, rose from its bed.' The contents of the sarcophagus were completely covered by linen shrouds. Carter quickly rolled them back, one by one… 'and as the last was removed a gasp of wonderment escaped our lips, so gorgeous was the sight that met our eyes: a golden effigy of the young boy king, of most magnificent workmanship, filled the whole of the sarcophagus.'

The only eye-witness account other than Carter's was written by James Breasted two days later. He had gone to the unveiling ceremony despite the illness which still incapacitated him and caused his doctor to protest.

From where I stood I could see on the opposite wall of the burial chamber, beyond the heavy timbers of the scaffolding, a painting of Tutankhamun's successor, King Eye [Ay], in the act of concluding the burial service over the body of the departed young Pharaoh… When the movie camera was finally ready, Carter took his place at the hoist nearest the King's feet, while Callender stood at the other hoist. Carter now gave the word, the hoists began to click, and we heard the faint rhythmic buzzing of the movie camera… The sarcophagus lid trembled, began to rise. Slowly, and swaying uncertainly, it swung clear… At first we saw only a long, narrow, black void. Then across the middle of this blackness we gradually discerned fragments of granite which had fallen out of the fracture in the lid. They were lying scattered upon a dark shroud through which we seemed to see emerging an indistinct form.

Breasted went on to describe the evolving scene of breathless excitement as Carter illuminated the sarcophagus with a flashlight while Burton followed his every move, filming the hidden interior in minute detail. Then complete silence reigned while Carter and Mace, with the 'routine efficiency of modern undertakers' assistants', loosened the shroud which covered the sleeping figure and carefully rolled it back.

The once white linen was scorched and blackened as if by fire, and in some cases it crumbled in their fingers. Under it was a second or inner shroud, less dark and discoloured, and beneath this…lay the King. Through the veil of the shrouding linen we could recognize the contours of his arms crossed at his breast, could see the profile of his face, and above it, at the forehead, an irregular prominence as of the projecting royal insignia…there at last was the King who had slept thus in the silent heart of the mountain for some three thousand two hundred and fifty years. All these momentary fancies and many more went thronging through the mind of an Orientalist as he looked down for the first time upon the undisturbed burial of an ancient Oriental sovereign who had died in the dawn of man's first spiritual emancipation.

Breasted's version of the most intensely poignant moment in the entire history of archaeology would ever remain the authoritative commentary among all the hundreds that have since found their way into print. He recorded his own thoughts, though they must have echoed Carter's, as the young monarch was revealed in the adornment of his funerary garb. The under-shroud was finally, with infinite care, rolled down to the feet. The onlooker gazed up and down the body, to the gleaming gold vulture's head and the rearing cobra of the forehead, to the eyes which stared as though from a body which still lived. And then he became aware of the whole body, glowing in the splendour of shining gold: the gold-encased arms and hands crossed at the breast, a gold and jewelled crook grasped in the right hand, the ceremonial flail, also of gold, in the left.

In the reverie of the moment, Breasted thought of those who had laid the king to rest, and wondered what they might have thought of the youth who ruled over them, he who was the victim of clerical and social forces beyond his control. What did his girl-wife Ankhesenamun, Akhenaten's daughter, think when she stepped down into the shrine? Was it she perhaps who took from the hand of a waiting servant an exquisite ivory writing palette, and placed it between the forepaws of the jackal guarding the innermost doorway, where Carter's men had found it lying just a year before? It had come from Amarna, made in the great days of that revolutionary city, where, for the first time in Egyptian history, prayers were offered up to the 'One and Only' god. The young queen, at any rate, had seen the hostile priests restore the old power. Perhaps they had caused Tutankhamun's death. Perhaps he had perished in the downfall of her father's great dream? The answers to such questions might be close to resolution. But Breasted had not anticipated the cunning of the king's servants or the perfidy of modern man.

The entire figure, wrote Breasted, 'was swathed in the gilded plumage of a protecting goddess'. He had not realized until he found time to reflect that this was not yet the king. 'What we saw was the outer coffin, some seven feet long and thirty inches high, cunningly wrought by the sculptor with the aid of the lapidary and the goldsmith, into a magnificent portrait figure of the king lying as if stretched out upon the lid like a crusader on his tomb slab in some European cathedral.' It occurred to the great Egyptologist, as he contemplated the scene which

Carter had created like some improbable masterpiece of set design, that there were probably several inner coffins within the last of which would lie the embalmed body. For the moment, the haunting figure presented to them would have to suffice. The face bore a striking likeness to the figures which had guarded the sealed doorway. The hands and insignia were beautifully modelled, 'entirely free and in the round'. The eyes were inlays of black and white stone. 'No anthropoid coffin lid heretofore known', Breasted concluded, 'can approach it as a work of art.' The day's work was done, Carter left the coffin lid suspended and closed the tomb for the night.

Carter had looked ill when the team went off to lunch before the raising of the sarcophagus lid. He told Breasted that he did not feel up to much. They sat together in an uncompleted tomb, number 41 on the official list, and Carter took Carnarvon's old chair at the head of the table. As the others ate heartily, Carter sorted moodily through a pile of correspondence, which included a note from Morcos Bey Hanna, new Minister of Public Works and the official ultimately responsible for Lacau's Department of Antiquities. He was a tough politician who had been imprisoned for treason, a sentence which imparted both charisma and respect in the prevailing anti-British atmosphere in Egypt. He disliked Carter with unconcealed passion and reinforced the bureaucratic efforts of the zealous Lacau in deluging the Englishman with demands and arbitrary instructions.

A few days before the ceremony, Carter and the Minister had agreed a schedule of work for the sarcophagus opening. Now, on the day itself, he had sent another version of the same agreed programme to Carter, couched in offensively dictatorial words. Carter handed it to Breasted who, on reading it, agreed that it was 'simply offensive in phraseology'. Carter murmured that the whole affair had made him sick as the work party joined the invited guests and made their way to the tomb at a few minutes to three o'clock.

Carter's senior advisers had sensed the danger of a showdown two weeks before. On the last day of January, Breasted, Gardiner, Lythgoe and Newberry addressed a joint letter to Lacau affirming that 'it is universally agreed that Mr Howard Carter is conducting his complex and very difficult task in a manner beyond all praise'.

The day after the opening of the sarcophagus, 13 February, the dispute reached a political climax in London and Paris. A question to the Prime Minister was put down by Dr Chapple in the House of Commons, asking 'what privileges and concessions had been extended by HM Government to Mr Howard Carter', and what obligations of reporting and photography rested on Carter in consequence. The Prime Minister, Ramsay MacDonald, replied that no privileges or concession had been given and that no conditions were therefore imposed.

Alan Gardiner had telegraphed the Foreign Office on 1 February predicting a crisis and asking the government to intervene. On the 14th he sent another message, 'Crisis apprehended has arisen.' In an exchange of views within the Foreign Office, there was sympathy for Carter: 'He is repeatedly burdened by petty regulations…and is unlikely to make more concessions.' Allenby was told to send a strong protest to Lacau. But there was reluctance to go further. 'Leave well alone,' advised the Senior Under-Secretary Lancelot Oliphant. 'One cannot help feeling that there are two sides to this question,' noted Mr Ingram.

In Paris, the Egyptian Ambassador released a press statement which hardly needed translating:

L'indignation universelle ne peut manquer d'accuellir cette nouvelle fermeture du tombeau due au refus des visites de personnes que Carter, contrairement à l'accord préalable et aux instructions officielles données, voulait injustement priviligier. Paris le 16 février 1924

The 13th had been set aside for a press view – for native

HOWARD CARTER

reporters only since European and American pressmen were subject to the *Times* arrangement – followed by a conducted tour for the wives and families of archaeologists and senior workers. On the morning of that day Carter awoke to a further batch of official communications, including a message from the Ministry of Public Works forbidding him to admit to the tomb of Tutankhamun the wives and families of 'collaborating scientists'. The Minister stated with beautifully rounded arrogance that he had dispatched an additional force of police to the tomb to ensure that his instructions were carried out. The order was subsequently confirmed by Lacau who added, 'Of course, they [the police] must execute this duty with all due courtesy.'

Carter's team, which included Merton of *The Times,* met at Luxor (according to Breasted 'in his hotel bedroom') to decide on a concerted course of action. Carter is said to have paced up and down the room almost bursting with anger, dictating one vitriolic retort after another while Charles Breasted typed furiously in an effort to keep up with Carter's staccato bursts. They had by now been joined by virtually every eminent archaeologist who was in Egypt at the time, along with other American and British scholars. After some twenty statements expressing the group's disdain for the Minister and its sense of outrage at his conduct, Breasted senior suggested that dignity would be better served by a calmer response. Carter finally agreed to sign a notice which was posted on the bulletin board of the Winter Palace Hotel at 12.30 p.m. on 13 February 1924. It read:

Owing to the impossible restrictions and discourtesies on the part of the Public Works Department and its Antiquities Service all my collaborators in protest have refused to work any further upon the scientific investigation of the discovery of the tomb of Tutankhamun.

I am therefore obliged to make known to the public that immediately after the Press View of the tomb this morning between 10 a.m. and noon the tomb will be closed and no further work can be carried out. (Signed) Howard Carter.

After the press view Carter, according to his own account, left the sarcophagus lid suspended as before, and padlocked the tomb.

Merton sent a telegram to his news editor at Carter's instigation. It read simply, 'Compelled to shut down tomb. Rely on you to give widest publicity to world's services and strongly attack Egyptian authorities.' The pages for 12 and 13 February were torn from Carter's diary: whether by him or by some well-meaning person after his death, it cannot be said.

The Times rose to the occasion on 14 February with an editorial which chastised the Department of Antiquities for its 'jealousy and interference'. Next day the newspaper published a letter affirming the reasons for Carter's action and placing the blame squarely on Pierre Lacau's intransigence and his department's bureaucratic policies. It was signed by Breasted, Gardiner, Lythgoe and Newberry. On 18 February renewed anti-British press outbursts were reported from Egypt. By then Carter had gone off to Cairo to set legal machinery in motion.

On 22 February a telegram was sent to Newberry from 10 Downing Street. It read: 'Urge Carter on highest authority to stop legal proceedings. Make amicable arrangement with Egyptian authorities.' Undeterred, on 25 February Carter rushed off with Mace to instruct solicitors. As late as 8 March, Whitehall was trying to induce Lady Carnarvon to intervene with Carter, but she was on her way to South Africa and could not be contacted.

The *Egyptian Gazette's* correspondent wrote: 'A pathetic note was provided by two of Mr Carter's trusted Egyptian foremen faithfully guarding a heap of their master's property, not far from the mouth of the tomb for the discovery of which they had served him with such unflagging fidelity and perseverance.'

Egypt should remember, said Breasted, as if writing a valedictory notice, that Carter's supreme achievement had brought the country greater prestige than it had ever enjoyed in modern times, and hordes of visitors to encourage its prosperity. The American academic who played the honest broker spoke of the 'arrogant, self-conscious, sweepingly victorious nationalists at the moment in unchallenged control of the Egyptian government.'

On the morning of 22 February, Charles Breasted left his father's sick-bed and rode to the tomb where he sat on the wall above the entrance waiting for the police chief and government representatives to arrive. He contemplated the irony of the situation: of actions on both sides which could so easily have been avoided and which now looked like dragging through a legal quagmire the most glorious of all the recovered treasures of antiquity. Just before 2 p.m. the expected official party arrived, led by the handsome, bushy-bearded Lacau who read out like the town-crier a letter from Carter in which he said that he refused to surrender the keys of the tomb. Then locksmiths set to work, sawing through the padlocks of the outer door and of the steel door leading to the antechamber. 'The rape of the locks' took until mid-afternoon. The precarious lid of the sarcophagus had not fallen as feared, but its retaining rope had stretched until the lid with its supporting cradle almost touched the sarcophagus. It was left as it was, hanging dangerously over the shrine it was supposed to protect. The officials replaced Carter's locks with their own and then went to the laboratory tomb of Seti II to repeat the exercise.

Afterwards, the younger Breasted rode over to Carter's home at Qurna. 'He looked disconsolate and worn,' he said, 'but was quite calm and evinced no rancour'. As Breasted left, Carter thanked him and asked him to tell his father that he, Carter, had decided to go to Cairo to fight the government decision in the Mixed Tribunals before which such complex cases of civil law were tried. He intended to fight on 'until they appoint me sequestrator of the tomb!'

Chapter 13

MACE'S STORY

Events of the 1923 - 4 season which led to the rupture of the always uneasy relationship between Carter and the Egyptian government have been subject to many interpretations, none of them flattering to Carter. The disappearance of vital pages from his diary helps to muddy the waters. Fortunately, however, there was another witness to those events who kept a detailed diary.

Arthur Mace was Carter's constant companion, his literary collaborator and close confidant, and his family tie with the redoubtable Flinders Petrie gave him an indirect but useful authority in the archaeological world. He was, in any event, a man of demonstrable independence of mind who would not allow loyalty to cloud his judgement, as his diary and particularly his letters to his family showed. A keen and humane wit illuminates these letters and sometimes shows through the factual diary record of the day-to-day work in the laboratory tomb. In February 1923, for example, he tenderly examined a child's garment which bore the king's cartouche and wondered, in a letter to his wife Winifred, if it was possible that Tutankhamun was a mere infant when he came to the throne. When the Queen of the Belgians visited them, he wrote that she travelled 'so incognito that she was recognized at once'. And of Carnarvon's death he wrote, 'I've seen a lot of him this winter of course and I had got quite fond of him. He was a queer person, but very likeable.' It is useful to re-examine the crucial month of February 1924 in the light of Mace's testimony.

The diary entry for 12 February, the day of the visit of the

231

Egyptian VIPs to see the raising of the sarcophagus lid, told of the arrival in the morning of the Under-Secretary at the Ministry of Works, Muhammad Zaghlul, and a 'panting' Lacau, and of the subsequent dispute about guests at the press show on the following day. A list of twenty visitors was agreed provisionally after 'some argument', to include the wives and families of Carter's senior assistants who were referred to as 'the scientists'. But Zaghlul said that he would have to telegraph his chiefs in Cairo for final assent. It was decided that Lucas the chemist was an official of the government and not of Carter's team and would therefore be placed on the official invitation list.

The VIP party assembled at 3 p.m. and was led into the tomb. Mace noticed that two Egyptians, one of them a junior police officer, had infiltrated the official group. Planks had been arranged for the visitors to stand on in the antechamber, so that they could look down into the sepulchral chamber. The Egyptian ministers fought for the front plank, but the successful combatants allowed Breasted to join them. The American was thus the only outsider to have a clear view, though after a while Lacau insisted that one of the Egyptian inspectors from his department should give way to Gardiner. The dispositions of Carter's team were set out by the immaculate Mace: three workmen to the east of the sarcophagus; Callender and a fourth workman to the west; Burton with his movie camera on the steps leading down; Mace himself on the north side of the sarcophagus, taking the 'official' note of proceedings; Carter directing. Then the process of rolling back the shroud was described, the breathless pause while Harry Burton tried out his movie camera, the gasp as the head of the coffin was exposed. The 'perfectly magnificent' funerary mask, the 'face of solid gold' as The Times called it, with its double uraeus of cobra and vulture representing the kingdoms of Upper and Lower Egypt. At long, long last, the young king lay before them, hands crossed upon the chest. Mace's words supplemented Breasted's, though he found it hard to write with proper detachment at that moment. As soon as the record of the sighting of the coffin had been made, however, Mace observed that the 'unauthorized' policeman who appeared in the tomb at the last moment handed to Valentine Williams of Reuters 'a full account of the whole proceedings'.

On the 13th, Mace went over the ground of the ministerial note and the indignant response of Carter and his assistants who had gathered at the former's Valley house. 'We felt that we must refuse to carry on any further work, as this was not only an insult to us, but a clear sign that the government were going to carry the policy of interference to even further lengths,' he recorded.

Carter, Lythgoe and Mace boarded Carter's Model T Ford (chauffeur-driven, since Carter never learnt to drive) and made for Luxor where Breasted, Gardiner and Newberry were gathered at the Winter Palace Hotel. On the river-bank, as they approached the hotel, they were intercepted by the Mamur (the chief of police) and one of his officers. It was then that the Mamur handed over the Ordre de Service signed by Lacau, forbidding the visit of the wives that afternoon. The critical part of the message read: 'His Excellency the Under-Secretary of State has just passed to me the order to forbid until further notice, entry to the tomb to all ladies who have not received ministerial authorization as journalists.' Three officers, Muhammad Effendi Shaaban, Antun Effendi Yusef and Ibrahim Effendi Habib, were detailed to prevent the entry of the said ladies, 'with all desirable courtesy'.

There followed a characteristic episode in which the police chief, anxious not to be late for another appointment, asked Carter if his driver could give him a lift. Carter replied that he would gladly help him 'as a friend' but that 'if he was taking anyone with him he could not lend it'. The Mamur hesitated, clearly wanting to take his officer along. Carter promptly told his driver to return home, and proceeded with his companions to the Winter Palace, where the notice was drawn up announcing the closure of the tomb. Before posting it on the notice-board, however, Carter and Mace went over to the river boat on which the Under-Secretary was staying, hoping even at the last moment to reach some kind of agreement. The minister was not aboard. They returned to the hotel and Carter posted the notice. As he did so, Rex Engelbach appeared, the Englishman in Lacau's department whom Carter liked and despised at intervals. He invited Carter to lunch and professed 'utmost sympathy', advising his fellow countryman to send a telegram to the Prime Minister, Saad Zaghlul Pasha. Having despatched the suggested telegram, Carter again called on the Under-Secretary, Muhammad Zaghlul. This time the junior minister was at home on his river boat and Carter told him officially that he had closed the tomb and proposed 'to take steps'. The minister, in Mace's words, 'seemed to think the whole thing was a joke'. Carter then returned with Mace to the hotel, calling on the Metropolitan's Harkness and Lythgoe on the way. Merton was waiting for Carter when the latter finally arrived at the Winter Palace, and the letter to *The Times* was composed in the names of the 'collaborators'. Merton telegraphed the letter that evening, the 13th. It was published two days later.

Mace's long diary entry for 13 February ended with an essay on the strange affair of the Mamur and his efforts to leave the tomb after Carter had refused him a lift. He appears to have commandeered a cab belonging to tourists, leaving the unfortunate sightseers stranded, and made for the nearby excavation site of Sir Robert Mond, the wealthy benefactor of the Egypt Exploration Society. After much toing and froing, the unfortunate police chief was stranded without transport at the locked and bolted tomb of Tutankhamun. He was forced to make his way back to Luxor by donkey. It was a fitting end to the day.

Next day, the 14th, was one of stock-taking on both sides. Mace called on Carter at 'the house' and discovered that a telegram had arrived from the Prime Minister, expressing complete approval of the actions of his ministers. Carter's *rais,* Ahmad Gurgar, had brought back news of a police reinforcement at the tomb, and a complaint that he was interfered with while attempting to sweep the entrance steps. Carter conveyed the latest news to Harkness and Lythgoe who received him aboard their houseboat.

On the 15th Carter went to the tomb to put his foreman's fears to the test. He was met by the Mamur who was armed with an order from Lacau stating that no one, Carter included, must be allowed into the tomb. On the 16th a wire arrived from Alexandria to say that Maxwell was on his way to Luxor. The French press in Cairo headlined a story that Carter's many crimes included bribery and the taking of commissions on tourist bookings at the Cairo and Luxor hotels. A disconsolate Carter spent most of the day with Mace, Breasted and Newberry. Maxwell arrived on the 17th. He went with Carter to the tomb and they were refused admittance.

On returning to Luxor, Carter sent a cable to Morcos Bey, the Minister of Public Works, at Maxwell's instigation, demanding entry and permission to carry out necessary maintenance work. 'If the government refused this his idea was to immediately issue a writ. In any case he stated that Carter should refuse under any circumstances to deliver up keys.' The next day a conciliatory message arrived from the Minister rescinding his earlier order and giving Carter permission to enter the tomb 'if he would prepare for visits'. Carter refused the offer 'unless an apology was forthcoming, and an assurance of no more interference'. On the 20th, Allenby arrived at Luxor to speak to Carter. News had come through on the previous day by way of Engelbach that all further visits to the tomb were 'indefinitely postponed'.

Mace was delegated to prepare a 'statement of case' and worked on his brief throughout the 21st, the day on which the Council of Ministers made an order confiscating the tomb and announcing that it would shortly be reopened by the government. Maxwell made an equally fateful decision. Acting on behalf of Lady Carnarvon, he instructed lawyers to issue writs against the Egyptian government.

There was still time to draw back from the brink, and Lacau at least seemed to be having last-minute thoughts of compromise. On the morning of the 22nd a telegram arrived from the Frenchman, asking Carter and his collaborators to meet him at the tomb at 2 p.m., when he proposed to open up. Later, a similar pressing letter arrived in the same hand. Carter was adamant in his reply. He failed to see why 'the tomb should be forced today', especially 'considering that the question of sequestratorship was to come up in the courts tomorrow, and the question of safeguarding the objects was not urgent.' At 1.45 p.m. a motor car drew up at Carter's home and a policeman emerged with a note from Lacau demanding the keys to the tomb. If the keys were not forthcoming, the policeman would be ordered to break down the entrance gates of the tomb. Carter returned the note with one of his own, refusing the keys and making another 'formal protest'.

There followed Mace's report of the 'rape of the locks', based on the eye-witness account of Ahmad Gurgar. With Lacau, Engelbach and another member of the Antiquities Department, Baraize, were the Mudir and Mamur, the commandant of police for the entire district, a member of the Department of Justice, a mechanic and assistants, thirty-three soldiers and policeman, camel corps, cavalry and infantry. After the locks had been sawn and filed, the tomb was entered by Lacau's official who were inside for about an hour. When they emerged, new government locks were fitted. The party then fitted new locks at the laboratory tomb of Seti II. Mace's last entry for the season was baffling. 'Telegram from Maxwell to say Court adjourned until 3.30.'

An affidavit was served on Lacau and the Antiquities Department – in effect on the government of Egypt – on 24 February 1924.

The pages of Carter's diary for this critical period had more the appearance of a mathematical exercise than a record of his movements. Nevertheless, there were useful notes between the statistics of payments to the work-force and receipts for artefacts sold to collectors and services rendered. He left for Cairo with Mace on Monday 25 February. Maxwell came down from his Alexandrian resort on the 29th. 'Meeting with Minister fixed for today,' said the entry of Saturday 1 March.

By effectively locking out Carter and the official excavators the government had put itself in an untenable position. The Antiquities Department was entirely dependent on Carter. No one else could take over the task of excavating the tomb at that late stage. As far as the legal position went, counsel explained that once the tomb had been discovered, Carnarvon's concession agreement became a contract which brought into play the standard clause 10 in all such agreements by which, in the case of tombs 'which have already been searched', the Antiquities Department ensured that the major share of finds accrued to Egypt while the foreign experts who were encouraged to carry out the work were entitled to the permittee's share which would 'sufficiently recompense…for the pains and labour of the undertaking'. In the case of tombs which were discovered intact, that is to say where there was no evidence of break-in even in antiquity, the entire contents would be the property of Egypt. Carnarvon had always held that there was indisputable evidence of the violation of the tomb of Tutankhamun and that clause 10 was therefore applicable. To complicate the matter, however, Carter's discovery was unique. There had been nothing like it in the history of Egyptian exploration.

According to James Breasted, Carter completely lost control of himself as the court proceedings ensued, and appeared 'so overcome by his misfortunes as to be incapable of major decisions'. The oriental, as the *Saturday Review* put it, had called his bluff. 'Mr Carter', said the same editorial, 'has fallen into what looks like a carefully laid trap.' To confound an already confused situation, thousands of tourists who had paid to see the body of Tutankhamun were milling round the Valley demanding that the tomb be reopened and the archaeologists told to 'Get on with it.' Carter's solicitor had appointed, as counsel for the Carnarvon estate, the English barrister F.M. Maxwell who less than three years earlier had prosecuted the present Minister of Public Works, Morcos Bey, and demanded the death sentence on him and his associates. It could not be described as an adroit choice.

Breasted wanted to withdraw from the affair but realized that only he could now achieve a settlement that was in the best interests of Egyptology. Acting as arbiter between the government and Carter he drew up conditions under which he hoped Carter would be permitted to return to the tomb. He succeeded in persuading the lawyers on both sides to agree to a postponement of the trial while the terms were being considered. The government accepted the proposals subject to the drawing up of a new agreement with Almina, Countess of Carnarvon, which would of course involve the contractual renunciation by the Carnarvon estate of any rights in the contents of the tomb. Carter refused the compromise. Though he had never himself claimed a share of the proceeds, as had Carnarvon, he was, in Breasted's words, 'overweeningly confident of a complete victory.'

Carter ignored Breasted's and his counsel's advice and, on his own initiative, withheld consent to a further postponement of the trial. 'He lost all control of himself and became very high-handed,' said Breasted, the man who had been a father figure to Carter from the outset of the excavation. On 4 March he gave Breasted a note addressed to the Egyptian Prime Minister stating his position in the most uncompromising terms. Carter's diary entry for 5 March observed that he met Breasted in the morning but refused an adjournment of the case due to begin on Saturday as he had received 'only promise and nothing definite – not even a letter'. He added: 'Breasted had in his pocket the letter I gave him yesterday for the P.M.'

The government was conciliatory and adamant by turn. So was Carter. Just before the case came to trial, the Prime Minister Zaghlul Pasha pre-empted Carter's claim that his inability to return to the tomb was putting the safety of the objects in jeopardy by announcing a 'gala' reopening with a hundred important guests on 6 March. Allenby and his wife were among the visitors, and they were greeted by the largest crowd ever seen at Luxor when their special train pulled in. Zaghlul was officially indisposed and unable to attend what was, in effect, a mass anti-British rally, designed to capture the headlines of every newspaper in the world that had it in for Carter; all that is except *The Times*. Carter was seen as the evil genius at the centre of a plot designed to deprive Egypt of its heritage. The lid of the sarcophagus which he had left precariously suspended was removed by Lacau's men and placed against the wall. The celebration banquet held afterwards lasted until dawn but by then Allenby was on his way back to Cairo to join the rest of the cast at the trial. Attempts were still being made to achieve a friendly settlement. *The Times* played down the anti-Carter crusade, reporting friendly negotiations on 3 March.

The case, The Estate of the 5th Earl of Carnarvon v. The Government of Egypt, began on 8 March 1924 with exchanges so furious and insolent on both sides that the court room came close to chaos. The timing of the event was unpropitious. The administration of Prime Minister Ibrahim Yahia Pasha had lost all credibility by the end of the year 1923, and much of the uncertainty which centred on the 'affair of the tomb', as it was called by the Egyptian press, in fact resulted from a battle between the new monarch, Fuad, and a tired and disillusioned premier.

Zaghlul, the massively popular nationalist leader who was released by Allenby from his exile in Gibraltar in March 1923, was elected to power by an overwhelming majority in January 1924. Now he prepared to visit London to discuss with Prime Minister Ramsay MacDonald the Sudan question and, quite possibly, though the matter was not on the official agenda, the question of Mr Howard Carter. March 15th, exactly a week after the opening of the trial, was the appointed day of the opening of Egypt's first constitutional parliament, and well before the great day arrived Egyptians of every class and persuasion were united in a frenzy of national joy. Zaghlul, the man who had challenged British rule, suffered exile, and won the day, was the hero of the hour. Britain, not so much in the shape of its High Commissioner in his splendid Field Marshal's attire, but of the unspeakable Carter, the Englishman who more than anyone had tried to rob the country of its legitimate inheritance, was in the dock. Even as the celebrations were being planned, a demonstration was arranged for the same day to protest against continued British rule in the Sudan.

Under the legal arrangements established by the British 'Protectorate' and still in force pending the laws to be promulgated by the new regime, a case concerning foreigners had to be tried by a mixed panel of Egyptian and expatriate judges, with a foreign referee and principal judge. Thus, the term 'Mixed Tribunals' was employed. The referee in this case was the American, Pierre Crabites, and, after a few days of heated argument, the two sides decided that Professor Breasted should act as mediator. The Egyptian press denounced the plaintiffs. The rest of the world press was far from sympathetic to Carter. The *Times* agreement had come home to roost.

Carter's case was recorded in the notes which Mace had hurriedly produced on 21 February, and which Carter subsequently used for publication in pamphlet form, though it never saw the light of day until Hoving used the document in his subsequent denunciation. The notes were made at the time of the 'wives' dispute and the government's accusation that Carter had deliberately left the tomb in a condition which endangered the contents; but they were particularly revealing of his state of mind at this time. He claimed that the closing of the tomb was 'a temporary measure' in protest against government 'insult'; that he had fully expected an apology so that his team could resume their programme; that his primary aim was to safeguard the objects in the tomb, an aim which the government was actively preventing him from carrying out; that the notice posted in the hotel was hurriedly drawn up and did not take account of 'all the relevant points'. He was backtracking even before he launched into ill-advised litigation.

On 11 March, Breasted met representatives of the Antiquities Department, and he believed complete agreement had been reached. In court, the government counsel announced amid the hubbub that his clients had accepted Professor Breasted's conditions, set out in his role as mediator. Carter agreed at last that his action should be withdrawn. Before the agreement could be signed, however, a complicated legal argument developed in the course of Judge Crabites' summing up. How was it, he asked, that Mr Howard Carter had relinquished the tomb *before* he had issued writs against the government? Could the court give back what Carter had voluntarily given up? Mr Maxwell, counsel for the Carnarvon estate, was indignant. He insisted that Carter was still in legal possession of the tomb when the writs were issued but the Egyptian authorities had come on the scene 'like a bandit'. There was stunned silence in the court room. Counsel for the Ministry, Maître Rosetti, protested vehemently. Judge Crabites thought the expression unnecessary. Maxwell stood his ground. The government promptly broke off negotiations. Breasted handed his resignation as mediator to Sir John Maxwell and Carter, the joint litigants, who declined to accept it. Few Egyptians were seriously concerned with the fate of the tomb or its royal occupant. Pre-Islamic history was not a significant ingredient of Egyptian thinking or learning. But the 'affair of the tomb' was enough to send crowds on to the streets in an orgy of anti-British rioting.

Breasted agreed to continue to mediate on condition that he be allowed to write a note to Morcos Bey dissociating himself completely from the use of the word 'bandit' and expressing his profound regret that such language had 'justifiably' terminated his negotiations. Sir John Maxwell and Carter approved and accompanied Breasted to the Minister's home. Morcos Bey was touched, but flatly refused to consider handing back the tomb to Carter. Instead, he urged Breasted to take over the concession and the direction of future excavations. He also offered the American any other concession in Egypt he liked to name. The offer was 'unthinkable', said Breasted. Further mediation was impossible. The court proceedings ended in stalemate. The Carnarvon estate dropped its action. The Ministry of Public Works refused to acknowledge a letter from Sir John Maxwell confirming that there was no claim against any of the objects in the tomb, though perversely the Ministry claimed that the communication amounted to a tacit admission that the estate had had a claim.

Carter saw Judge Crabites twice during Thursday 20 March, hoping, even at that late hour, to salvage something from his action. He also had a meeting with Maxwell in the afternoon. Next day he said his farewells to his American colleagues after breakfast at the Grand Continental. He went by the 9.15 train to 'Alex', where he boarded the *ss Vienna,* bound for Venice, his life's work in ruins, his future as uncertain as it had ever been.

Chapter 14

THE AMERICAN EXPERIENCE

CARTER arrived in England at the end of March 1924, a disillusioned and angry man, saddened that he had not been allowed to reach the superlative peak of his endeavour. The mummified body of Tutankhamun remained tantalizingly at the heart of the partly dismantled shrine, concealed in its anthropoid coffin as it had been for 3,300 years beneath a huge protective slate weighing one and quarter tons. The demise of Egypt's imperial age and most fascinating dynasty, even the king's lineage, remained wrapped in obscurity.

With the habitual optimism of a man who had always had to call on his own inner resources where others could turn to influential families and friends, he believed that he would achieve his objective in the end. He was convinced that the day would come when Egypt would admit its mistake and ask him to return. And when he was able to throw off the despondent feeling of rejection by Egypt and desertion by his fellow archaeologists, he basked unashamedly in the still-warm glow of fame and recognition. The resilience which had seen him through many a past crisis soon came to his rescue.

From the moment of the opening of the tomb there had been talk of a lecture tour of the United States and a visit to the museum in New York whose expert staff had given him such valuable professional assistance and loyal support through recent tribulations. Even so, some of his American colleagues had doubts. Soon after he had begun his literary collaboration with Carter in April 1923, Mace told a family friend, 'The question of lectures is going to be a rather serious one. I don't think Carter has ever given one in his life, and he doesn't in the least know how to set about it. Mace's reservations proved ill founded when Carter's first lecture in Edinburgh was such a success, and arrangements, discussed with Charles Breasted and other American colleagues in London in the summer of 1923, had given rise to a direct approach from the renowned agency of Lee Keedick during the chaotic last months in Egypt. He was booked to leave Southampton aboard the *ss Berengaria* on Saturday 12 April, within three weeks of arriving home from Egypt.

Edward Robinson was in London to greet him. Harkness was on his way from the United States. The American press was full of predictions – assurances even – that, following Carter's dismissal, the New York museum would be asked to take over responsibility for the clearance of the tomb. Robinson had denied such rumours, but he was anxious to keep abreast of every development. And there were other matters of pressing concern to the museum, such as the disposal of treasures promised by Carnarvon before his death and now in Almina's care.

Carter's first social engagement on arrival was with Eve at the Carnarvon's London home in Seamore Place. After a pleasant lunch for two, they spent the afternoon together before he went off later the same day (27 March) to Burlington House where he had been invited to meet a group of Fellows of the Royal Society. There were brief calls on brother William in Fulham between visits to his solicitors Messrs Hastie in the West End and Lincoln's Inn Fields, Harkness (who turned up with Lythgoe) at Claridges, and Porchester and Bethell at Seamore Place. On Saturday 5 April he joined Porchester's party, which included Eve and her husband Brograve, at the Boat Race. Meanwhile, Kenyon, the Director of the British Museum, wanted to hear about the Egyptian débâcle, as did his counterpart Harcourt Smith at the Victoria and Albert.

By the end of his second week in London, two members of the board of the Metropolitan were in town along with several senior members of the Egypt Department. There was no shortage of lunch and dinner invitations. He hired a chauffeur-driven Daimler for the last hectic days, and squeezed in a hasty evening visit to Walker's art gallery in New Bond Street where Charles Whymper's colour drawings of the Valley of the Kings, reproduced in the *Illustrated London News,* were attracting a good deal of attention. There was time, too, for dinner at the Savile with Percy White, and much talk of old times in Cairo, before packing his bags. He had hardly paused for breath since arriving in London. Yet, even in that brief interval, when the fate of the tomb still hung in the balance, he found time for yet more litigation.

The society into which fame and Carnarvon's patronage had launched him received him with courtesy, but not as one of its own. The bitterness with which he left Egypt was not assuaged by the knowledge that even *The Times,* which until recently had trumpeted his name, had already dropped him except for polite reporting of his comings and goings. Only Bruce Ingram's *Illustrated London News* retained the keen interest of old. His action in closing the tomb was not considered by his fellow countrymen to be altogether 'playing the game'. In any case, he was not and never would be a man to appeal to English middle-class society. He was too arrogant, too sure of his own convictions and abilities, too dismissive of others. He despised rather than resented the privileges and the advantages so often granted to people of little worth or ability. Even the closest of his archaeological colleagues such as Griffith and Newberry were uncomfortable with him.

By now, however, Tutankhamun and the extravagant wonders of his tomb had achieved a renown which was independent of the excavators. Press and public alike showed an insatiable appetite for the romance associated with the young king whose gilded and bejewelled accoutrements had startled the world in the past twelve months. Indeed, London, like Paris, Berlin, New York and the other great cities of the world, was awash with fashion and architectural themes which stated and recapitulated the current mania. The new Duchess of York was not the only bride of the day who went off on her honeymoon with a garment embroidered and printed with Egyptian themes in her trousseau. Such enthusiasm could have been harnessed to Carter's own advantage. Instead, he once more turned good fortune and hard work to his discredit.

The year 1924 was marked, above all, by the British Empire Exhibition at Wembley, representing the release of a national head of steam after the privations of the post-war period. The discovery of the tomb of Tutankhamun by Carnarvon and Carter was the most glamorous of all the modern achievements of the Empire, represented in an exhibition which was bedevilled from the outset by strikes and working disputes. Carter made it the occasion for another ill-advised and peremptory legal move, this time against Wembley Amusements Limited who had had the temerity to create, in the midst of England's premier sporting arena, a replica of the chambers of the tomb so far revealed. Reproductions of furniture and artefacts such as had graced the pages of the international press had been carved and cast by a well-known sculptor, Aumonier.

On 22 April, the *Daily Express* carried the headline, 'Carter's Wembley Bombshell – Attempts to close the Pharaoh's tomb'. In its report, the paper said that the organizers were 'astonished to receive a writ from Mr Howard Carter', who 'objects to the wood and plaster replica of the tomb in the amusement park...on the grounds that it violates certain copyrights held by him'. The tomb was said to be 'very like the real thing, filled with gilded tomb furniture, made of wood and plaster by Mr Aumonier'. On the same day Carter's solicitor, Hastie, wrote to Wembley Amusements, insisting that the model was made from Carter's 'plates and letterpress', that it was 'a legal fact' that he, Carter, had 'the right to control the situation', and that 'given permission of these points', Carter was willing to help in the presentation of a model which would be 'a real and worthy representation'.

On 23 April, the *Express* quoted Mr Molony, a partner in Hastie's: 'Mr Howard Carter's object in issuing a writ in connection with the model of Tutankhamun's tomb at Wembley is to make it clear to the public that he accepts no responsibility for the exhibits, and reserves his rights to the record of the work.' On the same date, Hastie's complained to Geoffrey Dawson, editor of *The Times,* about the 'mutilated report' of the firm's statement in the *Daily Express.* Dawson 'regretted' that he could not publish the solicitor's letter.

Carter assumed that the artist had used his copyright photographs to make the models, and instructed his solicitor to seek an injunction to have 'withdrawn from public gaze' any work which infringed that copyright. The case would be resolved while he was away, but its very conception showed Carter's lack of adroitness. Aumonier was able to show that he had used sources other than Carter's photographs as his references and the case was dismissed out of hand. But even before it arrived at court, Carter was once again punching the air, dissipating his hard-won savings and immense energy in angry, unprofitable dispute.

He was happy to see England's coastline fade along with the memory of recent events as the *Berengaria* made its way out of Southampton Water and the Isle of Wight gleamed in the sunshine of an early spring morning.

It was all very different in America. He landed at New York on Good Friday, 18 April, and moved into the Waldorf-Astoria. From the moment of arrival he was greeted as a celebrity. For the time being, he was the most famous man in the world. His lecture tour was booked to the limit in the USA and Canada, tickets were sold out even before he arrived, and every hostess from Boston to Baltimore sought him out as a party guest. His lectures were so oversubscribed in fact that he usually had to give repeat performances on successive days. Within three days of his arrival he gave two lectures at the Metropolitan Museum.

The first public talk was booked for the Carnegie Hall on the afternoon of 23 April. Tickets sold for as much as $5 each, an enormous price at the time, and the hall could have been filled twice over. In the event, about 3,000 people were allowed

in. The lecture was illustrated with some 350 slides made from
Burton's photographs, showing in detail the many works of art
already rescued from the tomb and flashed on to a screen with
great rapidity so that the audience was kept in a state of constant
wonder while Carter paced the stage with the assurance of
a well-rehearsed actor. He related the story of his earlier
disappointments, the moment of discovery in November 1922,
the painstaking opening up of the tomb and the magnificence
of the finds as he and Lord Carnarvon and American colleagues
searched chamber after chamber. There was none of the rancour
which some of his colleagues and acquaintances had expected.
There were no indiscretions. He spoke easily and with wit. The
voice had become more 'middle-English'. Only a Higgins in
the audience would have noted the occasional broad vowel
betraying the vernacular East Anglian accent with which he
had grown up. For the most part, a new confidence of manner
was accompanied by a voice of splendid volume and somewhat
forced enunciation which owed something to Carnarvon's
pervasive influence.

The New York *Tribune* was unkind about his correct Arabic
as well as his 'Oxford' English, making great play in its report
of the lecture of 'the *Sahawra*' (desert), and the way in which
he 'ashuahed' the audience about this and that on 'behawf' of
his colleagues. Americans had been fed so thoroughly with
reports and quotations from Metropolitan Museum staff that
they thought Carter was one of them until they heard his
voice. The *Tribune* commented that whoever it was who said
Carter was American should be 'captured, stuffed and placed in
a glass case and labeled the most inaccurate of human
observers'.

The critical essays of American reporters did nothing to
rob the public of its entertainment. They were entranced. The
lectures were covered by journalists from all over the world as
Carter made his way from state to state and coast to coast.
As he took them through the exploration of the tomb, in
Chicago and Washington and Detroit and all the main cities,

his audiences shared his humour and his tears. There was a Chaplinesque quality about his performance and it may be that his own admiration of the little clown who dominated the cinema of the day was cunningly deployed. There was a brief piece of cine film taken by Burton which showed Carter dressed in a suit and homburg hat. He carried a cane and walked stiffly along a path leading to the Valley of the Kings. As he passed the camera he turned to Burton, bowed, turned abruptly away and kicked his heels. It was a gesture of sheer joy which conveyed itself instantly to the audience. Demonstrating how mummified creatures were stored in the white ovoid boxes found in the tomb, he explained that it was just like the way Americans canned their food. A cane, carved with the figure of a captive with black headgear, was likened to Chaplin, 'even down to the little bowler he's wearing'. When he came to the moment of lifting the sarcophagus lid he spoke with hushed voice of the tears which came into his eyes at that most joyful moment of his life. The agent Lee Keedick had assessed both his man and the potential appeal of the tour well. He sold Carter for £1,000 a lecture, and almost everyone along the way made a profit.

'American Natural History Museum 3 p.m. Breasted 5.15 p.m. Trustee dinner of Met Mus. University Club 8.30 p.m.': so ran the diary for the 24th. It was at the University Club that the Metropolitan Museum honoured him with a dinner given by the board of trustees at which he was made an honorary life member of the Museum. In reply to the presentation made by the president, Carter spoke simply and well. The words seemed to come to him easily and with obvious sincerity: 'I beg to thank the Board on making me a life member of this noble institution. It is an honour of which I shall ever be deeply proud. My long association in Egypt with the members of their expedition has been for years a pleasant link between us, and, in that, my election adds an everlasting and much desired bond.'

A weekend visit to the Harkness home on Long Island was followed in the last week of April by two more appearances at

Carnegie Hall and two at the Brooklyn Academy of Music. On Thursday 1 May he went to Philadelphia for two days to give afternoon talks at the Academy of Music there. Back in New York he was able to indulge his favourite pastime, bringing his accounts up to date in his diary with a pyrotechnic display of arithmetic. In the first fortnight of his tour he had made more than £10,000, an enormous sum in those days. Press and public hung on his every word. He was the most popular European performer since Oscar Wilde, and vastly better rewarded.

On 5 May he went up to New Haven to lecture that evening. He left New York for Washington next day, travelling by way of Baltimore where he was due to deliver a talk on the 7th. On the first day in the capital (Thursday 8th) the Egyptian Ambassador, Yussri Pasha, called and after an exchange of salaams Carter went on to lunch with the laconic occupant of the White House, President Coolidge. Then came the mandatory call on Esme Howard, the British Ambassador. Coolidge asked him to return on Friday 9th to give him a private illustrated talk on the excavation of the tomb and the history of the Eighteenth Dynasty. A small select gathering awaited him in the east room of the presidential home. Carter was astonished and flattered by the President's familiarity with his work in Egypt and with the contents of the tomb. But there was a certain bravado about his confident manner at this time. As he travelled the length and breadth of that vast country he was worried by news which came from Egypt and he began to exhibit some of his less attractive traits.

The applause of crowded gatherings at Washington's National Theatre rang in his ears as he made for Boston on the evening of Saturday 10 May, glowing in the incandescent warmth of presidential and public esteem, savouring for the first time in his life the sweet aroma of unqualified approval. It was not in Carter's nature, however, to permit so uncomplicated a state of affairs to persist for long.

The actor Douglas Fairbanks waited with his son to present his compliments at the Museum of Arts in New York; back in

Boston, he met John Singer Sargent who had returned home to die. He went on to Pittsburg, Chicago, Cincinnati, Detroit, Cleveland. The Rockefellers and Henry Ford waited on him, as did Breasted, in Chicago.

Lee Keedick was at the Englishman's side for most of the tour. His notes, made at the time of the events in question, were handed to Thomas Hoving more than fifty years later by his son Robert. Hoving's subsequent portrait is plausible. It illuminates the undeniably dark and obdurate side of Carter's make-up. Keedick observed Carter's penchant for argument and conflict. Not even small children were exempt from his abuse. Everyone he met on his tour, from cab drivers to hotel porters, came in for criticism and invective. He told train drivers how they should control their engines, chefs how to cook, porters and doormen how to behave. It was conduct which swung dramatically from the whimsical to the absurd.

At the beginning of June he went north to Canada with an embarrassed Keedick at his side. Buffalo and Toronto, the first ports of call, produced the same ecstatic response as had followed him through the United States. In Montreal he gave three talks and lunched at the end of the second week of the Canadian tour with Lord Byng, the Governor-General. On the journey from Montreal to Ottawa the railway dining-car offered a comprehensive menu with one of those polite notes which invite customer observations. According to Keedick, he took out a pen and wrote juvenile protestations all over it, with ridiculous comments on the training and abilities of the dining-car staff. When the train pulled in he mailed it to the superintendent of the rail service.

It is unlikely that Lee Keedick, a man of some maturity and good sense, would have invented or exaggerated such stories. It was in his interest that Carter should be seen in a favourable light. His notes merely underline some of the undeniable and distinctly unattractive traits in Carter's character. In Egypt he was often provoked by people who were themselves arrogant, haughty and unprofessional. In America he was among friends and unstinting admirers but even so he could not resist the temptation to muddy the waters in which he himself must swim. Perversely, his bumptiousness in small, unimportant matters went side by side with extreme modesty which the American press found almost beyond understanding. Never, they noted, did he boast of his remarkable achievement. Never did he fail to give credit, sometimes of the most exaggerated kind, to his assistants. Yet, in the States and Canada and elsewhere, he would have advanced his own cause no end had he sometimes stopped to consider the import of his words, and allowed discretion to temper his observations.

In June it was arranged that Yale University would confer an honorary doctorate on him. On the 17th he went to New Haven where he stayed with Professor Williams, the Vice-Chancellor, to prepare for the following day's ceremony, the first and last academic honour that he would receive. He took it gratefully and with the dry diary comment of the 18th: 'Received degree.'

As the tour came to its triumphant conclusion events in Egypt were reaching a new and unexpected crisis. The self-effacing Carter whom the American public had to come to know and adore was about to find new ways of exercising his talent for making enemies and alienating friends.

While Carter was in America, Herbert Winlock had kept a watching brief in Egypt, looking after the interests of the Metropolitan Museum and, incidentally, those of Carter and the Carnarvon estate. The two men had been in regular communication by post. In May, Winlock wrote to say that he had been engaged in discussions with Mr Maxwell, the attorney for the estate, and his namesake Sir John Maxwell. A new lawyer, Georges Merzbach, appointed by Carter's solicitors to represent him and the estate, had also been engaged in the talks. Merzbach's advice was that, if the estate and Carter were ever to be allowed to resume the exploration and clearing of the tomb, they should confirm the promise of renunciation which they had made and withdrawn during the Cairo negotiations of the previous year. Merzbach convinced Winlock, who had been among Carter's most fervent supporters, that the demands of the Egyptian government were not unreasonable and that a conciliatory attitude was now essential. Sir John Maxwell disagreed. The barrister Maxwell had sent him a précis of a new contract proposed by the Egyptians. Both Maxwells thought it 'childish'. It was agreed that Sir John would advise his lawyers in London to withdraw formally the estate's letter of renunciation. He decided that the only course open to the British side was to fight the Egyptians, who had treated them as if they had 'done something wrong' and wanted to get 'everything for nothing'. Their tactic was to bring pressure on Pierre Lacau and they had chosen a good moment since the Director of the Antiquities Department had fallen out with his Minster Morcos Bey Hanna and was said now to be sympathetic to the Carter cause.

Lacau's alleged conversion went back to the events of the previous year when Carter, locked out by the Egyptians, took the first available ship to England. While he was in London he received a telegram in pre-arranged code from Winlock which told of a mighty storm brewing in Cairo. The decoded message told of Lacau's men returning on 30 March 1923 to the so-called 'lunch tomb', the empty cavern which Carter and his men had used as a canteen and storehouse, and finding at the rear an unlabelled sculpture of a head of a child represented as the Aten, the sun-disk, carefully protected in an empty wine box bearing the name Fortnum & Mason. It was the head of Tutankhamun at about nine years of age and was said to be the most beautiful work so far discovered, with its pedestal decorated with blue lotus petals and the head emerging from the flower itself. Rex Engelbach described it as a 'superior object of the Akhenaten type', the *pièce capitale*. It was assumed by all concerned that as it was unrecorded in the tomb index and unlabelled Carter must have secreted it away from the other stored objects with the intention of taking it eventually for himself or Lady Carnarvon. Carter replied to Winlock openly by telegraph and followed up with a letter which explained that not all objects had yet been entered in the index although they had all been given 'group numbers'. The piece referred to had been found in the debris of the entrance passage early on in the excavation and had been stored, with other early objects, in the empty tomb (number 4 in Carter's numbering system), where Lacau's men found it. It was only after the opening of the antechamber that he had been given permission to use tomb 15 as his storeroom, to which all subsequent finds were removed. The object in question had been in a very perished state and he and Callender had gone to great lengths to find its flaked decoration among the debris and had packed it away carefully to await attention at a later date.

By this time Carter had published with Cassell of London the first volume of the account which he and Mace had written of the discovery of the tomb and had not mentioned that particular object, which Carter conceded was the most important found in the first stage of clearing work. That could be explained by the fact that it was in need of special attention, and had not been photographed or indexed. In any event, the explanation pleased Lacau. The Frenchman's patience in dealing with the Egyptian and English hotheads around him had been put to a severe test and he had no wish to prolong the dispute.

By June 1924, the Americans had almost given up hope of finishing the work in the Valley to which they, as much as Carter, had become committed. Winlock returned to America to deal with Carter at first hand. Before he left Cairo, Lacau told him that the Minister, Morcos Bey, had reduced his demands. Carter must apologize for the 'bandit' remark in court and renounce any share in the treasures. An early demand that Carter should promise to be of good behaviour in future was dropped.

As soon as he arrived back in America at the end of May 1924, Winlock contacted Carter who was at Buffalo in New Jersey. He, Carter, must convince the Carnarvon estate of the need to renounce its claim to tomb objects and write a formal letter of apology to the government. Nothing short of those concessions would do. Nothing was to be gained now by self-deception or bandying words. The Egyptians believed that Carter quarrelled 'for the fun of insulting the Egyptian nation'. Perhaps it was a childish idea, said Winlock, but, as one of Carter's 'sincerest well-wishers', he was convinced that a conciliatory attitude was vital. And he pleaded that 'absolutely no comments of *any* sort' should appear in the press. He was only too well aware of Carter's tendency to use Merton's skills as a publicity agent through the columns of *The Times*. Lythgoe also appealed for compromise. Carter replied to both from the Statler Hotel at Buffalo, writing of 'sorrowful news' and of his sadness that he was the 'upsetting element' in it all – 'it was but an endeavour to carry out a duty.' But he was still adamant. There could be no going back, no renouncing of rights which might prejudice others in the future. 'I shall therefore retire – renouncing any claim whatsoever to the Tut.Ankh.Amen discovery,' he declared. He wrote of his 'broken heart', of his 'debt of gratitude' to the museum. He looked forward to seeing them all in New York in June. Lythgoe wrote back, refusing to allow that an 'old friend' should be allowed to 'wipe himself off the map'. It was not long before another of Carter's angry dissertations poisoned the warm relationship with his American partners.

While on the lecture trail he received from Cassell in London proofs of the pamphlet which his publishers had agreed to produce in a small quantity for 'private circulation', containing his statements and extracts from documents relating to the negotiations in Egypt. A tract much in the eighteenth-century style of political polemic, it examined every detail of the day-to-day discussions, arguments and attempted agreements which led eventually to the court room in Cairo. Though written in indirect language, it represented Carter as the man of peace. It attacked the Egyptian government and its individual ministers and described Lacau as 'a menace to the whole future of archaeology in Egypt'. The appendices which Carter had tacked on to the pamphlet included all the correspondence which he had exchanged with Winlock and other members of the Metropolitan's staff, including confidential notes and coded telegrams in connection with the 'lotus' sculpture in the Fortnum packing case. Winlock received his copy in the post on 1 July. Carter was due to call on him the same morning, having arrived in New York the day before, after a weekend with the Harknesses on Long Island.

Winlock did not mince his words. He was said to be a good writer of 'racy prose' but not ordinarily a man given to invective. As soon as Carter arrived at his office he took the offensive, telling the visitor that he wished to have nothing further to do with him. In chillingly measured words he told Carter that he had been used selfishly and with total insensitivity. The 'confounded pamphlet' was the last straw. Carter tried to justify himself. Rather than take the simple course of apology for printing confidential correspondence without consultation or acknowledgement, he argued that the pamphlet would 'arouse' the scholarly world so that Lacau could be 'ousted', and that firmness remained in his view the only way of dealing with the Egyptians. Winlock despaired. Carter would never change his attitude, but, unless he did, neither he nor anyone else would be allowed to complete the excavation of the tomb. Winlock warned Robinson, his director, of Carter's 'disgusting' booklet which could harm all their reputations. And he warned Edward Harkness of the dangers inherent in Carter's unstable character and temperamental outbursts. Winlock proposed to Harkness that the museum should try to persuade the Egyptians to permit a resumption of the tomb clearing on the basis of a division which gave the Antiquities Department first choice of all finds, with one in five of the remaining pieces going to the excavators. Harkness thought the idea worth trying.

Carter boarded the *Mauretania* next day, Wednesday 2 July, bound for London. Robinson had decided to travel with him. The recognition that had so long eluded him seemed to catch up with him on his transatlantic visit. Now he was rich as the result of a single lucrative and successful lecture tour, approved of for his modest, self-deprecating manner, for the credit he had given to his American colleagues, and his 'common touch'. But privately, those Americans who had been close to him in Egypt and had come to admire his high professionalism had seen and heard enough.

When they found themselves together at sea, Robinson and Carter rediscovered a rapport and the former asked once more that Carter give the Egyptians the apology which would set matters to rights. He also asked Carter not to circulate the offending pamphlet. Surprisingly, perhaps calmed by the benign sea breezes, Carter admitted defeat. In his cabin he wrote a message to Lacau, renouncing any claim or pretension to the tomb or its contents: 'I declare that I withdraw all actions pending and I authorize the representatives of the government to apply for them to be struck out.'

There was barely time for lunch with Newberry in London before Carter pitched anew into the legal battleground which now involved the Americans, as well as Egypt and the Carnarvon estate represented by Almina, Lady Burghclere and Mervyn Herbert. The American contingent was staying at Claridges. Matters were made more complicated by political difficulties facing the Conservative administration, which had taken over from Ramsay MacDonald's Labour Party following the 'Zinoviev letter' scandal, and an equally new Egyptian administration. Carter's Cairo counsel F.M. Maxwell was over for what turned out to be a legal jamboree. Carter made a note of his 'fees to date' in his diary: £1,384.

At their first meeting, attended also by Sir John Maxwell, Carter announced that he had bowed to the inevitable and asked the Countess to renounce for the second time her personal rights to any object. Maxwell insisted that the estate must maintain its right to a share, or to recompense. An agreed statement was eventually drawn up in the name of Lady Carnarvon. Dated 13 September 1924, it was addressed to His

Excellency Morcos Bey Hanna, Minister of Public Works. In it, she and Carter agreed to renounce all claims, but added: 'Lord Carnarvon's Executors are in a somewhat different position.' Her husband, in the course of ten years' research work in the Valley of the Kings, and with many disappointments, had spent about £45,000, an amount 'estimated by Mr Howard Carter'. There was regret at the 'misunderstanding' which arose in the previous year and a sincere desire for work to proceed. 'Moreover it is my own earnest wish that he, Mr Carter, should complete the work in accordance with the intention and wishes often expressed by the late Lord Carnarvon…'.

Finally:

> May I therefore make the suggestion that the renunciation by my husband's Executors should not be insisted upon, but that, when the work is finished, and the actual contents of the tomb fully ascertained, the share of those objects to which Lord Carnarvon's Executors are equitably entitled under the terms of the original Concession should be referred to the arbitration of two independent Archaeologists of recognized standing, one to be appointed by your Government and the other by the Executors, with liberty of course to them to appoint an Umpire should it be necessary.

It was the new counsel, Merzbach, who had suggested an 'equitable entitlement'. Merzbach, an old hand at the Cairo bar, knew that the Egyptian felt cheated if he could not bargain. In any case, it would not do to appear to neglect the interests of the estate. The Egyptian government was impressed by the approach, and counsel cabled back within a few days to say that the government was willing for duplicate items, 'as representative as possible of the discovery', to go to Lady Carnarvon. The message from the Cairo lawyer ended: 'My heartiest congratulations.'

Carter waited impatiently for an invitation from the new minister to return to the Valley. None had arrived after a month and he went off to Bath with the Robinsons. Later he joined Bethell at Highclere for a few days, lunched with Lord Montagu at Beaulieu, and went on a round Britain trip with William and his ailing wife Mary. They motored through central England, spending a few days at Malvern, touring the Vale of Evesham, and doing Stratford-on-Avon. Just before making a repeat motor tour with William in late August which ended in the Malvern hills, he noted in the precise way in which he always addressed financial matters: '11 a.m. purchased 4000 war bonds 5%.' There was a shooting party at Tellon House near Taunton (Carter had entered 'shooting' as his chief hobby in *Who's Who* though he had not used a gun seriously since the pre-war years of unemployment in Egypt), and a visit to the Empire Exhibition at Wembley with the Newberrys and Mrs Cosgrove, wife of a senior partner in his solicitor's firm. Here he was able to look again at the cause of his most recent legal débâcle, the 'Tomb' exhibit. He spent a few days with the Newberrys at Ightham in Kent before embarking on yet more lectures at Norwich and Rugby, at Newbury Grammar School, Westminster School and Eton.

In October he delivered a long-promised talk to the people of Swaffham. His home-town cinema had been decked out for the occasion with painted Egyptiana by William Carter. The cinema was reported 'full to overflowing' when Carter arrived to the thumping accompaniment of the 'silent film' pianist to give a slightly modified version of his American talk, complete with imitations of Chaplin and his now-practised account of the treasures of the tomb.

When he arrived back at the St James's flat he was in constant demand. Gulbenkian, the Duke of Alba, patron of the arts and the keenest of amateur archaeologists, the delightful Orientalist George Eumorfopoulos, Lythgoe and Robinson, Lady Burghclere, Oscar Raphael (a collector) and an assortment of lawyers queued up for his time and attention. His legal advisers had decided on litigation as the only course open to him in dealing with the Egyptians.

Back in July, the Duke of Alba had talked him into a brief lecture tour and the two men left for Madrid on 21 November, staying overnight at the Paris Ritz. Three lectures in the following week at Madrid, Barcelona and Toledo set Spain alight. Carter returned to England on Sunday 30 November just in time to be with his older brother William at the death of his wife. There was not time even to accompany Will, the brother who had become something of a father figure to him in his recent trials, to Mary's funeral at Swaffham on 8 December.

By mid-November, political events in Egypt began to dictate the terms of his own and Britain's presence in that country. Nationalist Prime Minister Saad Zaghlul Pasha, at the height of his popularity by 1924, had been warned by Allenby that his policy of appointing his most extreme followers to Cabinet positions, and allowing his own vanity rather than administrative efficiency to dictate the choice of ministers, was creating a dangerous situation for himself and the country. Good men were dismissed because they told the truth. Bad men were given important jobs for their sycophancy.

In October, while Carter was staying with William and Mary in London, Zaghlul had visited London with Allenby where Ramsay MacDonald's Labour Government was in its death throes. The vain, charismatic Zaghlul wanted to end British privileges which remained after the 1922 Declaration. He wanted to reduce the influence of British advisers, and to end the iniquitous policy of compensation to foreigners which followed from the old Ottoman 'capitulations'. One of the many demands for compensation that were doubtless in his mind was the claim of the Carnarvon estate. He also wanted to clip the wings of the British military establishment in his country, whose control was exercised by the Sirdar of the Egyptian Army and Governor-General of the Sudan, at that time Sir Oliver Lee Stack. Stack had been director of military intelligence in earlier times and he had highly placed enemies. The talks in London ended in failure. Zaghlul found a Foreign Office under Labour control as zealous as any Conservative administration in its protection of imperial interests. He returned home to learn that the MacDonald government had fallen and that a Conservative administration with Austen Chamberlain as its Foreign Secretary had taken over.

There was disappointment in Egypt at the failure of the Zaghlul mission, though outwardly the country was calm. But on 19 November, Lee Stack had been shot and fatally wounded on his way home from the War Office in Cairo. His ADC, Captain Campbell of the Black Watch, and the Australian chauffeur, Marsh, were all wounded too. Allenby was entertaining ex-Premier Asquith at the time, and soon after the shooting Zaghlul appeared at the High Commissioner's Residence to express his regret and sympathy. 'This is your doing!' exclaimed Allenby. Zaghlul turned and went away. But to the consternation of British officials, Allenby allowed the Prime Minister and government officials to attend the funeral service. Several of the British advisers resigned their posts. There were big anti-British demonstrations in Alexandria and Allenby reimposed direct rule under martial law. He also imposed, among other retributions, a fine of half a million pounds on the Egyptian government. The fine was paid, Zaghlul resigned, and Ziwar Pasha – huge of bulk, jovial, chain-smoking, Jesuit-educated and pro-British – became Prime Minister. King Fuad remained uneasily on his throne but Britain was in effective control once more. Allenby resigned, though he agreed to keep the deed secret until a suitable successor was found. Almost providentially, Carter was able to return to Egypt. It seemed he need not have made a single concession.

Lawyers, dealers and museum officials wanted to see Carter before he set off for Egypt to negotiate with the new administration. Mace, Harkness, and Breasted wanted to proffer advice, so did Sir Frederic Kenyon at the British Museum. Gulbenkian wanted Carter to accompany him to Sotheby's where there was a sale of Egyptian objects. A vital meeting with his barrister Maxwell at the Constitutional Club had to be fitted in at the last minute.

Carter left London with Mace on 10 December. The journey across to Paris was delayed by fog in the English Channel but little time was lost and they arrived at Alexandria on 15 December. Next day, in Cairo, he met the new Prime Minister Ziwar, who criticized his predecessors for their uncooperative policies concerning Carter and the tomb of Tutankhamun and promised his full support. Carter's response was to wonder whether he could withdraw Lady Carnarvon's letter of renunciation. Merzbach advised against such action. It would be interpreted as an act of bad faith. The memory of the consequences of precipitate action in the past may have suggested caution for once and Carter agreed to abide by his lawyer's advice. In any case, he was convinced that Ziwar, so 'kindly and cooperative', would agree to a share of the treasure. Merzbach also advised Carter to work quietly behind the scenes to exact a more equitable division of the finds from the government.

By midday on 16 December Carter was at the High Commission in Cairo where he was received by the second secretary Furness, having called on Merzbach earlier and run into the Prime Minister Ziwar 'by accident'. Furness told him that if he was to receive official support he must give an assurance that there would be no more 'private press contracts'. He promised that a clause would be written into the new agreement specifically excluding any such press contract. The arrangement with *The Times* was at an end.

Carter's diary, usually kept only for brief notes of appointments, contained a detailed account of the day's events:

From the few words I had with H.E. Ziwa[r] Pasha (P.M.) this morning, when meeting him by accident, and also from Merzbach and Furness at the Residency the air seems favourable for success with regard to amicable arrangements for all concerned, but may be requested to open the tomb for a short period in January for diplomatic reasons, merely to get a footing, mark [?] time, in which case should require a small credit of say £750 - £1000 to carry it through. One thing seems most imperative & that is stop proceedings – as this will be of no use whatsoever.

Allenby, his resignation still kept secret at the request of the Foreign Office, promised his full support and asked Carter to have the tomb ready for a public viewing for ten days in January. Clandestine meetings seem to have followed the visit to the High Commission and the meeting with Ziwar. The diary noted, 'Sharia Emir el Said, (R. over Bulaq bridge) between 5 & 6', but did not say who awaited him. In the next two days he called at the Palace to speak to King Fuad, and had tea with Madame Nequib. The diary recorded on 18 December: 'Furness said that the H.C. would be willing to open negotiations with the Egyptian Government on the basis of the continuance of the scientific investigation of the tomb of Tutankhamun with certain guarantees for the [Egyptian] government.' The guarantees seemed to involve once again the vexed question of the distribution of finds, a sure recipe for further argument and dissent.

In conversation with the Prime Minister and in company with the director of the French Archaeological Mission, M. Georges Foucart, Carter understood Ziwar Pasha to express his determination that 'excavator or discoverer should be fairly treated'. Foucart seemed intent on undermining his countryman, Lacau. Carter asked for an interview with the new Minister of Public Works, together with Merzbach, to draw up a new agreement. Ziwar said that he would like a letter from Carter first, setting out his proposals in detail. Madame Nequib, with whom Carter spent a good deal of time, seems to have had a part in negotiations which, predictably, were nothing like as straightforward as Carter had expected them to be. Merzbach was proving a tower of strength and he had a number of useful meetings on behalf of Carter and the Carnarvon estate. But it was not until Boxing Day, after a Christmas spent congenially with Percy White in Cairo, that Carter was able to report real progress. Furness told him then that the Prime Minister and the Minister of Public Works had expressed a willingness to 'discuss formally the tomb question'. On the 27th he noted: 'Phoned several times during morning for an interview with the P.M.' After seeing Madame Nequib on the 28th he was granted an interview with Ziwar. Georges Foucart was present and Carter was asked to put his ideas in writing.

A formal meeting was finally arranged in the first week of January 1925. To Carter's astonishment, the Egyptian side was represented not only by the powerful Minister of the Interior, Sidky Pasha, but also by Badawi Pasha, legal adviser to the old government with which he had had so much trouble, and by Pierre Lacau. Before the meeting, Carter was invited by Ziwar to a private briefing at the Muhammad Ali Club. There he told Carter that the Antiquities Department was still being difficult about one small matter – it wanted a further letter confirming the renunciation by the Carnarvon estate and Carter to rights in any treasures, even duplicates. The Prime Minister added that he would, of course, use his influence to see that some duplicated objects 'which would not interfere with the overall ensemble' were made available to Lady Carnarvon. Carter, fearing that he might once more find himself at the centre of international controversy, remained silent. When he told Merzbach of the volte-face before the meeting with the ministers, the lawyer remarked sadly that 'such an action by the Prime Minister was just about what one would expect – particularly in Egypt.'

At the meeting, Lacau was conspiratorial but Carter thought that Merzbach handled matters 'brilliantly'. It was still hoped that the government would undertake to give Lady Carnarvon some duplicates when work was completed. A letter was composed by Carter which Merzbach worked on before it was sent to the new Minister of Public Works, Mahmoud Bey. It was conciliatory and polite. It invited the government to grant a new concession on the understanding that the Countess renounced all previous claims and actions. It drew a response from the Minister of Works, dated 13 January, which 'though recognizing no obligation whatsoever in respect of the objects found in the tomb', proposed 'following the suggestion made by M. Lacau, immediately after the discovery' to give at its own discretion to Almina, Countess of Carnarvon, 'a choice of duplicates as representative as possible of the discovery, provided that such duplicates may be separated from the whole without damage to science'.

At last Carter could plan his return to the Valley, though on terms much less favourable than he had hoped for. Meanwhile, Sergeant Adamson, 'locked out of the tomb since the previous February', is said to have waited with the faithful workmen. Carter paid them up to date, though they had been called on to do only sentry duty. 'Paid Rais Ahmad Gurgar, Husain Ahmad, Gad Hassan and Hussain Awad their salaries due to Dec. 31st 1924,' he noted on the last day of the year.

Before he left London for Cairo, he had received a progress report from Qurna. It read:

Honourable Sir,
Beg to write this letter hoping you are enjoying good health, and ask the Almighty to keep you and bring you back to us in safety. Beg to inform your excellency that Store no 15 is alright, the Northern Store is alright. Wadain and House are all right, and all your work order is carried on according to your most honourable instructions. Rais Hussain, Gad Hassan, Hassan Awad Abdalal Ahmad and all the ghaffirs of the house beg to send their best regards. My best remarks to your honourable self, Longing to your early coming, Your most obediant servant,

Rais Ahmad Gurgar

Chapter 15

'LIVING IMAGE OF AMUN'

CHARLES Breasted described Carter's 'quiet' readmission to the tomb 'under conditions far less favourable than those which, during the previous spring, my father had endeavoured to secure for him'. The government, even though acting under direct British rule, had felt itself to be on firm enough ground to decree that in future *everything* found by excavators would be the property of Egypt. The ultimate effect, said Breasted, was to put a virtual stop to British and American expeditions.

Compensation for Lady Carnarvon, reluctantly agreed to, was confined strictly to the restitution of financial outlay. Britain was exercising waning authority through a tired and disillusioned High Commissioner who just wanted to retire and sought solace in drink. Many senior members of the administration handed in their resignation in consequence of Allenby's refusal to pursue and punish the perpetrators of Stack's murder. The country seemed powerless to protect its own interests. Carter and the Americans could work on the tomb if they wished. They would be entitled to nothing for their pains. It is little wonder that a few small, but none the less valuable, pieces found their way to London and New York.

On 15 January, Merton reported to London that Carter was on his way from Cairo to Luxor and proposed to reopen the tomb on the 25th. On that day the keys to the tomb and laboratory were ceremonially handed to him on behalf of the Ministry of Public Works. Next day, *The Times* carried Merton's account of the 'very simple ceremony' followed by Carter's brief inspection of the tomb and the Seti II workshop. But there was a first sign of damage resulting from the eleven-month hiatus. The pall which once covered the shrines, 'unique of its kind', had been left outside the Seti tomb by the Antiquities Department when Percy Newberry and his wife, who had been working at its preservation, were told to leave the site with the rest of Carter's team in 1924. It was inadequately covered and had been affected badly by sunlight.

Before resuming the dismantling of the coffins, Carter decided to work patiently on the objects in need of care and attention in the laboratory tomb, a task which took his team through the spring and much of the hot summer. Regular and proper arrangements now had to be made for receiving visitors, and it says much of Carter's change of mood that he cheerfully recorded more than 12,300 visitors to the tomb in the course of the season and 270 parties to the laboratory. Under the old dispensation he would almost certainly have closed the site at the very suggestion of so many sightseers holding up his work and hazarding the treasures.

Work proceeded calmly and without incident, greatly assisted by a permanent supply of electricity laid on at Lacau's instigation during the previous year. All the objects so far rescued from the burial chamber, first revealed in February 1923 when the wall adjoining the antechamber was pulled down, were treated and made ready for transportation to Cairo before the team was able to pause for breath. As Carter resumed work in the Valley, one of the latter-day saints of Near Eastern archaeology, David Hogarth, spoke to the boys of Westminster School. He told them: 'If the Egyptian Government had not been able to make an arrangement with Mr Howard Carter to continue the work he had begun there, they would not have found anyone else to go on with it. Yet Carter would not be entitled to anything he found.'

The archaeological establishment, never very sympathetic towards Carter, was beginning to see the injustice of his position. When he arrived in England in the summer, however, he seemed anything but depressed, enlivened indeed, by the prospect of things to come. A highlight of the vacation months was a return on 11 September to the New Oxford Theatre in Oxford Street where his lectures almost exactly two years before had attracted full houses. This time, Londoners and tourists crowded the theatre to hear a talk given in aid of the Egypt Exploration Society's Abydos Fund, entitled 'The Tomb of Tut.ankh.Amen from Anteroom to Burial Chamber.'

The following season's work began early in October 1925. In Cairo the Continental-Savoy Hotel had, he noted, given him the same room as 'poor Ld C used to have'. He called at the Cairo Museum on the first of the month and was horrified to discover that a fine silver stick, fellow to a gold stick found in the antechamber, was broken in its glass case. He was told casually that a European official had broken it while showing it to M. Capart. He was disappointed too to find that Lacau was away, but he spoke to a deputy who arranged for the electric lighting to be switched on in the Valley from 11 October. In an interview with Badawi Pasha at the Ministry of Public Works, Carter stressed the urgency of examining the royal mummy at the earliest possible moment. He proposed 25 October, when Professor Douglas Derry of Cairo University's medical school would be able to assist, along with the Egyptian Health Inspector Dr Saleh Bey Hamdi. Carter was told that Lacau must be present and would not be available until 10 November. 'Here is another delay for my work!' commented Carter.

The programme mapped out by Carter was to raise the nest of four golden burial shrines and the three mummiform coffins concealed within, which together formed the great sarcophagus. The three coffins, like the four enveloping shrines, fitted into each other with perfect accuracy. Separating them proved one of the most hazardous of all the delicate tasks involved in the tomb clearing. The lower halves of the inner coffins had become stuck to each other through the solidification of consecration unguents that had been poured over them. It was, therefore, necessary to split the coffins laterally so as to raise the upper half. The first coffin was opened in this way after two days of painstaking preparation on 13 October. Carter recorded the event:

> Upon careful inspection of the coffin as it rested in the sarcophagus, it was decided that the four original bronze handles (two on each side) were sufficiently well preserved to support the weight of the lid of the coffin and therefore could be utilized in raising it, that is if it were possible to remove the bronze pins by which it was fixed to the shell of the coffin.

Thus began the most emotive and sensational of all the tasks which Carter and his team undertook in the tomb of Tutankhamun.

The first of the three innermost coffins was made of wood, its gilded lid portraying the youthful king in all his magnificence. It would in itself have repaid the work of years but it marked only the beginning of eighteen days of glorious discovery. The second coffin, similarly constructed, was sumptuously inlaid with opaque glass to simulate cornelian, lapis lazuli and turquoise. The gilded image of the king showed him wearing the *nemes,* the striped blue-and-gold linen headcloth. The upper section was raised after much anxious preparation and after the mandatory photographic records had been made by Burton, on the 23rd. The third coffin thus revealed was covered with a red linen shroud. Carter and Burton removed the shroud in utter silence. As they did so they realized that the last of the burial vessels, the bourn of all their work and hope, was 'manifestly anthropoid in form' and made of solid gold. It was over 6 feet in length. Access was extremely difficult since it was fixed within the shell of the second coffin, the delicate inlay of which had to be preserved. Because of the enormous weight of the solid gold lid and the fact that the pitch-like oil used as a libation and preservative was at its thickest and most impenetrable within the coffin, the task of prising the lid open was both difficult and delicate. Even a sharp steel chisel made little impression. When they finally succeeded in releasing it, on 28 October 1925, neither Carter nor the others present, Burton, Lucas and Breasted, could believe their eyes. Carter's diary referred to 'the penultimate scene'. The mummy remained hidden by the solid gold mask, the 'mask of sad but tranquil expression, symbolizing Osiris'.

By 30 October Burton had made a complete photographic record of the actual coffin and its mummy. By the last day of the month, floral tributes, wonderfully preserved, and all the other movable objects on the exterior of the mummy had been removed for Lucas to treat. At last they looked down on the illuminated scene which was to make the image of Tutankhamun the most famous and photographed of all the kings of history. It was a sublime moment and Carter did his best to analyse it:

At such moments the emotions evade verbal expression, complex and stirring as they are. Three thousand years and more had elapsed since man's eye had gazed into that golden coffin. Time, measured by the brevity of human life, seemed to lose its common perspective... But it is useless to dwell on such sentiments, based as they are on feelings of awe and human pity. The emotional side is no part of archaeological research.

Carter was too close to the event to describe it dispassionately. James Breasted was better equipped to give a first, tentative account of one of the most awe-inspiring sights ever witnessed.

Four men, he said, could barely lift the solid gold coffin. In fact, it weighed 2,448 lb 2 oz. He went on:

The lid...again represents the King in all his splendid regalia: the face is a portrait; his garments above his crossed arms are encrusted with many-coloured semi-precious stones such as cornelian, turquoise and lapis-lazuli; while below his crossed arms he is enfolded by the protecting wings of guardian goddesses whose lovely forms are elaborately graven in gold, and envelop him with a luminous net of golden plumage.

Coffin and lid were wrought of solid gold which, at the exchange rate of that time, Breasted estimated to be worth in bullion alone, without reference to art or antiquity, about $243,000. 'How the portrait-face of the King was executed in the mirror-polished gold of the lid without leaving anywhere even the faintest traces of tool marks, is a great mystery,' he marvelled. And then there was the mummified body within, 'about 18 years old when he died', head and shoulders covered with the beautifully modelled mask of gold: 'No other relics of the goldsmith's art surviving from the ancient world, or from Tutankhamun's tomb itself, can compare with this coffin and mask. I looked upon them with amazement and reverence.'

Lacau and Egyptian officials were late on the scene, but they gazed with as much wonderment as Carter and his men on the opulent burial paraphernalia. The unbiased observer might reasonably think that at that moment Egypt would have reconsidered the question of compensation. Nothing was said or done, then or afterwards. Breasted's last words on the subject expressed his own dismay at the parsimony of the country that had gained so much without venturing a mite:

> The Egyptian Government ignored the suggestion that an appropriate way of rewarding Carter for his discovery and of recognizing his subsequent services and those of his American collaborators would be the presentation to the British Museum and the Metropolitan Museum of duplicate objects from Tutankhamun's tomb. It gave nothing to either museum.

Carter himself made no reference to the matter. He was now a wealthy man from the proceeds of his lecture tour and from the massive world-wide sale of the first jointly written volume of his book on the discovery of the tomb. He perhaps felt that he could adopt a dignified financial stance. In any case, he had taken the matter of compensation into his own hands, as later evidence would show.

Through the last week of October 1925 and the first week of November, helped by Burton and Callender, Carter meticulously prepared the coffin and its royal mummy for presentation to their Egyptian benefactors. When, on 4 November, he removed from the sarcophagus a golden bier with lions' heads and feet on which the last of the coffins rested, three years to the day had elapsed since the discovery of the steps which led to the tomb of Tutankhamun. In a life devoted to art and to dry and dusty work, this was Carter's labour of love. 'Today', he wrote, 'has been a great day in the history of archaeology…a day of days for one who…has longed to see in fact what previously has only been conjectural.'

At 9.45 a.m. on 11 November, Egyptian government officials, and Lacau and members of the Antiquities Department, joined Carter's team to see Professor Derry and Dr Saleh Bey Hamdi perform the most belated of autopsies. The day before, Carter had filled a page of his diary with a translation from Herodotus who observed in his travels in the fifth century BC the men of Egypt who practised the art of embalming: 'These persons, when a body is brought to them, show the bearer various models of corpses, made in wood and painted so as to resemble nature. The most perfect is said to be after the manner of him whom I do not think it religious to name in connection with such a matter.' Carter noted in parenthesis, 'No doubt the god of the dead, Osiris.' Herodotus went on to describe the method of embalming, the 'most perfect process'. After dealing with the brain and other soft tissues:

…the body is placed in natrum for seventy days, and covered entirely over. After the expiry of that time, which must not be exceeded, the body is washed and wrapped round, from head to foot, with bandages of fine linen cloth, smeared over with gum, which is used generally by the Egyptians in place of glue, and in that state it is given back to relations who enclose it in a wooden case which they have had made for the purpose, shaped in the figure of a man.

Just such a body, though encased in solid gold rather than wood, awaited Professor Derry. It could not be removed from the coffin without risk of damage and so the examination, described by Carter, was carried out as it lay:

10.35 a.m. In consequence of the fragile and powdery nature of the outer layers of wrappings, the whole of the exposed surface of the mummy except the mask was painted over with melted paraffin wax of such a temperature that it chiefly congealed as a thin coating on the surface and did not penetrate the decayed wrappings for more than a very short distance. As soon as the wax had cooled, Dr Derry made a longitudinal incision down the centre of the outer wrappings to just below the depth to which the wax had penetrated, thus enabling the consolidated outer layers to be removed in large pieces. The under bandages which were very voluminous were found to be equally decayed and fragile; in fact, as it eventually proved, the deeper and nearer the body, the worse the condition.

The meticulous examination, carried out in silence except for the measured words of the two medical men and occasional intervention by Carter, went on for eight days, during which only one of the original party, an Egyptian inspector, succumbed to fatigue.

Even after the removal of the decayed outer crust of wrappings, it was still impossible to lift the mummy from its coffin. Pitch-like material had gathered underneath the body and glued it to its gold surround. Derry decided to remove the wrappings *in situ,* layer by layer. As he did so, amulets and ornaments of solid and chased and inlaid gold were revealed. Each object was identified by a letter of the alphabet which was doubled up, tripled and then given numerical appendages as the count increased.

There was a large inlaid collar, built up in duplicate segments. An ornamented gold dagger with crystal-knobbed handle lay on the right thigh. A band of sheet gold was wrapped around the waist. An amulet of sheet gold reached from abdomen to pubis. A large gold bracelet, inlaid, lay open on the left thigh. An indication of the care exercised by doctors and archaeologists was contained in the discovery of a gold and beadwork object in fragile state lying on the left side of the abdomen. Work on the mummy ceased while molten wax was prepared and poured over the ornament so as to consolidate it. A large amuletic hawk of sheet gold with outstretched wings lay over part of the abdomen. Over the umbilicus was a resinous black scarab held by a gold wire pendant from the neck. A solid gold uraeus with the royal crown of the north also graced the left thigh, while the opposite thigh sported the head and neck of the vulture goddess Nekhbet. Burton made photographic records of every object as it was uncovered. 'Note orientation N & S of body,' 'Note orientation of certain objects such as vulture head and uraeus,' wrote Carter, hurried reminders of matters which must be dwelt on in less emotive circumstances.

Moving up the body, 'under the mask and covering the face' there was a fifth amulet, a hawk in chased sheet gold, identified as 'T' and not visible in Burton's photograph since it was hidden by the royal collar. 'Gradually, as the work proceeds, one is able to detect among the objects that which is purely religious and amuletic and that which was real and personal property.' Objects in both categories were, he wrote, 'magnificent', adding, 'but this is not the moment to describe them'. By the morning of 12 November the removal of further layers of disintegrating bandage had revealed more gold circlets over the umbilicus and above the knees; a massive bracelet of gold and cornelian on the right forearm; gold and faience beads from a broken necklace; a large bird plaque with fine gold inlay lying on the chest and covered with a single sheet of papyrus. The last object was the twenty-fifth, labelled 'Z', since the letter 'I' was not used.

The next group, 'AA' to 'ZZ', seemed to grow in magnificence as Derry removed more and more bandage segments, reaching ever closer to the mummiform body, coating the frailest objects with wax as they proceeded. Another collar lay over the thighs; a Meshura of gold and faience beads lay in confusion over the pubis, below it a gold circlet; a filigree gold dagger rested over the abdominal region, much finer and heavier than the weapon found earlier; another girdle of sheet gold; a group of five massive rings of lapis, gold, faience and chalcedony; another amuletic chased sheet gold collar; more amuletic objects of gold and other materials.

The afternoon of the 12th was devoted to uncovering the right arm and hand, the entire limb being fixed to the abdomen. The forearm was encircled by five resplendent bracelets. The fingers were covered with golden stalls. By the end of the day's work on 12 November they had reached the mummified remains of the lower parts of the king, and it was apparent that they were confronted by a young person. 'And a more detailed medical examination to follow will determine with certainty the exact age.'

Next day, the 13th, was devoted largely to photographing and measuring the king's body. The last wrappings were removed from the king's left forearm and hand, this time exposing more bracelets and a group of eight finger rings of gold and resinous composition, some with scarab bezels and others with the prenomen and nomen of the king. Some of the bracelets were of great intricacy and marvellous craftsmanship, and scale photographs were taken of them. Further anatomical examination revealed that the soft tissues of the body were in very brittle condition and gave the pathologists few immediate clues. To date, Carter noted, fifty-two groups of objects had been discovered (groups representing individual or composite objects found on particular segments of the wrapped body), mostly personal and religious jewellery, and all of the finest workmanship. So far the autopsy had only covered the lower parts. 'If therefore the upper parts and the head are proportionately rich,' Carter noted, 'we can begin to realize the wealth and profusion with which it seems to have been customary to adorn the remains of those ancient pharaohs buried in the royal necropolis.'

Press bulletins were issued daily as the examination went on. Merton, still officially on Carter's staff as publicity officer, although the *Times* arrangement was now ineffective if not defunct, was trying to cope with Egyptian political affairs as well as archaeology. The problems of dealing with the press came to the fore yet again as interest in the tomb reached another high point. The team assembled for the autopsy was suddenly besieged by press agents offering their services to anyone with a story to sell. They, rather than the journalists, became the current bugbear. But for the moment, such matters were no more than a passing irritation to Carter. He was preoccupied with recent discoveries.

'In all the material we have just seen we have a clear insight of the work of the skilled craftsmen of Thebes,' he wrote in a reflective moment. Tempted into spontaneous judgement, he thought the jewellery found in the tomb 'in many ways perhaps not so fine as regards finish as that of the Middle Kingdom jewellers, but if the technical skill be not so good, the refined taste displayed surpasses our expectations'. On another occasion there was an essay on amulets, admitting ignorance of many of the symbols found here and elsewhere which were intended to 'bring protection against injury on that journey into the underworld …enter into the realms of the dead, eat the food of Osiris…be guarded by Isis and Horus', etc.

Work went on for another five days until, on 19 November, the two physicians signed their notes and declared the examination complete. Lacau, who had been present for the whole of the time, left the day before for Cairo, taking with him the provisional report of the surgeons and Carter's archaeological bulletin. Carter noted that ninety-seven separate groups of objects had been found within the wrappings of the mummy, some groups including many individual pieces.

The gold plaques of the burial chamber bore benedictions of the old Heliopolitan gods addressed to the king as inheritor of Osiris's throne: 'Thy members are firm…thou goest out as a god…O Osiris Tutankhamun.'

The Times published in full the final 'official communiqué', constructed by Carter and Merton. It recorded the regret of the team that X-ray analysis had proved impossible since 'the gold coffin and the thick pitch-like material' were impervious to the rays. But it recorded the astonishing finds of the past month, made possible by the immaculate work of removing the 'carbonized' wrappings: the royal diadem with insignia of vulture and serpent on the head; amuletic figures round the neck; pectorals from the chest, including many amulets disposed in no fewer that sixteen layers, often with elaborate *cloisonné* enamel work; eleven magnificent bracelets on the arms, thirteen massive finger rings; two gold waist girdles, from each of which a beautiful dagger was suspended; gold funerary sandals; a great number of amulets. The world was once more astonished by the scale and magnificence of the discovery. But as for scholarship, there was a rider. Not a single document had been found. The discovery which more than any other in history had fascinated ordinary men and women the world over seemed fated to contribute only indirectly to the sum of knowledge of the ancient past.

In his report Derry wrote:

Little was it expected that a king of obscure origin with a short and uneventful reign should one day attract the attention of the whole world, and that, not on account of fame attaching to himself, but to the single fact that while the tomb of every Pharaoh yet discovered had been rifled in ancient times, that of Tutankhamun was found practically intact. In the confined space of this small tomb was contained an assemblage of royal possessions such as had never before been seen.

And Derry asked a rhetorical question that was to be echoed by Egyptologists ever after: 'What then must have been the contents of the tombs of Seti I, of Ramesses III, and others, in one of whose halls alone all the wealth of the tomb of Tutankhamun might have been stored?

Dr Derry prefaced his account of the actual autopsy by looking at the background to his work established by examinations of the remains of many kings in Cairo's Museum of Antiquities. He had recently examined the mummies which Winlock recovered from the Eleventh Dynasty temple of Nebhepetre Mentuhotpe at Deir al Bahari, from which none of the organs had been removed. Later practice was to make an abdominal incision after death and to remove the chief organs.

Another expert in the field, Professor Elliot Smith of London University who was Derry's predecessor at the Cairo medical school, had achieved unexpected public renown as a result of the *Daily Telegraph's* enterprise in asking him to write a series of articles in 1923 - 4 in which, by describing tomb discoveries in the context of history and pathology, he was able to drive a carriage and pair through the Carnarvon/*Times* agreement. An amateur Egyptologist of substance and one of the world's most distinguished anatomists, he had examined nearly all the royal mummies in the Cairo Museum, as well as priests and priestesses of the Twenty-first Dynasty, and described the methods of preparing and preserving corpses at different periods in his *Catalogue of the Royal Mummies*. Elliot Smith was the first to produce a full-scale book on the tomb discovery, published at the end of 1923 and providing some interesting if misleading commentary on Tutankhamun's reputed ancestors. When it came to the performance of the autopsy on Tutankhamun, Derry had the advantage of Elliot Smith's as well as his own extensive experience in following the common system of preparing and bandaging royal mummies. He was able to describe, for instance, the individual bandaging of fingers and toes, after which gold sheaths were adjusted to lie over the exact positions of the nails, before the whole foot or hand was bandaged again.

What of the king's age? Derry's evidence was chiefly orthopaedic. He wrote: 'Tutankhamun, from the evidence of his lower limbs, would appear to have been over eighteen but below twenty years of age at the date of his death.' Later, by comparative anatomical study, he said the king 'was evidently over seventeen'.

But in a family where platycephalic skulls and effeminacy in portraiture gave rise to suggestions of an inherent glandular defect and even to a cultivated transvestism, it was the head which caused most debate at the time, and ever since has contributed to academic argument and controversy. It is a debate which raises universal questions of historical judgement based on preserved visual evidence. It is impossible to go too deeply into the voluminous arguments that have ensued about the effeminate looks of Tutankhamun and his supposed relations in the royal family of the Amarna period, without asking if some far distant generation of people might judge the appearance of twentieth century mankind by reference to, say, the portraiture of Picasso or Henry Moore. All the same, the debate which began with the discoveries of Petrie and the German Oriental Institute at Amarna prior to 1914 is perhaps the most fascinating, certainly the most persistent, of Egyptological topics.

Elliot Smith had been the first to examine the mummy of the heretic king Akhenaten, in 1907. Now, in 1925, Derry found the general shape of the head of Tutankhamun to be so like that of his reputed father-in-law that it was 'more than probable that there was a close relationship in blood between these two kings'. The remarkable shape of the Akhenaten skull had led Elliot Smith to the conclusion that the king had suffered from hydrocephalus, but later research was to throw doubt on that diagnosis. Unusual size was the determining

factor in Derry's belief in consanguinity. The exceptional
breadth of Akhenaten's skull by Egyptian standards (154 mm)
was actually exceeded by Tutankhamun's. Derry declared that
a blood relationship was 'almost a certainty'. Was it possible,
since he married Akhenaten's daughter Ankhesenpaaten
(Ankhesenamun after the return to Thebes and Amun worship),
that the young king whom Carter believed 'may have been of
the blood royal', with some indirect claim to the throne on his
own account, or perhaps 'a mere commoner', was in fact both
the son and son-in-law of Akhenaten? The possibilities were
intriguing, even for those newspapers and their readers who
were not habitually attracted to the ins and outs of ancient
history.

Theories were profuse. Was it possible that the kings were
brothers and not father and son, or that Tutankhamun was
simply a son by an 'unofficial wife', or the son of Akhenaten's
vizier, the 'Divine Father' Ay, who became king after
Tutankhamun? If the latter possibility held, then his mother
would have been Ay's principal wife Tiye. And Ay and Tiye
were the possible parents of Nefertiti, the royal wife in whose
eloquent beauty many saw the foundation of Tutankhamun's
handsomeness. Years later, the debate begun by Elliot Smith,
Petrie, Gardiner and others in the first decade of the twentieth
century, produced persuasive protagonists of Amenophis III as
father rather than grandfather of the boy-king, either by his
chief spouse Tiye or his daughter-wife Sitamun (a not
uncommon duality in ancient Egypt). Such conjecture is the
stuff of popular writing and in this case it has spawned a vast
library. Indeed, within a few years of the revealing of the young
king, Agatha Christie was making dramatic use of ancient
Egypt's most famous family in her stage play *Akhnaton*.

Carter, by the time he reached the third volume of his
account of the tomb discovery, surmised that Akhenaten
reigned for between seventeen and eighteen years after the
forty-year sovereignty of his father Amenophis III, followed by
Tutankhamun's tenure of just over nine years, a reign which

began in honour of the Aten or sun-disk as Tutankh*aten*, 'Living Image of the Aten', and ended with a pathetic attempt to eradicate image and heresy and return to the worship of the old Theban god Amun, Tutankh*amun*. The reappraisal of religious dogma had political overtones. New anthropomorphic likenesses showing the animal god-figure with Tutankhamun's face were not enough to restore his memory to favour. At his death they were disfigured by conservative priests and their followers, along with the tombs of the apostate kings who had gone before. Statues were smashed, names eradicated and substituted, and Tutankhamun's face replaced by that of the successor kings of common blood, Ay and General Haremhab.

But regnal terms and the order of succession were still in doubt, as were Tutankhamun's exact place and year of birth. There was one piece of evidence as undeniable in its artistic force as it was unprovable in scientific terms. The mask in which the young king was revealed to the world bore an uncanny resemblance to one of the best-known of all human sculptures, the bust of Queen Nefertiti, wife of Akhenaten. There was none of the written evidence such as Egyptologists dearly hoped for in the tomb. And conjecture was made difficult by the possibility of co-regencies at the beginning and end of Akhenaten's reign.

Modern scholarship suggests the probability that Amenophis III came to the throne in 1391 BC and reigned until 1353. Circumstantial evidence pointed to Akhenaten's succession, however, as dating from 1358, so that there may have been a period of co-regency of father and son. At the other end of the reign, Akhenaten was believed to have been succeeded by the minor Tutankhamun in about 1333 (some prefer a date closer to 1340), but another king appears in the last two years at the end of the reign, Smenkhkare, son-in-law of Akhenaten and putative brother or uncle of Tutankhamun, thus suggesting another co-regency. Archaeologists and medical experts would argue the nature of this or that relationship, or date of birth or accession or death, as time went on. Advances

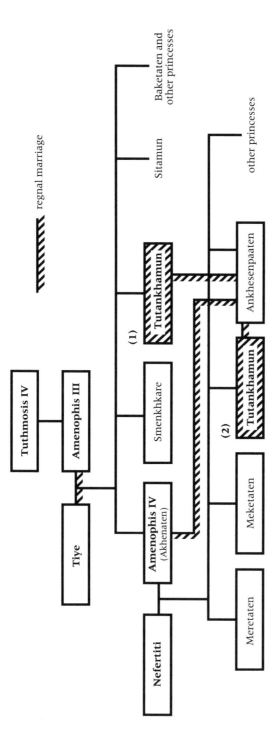

regnal marriage

Note. Smenkhkare, probable co-regent of Akhenaten and perhaps of Tutankhamun, is ignored except for his position as the son of Amenophis III, to avoid unnecessary complication.

Alternative family and marital relationships of Tutankhamun based on the propositions that he was (1) the son of Amenophis III, and thus the brother (or half-brother) of Akhenaten, and uncle and brother-in-law to his wife Ankhesenpaaten (Akhenaten having taken his own daughter as consort), or (2) the son of Akhenaten and thus full or half-brother to his wife Ankhesenpaaten, daughter of Akhenaten and Nefertiti.

in medical science made possible serological tests and X-ray examinations which were impractical at the time of Derry's examination.

Expert re-examination of inscriptions from the tomb and coffin carelessly excavated in 1907 by Theodore Davis near the grave of Ramesses IX added fuel to the debates. Davis thought it was the tomb of Queen Tiye; Weigall was convinced that the bones belonged to Akhenaten, brought from Amarna when the city was abandoned. Engelbach favoured Smenkhkare. Medical evidence first supported one and then the other. Norman de Garis Davies, surveyor to the EES expedition, joined the regent Smenkhkare's lobby. Late twentieth century scholarship has leaned toward the theory that the coffin was designed for one of the royal daughters of Amarna, perhaps the eldest Meretaten or Meketaten, or even their mother Nefertiti, and later adapted for one of the kings, Akhenaten or Smenkhkare. Vitally, the latest evidence points to abnormalities in the remains which suggest the same eunuchoidal characteristics associated with surviving sculptures of Akhenaten. The facial skeleton closely resembled Tutankhamun's. Serum tests on the body found in Davis's tomb (number 55 in the Valley catalogue) showed the same blood group as Tutankhamun's, A2 with serum antigen MN. Proof, it was said, that whether the body was that of Akhenaten or Smenkhkare, and most experts favoured the latter, it was the body of Tutankhamun's father or brother. The world was prepared to allow that the last words on the subject had been spoken, until the Russian scholar Perepelkin demonstrated that texts found in tomb 55 showed that the coffin was made for 'The Royal Favourite' Kiya, a secondary wife of Akhenaten and the candidate of some experts as the likely mother of Tutankhamun. And texts found at a temple of Amarna by Sir Leonard Woolley in 1922, and ignored ever since, showed that Kiya's fall from grace had resulted in her name being expunged from monuments and replaced by that of Princess Meretaten, while Kiya's inscription on the coffin of tomb 55 was modified to apply to the king. Perhaps that tomb had become a vault for

the disgraced royal family after the reaffirmation of the old
faith and the move, under Tutankhamun's sovereignty, back to
Thebes.

A flimsier argument at the time, that a granite lion in the
British Museum bore an inscription in which Tutankhamun
made reference to Amenophis III as 'father', thus 'proving' that
he was Akhenaten's younger brother, received some support.

Whatever the truth of the matter, Carter's description of the
court he had played such a prominent part in unveiling since
his earliest days in Egypt when he dug with Petrie at Tal al
Amarna remains among the most profound of all the words
spoken and written on the subject, tracing as he did the
succession and the supposed family relationships from the time,
fourteen centuries before Christ, when 'Akh.en.Aten, Gallio
of Gallios, dreamt his life away'. Carter's story, too, of the
young king's marriage to Ankhesenpaaten, the daughter of
Akhenaten and therefore perhaps his own sister or blood
cousin, touches a universal note of romance. He tells of her
widowhood and search for a royal husband in a letter to the
Hittite king Suppiluliumas just after the latter had conquered
Carchemish:'Why should I deceive you? I have no son, and my
husband is dead. Send me a son of yours and I will make him
king.' And then:

> Did the Hittite prince ever start for Egypt, and how far did
> he get? Did Ay, the new king, get wind of Ankh.es.en.Amen's
> schemings and take effectual steps to bring them to naught?
> [She had of course changed her name along with her
> husband in his last days.] We shall never know. In any case
> the queen disappears from the scene and we hear of her no
> more. It is a fascinating little tale. Had the plot succeeded
> there would never have been a Rameses the Great.

Perhaps, if subsequent scholarship holds water, it was the queen
mother Nefertiti who wrote in her widowhood to the Hittite
king begging for a royal husband and not her daughter, as

Carter and other Egyptologists had assumed. A modern scholar has summarized the likely denouement in a manner which Agatha Christie might have envied. He recalled that at about the years 15 - 16 of his reign, Akhenaten elevated his eldest daughter's husband, Smenkhkare, to the throne as his co-regent. Before that event, or in consequence of it, Nefertiti left her husband and the royal city of Amarna, and Smenkhkare and his (Akhenaten's) daughter Meretaten occupied his affections, Smenkhkare appearing 'more as a mascot than a legitimate partner in the kingship'. Akhenaten died within two years, in year 17 of his reign, and Nefertiti saw her opportunity. The Hittite king Suppiluliumas to whom, as Carter had noticed, she wrote in search of a princely husband who would rule over Egypt, sent her one of his sons. But as the prince approached the frontier in Egypt, unidentified assailants waylaid him and killed him.

It does not require much imagination to conjure up the Machiavellian hand of Smenkhkare in the bloody deed. It was probably Smenkhkare's last move; he and Meretaten disappear so swiftly that one cannot help but wonder whether the enraged Nefertiti effected their downfall more cunningly than they had plotted the murder of her fiancé. At any rate, Nefertiti appears at Amarna, champions the claim to the throne of the hitherto obscure Tutankhamun, marries him to her third daughter Ankhesenpaaten and, in conjunction with Ay, manages to carry on a semblance of ordered rule at Amarna for about two years. It may well be that the event that precipitated Tutankhamun's capitulation and withdrawal from the city in his third year was her death.

An even more recent critical analysis of a debate which has endured for nearly three-quarters of the twentieth century makes two points of the utmost significance. That analysis, appearing in the journal *Antiquity*, stresses that comparison of blood groups of various members of the royal family who followed on from the reign of Amenophis III, while 'no doubt justified' in suggesting filiation, 'cannot under any circumstances prove it'. The author demolishes much of the 'serological evidence' on which many an edifice has been built with the words: 'In comparisons of this sort, a negative result will immediately suffice to disprove filiation…but a positive result may be nothing more than a coincidence.' The same author argues: 'If Tutankhamun is accepted as the son of Akhenaten, natural curiosity will lead one to ask who his mother may have been. The truest answer seems to be that we do not know.' If he was the son of Nefertiti, why did his name never appear on monuments together with the six daughters of the principal queen?

As with so many of the questions surrounding Tutankhamun, there comes a point where further conjecture is unprofitable. In Carter's words, 'The mystery of his life still eludes us – the shadows move but the dark is never quite uplifted.' And then again, 'Let us put aside the tempting "might have beens" and "probablys" and come back to the cold hard facts of history.' Most of those cold hard facts are still accessible in Carter's simple, unpretentious and unique account of the discovery of the tomb.

Chapter 16

'A MYSTICAL POTENCY'

THE uncovering of the gold coffin and the mummified remains of the young king marked the high point of Carter's life and career. Here, surely, was the moment in life when past conflict should give way to present achievement, when the brilliant climax of a long and hard career, at the very core of which was the vision of the serene young face of the monarch, might be expected to offer up a future of contentment; even, perhaps, of comfortable retirement. No such thoughts seem to have entered Carter's mind. He worked on as conscientiously as ever, and seemingly as indifferent as ever to the opinion of those who might smooth his path to social and academic recognition.

Through late November and December 1925 he and his diminishing band of colleagues worked on the clearing of the gold coffin, designated article number 255, and the restoration of objects found on the mummy. Callender and Lucas were now his chief support, the former always at his side, while Lucas worked away in his laboratory tomb nearby. Mace, whose family had been with him for much of the time at Luxor, was too ill to continue by the end of the 1924 season.

The Americans, most of whom had wives in attendance at the Winter Palace Hotel and the Expedition House, had led a largely separate social life, though every now and again they came together for a game of bridge or an outing. Letters exchanged by members of the Mace family, which came to light sixty years later, gave the best of all insights into social life at Luxor: the outings on the Nile, visits to the mortuary temple of Ramesses III at Madinat Habu, to the great Ramesseum and the Colossi of Memnon, the disputes of Mrs Lythgoe and Mrs Burton who both wanted to be queen bee in the Anglo-American matriarchy, the largesse of the millionaire Harkness, donkey rides, the journeys from the Valley to Luxor aboard a 'coach' built on the chassis of an early Ford saloon, the comings and goings of important visitors such as Prince Arthur of Connaught, the Astors and Sir Rider Haggard.

At Christmas time in 1923, Carter had taken Winifred and Margaret Mace for a ride in his car, into the Valley, 'deep and frightening', and on to the tomb where Winifred noted 'the blaze of gold and glorious blue faience' of the interior. Carter opened up and led their gaze to the shrine with its 'beautiful untarnished gold doors', and then the alabaster vases. They could see the laboratory tomb where Mace was at work, 'So I could see my Father,' Margaret wrote, 'treating the Chariots – they were gorgeous, gold, with gold pictures of people, Negroes, Asiatics, prisoners and outside ornamentation of lotus flowers, daisies, lotus leaves in faience, glass and cornelian. The wheels were covered in sheet gold.' Winifred supplemented her daughter's description: 'here Arthur reigns supreme...the chariots are gorgeous...I have never seen such things.'

Christmas 1923 had been a relaxed time, despite Carter's dispute with the Egyptians and the memory of Carnarvon's tragic death. The Maces had a party at the Winter Palace Hotel and afterwards Carter joined them for dinner and parlour games at the Expedition House which they had decorated with streamers. The Metropolitan Museum site house was the social centre of the Valley but its typically American bustle was far removed from the turmoil of the archaeologists' work in the great heat of the Egyptian day and the cold of its nights, allowing of little respite and causing much aggravation. Mace's work in the laboratory, his help with the press and VIPs, the urgent collaboration with Carter in writing their joint account of the discovery of the tomb, contributed to his exhaustion. His health was more fragile than Carter's and in May 1924 a rapid deterioration gave rise to a hurried departure to England.

Left: Queen Hatshepsut from the temple at Deir al Bahari, a water-colour by Carter.
Right: Carnarvon, Evelyn and Carter.

Carter escorts a party of government officials to the tomb.

A last view of the tomb entrance and Carter's surrounding excavations on the adjoining tombs of Merneptah and Ramesses II, before the Valley floor was reshaped to provide facilities for the vast influx of tourists.

Anubis guarding the entrance to the Treasury.

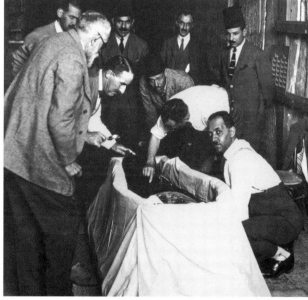

Left: Carter and Callender open the door of the inner shrine to reveal the sarcophagus.
Right: Unwrapping the mummy of Tutankhamun in the innermost coffin of solid gold following the removal of the outer coffins in November 1925. (*From left to right*): Pierre Lacau, Carter, Dr Derry and Dr Saleh Bey Hamdi.

Carter and an assistant separate the mummy from the walls of the coffin to which it was glued by resinous consecrating oils that had been poured over the inner coffin.

The life-size guardian statues, from the north wall of the antechamber, which protected the sealed entrance to the burial chamber.

Ritual representations of the king emerging from their wooden coffer.

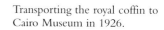

Transporting the royal coffin to Cairo Museum in 1926.

Model of the king's boat from the Treasury.

Fifty years on, Lady Evelyn, now Lady Beauchamp, sees the gold mask of the king at the anniversary exhibition of 1972 at the British Museum.

Carter at work on the gilded mask in the second coffin.

Detail from the gilt throne showing the king and his young queen, Ankhesenpaaten (later Ankhesenamun), under the rays of the sacred sun-disk.

Christmas 1925 reverted to normality as far as Carter was concerned. The work of clearing the tomb took precedence over holidays. Carter's diary was matter of fact. After the disappearance of the surgeons, H.R. Hall, head of the Department of Egyptology at the British Museum, arrived for a brief visit to the tomb. Otherwise every moment was devoted to the preparation of coffin and mummy.

The period 16 - 31 December was dismissed in a single sentence: 'Completed the gold coffin 255 and gold mask 256a.' On 31 December Carter and Lucas left for Cairo with three cases containing coffin, mask and the objects found on the body, which were handed over to the museum. The king's body was replaced in its outer coffin within the stone sarcophagus and left to rest in the burial chamber of the tomb, where it was to remain for ever.

Carter decided to carry on with restoration work until the end of the season, though the Ministry of Public Works announced that the tomb would be open to the public from 15 January 1926. *The Times* reported Carter as estimating that the gold found on and in the coffins was worth £40,000 – well over a million pounds in the language of the late twentieth century and almost exactly equal to Carnarvon's investment. Carter finally arrived in England on 28 May to a strangely quiet homecoming.

In fact, the arrival at his London home was so unremarkable that he was able to conceal his presence from the academic world which had expected him to give the Royal Institution lecture on 12 June. The gruelling season had left him in a state of physical exhaustion and *The Times* announced three days before the lecture was due to be delivered that he had been 'detained in Cairo'.

When he was sufficiently recovered to advertise his presence he became embroiled in yet another dispute. If old arguments rumbled on – in March his solicitor Hastie told William Lint Smith of *The Times* that he no longer acted for Carter and wished to have no further dealings with him – the latest contretemps was one in which the merits of Carter's position could not, for once, be doubted. On 10 April, while the autopsy on Tutankhamun's mummy was in progress, the *Morning Post* carried a story headed 'Uncanny Incidents' and 'Coincidence of Mark on Tutankhamun's Face'. The report was inspired by the death of a distinguished French antiquarian, M. Bénédite, but quoted Arthur Weigall at length in what was clearly a sensational attempt to seize on the notion of an ancient curse.

> In conversation with a *Morning Post* representative yesterday, Mr Arthur Weigall, the famous Egyptologist, who had made a special study of Egyptian superstitions in general and of Tutankhamun's reign in particular, pointed out that the object of the curses sometimes attaching to tombs was to terrify the tomb robbers of the period, who might smash up the mummy in searching for jewellery or otherwise damage the tomb in such a way that the dead man's identity would be lost. Such an event, in the opinion of the Egyptians, would injure the welfare of the spirit in the underworld...

The most eminent archaeologists now habitually hitched their wagons to Tutankhamun. Weigall was no exception. 'While I cannot exactly say that I subscribe in believing in the efficacy of such curses, I must admit that some very strange things – call them coincidences if you will – have happened in connection with the Luxor excavations,' said the man who had succeeded Carter as chief inspector for the Luxor region and who now dogged his path as special correspondent of the *Daily Mail*. The 'things' or 'coincidences' to which Weigall referred harked back to the canary-and-cobra legend which Carter insisted was a perfectly explicable event given the attraction of birds for most predatory creatures in the wild.

More remarkable was Weigall's own contribution to the store of local superstition. He told the *Morning Post* correspondent, presumably Bradstreet, of the fate of a local citizen who at Karnak smashed the statue of the goddess Sekhmet, employed in legend by the sun-god Re to destroy mankind. Weigall alleged that he inquired into the deaths of infants on the day of the iconoclastic act and found that a boy had died, the son of 'he who had smashed the statue.' Then there was the story of Carnarvon's first visit to the tomb, 'in very gay mood' and uttering 'jocular remarks'. Weigall had turned to H.V. Morton of the *Daily Express* who stood just behind him and said, 'half jokingly, if he goes down in that spirit I give him six weeks to live'. Six weeks later, according to Weigall, when Carnarvon died, Morton reminded him of his words.

The newspaper had led its contentious story with another reference to the fate of the Earl of Carnarvon. A mark which Dr Derry had found on the face of Tutankhamun was described by the newspaper, without quoting a source, as being in 'exactly the same position' as the insect bite which killed his lordship. In view of the impetus which the *Morning Post* article gave to the story of the 'curse of the Pharaoh', the precise words of the official medical report deserve quotation:

On the left cheek, just in front of the lobe of the ear, is a round depression, the skin filling it, resembling a scab. Round the circumference of the depression, which has slightly raised edges, the skin is discoloured. It is not possible to say what the nature of this lesion may have been.

There is no medical indication of the exact position of the insect bite which indirectly gave rise to septicaemia in Lord Carnarvon, and ultimately to the fatal pneumonia, but even if it was on the left cheek it would surely stretch the theory of coincidence too far to suggest that Tutankhamun was stung in precisely the same place, giving rise to the lesion identified after 3,000 years. Even so, the popular notion of the 'curse' which was first aired by the press at the time of Carnarvon's death and supported by the most distinguished occultist of the time, Sir Arthur Conan Doyle, was now given scientific credence by Weigall.

Within six months of Porchy's death, the theory was given superficial support by the sudden death of one of his half-brothers, Aubrey Herbert. Blind for the last nine months of his life, Aubrey took the advice of the Master of Balliol, who insisted that there was a close connection between eyes and teeth, and had several teeth extracted. Septicaemia set in, as with his brother's insect bite, and he died at the age of forty-three in September 1923. Seven years later, the other half-brother, Mervyn, died suddenly at the age of forty-one. Such deaths, though perfectly explicable, led inevitably to mystical speculation. Marie Corelli averred that 'the most dire punishment follows any rash intruder into a sealed tomb'.

In the interval, Winlock in America fought a rearguard action against the 'wild rumours and fanatic tales' which appeared almost daily in the press and caused widespread public fear, even keeping his own record of events the better to pour scorn on each allegation as it arose. He had little success.

Whenever an Egyptologist or tomb visitor died, whatever his or her age or condition, the 'curse' was said to have struck again. The public's fascination was likened by one well-known writer of popular archaeological studies to the 'curse of the Hope diamond' and the 'curse of the monks of Lacroma'. A friend of Carnarvon's died while on a visit to the tomb. A member of the deposed Egyptian royal household was murdered in London. A workman at the British Museum was supposed to have died while labelling objects from the tomb. Winlock observed that Carnarvon's friend was ill before he arrived in Egypt, and that many tourists who went to Egypt were retired people voyaging for their health. The Prince Ali Kamal Fahmy Bey, who was murdered by his wife in the Savoy Hotel, could only have been at the tomb as a visitor, never in an official capacity. There were never any objects from the tomb in the British Museum.

From 1926 onward there was a succession of deaths to feed the widespread appetite for mystery. Bethell, Carnarvon's secretary, died in his bed of a coronary thrombosis His father, the seventy-eight-year-old Lord Westbury, committed suicide by jumping from his seventh-storey apartment in London. The surgeon Sir Archibald Douglas Reid died while arranging to X-ray a mummy (though not that of Tutankhamun or a member of his family). An American named Dr. Carter died suddenly and unaccountably. Mace, Breasted, Aubrey Herbert, two of Merton's assistant reporters on the *Times* staff, and others, would add to Winlock's growing list. In 1933, the German Egyptologist Professor Steindorf compiled a pamphlet on these deaths. After investigating their backgrounds, he decided that none of the people or events could possibly be ascribed to the invasion of the tomb or the removal of its contents. Carter was quoted as saying that it was false to pretend that the protective formulae inscribed on the manikin figures in the burial chamber were curses. They were intended solely to 'frighten away the enemy of Osiris (the deceased) in whatever form he may come'.

An observant visitor in 1925 was Henry Field, a young Anglo-American anthropologist. Field was travelling with Dr L.H. Dudley Buxton, under whom he had studied at New College, Oxford, and the two men were going to Mesopotamia to meet Gertrude Bell and visit Woolley at Ur. They were equally keen to meet Carter on the way. In a book written thirty years later where he put 'curse' theories into a more intelligent perspective, Field also described a night in Cairo – enjoying the delectable food and wine of Shepheard's, observing Russell Pasha the much-feared chief of police at a nearby table, while outside mangy dogs barked and 'beggars begged for baksheesh; dirty little urchins tried to sell their sisters, dirty little sisters tried to sell their brothers.'

Buxton and Field went to the tomb with James Breasted:

> Buxton and I waited on dust-covered boulders near the entrance, trying to appear nonchalant. Howard Carter ...had the reputation of tearing to shreds the cards of would-be visitors. But Mr Carter was friendly. He was smiling as he led the way into the most publicized tomb in

history. He talked of the discoveries and excavations and Buxton listened with fascinated attention, but my mind was on one subject only.

Carter asked the young man what was making him restless, then smiled and told him to lift the sheet by his right foot. Field lifted the dirty linen sheet, and 'stared with dazzled eyes at the blindingly beautiful carved mass of gold that had held the mummy of the young king'. Years later he saw the mask of gold in the Cairo Museum, 'but it would never again seem so magnificent as in that moment, in the ill-lit shaft cut into the hillside of the Valley of the Kings'. He would never forget either the affability and kindness of Carter, the older and famous man conducting a young unknown graduate on the most famous of all tours. Then he wrote of the 'superstition that calamity would befall those who dared to break into the gold-filled tomb of Tutankhamun'. He recalled the story of the paperweight given to Carter's friend, Sir Bruce Ingram. The paperweight consisted of a mummified hand, its wrist still bound with a copper bracelet set with a scarab which bore the words in hieroglyphic 'Cursed be he who moves my body. To him shall come fire, water and pestilence.' Soon after he received the gift, Ingram's country home was burned down, and after it was rebuilt flood-water swept through it. He returned the paperweight to Egypt. 'To call this superstition combined with coincidence is the easiest and also the most scientific way out,' Field declared, adding, 'Nevertheless, there have been many times when I have hesitated before the locked and sealed doors of the past. Something grips the imagination then and holds one back. It is not a pleasant sensation. That day at Luxor, in King Tutankhamun's tomb, I knew it for the first time, and never more powerfully.'

As for Weigall himself, the archaeologist who won early approval for his work in the Inspectorate and returned to Egypt in 1923 as correspondent of the *Daily Mail,* he died of a fever, a common affliction in Egypt, becoming number 21 on the list of 'victims'. But Winlock pointed out that the man who gave succour to the 'curse' theory had never been invited to the tomb except on public occasions, and that he had no official position. Protest was in vain, however. Public interest in the tomb had switched largely from the artistic splendours of the Amarna period and its immediate aftermath in the Eighteenth Dynasty to the perpetual threat of a pharaonic curse. Carter's disdain turned to fury, but like Winlock he could do nothing to curb the public's craving or diminish the efforts of the press to satisfy its appetite. He quoted Sir Alan Gardiner in admitting the idea of 'a mystical potency' inherent in the image of things Egyptian, and he wrote of a determination to avoid 'gratifying the excitement of a morbid curiosity' in disturbing the religious paraphernalia of the young king. 'I am still alive,' he would reply when, almost daily, he was asked about the death of some obscure archaeologist or museum official. The fact was, though nobody wanted to hear it, that even a decade after the opening of the tomb, all but one of the five men and the single woman present had survived.

It was just as well that journalists did not at the time have access to Carter's notebooks which, ironically, might have provided powerful support for metaphysical speculation. One newspaper report referred to the words on a candle base at the shrine of the god Anubis, 'I am the protector of the dead.' The reporter added words of his own: 'I will kill those who cross the threshold...' Just before he left for England in May, Carter wrote in his diary a strange tale of the jackal Anubis, zoomorphic god of the dead:

May 1926. In the hills behind my house [at Western Thebes], I saw a pair of jackals...making their way towards the cultivated land. They probably had cubs in the hills as otherwise it was early for them to descend to inhabited and cultivated quarters. But the great interest was, while one of them was of normal size and colouring, the other – I was unable to tell whether dog or bitch, as they did not approach nearer than 250 yards – was totally black, much taller and attenuated, resembling, though tail not quite so bushy, the type...found upon the monuments. This is the first example of that colouring and of that type of jackal I have seen in Egypt in over 35 years experience in the desert, and it suggested to me ...the old and original Egyptian jackal only now known to us as Anubis.

Beneath the diary entry was a simple yet evocative thumbnail sketch of the creature, dense black with pricked ears, as seen through his Zeiss glasses. There was little opportunity to draw nowadays, but whenever the chance presented itself he showed that the sense of line and form which characterized his tomb drawings some forty years in the past had not deserted him as archaeology gained the ascendancy over his first love.

During the summer recess of 1926, Carter made his customary visit to Highclere Castle. This time, though, he had work to do. Lady Carnarvon had decided, in compliance with her late husband's will, to dispose of some of his fine collection of antiquities. To paraphrase the legal jargon of the will, Carnarvon's stated wish was that his 'entire Egyptian collection' would go to Almina, and he asked her to give one object each to the British Museum, the Ashmolean and the Metropolitan Museum. The gift to the last institution was specified – 'a fragment cup of blue glass, Tothmes III'. There is no truth in the later assertion by Hoving that he intended the entire collection to go to the British Museum. *But,* 'if my wife is forced to sell', Mr Carter should have sole charge of the negotiations and should fix the price. If, on the other hand, she decided to keep the collection, 'for my son or for the nation', she should 'consult Dr Gardiner and Mr Carter'. When it came to a decision to sell, however, it was Albert Lythgoe, representing the Metropolitan Museum, who joined Carter in August to pack the precious items and advise Lady Carnarvon on their disposal. The estate's solicitor contacted the British Museum, whose trustees must approve large purchases and whose methods in those days were not dynamic. The sum arrived at by Carter, about £40,000, could not be approved in the allotted time, 4 p.m. on the day of the solicitor's approach. The collection in its entirety was offered to the Metropolitan for the equivalent figure, $145,000. The New York museum struck one of the most profitable and most secretive bargains of its existence, and Carter assuaged his conscience over the failure of Egypt to compensate the one institution without whose experts he could not have accomplished the effective clearance of the tomb.

Carter was back in Egypt on 27 September 1926 ready to begin a new season's work in the 'room beyond the burial chamber'. Lucas, now in sole charge of the laboratory after Mace's retirement, was still a close and loyal companion, even though he had arrived on temporary loan from the Ministry of Public Works four years earlier. There was a fortnight of discussions and informal meetings with ministry officials in order to agree a programme for the clearing of the store chamber, which Carter was later to describe as the 'innermost treasury'.

The tomb would remain closed to the public until 1 January 1927, after which it would be open for three days a week until 15 March. There was also a brief interval of friendly dispute with fellow countrymen Quibell and Frith who had been alienated by Carter's angry disputes with their chief Lacau, but who now sought his views on a horse skeleton they had discovered at Saqqara. 'Allowing for certain shrinkage, its height to withers is 160 cms = 60 ins = 15 hands,' he noted, 'which seems abnormally high for a horse of the Ramesside period as Frith and Quibell appear to date it.'

When he and Lucas arrived at the tomb they discovered that rats had found their way under the wooden gate of tomb 15, the laboratory. In the event the invaders had done little harm, though Carter remarked testily that they 'might have done' and that 'a little sand placed at the base' would have prevented possible damage. There were still finishing touches to be put to the royal mummy and the outer coffin in which it was to rest henceforth. On 23 October he wrote: 'The first outermost coffin containing the King's mummy, finally rewrapped, was lowered into the sarcophagus this morning.' They were now ready to begin the investigation of the room to the north of the burial chamber. In a farewell to the object of all his ambition and desire, Carter quoted the great nineteenth-century Egyptologist Sir Gardner Wilkinson on the burial of the dead:

> Love and respect were not merely shown to the sovereign during his lifetime, but were continued to his memory after his death; and the manner in which his funeral obsequies were celebrated tended to show that, though their benefactor was no more, they retained a grateful sense of his goodness, and admiration for his virtues.

A new inspector in the Antiquities Department, Tewfiq Effendi Bulos, arrived to see the last preparation for the lying in state of the mummy, photographed at every stage by Burton who turned up at Luxor on 16 October. On the 24th Burton moved his photographic equipment into the store-room (Carter's 'treasury'). When it was first discovered back in February 1923, the chamber had posed a challenge to Carter's sense of discipline. Unlike the other chambers, its opening had not been sealed in antiquity. The temptation to wander among its array of burial objects was immense, and so Carter had ordered that the entrance be barred by wooden planks so that he and his men would not be distracted. Now they were able to study it in detail.

In the entrance itself was the black figure of Anubis, couchant on a gilt pylon resting on a sledge (or palankeen) with carrying poles. On the ground before the jackal god was a reed torch on a clay-brick pedestal, bearing the incantation 'to repel the enemy of Osiris, in whatever form he may come'. Behind the figure of Anubis a head of a cow stood, another symbol of the world beyond. Along one wall was a heap of black, shrine-shaped chests, all closed and sealed save one. The open chest contained statuettes of the king, swathed in linen and standing on leopard-back. The thought of what the other chests, 'sinister' chests, might contain 'beggared the imagination'. In the event, they contained statuettes of the king in his divine pursuits. The panting, sweating team rescued a number of model ships, their sterns all facing west, equipped with cabins, look-outs, thrones and kiosks. In front of the chests they found more ethereal offerings, boats with rigged and furled sails, resting on a wooden model of a granary. And beneath the pile of chests, in the south-west corner of the room, was a huge oblong box containing a figure of Osiris swathed in linen.

On the opposite side of the room was a row of caskets ornamented with ivory, ebony and gilt, and vaulted boxes of plain wood painted white, containing jewellery; excepting one, which contained an ostrich-feather fan with ivory handle, a relic of the young king 'as perfect as when it left his hands'.

Other objects in the 'treasury' included more model boats, an ornamented bow case, two hunting chariots dismembered and stacked like the chariots in the antechamber, miniature coffins, and more of the wooden 'houses' for *shawabti* figures. Many of the objects were undisturbed, but Carter was sure that thieves who knew what they were about had entered the little room. In 'their predatory quest' they seemed to have done little harm apart from rifling the treasure caskets and scattering a few beads in nervousness or haste.

But one other object of first importance remained. 'For there, standing against the east wall, and almost reaching the ceiling, was a large gilded canopy surmounted with rows of brilliantly inlaid solar cobras.' The canopy, supported by four square posts and mounted on a sledge, shielded a shrine-shaped gilded chest containing a canopic box which in turn offered alabaster compartments into which four mummiform containers of solid gold, holding the king's viscera, fitted. Against each of the panels the figure of a goddess – Isis, Nephthys, Neith and Serket – stood sentinel, guarding a particular part of the royal body.The four sides of what is generally known as the Canopic Chest are incised with hieroglyphs stained with black pigment in evocation of the formulae pronounced by each of the protecting goddesses in addressing the four sons of Horus: Imset, Hapy, Duamutef and Qebehsenuf. That remarkable discovery, the last to gratify the world's insatiable demand for gold embellishment and deep mystery, brought Tutankhamun and his tomb back to the front pages of the press. Even among the unimagined treasures of the tomb, it stood out as a major work of art and design. 'Besides the material just recorded,' Carter wrote in conclusion, 'there must have been a wonderful display of riches in those treasure caskets, and would still have been, were it not for the selective activities of the dynastic tomb-plunderers.'

Carter lingered over the meaning of the little room which he called the treasury, referring to the Turin papyrus with its plan of the tomb of Ramesses IV in order to explain its many mystical features. 'Although that document belongs to a reign some two centuries later than Tutankhamun, it does throw light upon his tomb.' Dimensions and elevations are given as in an architectural specification: 'drawn with outlines, graven with chisel, filled with colours'. There are notes on the back of the papyrus, including a heading, 'The measurements of the tomb of Pharaoh, Living, Prosperous, Healthy.' The burial chamber is described as 'The House of Gold, wherein One rests'; and that chamber is provided 'with the equipment of His Majesty on every side of it, together with the Divine Ennead which is in Duat' (Ennead being the divine synod of nine gods, Duat the nether world).

By comparison, Carter noted:

It therefore becomes fairly clear from the data quoted, and from the collection of material found in the little room beyond the Burial Chamber, that it combines several chambers in one: The *Shawabti-place; the Resting-place of the God's;* at least one of the two *'Treasuries';* and *'the Treasury of the Innermost'*.

The diary for October 1926 contained notes on the orthodox religion and the deities of ancient Egypt which showed an understanding born of long years of copying and working at the inscriptions and sacred objects of the tombs. 'The nucleus of Egyptian religion,' he wrote, 'was monotheistic.' But with that central god (who was no less than the sun-god) were grouped other deities. With him, eight major deities formed the Great Ennead (set of nine), all of whom were looked upon as direct descendants of the Great God. In addition to this there was a second or Lesser Ennead, 'who, though in direct line of descent from the sun-god, were more remotely related'. He listed the Great Ennead; Re, the sun-god, created from primeval waters; Shu and Tefenet, spat out from the mouth of Re, who supported the heavens; their children Geb and Nut, the earth and sky, and their offspring Osiris, Isis, Seth and Nephthys 'whose children are many on the earth'. Then came Horus, Toth, Anubis, and so on of the Lesser Ennead.

For the rest of the year, notebooks and diaries witnessed Carter's increasing preoccupation with the lessons of the artefacts he had discovered, with the pantheon, the myths, hieroglyphs (which he copied with a fine confident hand), etymologies of Egyptian words, and the organization of early Egyptian society. There was even space and time to devote to a fascinating piece of modern etymological detective work, quoting E.W. Lane on a drinking potion of the Nile boatmen in his *Modern Egyptians,* 'Boozeh or Boozah, an intoxicating liquor made with barley-bread'. The tomb itself seemed to have little more to offer.

At the end of October a young Frenchman, Henri Landauer, arrived at Luxor at the invitation of Lacau, as assistant to Carter and Lucas in the store-room. Through November and December, the surviving contents were cleaned and brushed up ready for the laboratory where, under the expert eye of Lucas, they were consolidated and made ready for their final journey to the Cairo Museum.

Press interest had waned to the point where few correspondents now bothered Carter, and even Merton, always under a cloud as far as his chiefs in Printing House Square were concerned, was away in London defending his actions during recent political troubles and explaining why he had not been able to send the paper a description of the removal of the king's body from the tomb to the Cairo Museum at the end of the previous year. As a consequence of the lessening of publicity interest, Carter was able to keep the contents of the store-room from the world until 4 December, when a communiqué agreed with the Antiquities Department was issued by the *Egyptian Gazette,* detailing the latest treasures. By the end of the year, a renewed interest on the part of government, press and public was apparent. Government ministers and their friends, as well as officials of the Antiquities Department, came and went without a suggestion of Carter losing his temper.

Tea with the Newberrys and an afternoon at the inaugural ceremony of the new broad-gauge rail link from Luxor to Aswan marked the only social engagements in three months. The tomb closed just before Christmas, on 19 December, after a visit from delegates to the XIVth International Navigation Congress. Carter, Lucas and Landauer celebrated together at the Winter Palace on the 25th. Work recommenced on the 30th. An enigmatic note in the diary for that day referred to the 'preserving and recording of materials and objects discovered buried in a hole'. On the last day of 1926 King Fuad visited the tomb and laboratory, excited by reports of the latest discoveries.

The New Year opened to more disturbances from the large crowds attracted by publicity given to the spectacular treasury artefacts at the end of the year. The public was now admitted to the tomb on three weekdays, Tuesdays, Thursdays and Saturdays, from 9 a.m. to 12 noon. By 9 February Carter's diary announced his departure for Aswan 'owing to demands from visitors'. He returned to the laboratory tomb twenty days later to find Burton and Lucas still hard at work photographing each item from every angle before it was packed ready for the journey to Cairo. Exhausted and for the first time beginning to feel the effects of so many years spent in the heat and turmoil of Egypt, he looked forward to the summer vacation in England. On his way, he stayed overnight at the Cairo Residency at the invitation of the new High Commissioner, Sir George (later Lord) Lloyd. Allenby, driven to despair by the politics of his own government and the administration he had been asked to oversee, had left for England in June 1925. He learnt from a Reuter cable that his successor was to be Lloyd, who had served as one of his intelligence officers in the 1914 - 18 war. Carter arrived in London on 3 May 1927.

Chapter 17

OF THE LIVING AND THE DEAD

I⊤ was a weary, more placid Howard Carter who set out to complete his life's work with the clearance of the last compartment of the tomb, the Annexe.

He was back in Cairo in mid-September 1927, in conference with officials of the Antiquities Department and the government. He had to sign a new agreement annually now, acting always on behalf of Lady Carnarvon who still shouldered the legal and financial responsibilities for the excavation undertaken by her late husband, even though she was no longer mistress of Highclere. The new season started officially on 15 September. 'During the last days of November 1927, we were able to begin the final stages of our investigations.' Those final stages were to last, on and off, for another five seasons.

The first six weeks were devoted to laboratory work on the Anubis shrine and the smaller artefacts of the Treasury, watched over for much of the time by Rushdi Effendi, the inspector for the Luxor region, and several of his junior colleagues. Burton joined the team on 15 October and Landauer turned up a few days later, in time to help with an influx of visitors. By the end of November they were ready to shift the roofing sections of the dismantled shrines which had been stored at the southern end of the antechamber, preparatory to returning to the annexe at the western end. This was the chamber they had allegedly invaded on the 'long night' of 26 - 7 November 1922, forcing the upper part of a sealed doorway, the lower part having been breached by robbers nearly four millennia earlier. On 30 November 1927 they were able to remove a few objects from the threshold and to step into the chaotic jumble which would occupy Carter and his men for the next four years.

'Strange and beautiful objects incur wonder and praise, conjecture and fair words,' Carter wrote in his diary, as he planned the twenty-first chapter of the book in which he recounted, as he worked, the stage-by-stage clearance of the tomb. When it came to the final draft, he replaced the word 'incur'; 'Strange and beautiful objects call for wonder...' He believed that his book should convey in the simplest terms not merely the facts of his discovery, astonishing as they were, but also his own true emotions as he uncovered each chamber and each object. As he reminded the reader several times in the final text, he was anxious to avoid the complexities and Egyptological refinements which would have meant nothing to the lay mind and served only to make his story the harder to follow.

Breasted and Gardiner helped to decipher the four seal impressions which remained in the plaster skin of the upper doorway, announcing by his coronation name the young occupant of the tomb:

The King of Upper and Lower Egypt, Nebkheprure, who spent his life making images of the gods, that they might give him incense, libation and offerings every day.

Nebkheprure, who fashioned [made images of] Osiris and built his house as in the beginning.

Nebkheprure – Anubis [probably when understood as the king as in the case of Osiris], triumphant over the nine bows.

Their Lord Anubis triumphant over the four captive peoples.

But Carter was at pains to explain that his academic friends were only partly responsible. He eventually rendered the seals in his own way, with minor changes.

Carter was fascinated by the thought of the incursion of

thieves with inside knowledge all those centuries before. 'There was something bewildering, yet interesting, in the scene which lay before us. The incongruous medley of material, jostled in wanton callousness and mischief, concealed, no doubt, a strange story if it could be disclosed.' The electric lamp bathed the chaotic room in golden light, showing up individual items among the heap of funerary objects. Here a chair 'like a faldstool, decorated in the taste of a distant age', there a bedstead, not much different from those used by Nile dwellers at the present day, a vase, a tiny figure; weapons, baskets, pottery, alabaster, boxes, boats; a broken box bulging with beautifully carved boats; lion, ibex, fan, sandal, glove – all 'keeping odd company with emblems of the living and of the dead'.

Carter's thoughts of skilled if not exactly pious hands at work in some distant age of supreme craftsmanship soon gave way to a sobering assessment of the task that lay before him. At a conference with his French and British assistants, it was decided to form into two groups, an inner group of 'treasure hunters' who would make their way head down, in line, inch by inch, through the mountain of objects, supported by rope slings under the armpits which would be held, puppet-fashion, by a second group of workmen in the antechamber. Thus the objects would be collected and removed one by one, uppermost first, while the danger of anyone slipping and causing a heavy artefact to fall, or the entire heap to collapse, was avoided.

In tackling the problem in so systematic a way, the excavators were able to build up a remarkable picture of both the original order of things, and of how the final chaos came about. It was concluded that there had been two robberies: the first by the infamous metal robbers of the Valley whose only interest was in gold, silver and bronze; the second by very specialist thieves whose mission was to find the rare and expensive unguents used in the burial process and contained in stone vessels. The annexe was, indeed, the store-room proper, intended for housing the oils of unguents, the wine and food, for the journey to the underworld, but materials belonging to the burial chamber and the treasury had overflowed and been stacked on top of the original contents. The two robberies had then compounded the confusion until the unholy jumble was created which would greet Carter and his men some 3,500 years later.

Why had so many quite insignificant vessels been tampered with? asked Carter. Why were some of them left empty on the floors on the chambers, while others were discarded in the entrance passage? The greases and oils used in those days, Carter guessed, were of far greater value than could be imagined in the present. Their value explained the fact that the tomb had been twice reclosed, as he had postulated when he first inspected the sealed entrance and inner doorway. The odd basket and alabaster jar found scattered on the floor of the antechamber, and the solitary *shawabti* figure leaning against the wall, had, he felt sure, come from the annexe and been left behind by thieves either inadvertently or for their later convenience.

As it happened, the chemistry and significance of one jar of 'cosmetic' found in the tomb had been discussed at the annual meeting of the British Association held in August 1926. The authors of the paper, Mr Chaston Chapman and Dr Plenderleith, described the fatty content of the jar as rather sticky and presenting the appearance of 'a heterogeneous mixture, consisting of yellow modules, together with a chocolate-coloured substance'. It melted at body temperature giving off a 'faint yet distinctive odour' which the chemists likened to coconut. After careful analysis, the substance was said to be about 90 per cent neutral animal fat and 10 per cent resin or balsam.

At the conclusion of his work on the annexe and the dedication of his remaining energies to the objects in Lucas's laboratory tomb, Carter permitted himself a sweeping historical summary:

Nothing can ever change the fact that we have undoubtedly found evidence in this tomb of love and respect mingled with want of order and eventual dishonour. This tomb, though it did not wholly share the fate of its kindred, though mightier mausoleums, was nevertheless robbed – twice robbed – in Pharaonic times…I am also of the belief that both robberies took place within a few years after the burial. Facts such as the transfer of Akhenaten's mummy from its original tomb at Amarna to its rock-cut cell at Thebes, apparently within the reign of Tutankhamun; the renewal of the burial of Tothmes IV, in the eighth year of the reign of Haremhab [Horamheb], after it had been robbed of its treasures throw considerable light upon the state of affairs in the royal necropolis at that Age. The religious confusion of the State at that time; the collapse of the Dynasty; the retention of the throne by the Grand Chamberlain and probable Regent, Ay, who was eventually supplanted by the General Haremhab, were incidents which we may assume helped towards such forms of pillage… The wonder is, how it came about that this royal burial, with all its riches, escaped the eventual fate of the twenty-seven others in the Valley.

Visitors still came from every quarter. On the last day of 1927 the King of Afghanistan arrived with his court entourage. On 6 January 1928 Egypt's restored Prime Minister, Sarwat Pasha, appeared, and two days later the tomb was opened to the public. It was time to pack the latest batch of antiquities from the laboratory and dispatch them to Cairo while Carter himself set off in the same direction to meet Carnarvon's sister, Lady Burghclere. The last of the visitors requiring his personal attention was the dowager Sultana Malek, who turned up on 13 January. Carter returned to Luxor from Cairo with Lady Burghclere in order to greet Umberto, the Crown Prince of Italy, in the first week of February.

High-level guide work had taken over from the exhausting routine and political bickering that had absorbed so much of his energies in recent years. A change of life-style might have seemed desirable and, on the surface, he coped well. But the inimical life he was now compelled to lead in his adopted country soon took its toll on his health. Like most of his generation he had smoked habitually for years and 'chestiness' became evident in his breathing. He took Lady Burghclere upriver to Aswan in early February and returned to his house at Qurna at the end of the month with a heavy cold. He was in bed for almost the whole of the next month, attended by his faithful servant Abdal-Asl Ahmad Said. He was up and about by the end of the month for the arrival of Princess Mary, daughter of George V, and her husband Viscount Lascelles, taking them on a tour of the Valley and to the cliff-top tombs of Thebes in which he had spent so many profitable years in his youth. The Sultana Malek, most enthusiastic of all the members of the Egyptian royal household, returned in April and Carter took her to Deir al Bahari to see the restored wall drawings. He was in London for the start of summer, exhausted by social duties.

Before he said farewell to Burton and Landauer and closed the tomb for the hot season, he received news of the death of Mace, his literary collaborator and, along with Burton and Callender, among the closest of his companions. Quiet and unassuming, Arthur Mace was as far removed temperamentally from Carter as from his cousin and mentor Petrie. He was sound in judgement, stable in personality and easy-going in manner, qualities which were in short supply in the American and British communities at Thebes. His work on the first volume of the *Discovery of the Tomb of Tutankhamen* [*sic*] had been seminal; indeed the manuscript, though unquestionably a joint composition, was in his handwriting. Like Burton, he was blessed with a determined wife – archaeologists' wives in the pioneering days between the two Great Wars were traditionally forceful – but in Winifred, Mace found a partner who would share his devotion to travel and to Egypt and archaeology: a perfectionist in her own way who expected sometimes impossibly high standards in others and was always openly delighted when she found that her husband could measure up to her values.

When Mace joined forces with Carter in January 1923, he described his new chief as 'a queer chap', adding that he was 'very nervy sometimes from the responsibility (I don't wonder), but he's always very nice to me.' Carter, on hearing of his colleague's death, sent Winifred a telegram saying that he was 'a man for whom I had great respect'. There was something of a lack of generosity in Carter's last tribute to the man who had been his *alter ego* in the first two years of tomb discovery and clearance. He owed Mace a large debt. If, as is often claimed, their joint work on the discovery of the tomb published as Volume One in 1923 is among the finest popular accounts of an archaeological excavation ever written, then a substantial part of the world's appreciation belongs to the gifted and modest A.C. Mace, as did the gratitude of Carter. But generous words never came easily to Carter. When his elder brother William lost his wife Mary in December 1924, Carter had said farewell to a favourite sister-in-law with a note in his diary, 'Willie lost his wife.' Such impersonal words were typical of Carter and now marked his response to the death of Mace in a Sussex nursing home.

Mace was inevitably given an honoured place in the long list of people associated with the tomb who were held by the popular press to be victims of the 'Pharaoh's curse'. He was exactly the same age as Carter, fifty-four years old, when he died. If Carter could find no more than prosaic words of acknowledgement when he heard of his colleague's demise, he did find some of his old ire when journalists insisted on stoking metaphysical fires which had, in the past, led to thousands of superstitious people destroying, or sending to museums, any Egyptiana they could find in their homes, however insignificant. Mace had suffered from pleurisy and pneumonia in recent years and Egypt had taken its toll. That, Carter insisted, was all there was to it.

The demands of everyday life soon drew him away from the latest 'death' controversy. The Spanish government, on the recommendation of the Duke of Alba, had wanted to give Carter a decoration in 1923 to mark his contribution to history and archaeology, but the British government – always wary of civil awards by foreign governments – referred the matter to Buckingham Palace and with royal approval turned down the offer. Not to be outwitted, the Duke booked him for a second lecture in Madrid in May. At the earlier address in 1924 Carter had left his audience at the point of discovery of the 'quartzite sarcophagus'. The royal patron took the chair as Carter once again kept his audience in rapture with his account of the subsequent dismantlement of the nest of coffins, the discovery of the mummy, and the ritual application of unguents before burial.

He returned on cue to Egypt, the land that was now his first home, on 25 September 1928. As he arrived at Kasr Carter he spotted a second example of the rare, almost extinct black jackal that he had noted two seasons before. 'This is now the second example of this animal that I have witnessed, in both cases resembling in form and in colour the Anubis-animal far more than the jackal of these parts.'

Lucas arrived on 8 October with a high fever and after ten days Carter called the doctor, who sent the patient to the Anglo-American hospital in Cairo. Paratyphoid was diagnosed. Carter developed a severe cold which prevented him from working at 'full steam', his automobile broke down among the sand dunes, and – suspiciously he thought – the hospital could give him no definite news of Lucas's progress. Burton arrived from Italy on 5 November, and promptly became ill. He took to his bed at the site house, attended by a nurse sent from Luxor, while Carter worked on alone, 'examining, repairing and recording a number of miscellaneous objects'. His temper exploding in several unaccustomed directions, he might well have begun to wonder if his dismissal of the 'curse' theory was entirely justified. If so, he gave no indication of a change of mind in diaries and notebooks. Only his growing dissatisfaction with colleagues and work-force became more and more evident.

On 15 November 1928 he wrote: 'Having a lot of trouble from stupidity on the part of the *Raises* and men. It seems that they get more stupid as they get older and slacker having been perhaps too long with me.' His notes showed how sadly his own intemperance and lack of generosity grew with the passing of the years. His workmen had been among the most loyal and devoted of employees, running the gauntlet of their own countrymen's anger when their chief's activities and ill-considered outbursts had brought official displeasure on them all. The *rais* Ahmad Gurgar and his companions, who had longed for his 'early coming' when he left them in 1924, were now blamed for the depressing state of inactivity which, in truth, marked the anti-climatic end of discovery and the onset of routine preservation work.

The mood of despondency was caught by terse correspondence between William Lint Smith and Merton, whose recovery from jaundice had demanded a long convalescence in the Mediterranean climate of Alexandria. Merton was still officially Carter's publicity agent. The efforts of *The Times'* management to contact both Merton and Carter's solicitor at the same moment brought past and present together unpropitiously.

On 1 November 1928, the London solicitors Frere Cholmeley & Co. of Lincoln's Inn Field responded to a letter which Lint Smith had sent to Carter's erstwhile solicitor, Hastie: 'Messrs Hastie wish us to inform you that they no longer act for Mr Carter and do not want further communications connected with his business addressed to them. Though we have not done anything for Mr Carter lately, we imagine that we are still his London solicitors.' The newspaper's management files referring to Carter's legal representation contained a note of two bonus payments of £100 each made to Merton in April 1923 and September 1925, both for his work on the Tutankhamun discovery.

As Merton returned to Luxor to keep the press at bay, Carter went to Cairo for consultations with the Antiquities

Department. *The Times'* Foreign News Editor, Deakin, had decided to find a replacement for his Cairo man. It was the culmination of long-felt dissatisfaction with Merton's work. Even at the height of the Tutankhamun story in 1923, when he was receiving handsome bonuses, Deakin had told the editor that there was 'no marked improvement in Merton's own service to the paper'. And in 1924, Sir William Tyrrell of the Foreign Office had reported to Geoffrey Dawson some 'unwise remarks' made by his correspondent. In November 1926, the editor cabled a complaint to Merton that he had failed to report the 'reburial' of the body of Tutankhamun after the autopsy and that he had failed to describe the finding of the contents of the annexe, reported in other journals. 'As a correspondent Mr Merton is not satisfactory. His long cables are frequently badly constructed... His political geese may become swans at any moment...' Dawson observed in an internal memo.

Merton's suit was not entirely threadbare. He had suffered extremely poor health during most of this period. Indeed, he was in a sense the first victim of the tomb's alleged blight on intruders, requiring an operation soon after the initial discovery, and later being struck down with hepatitis. He had been responsible for the major early dispatches which brought credit to the paper, not to mention considerable profit from syndication. In subsequent years he worked on despite sickness. Carter's diaries and notebooks make no mention of Merton's plight.

Germany had taken Britain's place in the Egyptian spotlight, with renewed demands in the press for the return of the Nefertiti 'head'. The *Sunday Times* sported the headline 'Bargain Bust for Lovely Queen'. It was a strange feeling for Carter not to be in the eye of the storm. In Cairo, the question of the Carnarvon settlement came up again in discussions with the Ministry of Public Works. Carter discussed the matter with Lady Carnarvon and Frere Cholmeley in London in the early Summer of 1929. When he returned to Cairo in September 1929 he was armed with draft proposals to present to the

Egyptians, taking account of the Carnarvon's estate's demands, the conditions under which he would continue to work on behalf of the Egyptian Ministry, and the need to recompense the Metropolitan Museum for its considerable investment of personnel and expertise in the tomb. As a result, no work was done during the entire season. Negotiations went on day after day for six months. By the end of the season he had come to an understanding 'with regard to favourable conditions for the completion of the remaining work'. Not until the start of the following season was agreement reached on the vexed question of compensation for the estate. Egypt eventually offered to pay £34,000 to Carnarvon's heirs. The sum of £35,979 was finally established by royal decree signed by King Fuad on 3 July 1930, covering expenses incurred and proved from the inception of work late in 1922 until the termination of the Carnarvon involvement in April 1929. Compensation for the Metropolitan Museum was left in abeyance. Kenyon of the British Museum expressed to the Foreign Office his surprise that the Egyptians had taken what for them was the most expensive way out. 'It seems the Egyptian government prefers to pay the estate out of its own pocket, rather than charge Britain for a liberal grant of duplicates.'

While those negotiations were in progress, Merton received notice of dismissal from *The Times.* Lint Smith's letter, dated 1 November 1929, gave several reasons for the termination of his appointment – unnecessary expenses, unnecessary and prolix cables, taking sides too frequently and too readily. His recent work in Palestine, where the British mandate was under attack from Arabs and Jews, was said to be 'very disappointing'. Whatever the justification for the decision of *The Times'* management, Merton was outraged. On 28 May his solicitor issued a writ for 'printed libel', a common procedure in those days, dependent on the willingness of secretaries and others to witness the offending words, and in this instance described by Lord Justice Scrutton as a 'rather rubbishy' typewriter case. Whatever its merits, the case was destined to keep lawyers on both sides busy for the following two years, during most of which Merton commuted between the Turf Club in Cairo and the tomb, standing in for Carter when the latter found the tedium of sorting and docketing the store-room artefacts too much and went off himself for a few days' respite in Cairo. The former Egyptian Minister in London, Dr H. Mahmud, revealed to *The Times* that while Merton worked for that newspaper he was paid not only by Carnarvon and Carter for extra-mural services, but also by the Egyptian royal household which made an allowance of £200 a month in addition to an initial payment of £1,000. Precisely what service Merton rendered for those emoluments was never made clear.

Eventually *The Times* offered Merton £1,000, which the newspaper's own lawyers mistakenly passed on as £10,000 before realizing their mistake and correcting it. In March 1932, the offending words of Merton's notice of dismissal were eliminated from the records and replaced by words which referred to a 'retrenchment scheme in Egypt', and thanked him for his 'loyal service'. The sum paid to Merton in compensation and costs was £5,936 and a few shillings.

At the start of the proceedings, both Merton and Carter had been put up for membership of the Savile Club in London. Merton's proposer was Ralph Walter, director of *The Times*. Carter, familiar as a guest at the club over the years, was proposed and supported by a group which included his old Cairo acquaintances Percy White and Edward Boulanger, Ivor Back, consultant surgeon at St George's Hospital, and Ernest Louis Franklin, banker, philanthropist and collector.

In the last two seasons, 1930 - 1 and 1931 - 2, Carter laboured under increasing burdens of depression and physical strain. His waspish manner returned. Time and again in his notes he complained of the presence of Egyptian inspectors standing over him and asking questions about his activities. More and more his diaries filled with details of important visitors: 'Our work was temporarily stopped owing to the arrival of the Crown Prince of Sweden whom I was obliged to attend during his three-day visit.'

Egypt had been in a state of almost constant political upheaval during the decade in which he had realized his life's ambition and completed the task which a Janus-like fate had assigned to him. Hard toil, climate and contentious debate had taken a severe toll on his strength. Colds came more often and more severely than in the past, and he found it ever harder to work at full speed. But Egypt had claimed him in spirit, and though he could afford to live in London and lead the congenial life of the well-off celebrity, the prospect of such a life did not attract him. In his prosperous fifties he remained a solitary man, ever more distant from his family, sure of his own capabilities and too often dismissive of others'; moody, taciturn and suspicious, victim in part of England's class-infused society which took more account of background than of achievement in life, but even more, victim of his own uncompromising nature.

There were women in his life; brief affairs, desultory and seldom blossoming into companionship. Howard Carter had few if any confidants, and his family is generally marked with his own trait of taciturnity, but his brother William, respected as an artist and friend by several distinguished academicians and fellow painters, let it be known that he was not entirely chaste. Others who knew him well enough, however, thought him sexless. The influences of his youth were not unique, but neither were they normal. The deprivation of parental care in infancy and the overweening attentions of two maiden aunts, the lack of formal schooling and consequently of games and group activities, and the attentions of earnest Egyptologists at an age when other young men's thoughts and fancies turned elsewhere, doubtless had their effect.

Gertrude Caton Thompson returned to the Valley in 1930 with her friend Elinor Gardner, wife of the Wykeham Professor of Ancient History, to cast an expert eye on the Englishman who had become Egypt's most familiar, if least popular, expatriate citizen. The two women stayed at the Savoy Hotel, 'because of its beautiful garden', but they wanted something more of Egypt than Cairo and the Fayum and so made their way to the Valley. Carter received them with polite indifference. Thompson commented that, 'At Thebes Howard Carter was still at work seven years after the discovery of Tutankhamun's tomb, as we found him repairing some of the coffin-cases. He showed us the multitude of things still awaiting attention and I pitied him cooped up for years in the electrified darkness of the tomb.'

Others in the ensuing years noticed him cooped up not in the laboratory tomb, making endless notes on the shrines and artefacts of the store-room and antechamber, but in the Winter Palace Hotel where he was able at least to indulge his lifelong love of a comfortable armchair, as one visitor put it, 'sitting in the foyer, sunk in gloom and talking to no one'.

Egyptologists began to point to the artistic wonders of Carter's discovery, and to compare them with the paucity of archaeological gains. Alan Gardiner, for example, was to say 'the discovery had added very little to our knowledge of the history of the period. To the philologist the tomb was disappointing as it contained no written documents.' Gardiner's work in Carter's advisory team was indispensable, but Carter was not well disposed towards him, saying on one occasion, 'The more I see of him the less I like him.' For his part, Gardiner greatly admired Carter's work, calling him a near-genius in 'the practical mechanics of excavation'. He told the writer Leonard Cottrell:

But as a revelation of the *artistic* achievement of the period, the discovery was quite unparalleled. Nothing like it had been discovered before, and, in my opinion, it is extremely doubtful if any comparable discovery will be made in the future. The fact that, after a superficial looting, it remained untouched for 3000 years was probably due to a lucky chance. When, many years after Tutankhamun's burial, the hypogeum of Ramesses the Sixth was being tunnelled out of the hillside above the tomb, the stone chippings from the excavation buried the entrance to Tutankhamun's much more modest sepulchre, which thus escaped. The value of the discovery to archaeology lies not only in the wealth of objects it revealed, but in the fact that these lovely things were recorded and preserved with such consummate skill.

There was inevitable qualification. The results of the greatest discovery in the history of Egyptology, 'made by an Englishman', had never been properly published, in the scientific sense of a detailed description of every object. 'In 1926, Carter told me,' wrote Gardiner, 'he estimated that such a publication would cost £30,000.' In 1950, when he raised the matter, Gardiner estimated that Carter's figure would by then have reached £100,000. What it would cost at the end of the inflationary twentieth century is a matter for day-to-day conjecture, but it could hardly be less than a million pounds. Who would finance such a publication today? asked Sir Alan. Seventy years on from the discovery of the tomb, the Griffith Institute, within the Ashmolean at Oxford, is engaged on the painstaking task of a full and accurate record of Carter's achievement. This posthumous tribute will be the ultimate reward for Carter's life of labour, of lonely devotion to a cause in which he had singular faith, and which he realized with the financial and moral support of the one true friend of his entire life, Lord Carnarvon.

Was there no other true friendship among all the people he came to know in Egypt, England and America? Not a single love-affair or even female companion? Not even an 'indiscretion'? Had he lived in France, such questions would only be asked rhetorically; a paramour here and there would hardly be thought worthy of comment. In British public life, however, there is seldom much evidence of the sexual expedient. Answers to questions which most other peoples treat light-heartedly embarrass the English and must necessarily be based more on rumour and supposition than fact.

The young man's early fancies seem, however, to have

flagged before they were given much of a rein. Back in the 1903 season, at the time of his appointment to the inspectorate and the discovery of the royal chariot, while he worked 'experimentally' on the tomb of Tuthmosis IV on behalf of Theodore Davis, Carter went off to Cairo, pleased with his efforts on the American's behalf and looking forward to a few days with some old friends. It was an interval which gave rise to a revealing essay. His unnamed friends had invited him to dinner at the Hôtel d'Angleterre and among the guests was 'a charming young lady whom it was my pleasure to sit beside'. There was the usual 'perfunctory' introduction and neither quite knew who the other was, but he found his table companion an excellent and amusing conversationalist, 'particularly so on the subject of her experiences during a sojourn in Upper Egypt on one of Cook's Nile boats'. Carter sat silent while the young woman at his side talked of her fascinating journey and of seeing the 'wonderful royal chariot' in the Valley of the Kings. Had he, Carter, ever been to the Valley? Had he heard of the discovery of the chariot? Carter replied in the affirmative. 'I am the luckiest woman on earth!' she exclaimed. 'And from her expression I vaguely discerned the symptoms of another mystery,' wrote Carter. 'Would you believe it!' she said. 'I was present in that glorious Valley when the discovery of the chariot was made, and I saw it drawn out of the Pharaoh's tomb by three white camels!' 'Oh! Madam!' Carter retorted. 'I must indeed congratulate you!'

The young man's conclusion to the half-imagined tale told by the 'fascinating' girl he met in Cairo was a sarcastic note to the effect that the 'remnant of a royal chariot' was for years after dragged about by 'those mysterious and somewhat ungainly milk-white beasts of burden'. He agreed mundanely with Professor John Tyndall: 'When people are of this frame of mind, the story of Jack and the Beanstalk may be maintained in the face of all the facts in the world.'

On his return to London following the closure of the tomb in 1932 Carter was operated on for a serious bladder condition and Hodgkin's disease was diagnosed. For some time afterwards, he was looked after by a handsome young man whose name no one seems to have remembered. Implied suggestions of homosexuality are implausible, for there would have been plenty of opportunity for practice, and rumour, in Egypt. There was talk among acquaintances, especially at the Chelsea Arts Club to which William often took him, of a young Frenchwoman in the King's Cross area of London. Others spoke of a women friend who lived on the south coast near Brighton. If she existed, the same woman could well have moved between the two addresses. The same whispered confidences from the past suggest that on his many visits to the Burton home in Florence over the years, Carter came to know a few Italians and expatriate Britons, but there is no suggestion of friendship or sexual encounter. The same has to be said of his journeys home across Europe with Carnarvon in the years immediately before and after the First World War. At that time, he was essentially his lordship's servant and he was in no position financially to share his patron's enthusiasm for expensive women or for the passing pretty face, but he seems to have had an eye for one and there is no reason to suppose that he did not enjoy an occasional fling.

More importantly, what of the rapport which undoubtedly existed, at any rate for a year or two, with the beautiful and aristocratic Lady Evelyn? He was certainly a frequent caller at her London home in the decade after her father's death, and perhaps there is significance in the fact that in 1930 he had moved from St James's to an apartment in Prince's Gate Court, practically next door to Evelyn's married home. Even so, according to his diary, he called as frequently on Evelyn's aunt, Lady Burghclere, and there is no evidence that either received him more than politely or with anything other than a genuine desire to learn more about his work at the tomb which was so much part of all their lives. There was, all the same, the effusive letter written soon after the discovery, expressing the feelings of a sensitive eighteen-year-old girl at a moment of high emotion; a moment shared with almost all the world. Intrigued by persistent rumour connecting her mother with the archaeologist, Evelyn's daughter Patricia when she grew up asked pointedly, 'Is it true?' Lady Beauchamp, as she was then, replied, 'At first I was in awe of him, later I was rather frightened of him.' She told her daughter that she believed Carter had 'a chip on his shoulder' and that she resented his 'determination' to come between her father and herself.

Could there have been any substance in subsequent insistence on an 'affair'? Patricia, now Mrs Leatham, is adamant, believing that the congratulations intended in Evelyn's letter had taken on in all innocence the appearance of a panegyric: 'At the time of those allegations, mother had had a second stroke,' she said, 'and was unable to act independently. Otherwise I am sure she would have taken legal action to prevent publication of the story.' The daughter of course would remain loyal to the memory of her mother and father, and her testimony cannot be gainsaid. She was close to her mother and had no reason to conceal or to varnish the truth. That there was an emotional tie between her mother and Carter cannot, however, be doubted. Evidence of that fact was manifest as much after Carter's death as before.

Fame gave Carter a sporadic place on the 'country house' circuit and rare visits to Norfolk were sometimes spent with the Colman family of mustard fame, who had shown a great interest in his work; sometimes too with the new generation of Amhersts at Foulden Hall, on the old Didlington estate. He visited his boyhood home occasionally – a cousin, Annie, went to live at the Sporle Road cottage after Aunt Kate's death – but he usually stayed with Verney's widow Audrey at North Creake near Swaffham.

In 1932, soon after the ending of his Egyptian contract, he once again moved his London abode from Prince's Gate Court to a finely appointed apartment just round the corner by the Royal Albert Hall in Kensington Gore, 49 Albert Court, and the Grill Room of the Hyde Park Hotel nearby became the focus of his social life in London. The head waiter was pointedly obedient while Carter's invariable response to the respectful attentions of the *Maître d'hôtel* was *'Pas mal.'* On one occasion when he was eating in the Hyde Park, John Drinkwater approached him and said that a mutual friend, Axel Munthe, was coming to stay for the weekend; he wondered if Carter might be free to join them. Carter declined, boasting to the poet that he had once thrown Munthe out of his house in Egypt. Drinkwater said: 'How sad. My wife was very impressed with him.' 'Exactly!' replied Carter. Munthe's enthusiasm for Egypt occasionally leapt from the pages of his famous *Story of San Michele,* as when he related how he had put a cobra in a state of catalepsy in the temple at Karnak. He had been proud to call at 'Castle Carter' soon after the publication of his book in 1929.

Egypt and *his* tomb were in his blood. He continued to winter in Luxor, living in the house in the Valley, his old servants in attendance, or at the Winter Palace where he still sat in isolation, increasingly contemplative and lonely. On 17 March 1931, the Antiquities Department acknowledged the last large consignment, thirty-nine cases of objects from the tomb, signed for by Lacau's deputy.

On 22 July, *The Times* reported one of the last significant public appearances of the man who had already begun to fade from view when Flinders Petrie asked him to lecture at University College. Aided by 600 slides he produced a *tour de force* under the eagle eye of his first master in Egypt. There was a final mystery, Carter was reported as saying:

> Among the treasures of the tomb were two miniature burials of stillborn children, both nameless but buried in their father's name. If they never reached the earth alive, was that the result of abnormality, or was it the result of political intrigue? Was there a crime committed? That, and the preceding question, Dr Carter feared, would never be answered, but what might be inferred was that had one of

those babes lived there would never have been a Rameses dynasty. Thus it was that the famous dynasty passed into the hands of the Great Chamberlain, who in turn was supplanted by Tutankhamun's general, Horemheb, who founded the 19th dynasty.

The embryonic babes had been found in the so-called treasury, in tiny gold coffins within a blackened wood box, placed side by side and head to foot. The inscriptions of the coffins referred only to an Osiris, giving no clues as to the worldly names of the occupants had they lived. Later examination showed one foetus to be 'probably' of six months' development, the other seven months.

The last rites of the tomb clearance were read out six months later by the newspaper which all along had been at the heart of the Tutankhamun story. On 2 February 1932, *The Times* reported: '1 February. A last consignment of finds, including fragments of the great golden shrine, left for Cairo today. With this consignment Mr Howard Carter's 10 years' work on the tomb is ended.'

There was a leading article on 3 February, headed 'Tutankhamun – the Last Phase'. One of the most successful and certainly one of the most exciting episodes in the annals of archaeology had come to a close.

MR HOWARD CARTER, the hero of it all, has the satisfaction now of seeing his work completely finished. He and the late Lord Carnarvon planned it, and for a long time they toiled with no results; then came clear indication of the quarry, and the death, in the moment of triumph, of LORD CARNARVON...MR HOWARD CARTER's achievement has a magnificent finality about it... He has recovered the romance of a dynasty of which not much was known before, the brief happiness of a young King and his consort; and he has proved once more the eternal power of mortality to touch the human heart.

Capitals and all, the reader would have forgotten that requiem when, two years later, in October 1934, the same newspaper announced that Mr Carter was returning to the Valley to resume his work there. It was a false alarm, though Carter was to live, hovering between Egypt and England, for another five years.

Callender's death, more than any other event, seemed to signal the end, for three decades at least, of public interest in the boy-king of ancient Egypt and his English trumpeter. As far as it is known, Arthur Callender died in Egypt in 1937. Remarkably, his death was never recorded by the official registry of Great Britain, neither was it reported to the Consulate in Cairo or Alexandria. For whatever reason, Callender's death, at the age of sixty-one, was kept a closely guarded secret, and from Carter, with whom Callender had shared a house for fifteen years, there was silence.

The discovery and clearing of the tomb of Tutankhamun took place contemporaneously with Woolley's excavation of Ur. It is an interesting commentary on British attitudes to achievement in general, and to academic deeds in particular, that Woolley arrived home to a knighthood, honorary degrees from major universities and a government appointment in India, while Carter met a curtain of silence. To the end of his life, the single acknowledgement of his achievement was the degree awarded by America's Yale University. It is tempting to analyse the thought processes of the 'establishment' and of those institutions which tapped their heels in the face of the most spectacular revelation of ancient kingship. If he was a difficult, waspish man, it is hard to find words for the politicians and colleagues whose envy and snobbery are demonstrated in equal measure by their failure to honour his achievement.

By 1936, the story of the heretic city of Amarna, into whose cult of sun-disk worship Tutankhamun was born, had become public property. Agatha Christie's play *Akhnaton* reached the London stage, bringing all the devices of popular theatre to bear on the effete king and his queen Nefertiti, and the apostate beliefs which their children grew up to embrace, and finally to reject. Agatha, who met her husband Max Mallowan at Woolley's Ur of the Chaldees, discussed the plot endlessly with them and other archaeologists whom they had met at Woolley's latest site, Atchana, and at Nineveh where Max dug in the thirties. Nobody ever sought Carter's opinion, on that or any other matter pertaining to the piece of ancient history which he, more than anyone, had made intelligible.

The Middle East, like Europe, was overtaken by the rise of fascism in the thirties, but as his compatriots bemoaned the passing of a world which their country and empire once dominated, Carter contemplated a more distant and vastly more romantic empire of the past, displayed now for all the world to see in Cairo's splendid new museum. His own name was hardly evident though. The tomb and its contents had become Egypt's, rightly but sadly all the same for the man who had given almost all his life to their recovery.

In 1936, the young Prince Farouk returned to Egypt from his military apprenticeship in England, to take the throne on the death of his irascible father, Fuad. Soon after, Carter was asked, though in an unofficial capacity, to take the young monarch on a tour of the tomb. One member of the royal party was a prince on the maternal side of the family, seventeen-year-old Adel Sabit, who was to become the king's biographer. He was to provide the Egyptian native view of Carter in his declining years, formed in the midst of a feud between the new Queen Farida, and her mother-in-law, the dowager Queen Nazly:

> ...during a week of constant visiting of temples and tombs, when we were accompanied by such illustrious personages as Howard Carter... the feud continues... Howard Carter is a forceful and vital personality, but grumpy and rather dour with people, tourists being his pet aversion. Carter can nevertheless be a charming and interesting man when he is not thundering imprecations on the Egyptian government's

Antiquities Department, with whom he has a long-standing feud.

Carter, it seems, improved on the bizarre tale which he had told Charles Wilkinson many years before, that he proposed to search for the tomb of Alexander. Now he told his royal guests that he had found the tomb but intended to keep its whereabouts to himself. 'The secret will die with me,' he promised. Adel Sabit's memory played him false in at least one respect. He believed that his visit to the tomb was in 1941. If that were so, it would certainly have proved the supernatural theories which Carter rejected so vehemently. 'The sentiment of the Egyptologist…is not one of fear, but of respect and awe… entirely opposed to foolish superstitions.' By 1941 Carter had been dead for three years.

His end came suddenly, on 2 March 1939, at his London home, at the age of sixty-five. His doctor ascribed death to cardiac failure and lymphadenoma (medical description for Hodgkin's disease). His niece Phyllis was at his bedside.

He enjoyed a good press at the end, but even in obituaries journalists insisted on the perverse superstitions which dogged his achievement. One of Britain's leading provincial newspapers, the *Yorkshire Post,* spoke for the rest, quoting the alleged tomb inscription, 'Death shall come on swift wings to him that toucheth the tomb of a Pharaoh.' Had he been able to respond, Howard Carter would assuredly have repeated words he had used so often on the same subject, 'Tommy-rot.'

His burial, on 6 March, took place at Putney Vale Cemetery in the presence of nine mourners. It was a modest plot, grave number 45 in block 12, with a headstone which read simply:

HOWARD CARTER

Archaeologist and Egyptologist

Born May 9, 1874 – died March 2, 1939

His surviving brother William was there, and the cosmopolitan George Eumorfopoulos paid his respects. Two archaeologists who had assisted him briefly in the twenties were present, and there was a lone woman, Lady Evelyn Beauchamp.

Chapter 18

AFTERMATH

I N his last will and testament, made on 14 July 1931 while he was living at Prince's Gate, Carter named Henry (Harry) Burton, of Via dei Bardi in Florence, and Captain Bruce Ingram, editor of the *Illustrated London News,* as his trustees. He charged them with the task of ensuring that the house and estate he occupied for so many years at Alwat al-Diban in the Valley of the Kings, purchased from the Egypt Exploration Society and extensively developed by him, with all its contents, should go 'as soon as possible' to the Metropolitan Museum of Art. After the customary tokens to his trustees, and to his long-term servant Abdal-Asl Ahmad Said, he left all other properties, shares and money (mostly held by the National Bank of Egypt) to his niece Phyllis Walker.

He added: '…and I strongly recommend to her that she consult my Executors as to the advisability of selling any Egyptian or other antiquities included in this bequest…' His niece took his advice. Burton and Ingram, confronted by the certain knowledge that among the many objects purchased legally from dealers there were important pieces in Carter's collection which came from the tomb, asked Newberry for his advice. Newberry consulted Alan Gardiner.

The implication of the posthumous discovery of Carter's hoard was complicated by the fact that an ex-employee of the Cairo Museum, Salim Bey Hassan, was at the time taking action for libel against a local newspaper which had accused him of complicity in the wholesale theft of objects. In the course of that action, counter-accusations were made naming several British employees of the Antiquities Department, in particular Rex Engelbach. Furthermore, Lacau's successor, the kindly Abbé Drioton, had decided to retire and Engelbach was the principal candidate for the job. Unfortunately, Engelbach's academic qualifications were not deemed to be adequate and Newberry was trying to persuade the Vice-Chancellor of Liverpool University to bestow an honorary MA on the man everyone in the British camp wanted to occupy the seat of Director-General. The last thing any of the actors in these interconnecting dramas wanted was another scandal involving Carter's embarrassing possessions. Gardiner sought the advice of the Foreign Office, which – with impending war with the axis powers in the wind – was understandably reluctant to become involved in an archaeological *cause célèbre*.

It took nine months for any kind of resolution to be reached by which time the countries chiefly involved were locked in the early skirmishes of the Second World War.

By November 1939, Engelbach had taken over at the museum and Burton sent him a list of the objects concerned and asked his advice. It was an imposing catalogue.

1 green–blue glass headrest
1 large *shawabti,* green faience
1 pair lapis *shawabti*
1 small libation glass
1 sepulchral dummy cup, faience
1 ankle amulet
9 gold–headed nails
3 gold ornaments for harness
1 metal tennon

Engelbach, after setting out Burton's list, wrote of the collection of 'figurines, small amulets...more importantly...a large turquoise blue glass headrest, bearing the cartouche of Tutankhamun, worth many thousands of pounds'. Engelbach suggested that if the articles could be returned to Cairo by 'diplomatic bag' he would replace them without fuss.

Although it did not follow that any of these pieces were necessarily secreted from the tomb on the 'infamous night' of 26 - 7 November 1922, it was now proven beyond doubt that Carter had taken the matter of compensation into his own hands at some stage.

The archaeologists involved agreed that the details of the 'illicitly exported objects' should be suppressed in order to prevent an international scandal. Even at that late stage, however, there was disagreement as to how the matter should be handled. Burton thought it best that Miss Walker should quietly 'present or sell' them to the Metropolitan Museum. The Foreign Office diary for 7 December 1939 contained the remarks of Under-Secretary Laskey: 'I suppose the objects must be returned... My own inclination is to have them dropped into the Thames.' As for the plan to return them by diplomatic bag, 'I don't like the idea of making HMG an accomplice.' The redistribution of these pieces, and of others known to have been in the Carnarvon collection, suggests that while the most important objects were sent back to Egypt and replaced by Engelbach (who remained silent ever after on the subject), others did find their way to New York.

Gardiner must have been reminded of an occasion in December 1922, just before Lord Carnarvon and Almina left to spend Christmas in England. A fortnight after the opening of the first door to the inner chambers, Porchy threw a party at the Winter Palace Hotel, at a time recalled by Valentine Williams of Reuters as 'the most brilliant season Luxor had ever known'. Gardiner was present, as was the young artist Charles Wilkinson, and they observed his lordship openly handing round objects from the tomb.

In fact, Carter was at no great pains to conceal the objects which he had taken for himself in payment for work done and in unspoken retribution for Egypt's obduracy. On the desk of his London home he openly displayed a delightful blue faience *shawabti* figure of Tutankhamun. A tiny figure of the dog Anubis found its way to the Griffith Institute at Oxford, but when embarrassed officials checked the records they found that Carter had made out a card for the item in the meticulous index which he had kept of all the tomb's artefacts. Mace's daughter Margaret, Mrs Orr as she became, recalled in later life her girlhood visits to Carter's home in Kensington in the company of her mother. 'My mother disapproved of Carter,' she said in a newspaper interview. 'We visited him years later and he had pots and things. She said to me, "Did you see all that? It's disgusting." At the time I didn't know what she meant.'

The return of a nationalist government to power in 1930 had given rise to a new law, forbidding the removal of any article from Tutankhamun's or any other tomb without the sanction of the Antiquities Department, even of duplicates. Whether the objects which came into the possession of the Carnarvon and Carter estates were taken out of Egypt before or after that all-embracing law cannot be said for certain, but it is probable that Carter took them at different times, most probably at moments of extreme anger and frustration. At the time of the resumption of nationalist power, Professor Capart had made an independent evaluation of duplicates provided by Carter in order to give the Egyptian government a sum to work on when it agreed to compensate Lady Carnarvon, and the Belgian's assessment was almost exactly the same as Carter's, about £37,000 sterling.

Thomas Hoving, in subsequently piecing together evidence from several sources, including the curators of American museums, lists the disposal of seventeen items, 'described in his [Carter's] own notes', to the Metropolitan Museum. 'Some were purchased by the Metropolitan – either from Lord Carnarvon's estate or from Howard Carter during his lifetime or from Carter's estate in 1940,' writes Hoving. 'Others were given by Carter to the museum.' Yet, in all the years the museum had possessed the objects in question, it had never publicly acknowledge their provenance. Perhaps the Metropolitan Museum was conscious of a shared responsibility over the possession of illicit treasure? Certainly it has always kept a quiet counsel in the matter. At the fiftieth anniversary celebrations of the discovery of the tomb in 1972 - 3, the museum staff's response to questions smacked more of the CIA than of a respected academic institution, and with the approach of the seventieth anniversary, the successor staff has made it equally clear that its attitude remains the same. Hoving's list included a few items taken for scientific analysis, such as dried embalming fluid, fragments of gilded wood, fabrics, pieces of matting and so on. But there were more tangible objects, such as two 'beautiful finger rings of blue faience with cartouches bearing the King's coronation prenomen; two silver and two gold nails from the royal coffins; a bronze rosette; a broad collar of blue faience beads; a bronze puppy.' Such pieces, Hoving thought, amounted to no more than 'a minor archaeological indiscretion', presumably as much on the part of his employers, the Metropolitan Museum, as of Carnarvon and Carter whose money and labour had brought them to the light of day.

But that list was merely the tip of the Metropolitan iceberg. Ten works, listed by the museum as probably from the tomb of Tutankhamun, Hoving describes as 'masterworks in any lexicon of ancient Egyptian art'. The second list is imposing. A solid gold ring, engraved with the prenomen, was presented to the museum in December 1922, just after that night spent in the tomb at the end of November, and the frenzied clearing of the passage leading to the antechamber when Carter told his chief that he could see 'wonderful things'. Winlock's notes said that the ring had been on the Cairo art market since 1915, an improbable claim. Carter's diary for December 1922 showed purchases of antiquities valued at £1,000 and sales amounting to £435. Then there was a superb inlaid golden fan or sceptre; two painted and carved ivory cosmetic boxes in the form of fanciful ducks; an ivory dog, carved in the act of running and with a movable lower jaw and collar with leash attachment; an alabaster perfume jar; a paint palette and an ivory writing palette. The last contains, on a sliding slot designed to take the brushes, a hieroglyphic inscription which reads, 'The King's

Daughter of his body, his beloved Meretaten, born of the Great Royal Wife Neferneferuaten Nefertiti, who lives forever and ever.'

Hoving recalled Carter's words to Lythgoe in 1926, when asked where he thought some of the pieces in the Carnarvon collection came from: 'The tomb of Amenhotep [Amenophis].' Nearly fifty years on, in March 1988, the uncertainty surrounding those artefacts which found their way abroad was underlined by the discovery of more treasures in a cupboard at Highclere, jewellery and other pieces, which were headlined as 'Treasures of Tutankhamun' although they were said to have come from the tomb of Amenophis III, 'emptied by Lord Carnarvon in 1915'. Of course, the latter tomb was emptied not by Carnarvon, who was at Highclere in 1915, but by Carter who remained in Egypt.

At that time, the curator of the Highclere collection published in *The Times* a list of objects which Carter had compiled when he visited Lady Carnarvon with Lythgoe in November 1924 and prepared the main items in the collection for safe-keeping in the vaults of the Bank of England. It is impossible to identify particular objects from that list, but its very generalized headings, such as 'Sculpture' and 'Stone visages', could easily have embraced some of the pieces which have since found their way to America.

Two other items are cited by Hoving in his catalogue of uncertain provenance: a famous leaping horse figure carved in ivory and painted reddish brown with black mane, probably part of a once more elaborate composition; and a gazelle, about six inches in height, with the alert, nervous look of that most winsome of wild creatures. According to the records of the museum, quoted by Hoving but not otherwise vouchsafed, these two 'lovely animals', purchased from the Carnarvon estate in 1926, 'may have come from Tutankhamun's tomb'. A letter from Carnarvon to Carter dated Christmas Eve 1922, sent from Highclere to Luxor, is also on the Metropolitan Museum file and is quoted by Hoving in evidence of a 'purely Egyptological joke', shared by patron and servant. Carnarvon had received congratulations from every corner – the most important of them from the 'Jockey Denoghull' (a play, presumably on Donague). He had, he said, put the aerial (gazelle) and horse, *bought* in Cairo', in a wall case at Highclere. On close examination, Carnarvon had decided that these unmarked pieces were 'early Eighteenth Dynasty from Saqqara'. He had already inquired of Carter whether there might be any more 'unmarked stuff' in the tomb.

Other articles related to Tutankhamun are on display at other American museums, notably Brooklyn, Cleveland and Cincinnati, and the Kansas City Art Gallery. One magnificent work, a gold ornament representing the young king aboard his war chariot, was presented to the Cairo Museum by King Farouk in 1952, prior to his abdication. And Farouk is described as the 'conduit' for 'four or five other Tutankhamun objects removed by Howard Carter and taken to England'. According to Hoving, his will 'specified that the pieces – rings and gold and faience – be bequeathed to his niece, Phyllis Walker, who, when she discovered their true provenance was appalled and, through the executor of Carter's estate, handed the rings over to Farouk.' In fact, the will says nothing of any specific piece of Egyptiana, referring only to 'property real and personal'. As his diary for the season 1929 - 30 shows, he was worried even at the last by the fact the Metropolitan Museum had received no recompense for its enormous contribution to the work at the tomb, 'at their own sacrifice', at any rate up until April 1929 when the Egyptian government took over responsibility from the Carnarvon estate.

When the Ministry of Public Works showed that it had no intention of taking up Carter's plea on behalf of the museum, it is very probable that he took matters into his own hands. Some of the items in the Metropolitan Museum undoubtedly answer to descriptions in Burton's list, and suggest that Phyllis Walker took Burton's advice and sold or gave to that institution some of the lesser pieces left to her.

The onus for clearing up the entire question of the provenance of Tutankhamun artefacts in the Metropolitan Museum, seventy years after the discovery of the tomb, rests entirely with the directorate of that museum. Until it acts like other great institutions in its field, such as the British and Ashmolean Museums, and places on public record all relevant correspondence, it will be heard to cry *mea culpa*. In the absence of a clear statement of the museum's own position, no accusations made by its servants against Carnarvon or Carter could be entertained for a second in any court of law.

It is for Egyptologists and the custodians of museum collections to distinguish fact from conjecture in all these accusations. Carter traded so much Egyptian material over the years that some of the objects are almost certainly traceable to the market place. Equally, there can be no doubt that he and Lord Carnarvon were not too scrupulous in the observation of the Egyptian antiquities law, particularly, in Carter's case, when he felt himself to have been unjustly treated.

The question which would henceforth bedevil descriptions of the great achievement of Carnarvon and Carter remains unanswered. That they returned to the tomb on the night of 26 - 7 November 1922, as claimed by Hoving, is now proven. Indeed, final affirmation was provided in 1981 when the journalist John Lawton, who took Sergeant Adamson back to the tomb to relive the recollected events of sixty years before, examined the diary of Mervyn Herbert, Carnarvon's second half-brother, in the Bodleian Library at Oxford. Describing the automobile drive to the opening ceremony on 29 November 1922, Herbert noted: 'Porch whispered something to Evelyn and told her to tell me. This she did, under the strictest promise of secrecy. Here is the secret. They both had already been into the second chamber! After the discovery they had not been able to resist it – they had made a small hole in the wall (which afterwards they filled up again) and climbed through. The only others who know anything about it are the workmen.'

That of course does not prove that anything was taken from

the tomb at the time. There remains the testimony of Sergeant Adamson that they could not have entered the antechamber or the chambers beyond its north and west walls that night for the sheer accumulation of objects which would have barred their way, and that in any case they would have had to step over his sleeping body in order to do so.

As it stands, Adamson's account must be treated with caution. For several years, the ex-military policeman lectured to lay and expert audiences in Britain and abroad and impressed everyone who heard him with the clarity of his recollection and the simple truthfulness with which he conveyed his story. Yet, in the ten years during which he claimed to have been the tomb's official guardian, not a single member of the team – not Carnarvon or Carter or one of the Americans – mentioned the English soldier in their midst. It must be supposed that the experienced reporters who spent two or three years in a vain attempt to break *The Times'* news monopoly would have tried to interview the one man who, with a discreet word or two, could have told them all they needed to know. Not one of them ever mentioned him, at the time or in reminiscence. The photographs and slides used by Adamson, and subsequently to illustrate books and articles devoted to his adventure, were all official pictures from newspapers and magazines which had received the *Times* service. Of the thousands of photographs taken inside and near the tomb, not one showed the guardian policeman.

Richard Adamson ended his life at the Star and Garter Home for disabled servicemen at Richmond, and the superintendent of that famous establishment in the last two years, Major Harris, had no doubt of the man's sincerity and honesty. But Adamson did not begin to tell his story until after the death of his wife in 1966. Not even his own children knew of his remarkable adventure until then. Unfortunately, his story, fascinating though it is, cannot without further elucidation be used in confirmation or disproof of the events of that 'day of days'.

There may still be useful evidence in the private records of the families of Carter and his assistants. Among the mysteries which continue to lurk in dark corners of Carter's strange story are the deaths of his two closest colleagues – 'Pecky' Callender, said in archaeological directories to have died in 1931 though in fact his decease was not until six years later, intestate in Egypt, and Harry Burton. Burton died at Assiut in Egypt at the age of sixty in 1940, soon after he had attended to Carter's last affairs. His will was proved at Llandudno in Wales but it said nothing of his possessions, except that he left them to his wife Minnie. But there were two unpublished codicils to the will, proved in the High Court separately from the will which was resealed by the Cairo Supreme Court on 16 July 1941.

Historically, a perhaps more important bequest from Carter to his niece was the manuscript bearing his own notes and corrections of his *The Tomb of Tutankhamen*. In 1972, that version of the book was published in Britain, followed in 1982 by a further edition introduced by the archaeologist John Romer who described it as 'one of the finest works of popular archaeology ever written'. Romer told how he, a generation after Carter, working among the royal tombs of the Valley, knelt to read his measuring tape: As he did so he saw 'a shiny vertical line' at the precise spot on the wall that he was seeking. Next to that pencil mark were the initials 'H.C.' and the date '1917'. Few tombs escaped his attention. 'It was not surprising that Carter had been there before me,' said Romer, and he quoted Théophile Gautier's novel *The Romance of the Mummy,* written in 1854, whose fictional aristocratic patron Lord Evandale he described as a *déjà-vu* caricature of the 'cold, handsome' Carnarvon. But Gautier's Egyptologist, Ramphius, 'with a face like an ibis and a predilection for obscure religious texts', was far removed from Howard Carter, 'a robust and practical man, recognized by his contemporaries as an expert fieldworker, an acute observer of desert landscape and one of the finest archaeological draughtsman ever to have worked in Egypt'.

It is a suitably uncontroversial note on which to bid farewell to a great and much neglected archaeologist; to an instinctive student of ancient Egyptian art and language, whose career began in the shadow of his country's obsession with 'class', an embittered man who might have responded better to the heady music of passing fame had it been accompanied by the unaffected embrace of his contemporaries.

APPENDIX 1

Almina Countess of Carnarvon

Publishing economics make it necessary to keep within accepted limits of relevance in writing a biography, and in this work the temptation to write at length about the fascinating woman whom Carnarvon married in 1895, was resisted with conscious effort. On reflection, however, a brief supplementary note is called for so that the bare bones at least of an important aspect of the story of the search for the tomb are available to the reader.

Contemporary records give us colourful glimpses of the 5th Earl of Carnarvon in the last decade or so of the 19th century and the early days of the 20th, but we seldom read of his wife, the petite, beautiful and immensely wealthy Almina, the 'Pocket Venus' of Highclere. Yet it was her infusion of money into the almost empty coffers of the Carnarvons that made possible the costly search for a long forgotten tomb.

Almina Victoria Marie Alexandra Wombwell was born on 14 April 1876 at 20 Bruton Street, London, officially the daughter of Frederick Charles Wombwell and his wife Marie Felice ('Mina'), though in fact her natural father was the bachelor Baron Alfred de Rothschild, joint head of the world's richest banking dynasty. The long affair of the immensely wealthy Rothschild with the wife of a respected man of business, the fourth son of Sir George Wombwell (the 3rd baronet), was devoted and open. No effort was ever made to conceal the relationship or the illegitimacy of Almina, her name conjoining the abbreviations of his first name and her nickname 'Mina'.

341

Religious orthodoxy, however, prevented a legal union. Her family was ardently Roman Catholic and Rothschild was a strict Jew, so that there could be neither divorce nor marriage outside the faith. A relationship well known in English society for its devotion and loyalty remained an 'affair' to the end of the parents' lives.

Almina was just 19 when she married Lord Carnarvon at St Margaret's, Westminster, on the bridegroom's 29th birthday, 26 June 1895. It was the society wedding of the year and reports of the spectacular wedding dress, of the exotic pink of the bridesmaids and the bride's going-away ensemble, caught the imagination of the press. It became known as the 'pink wedding'. In those days the Carnarvons maintained a London home at 13 Berkeley Square and an apartment in New York, as well as Highclere Castle. Their first son, Henry George Alfred Marius Herbert (Lord Porchester), was born in 1898. Almina and the child spent much of those early years at the London home while Carnarvon engaged in the familiar sports of Highclere and its surroundings, shooting, fox hunting and horse racing. Indeed, when he was not engaged in blood sports and the sport of kings at home, Carnarvon was often away on long continental trips, taking Europe by storm in his fast and luxurious Panhard motor car, enjoying the fun of the gambling salons and the company of the 'fillies'. In the last quarter of Victoria's reign, when the Prince of Wales dominated the London social scene, it was no surprise to London society that the wealthy young 'Venus' of Highclere was herself in demand. When she travelled abroad her wardrobe was extravagant in the extreme – a more or less standard baggage containing large feathered hats, crocodile leather handbags, furs galore, the precise number of seventy-two pairs of shoes, cushions to insure against discomfort even in the best hotels, a footstool and perhaps the ultimate symbol of self-indulgence, her personal chamber pot.

A daughter was born in 1901, Lady Evelyn Leonora Almina Herbert. The boy Porchester spent more and more time at grandma 'Mina' Wombwell's home round the corner from

Berkeley Square in Bruton Street while his mother moved between the two houses and her own father's magnificently furnished home in Seamore Place. Grandma Wombwell spoke French as her mother tongue (her maiden name was Boyer) and insisted on it when the grandchildren were present so that Porchester grew up with a native command of the language.

The children were seldom in the company of their parents. When at Highclere they lived on the top floor of Barry's domestic essay in Gothic revival architecture, shut away with Nanny Moss in an enclosed community with nursemaids and servants. As Porchester was to observe in adulthood, 'seldom seen and never heard'. As the children grew up, however, Carnarvon became increasingly devoted to Evelyn. As a young woman she was the apple of his eye and at an early age she started to accompany him on his European and Egyptian trips, looking it was said, a mirror image of her mother in face, figure and dress.

It has been suggested that Carnarvon struck a hard bargain with Alfred de Rothschild by way of his daughter's marriage dowry. In fact, little or no effort was required. The Baron's generosity to his daughter was spontaneous and unstinting. The £250,000 he settled on Almina was followed by £150,000 to pay off Carnarvon's gambling debts. His largesse was not confined to his own daughter. In 1918, the year of his death, he gave Porchester and Evelyn £50,000 each; and in his will he left a large part of his estate, valued at £1.5 million, to Almina and her two children. As Porchester recalled in his memoirs, Almina only had to ask for money – ten or twenty thousand pounds at a time – to provoke a sympathetic response; 'Oh puss-cat, I gave you ten thousand pounds only last week. Whatever have you done with it, my darling child?' Porchester, Rothschild's natural grandson though referred to as his 'godson', was also a welcome visitor at the city bank in time of financial difficulty.

Little wonder that the adored, hopelessly spoilt Almina was never able to keep track of money. Yet her besetting sin was not so much extravagance as generosity. She neither boasted nor protested at the immense contribution her family's wealth made to the search for Tutankhamun's tomb and the subsequent clearance, though she was never consulted about its progress or financing. At the same time, she was unmoved by the treasures that Carnarvon secreted to Highclere and was only too ready to dispose of them after his death; and she sold many of the paintings and drawings her father had left her. But when all was said and done her most spectacular use of the family fortune was in the setting up of nursing homes which became famous for their medical excellence, for the warfare they engendered in the consultant ranks of the medical profession, and for profligate expenditure.

At the outbreak of the Great War in 1914, while Carnarvon's thoughts still lingered in Egypt, Almina invited the Secretary of State for War, Lord Kitchener, to Highclere and suggested turning the house into a military hospital. Kitchener thought it a good idea and thus was born her long and costly association with the higher reaches of medical practice. The Earl suggested a new telegraphic address – 'Amputate, Highclere'. In the war, Highclere military hospital became for Almina a personal mission of patriotism and service in which the rehabilitation of casualties from the battlefronts was her consuming interest. Commercial vehicles were converted into ambulances and she went with them to collect battlefront casualties off ships at Southampton. Encouraged by the success of the venture, she soon opened another private hospital at Bryanston Square in London. Shortly after the war she opened yet another, Alfred House in Mayfair, in honour of her father, an establishment that claimed members of the royal family among its patients.

Peace and the resumption of Carnarvon's interest in Egypt widened an already unbridgeable gulf in the interests of Earl and Countess. According to Porchester it was only the devoted interventions of his sister Evelyn that kept them together in the frantic years of the discovery of the tomb, amid the renown and controversy that went with it. Almina made a brief visit with her husband to the Winter Palace Hotel at Luxor in the 1919 - 20 season. From then on she devoted herself to her nursing homes and to her own friends and acquaintances, far removed from the world of Egyptology. Professional retainers and friends in the medical world were legion in the memories of patients and admirers such as Lord Moynihan, Wilfrid Trotter, Sir Maurice Cassidy, Sir Cedric Lane Roberts, Sir Benjamin Rycroft, Sir Archibald MacIndoe; and among the patients, the Duchess of Windsor. With most she was on terms of close friendship. For a few of the doctors who walked the wards of her nursing homes, she professed undying enmity.

In post-war years Almina resumed the visits to Paris that were a feature of her childhood, and before leaving London she was asked by a woman friend, Mrs Dennistoun, if she would deliver a package to her estranged husband then living in the French capital. Lt Colonel Ian Onslow 'Tiger' Dennistoun, a retired Grenadier Guards officer, was invited to join her at the Ritz where she was staying. The man who confronted her turned out to be emaciated, half starved and apparently living in a cold and dirty garret. Almina's generous instincts were activated with electrifying effect. She supervised new accommodation and put her new-found friend on a diet that would have made eyes pop at Fortnum's. It seems that she had lost no time in informing Carnarvon of her new liaison, and the couple were together in Paris when her husband became desperately ill in Cairo in 1923. The High Commission in Cairo and the Embassy in Paris had difficulty in locating her and when she was found she was, according to family report, 'not pleased' at being asked to leave Dennistoun in order to respond to an urgent call to be at the Earl's side. In the event, she hired a private plane and reached Cairo just in time to join her children at the deathbed and to accompany the body on the journey to Highclere for burial. She returned to Paris as soon as she could after the interment, and she and Dennistoun were married on 19 December 1923. Almina settled £100,000 on the Colonel as a token of her affection.

The dowager Lady Carnarvon moved out of Highclere soon after Porchester succeeded to the title, though her son allowed her a grace-and-favour residence on the estate which she used on the occasions she met Carter after the death of the 5th Earl. From then on she freewheeled to a state of penury. She lived happily as the wife of Dennistoun, though calling herself Almina Carnarvon, at a spacious house on the Isle of Wight, while her nursing homes fell into decline. She was said to be grief stricken at the death of 'Tiger' Dennistoun in May 1938. He was a life-long sufferer from asthma and had enjoyed hardly a moment of good health in their 15 years of marriage. After his death, Almina took a rented house in Regent's Park before moving in 1943 to a small picture-book thatched cottage in Somerset, with six acres of fruit orchard and pasture land. The 6th Earl contributed half the cost of the new home, which she sold after five years to pay off her mounting debts, without consulting him. When he discovered what had happened, Carnarvon wrote to his mother in green ink calling her 'a scheming swindler'.

During the Second World War, following the move to Somerset, Almina had met Mrs Anne Leadbetter who became her companion housekeeper. Together with her son Anthony, the two women moved into an end-of-terrace home in Bristol. In 1951, the debts of the lady of the 'Pink Wedding', mistress of Highclere and friend of the royal family, who had enjoyed wealth and privilege on a regal scale, became such that her own son was compelled to call in the receiver. But not even a bankruptcy order could mitigate her wilfulness or her extravagant behaviour. Her son allowed her an income of £150 each month from which Mrs Leadbetter's housekeeping bills had to be paid, but Almina still wrote cheques to help the needy and those who simply took her for granted, sometimes giving them a few shillings, sometimes hundreds of pounds. She still rented villas in the South of France, usually paid for by the 6th Earl of Carnarvon, the son who through most of his life had veered between tears and laughter at the conduct of his impossible mother. The young Anthony Leadbetter who became her godchild recalled in later life that he was always responsible for tipping porters and hotel staff. And to the end, in regular phone calls to her son and to daughter Evelyn, Lady Beauchamp, she referred to her last homes in Somerset and Bristol as her 'cabbage patch' – a description which she thought might make them feel suitably guilty. She died at the Frenchay Hospital in Bristol on 28 May 1969 in her 93rd year. Anne Leadbetter, the constant companion of her later years, had died six weeks earlier, her daughter Evelyn three years later, in 1972. Her true claim to immortality was one that she was hardly conscious of in life: that without her money the tomb of Tutankhamun would not have been discovered, not at any rate by Lord Carnarvon and Howard Carter.

APPENDIX 2

Itinerary of the discovery and clearance
of the tomb

1915
April
18 Authorization for Earl of Carnarvon to dig in Valley of the
Kings signed in Cairo by Daressy, Acting Director-General
of Antiquities Service and Howard Carter

1917
November
16 Authorization renewed for one year. Signed by P. Lacau
and Howard Carter

1918
November
26 Renewed for further year. Signed Lacau and Carter

1919
March
Carnarvon arrives at Valley of the Kings. He and Carter
continue digging in triangle close to tomb of Ramesses VI.
Small cache of alabaster jars found bearing names of
Ramesses II and Merneptah. Home in autumn

1920-1
Fruitless continuation of search but on January 26, 1921,
authorization for further year signed by Daressy and Carter

1922

February

12 Authorization for further year from 16 November 1921 signed by Lacau and Carter

October

Carnarvon agrees to finance 'one more season'

5   Carter leaves London for Marseilles on *ss China*

28 Reaches Luxor

November

1   Excavating NE corner of tomb of Ramesses VI

3   Clearing 3ft soil beneath workmens' huts

4   Workman encounters steps

5   Stairway and sealed door found

6   Carter telegraphs Carnarvon

8   Message from Carnarvon. Coming out with Evelyn

18 Carter to Cairo to meet Carnarvon and Lady Evelyn

21 Returns to Luxor

23 Carnarvon and Evelyn to Luxor

24 Stairway cleared

25 Sealed door removed

26 'Day of Days'

29 Official opening

30 *The Times* illustrates first treasures of tomb

December

4   Carnarvon and Lady E return to England

21 December, world press corps arrives at Luxor

22 Carter agrees to guided press tour

22 Carnarvon in audience with King, Buckingham Palace

1923

January

10 Carnarvon's agreement with *The Times* for exclusive coverage announced

February

12 Egyptian government ultimatum demands 'strict neutrality' in reporting of finds

15 Authorization for further year signed by Carter and Lacau
15 Carter announces antechamber cleared, work to begin on burial chamber
16 Opening of King's burial chamber
18 Queen of the Belgians arrives by special train
21 Increasing animosity between Carter and Carnarvon revealed
22 World press carries first stories of 'amazing sight' of young king's body

March

6 Carnarvon bitten on cheek by mosquito. While shaving at Winter Palace Hotel cuts small pimple with razor
18 Evelyn informs Carter her father confined to bed
22 King George V sends message to Carnarvon
26 Almina, Lady Carnarvon arrives at husband's bedside
30 *The Times* reports Lord Carnarvon suffering from lobar pneumonia; cause for anxiety

April

5 Death of Carnarvon
27 Carter informs M. Lacau, Director Service des Antiquités, that family of late Earl wishes to continue clearance of tomb in his memory. Carter and Lacau agree that further work shall be regarded as *déblaiement* (clearance) and not *fouilles* (excavation). Letters of agreement exchanged, dated April 27, July 12, 1923 (see below)

May

24 Carter leaves Cairo for England

June

16 Carter at Highclere. Almina Lady Carnarvon agrees to renew concession

July

12 Lacau confirms authorization for work to continue in name of Lady Carnarvon for further year, until 1 November 1924. 'It may be renewed if the work is not completed'. Carter acknowledges with copy of new agreement signed Almina Carnarvon

October

8 Carter returns to Cairo, on to Luxor. Discusses with Quibell, acting for Lacau, desirability of preventing press complaints. Also avoidance of friction with regard to visitors. Daily press bulletin to be issued by Press Bureau. Carter proposes Merton of *The Times,* taken on to his staff, should cable *The Times* story in evening and given to Egyptian papers early next morning. Opening of tomb once a week for 'small number' of visitors

11 Lacau issues note on ways to avoid further problems with visitors and press. Countersigned by Carter

17 British Residency at Ramleh warns Carter, new arrangements will 'cause disappointment to many tourists'

19 Work on burial chamber resumes. Work of dismantling the 4 shrines begins; world-wide interest

31 Quibell warns Carter, 'certain British newspaper correspondents' threatening to cause trouble

November

13 Quibell, acting for Director-General Antiquities, tells Carter that representatives of the department will henceforward be present in the tomb at all times to 'supervise operations'. Press matters to be dealt with by Ministry of Public Works

15 Carter writes to Lacau. Agrees to proposals in Quibell's letter but insists 'the present arrangement is without prejudice to such rights as have been ceded to Almina Countess of Carnarvon'

17 Carter returns to Luxor and resumes work on tomb

20 Carter receives letter from Lacau questioning reservations of the rights accorded to Countess of Carnarvon. '....the Government fails to see its relevance to the measures in question'

21 Carter receives further letters from Ministry of Public Works stressing 'strengthening' of supervision of tomb and press matters. Asked to provide list of members of his staff

December

3 Writes formally to Quibell and Ministry

13 Lacau and Carter in dispute. Lacau announces that 15 'native ladies' wish to visit tomb

15 Ministry of Public Works summons Carter to Cairo. Angry exchanges with Egyptian officials

20 Carter protests to Director-General, Antiquities Service 'I must warn you that if, as you threaten, you ignore my protest I shall reluctantly be compelled to take action in defence of the interests of the executors of the late Lord Carnarvon'

1924

January

12 Carter receives letters clearly intended to cause resentment from Quibell and others. When work on outer coffins reaches certain point that allows access to mummy, 'all work must cease and H.E. Minister of Works be alerted'

13 Carter promises to communicate with authorities 'few days in advance ' of success of undertaking

In last days of January government of Yahia Pasha falls and nationalist administration of Saad Pasha Zaghlul takes over, with new Minister of Public Works, Morcos Bey

February

Carter resumes work. Shrine revealed with two large doors leading to 2nd, 3rd and 4th shrines and sarcophagus

4 Carter writes to H.E. Morcos Bey, Minister of Public works: 'Beg to inform Your Excellency that I was able to uncover sarcophagus yesterday... May I suggest...official opening February twelfth?'

8 Communique jointly issued by Ministry and Carter announces sarcophagus will be on view at 3 pm Tuesday 12 February in presence of Ministers and Director of Antiquities. Press to be admitted on morning of 13th. Following four days to be devoted to making of records by Mr Carter and 'necessary preparations' for reception of 'authorised visitors'

11 Personal note from Prime Minister Zaghlul. 'Kindly send me, by tonight, your proposals for such a list' [of Carter's personal

guests]. Dispute over inclusion of families of 'collaborators'

12 Message from PM: 'No wives' to be admitted on following day, 13th

12 Special viewing for VIP's at opening of king's sarcophagus. 'A gasp of wonderment'

13 Dispute continues between Carter and Egyptian government. Questions in House of Commons. Carter posts notice in Winter Palace Hotel, 'all my collaborators have refused to work any further upon the scientific investigations...'

14 Professor Gardiner asks British government to intervene

14 Angry exchanges between Carter and PM Zaghlul

15 Lacau issues Ordre de Service, announcing closure of tomb

18 Minister of Public Works to Carter, 'one last chance'

19 Carter to H.E. Minister of Public Works: 'In order to safeguard contents of the tomb I am commencing proceedings in the Mixed Courts to-day'

22 Lacau to take possession of tomb 'this afternoon', demands keys to tomb. Carter refuses to hand over keys. Government calls in locksmith to tomb and laboratory. Matter of sequestration referred to Mixed Courts

March

8 Start of legal proceedings in Cairo. Estate of 5th Earl of Carnarvon v Government of Egypt. Carter renounces further work on tomb

April

British Empire Exhibition, Wembley

18 Carter leaves on lecture tour of America

22 In absentia, Carter issues writ against Wembley Amusements Ltd for infringement of copyright on furnishings and artefacts of tomb

December

Carter returns to Egypt to negotiate with newly formed Egyptian administration

1925
January

Carter to Luxor. Draws up new agreement on behalf of self and Carnarvon estate. Carter and estate would not be entitled to any articles from tomb. Carter obtains letter from Antiquities Service (13 Jan) offering Lady Carnarvon, 'at its own discretion...a choice of duplicates as representative as possible of the discovery'

25 Keys ceremonially handed to Carter. But damage caused when pall used to cover shrines left in open when Carter's staff dismissed from site 11 months before

February

Carter returns to England

October

10 Opening of 1st coffin

28 Third coffin with golden death mask revealed

November

11 Professor Derry and Dr Saleh Bey Hamdi carry out autopsy on c.3,200 years old mummy

December

31 Carter hands over to Cairo Museum 3 coffins, mask and items found on body

1926

Summer

Lady Carnarvon decides to dispose of some of her husband's collection of antiquities. Carter to have sole charge of negotiations

September

27 Carter begins clearance of last chamber, the Treasury. Tomb to be closed to public until 1 Jan 1927. Afterwards, to open three days a week until 15 March

October

23 Outermost coffin containing mummified body of king lowered into sarcophagus within tomb

24 Burton begins photographing the treasury. At entrance Anubis, the jackal, protector of dead, couchant on gilt pylon with palankeen. Pictures astonish the world

1927
February
Carter returns to Luxor but crowds coming to see magnificent finds in Treasury cause him to depart for Aswan. Does not resume work until September 1927. 'Strange and beautiful objects'
December
30 Amir of Afghanistan, described in press as 'King', visits tomb

1928
January
13 Carter and Lady Burghclere, Earl's sister, greet Crown Prince of Italy, Umberto
September
Annexe cleared. Work in laboratory tomb resumes

1929
January
Carnarvon involvement terminated by Egypt. Agreement reached on compensation to Carnarvon estate for work since 1922. Egyptian government offers £34,000. Compensation for Metropolitan Museum of New York left in abeyance
November
1 *The Times* decides to dismiss its Egypt correspondent Merton Final clearance of laboratory tomb begins

1930
July
3 Sum of £35,979 finally settled on Carnarvon estate by royal decree, signed by King Fuad

1931-2
Carter back and forth to Valley of Kings to receive guests and engage in ongoing disputes with officials

1932
February

The Times reports last rites as final consignment of finds leave for Cairo. 'Mr Howard Carter's 10 years' work on the tomb is ended'

CHAPTER NOTES

ASAE   Annales du Service des Antiquités de l'Egypte
EES   Egypt Exploration Society, earlier EE Fund
FO   Foreign and Commonwealth Office
GI   Griffith Institute, Ashmolean Museum, Oxford
IO   India Office and Records (British Library)
JEA   Journal of Egyptian Archaeology
L/P&S/   India Office, London/Political & Secret
MDAIK   Mitteilungen des Deutschen Archaeological Instituts
         Abteilung
MMA   Metropolitan Museum of Art

Titles of works referred to frequently are abbreviated thus:
Discovery: Carter and Mace, *The Discovery of the Tomb of Tutankhamen,*
         1977
The Tomb: Carter, *The Tomb of Tutankhamun,* 1972 edn
Notebook: Carter's unpublished notebooks in Griffith Institute,
         numbered 15 - 20, containing Sketches I - XIII
An Account: Carter, *An Account of Myself,* in *Notebook 15,* GI
Pioneer: Breasted, *Pioneer to the Past*
Untold Story: Hoving, *Tutankhamun, The Untold Story*

Introduction   pages xv - xxv
page
xvi   Quote, 'wretched lack of magnanimity', Jon Manchip
         White, *Discovery,* Intro, pxxviii
xvii   Metropolitan Museum, correspondence with author,
         20 June, 1989

Egypt at the age of seventeen-and-half.' Dr Patricia Spencer, secretary of the EES, agrees with me that although some of Carter's letters to members of the Society appear to bear the year date 1890, a reading of them suggests 1891 [author]

14   '...not a gentleman', letter from F.L. Griffith to J.E. Newberry, *GI,* dated 2 Feb. 1891. Letter actually reads: '... If you come across a colourist (eye for colour must be the chief qualification added to drawing) who would like a trip for expenses paid and nothing else, I should be much obliged if you would ask him to call... It seems to me that as cost is a great consideration it matters not whether the artist is a gentleman or not...'

15   With Petrie in Egypt: Carter, *The Tomb,* p111. And see Drower, *Flinders Petrie,* p172f. Grenfell to Miss Edwards: *EES* corr., 8 Jan. 1891 (IIId.31)

Chapter 2 *'My great desire',* pages 16 - 39
page
16   Egypt and the British 'Protectorate': see Marlowe, *Spoiling the Egyptians,* chapters 11 and 12, for a concise analysis of events leading up to the British occupation in 1882

16   Salisbury, *ibid,* p260f

16   Cromer: Sir Ronald Storrs, *Orientations,* (1937) p191f

16   Khedive Tewfiq [Taufiq] and British: Marlowe, *op.cit.,* p260f; and Winstone, *The Illicit Adventure,* p3f

16   Mariette, Maspero, Grébaut: Marlowe, *op.cit.,* p12, Winstone *Uncovering the Ancient World,* p116f; and Drower, *op.cit.,* p40f

17   Carter in Egypt: Carter, *An Account,* and Drower, *op.cit.,* p191f

18   Royal cache: Maspero, *La Trouvaille de Deir al Bahari.* Also *Discovery,* p69f, and see Romer, *Valley of the Kings,* chapter 14

18   Chronology and king lists: Petrie, *A History of Egypt* vol 2; Baines and Malek, *Atlas of Ancient Egypt;* and Reeves, *The*

Complete Tutankhamun

19   Manetho, Herodotus, et al: Winstone, Uncovering the Ancient World., p213f

19   Exciting Discovery: Emery, introduction to Archaic Egypt

20   Giza and Bulaq museums, Drower, op.cit., p168f

20   Petrie, et al: ibid., p168f

21   Newberry and Griffith: Carter, An Account

21f   Archaeological Survey of Egypt: 'Scheme for carrying on the survey' and first and second season's reports, EES, 1890 - 1/1891 - 2

21f   Tal al Amarna, 'Akhenaten's city': Carter, Discovery, p41f

22   Poole, Petrie, Grenfell, Miss Edwards, Grébaut, Willoughby Fraser: EES corr., 1891 (see in particular IIId.31); and see Winstone, op.cit., p134

22   Chester, Swaffham Museum records, and Drower, op.cit, p40f

22   Bani Hasan [Beni Hassan]: EES reports. And McCall, op.cit., and Drower, op.cit., p172f

22f   Copying methods: Carter, An Account; and Winstone, op.cit., p315f

23   First impressions, Carter op.cit

24   Al Bersheh [Bersha], ibid, and McCall, op.cit.

24   Wall drawings of al–Bersha, Collection in EES library

24f   Chapel of Djehutihotpe, Carter, op.cit.

25   Tent life, ibid

26   Lost and undiscovered tombs, ibid

27   Petrie's regime: Drower, op.cit., p319

28   Akhenaten's city, Carter, Discovery, p41f. And see: Aldred, Akhenaten and Nefertiti, p27f

28   Fraser and Blackden: EES second season's report

28   Petrie and Grébaut: Drower, op.cit., p186f

28   Carter's status; Carter, An Account, and Discovery p41f

29f   Carter at Amarna, Carter, ibid

30f   Lepsius, Amarna: Letters: Winstone, op.cit., p163f

31   Petrie's philosophy: Carter, An Account, and Drower, op.cit.

34   Fraser and Blackden, Newberry: Carter, op.cit.

37   Chester: ibid

37   Death of Samuel John Carter, *ibid*
38   Carter quotes, *ibid*
38   Grébaut, de Morgan, Khedival decree; Drower, *op.cit.*, 186f, and Winstone, *op.cit.*, 211f
39   Carter quote, Carter, *op.cit.*

Chapter 3 *'The Promised Land'*, pages 40 - 50
page
40   Petrie and assistants in London: Drower, *Flinders Petrie*, p200f
40   Amelia Edwards: *ibid*, introduction, and p46f
41   Petrie's packing cases: Carter, *An Account*
41   Dissention in EES, personalities: *EES* corr., 1884 - 92, and Drower, *op.cit.*, p58/201
42   Miss Paterson: *EES* corr., (XIId.10)
43   Amherst and Amarna fragments: Aldred, *Akhenaten and Nefertiti*, p54
43   Return to Egypt: *EES Survey Report*, 1892 - 3 by Percy E. Newberry (20 April 1893), and see Carter, *An Account* (does not mention presence of Newberry's brother John, contained in Percy Newberry's report)
43   Carter's retort, *ibid*
44   Germans at Amarna: Aldred, *op.cit.*, p59
44   Carter quotes: Carter, *op.cit.*
44f   *Notebook, ibid*
45   New tracing method, *ibid*
45   Timai al Amdid: *ibid*, and Drower, *op.cit.*, p282
45f   Roger: Carter, *op.cit.*, and Drower, *op.cit.*, p282. Project abandoned: *EES Survey Report*, 1892 - 3
46   Amarna, Carter, *op.cit.*
46f   Al-Bersha, *ibid*
47   Quote, *ibid*
47f   Shaikh Ayd and goose story, *ibid*
48f   Petrie on Naville and others: Drower, *op.cit.*, p282f
50   Deir al Bahari, Carter, *op.cit.*

Chapter 4 *'Didlington up the Nile'*, pages 51 - 66
page

51   Work at Bersha and Deir al Bahari, letter to Newberry: *EES Survey Report*, 1892 - 3, 4 Jan - 7 April; and *EES* corr., 1893

51   Work procedure, brother Verney: Carter, *An Account*

52   Sculptures etc., Carter's artistry: Some of Carter's finest work was done between the years 1893 - 9 when he served as draughtsman to the expedition of Naville at Deir al Bahari. He copied all the scenes then visible on the temple of Hatshepsut, for reproduction by collotype in Naville's folio volumes, *The Temple of Deir al Bahari*, 6 vols, EES, 1895 - 1908. Carter also painted many facsimile water-colours of scenes and hieroglyphs from the tombs of Bani Hasan and al-Bersha, and he produced works for sale and in response to private commission. A few are held by the EES, the Ashmolean Museum, the Victoria and Albert Museum and private collectors. The majority are widely dispersed, and there is no comprehensive index

53   Hoving, *Untold Story*, p27

53f   Carter's work:
        From the catalogue of drawings and paintings in the Victoria and Albert Museum, 1990: 'Head of Queen Makare Hatshepsut': water-colour, detail from copy of painted low relief in mortuary temple of Hatshepsut, Deir al Bahari, 'Offering of vases of Amon'. Signed Howard Carter. Date, [?] 1893 - 6. Provenance, Lady Loch, daughter of 5th Marquess of Northampton, purchased Christies 20 May 1975. 'Royal Cartouche of Queen Makare Hatshepsut': water and body colour on green card, formerly part of original mount of above. Detail and provenance, the same as above. 'Head of Queen Aahmes Nefertari': Copy of painted low relief in mortuary temple of Hatshepsut, Deir al Bahari. Signed and dated: Howard Carter – 1896. [Nefertari was the wife of Tuthmosis I, who reigned 1512 - 1504 BC, and

mother of Hatshepsut.] Provenance, Lady Loch. Purchased Christies 20 May 1975. 'Pair of pelicans' water-colour. Signed and dated, Howard Carter – 1899. Purchased Caroline Smith (ex-P Heathcote-Williams) Feb. 1979 Naville: *EES,* Naville's Report 14 December 1894 (Xid16) Work on Temple, *ibid;* and *EES* corr. 1 Dec – 14 March, 1894

54   Hogarth/Naville: *EES* reports 18 Jan/18 March 1895

54   Railway for Daressy expedition: this was the adaptable, so-called Decauville track which was to serve Carter well in his later work in the Valley of the Kings

55   Naville to Paterson: *EES* corr. Jan-March

56f   'Didlington up the Nile': Notes from unpublished journal of Alicia M.J. Amherst, Dec 1894 - June 1895, incl., British Museum
EES exhibitions: Fund catalogues

61   Naville/Grueber/Carter: *EES* corr., 1 Aug 1895, Carter to Miss Paterson from 428 Fulham Road; 8 September 1895 from Didlington Hall

61   Horniman: *EES* corr., Naville to Grueber, 22 Jan. 1896

62   Home visits, weddings; Carter, *An Account,* and Swaffham Museum

62   Crissocopolu: *EES* contract, 12 Dec 1897

62   Deir al Bahari: *EES* corr. 1896 - 7

63   Somers Clarke/Hilton Price: *EES* corr. Price to Grueber, Cairo 18 Nov. 1898; Somers Clarke to Price, Luxor 15 Nov. 1898

63   Marquess of Northampton: EES, Carter to Grueber, 31 Dec. 1898

64   Carter in 1896: *ibid,* and Carter, *An Account*

64   Spielberg, Newberry: Drower, *Flinders Petrie,* p250

64f   Carter and Naville: *ibid,* p218f, 250

65   Brown: Carter, *op.cit.*

66   Carter to Paterson: *EES* corr., 23 Nov. 1898; re. Punt Terrace drawings, 29 66 Jan. 1899. Salary: *EES* corr., Carter to Paterson, 9 March 1899

66   Inspectorate, Maspero, de Morgan: *ibid,* and Carter, *An Account*

HOWARD CARTER

82 Visitors, Cromer etc: *ibid*
82 Quote, *ibid*
84f *Temple of Deir al Bahri,* EES book in 6 vols: Part I, September. 1895; Part II, Dec. 1896; Part III, 1898; Part IV, 1901; Part V 1906; Part VI, 1908
84 Grueber to Miss Paterson 22 June; Carter to Grueber from Luxor 30 June: *ibid*
85 Madinat Habu, 'A new life': *ibid*
87 Loret: *Discovery,* p84
87 Maspero and Carter's removal: Breastead, *Pioneer,* p155f
87f Newberry, Carter's version of Saqqara incident: *GI* file, correspondence and telegrams, Jan. 1905, between Carter, the Earl of Cromer (Britain's Resident and Consul-General), M. Maspero, and summary of official inquiry, with contemporary French newspaper reports
88 Character: Reeves, *The Complete Tutankhamun,* p42
89 Director-General, James Quibell
92 Carter's refusal: Newberry, 'Howard Carter', *obit., JEA 25,* 1939
93 Quibell and Carter: Drower, *Flinders Petrie,* p261
93 Carter to Maspero: *GI,* letter 21 Feb. (No.240)
93 Breasted: *Pioneer,* p155f
94f Tomb of Yuya and Tuya: *ILN,* Supplement to 17 March 1906
95 Carter to Newberry: *GI,* letter dated 'September 1907'

Chapter 7 *A 'true Etonian' at Thebes,* pages 96 - 110
page
96 Lady Burghclere: *Discovery,* introduction, p9. Porchy's sister attributed much of her brother's natural charm and personality to the 'devoted affection' lavished on him and his sisters by their aunts Lady Gwendolen Herbert and Eveline, Lady Portsmouth. It was, she said, at the Portsmouths' home at Eggesford in Devon among the horses and hounds, and 'probably the most popular M.F.H. in England' (Lord Portsmouth) that he was transformed into a 'hardy young sportsman'

96   Carnarvon family background: *ibid,* and see Fitzherbert, *The Man Who was Greenmantle,* p6f. I am also grateful for permission to use the research of Henrietta McCall in her unpubl. dissertation (chapter 3)

98   Carnarvon's desire to excavate: Lady Burghclere, *Discovery,* p29f

99   Carter's house: From the moment of his meeting with Carnarvon, Carter began the construction of a site house close to the EE Fund's abandoned mud-brick site house at Qurna. The house was finally built in 1910. Bricks were sent out by Carnarvon's suppliers, and were inscribed 'MADE AT BRETBY ENGLAND FOR HOWARD CARTER THEBES AD 1910'. Nicholas Reeves to author, 9 October 1990

99f   1906 - 7: for Davis's excavations at this time and discovery of Tutankhamun relics, see Romer, *Valley of the Kings.* Drower in *Flinders Petrie,* p311, observes that in 1908, Petrie started to explore the Valley in search of sites. Arthur Weigall, who had succeeded Carter in the Inspectorate, and Mrs Weigall were hospitable to Carter who was working nearby for Davis, with the artist-clergyman Norman de Garis Davies and Mrs Davies

100   Deir al Bahari: Carter, *An Account;* and see *Discovery,* p69f, and Carnarvon and Carter, *op.cit.*

101   Kamose tablet, Hyksos: See Winstone, *Uncovering the Ancient World,* p227

101   Carnarvon's Egyptian collection: Burghclere, *Discovery,* Intro, quotes Budge in *Tut.ankh.Amen,Amenism,Aten[n]ism, and Egyptian Monotheism* (1923)

102   First five years: Carnarvon and Carter, *op.cit.,* introduction

102   Carnarvon, quote: Burghclere, *op.cit.*

102   Blue faience cup: Romer, *op.cit.,* p210, discovery attributed by Davis to Edward Ayrton, another of Petrie's protégés

103   Carnarvon's accident, 26 August: *The Times,* 1 Sept. 1909; and see Burghclere, *op.cit.,* and Carnarvon, 6th Earl of, *No Regrets.* Accounts are not always consistent

CHAPTER NOTES

103f   Employment at Abydos: *EES* corr., Carter to Grueber, Luxor, 7 October. 1909

104   Winlock: quoted in *Untold Story,* chapter 4
Hoving, quoted: *ibid,* p51

105   'Pocket Venus', Almina Countess of Carnarvon: see Appendix 1 in this edition [author]; and see Colins and Ogilvie-Herald, *Tutankhamun and the Exodus Conspiracy*

105   Temple of Ramesses IV: Carnarvon and Carter, *op.cit.,* p8f

105   Home visit, Carter, *An Account*

106   Hogarth, Woolley *et al:* Winstone, *Woolley of Ur,* p24/37

107f   'Five Years' Exploration': *The Times Literary Supplement,* 23 May 1912, p216

108   Sakha: Drower, *op.cit.,* p72f. See also, Reeves, *The Complete Tutankhamun* p46: 'The following year [1913], having failed in their attempts to dig at Dahshur, Carnarvon and Carter turned their attention to another Delta Site, Tell el Balamun. There were no snakes, but, as at Sakha, the yield was uninspiring'

108   Movements 1912 - 15: Carter, *An Account, Notebook 16,* and McCall, *op.cit.* 108 Concession: *Discovery,* p76, 'actually received the long-coveted concession' in June 1914 – in fact, the concession agreement was dated 18 April 1915. Also, see Newberry, *obit., JEA 25* (1939)

109   Death of Fanny Carter: 19 December 1913

110   Artefacts: Davis, *Tomb of Iouiya and Touiyou*

110   Donated to Metropolitan Museum: McCall, *op.cit.*

Chapter 8 *King's Messenger,* pages 111 - 129
For background to this chapter see FO371/3202-4, EEF at Amarna, Antiquities Service/Carnarvon Antiquities; and FO371/3711/3724-29, Armana, Egypt, Curzon's views, Professor Breastead's visits to Egypt and Mesopotamia
page
111   War with Turkey and annexation of Egypt,: Cabinet Papers *CAB41/35,* Foreign Office file *FO371/2930* and *FO 822*

(Arab Bureau), India Office *L/P&S/18/B222;* this and other documentation cited in Winstone, *The Illicit Adventure,* p124f and notes, p432f; and see Sir Ronald Storrs, *Orientations*

112 Carter in Cairo, *An Account*

112 Imitation of Carnarvon, McCall, *op.cit.*

113 Contemporary archaeologists and their work: See Seton Lloyd's *Foundation in the Dust* (Oxford, 1907), and author's *Uncovering the Ancient World* (London, 1985)

113 Germans at Amarna: Aldred, *Akhenaten,* p59

114 Carter in 1914: *Discovery,* p75f

115 Tomb of Amenophis I/Ahmosi Nefertere: 'Report on the Tomb of Zeser-ka-Ra Amen-hetep I, Discovered by the Earl of Carnarvon in 1914', *JEA 3* (1916) p147-154. In fact, discovery made by Carter, Carnarvon was in England

115f Literary masterpiece, quotes from: *Discovery,* p60f

116f War in Egypt: Military and academic personalities. See Winstone, *Illicit Adventure,* p173f

118f Miss Paterson to Olza: *EES* corr., from Fund's new offices at 37 Great Russell Street, 7 October. 1915

119 Tomb of Amenophis III: Reeves, in *British Museum Society Bulletin,* No.61, Summer 1989, p28f

120 King's Messengers: Foreign Office Establishment records, FO Library; FO Lists. And see Wheller-Holohan, *The History of the King's Messengers,* and Antrobus, *King's Messenger, 1918 - 1940*

121 Army intelligence operations: Winstone *op.cit.,* Ch.9, 'The Intrusives'

121 Winter of 1916: *Pioneer,* p320

122 Adventure at Qurna: *Discovery,* p79f

123f Carter quote: *ibid,* p82

124 Military situation: Winstone *op.cit.*

125 'Our real campaign', excavations in 1917: Carter *op.cit.* p82f, and Romer, *Valley of the Kings,* p245f

125 Alexander the Great, Wilkinson's version: *Untold Story,* p58

126 1917 - 21 season: *Discovery,* p81f; and McCall, *op.cit.*

129   Death of Martha Joyce Carter at Churchfield Mansions, Fulham. Births and Deaths registry

129   Resources and expenses: See Reeves, *The Complete Tutankhamun,* p46f. Also, McCall, *op.cit.* and Colins and Ogilvie-Herald, *op.cit.,* chapter 25. According to Dr Reeves, ex-Curator of the Carnarvon collection and archive at Highclere, Carnarvon's anticipated team in 1912 included his personal physician, Dr Johnson, Lady Carnarvon's maid, and a cook, as well as Newberry and Carter. Remarkably, Carter's pay had risen from £400 a year in 1907 to £200 a month in 1911. Against this, Baron Rothschild died in 1918 leaving his daughter Almina, Lady Carnarvon, his Mayfair mansion valued at c.£500,000. There was also the wedding dowry of £250,000 twenty-three years earlier, as well as a substantial sum to the groom and the elimination of Porchy's gambling debts. Allowing for Egyptian exploration and the upkeep of Highclere, it does not seem that the Earl's early disciplines at the hands of his aunts embraced frugality. See Appendix 1

Chapter 9 *'Tomb of the Bird',* pages 130 – 140

page

130   Need for caution: see note to p109 above

130   Carnarvon's decision: Reeves, *The Complete Tutankhamun,* p50

130   Maspero's view: *Discovery,* p76

131   Map of Valley: *Pioneer,* p300f

131   Carter's interview with Carnarvon: *ibid.* And Cottrell, *The Lost Pharaoh,* p149f

131   Carter's resources: see Reeves, *op.cit.,* p47 for details of Carnarvon's correspondence with Wallis Budge of British Museum respecting the purchase of antikas through Carter's mediation. For example: Budge to Carnarvon, 'Morgan had bought the Coptic mss you refused for 80,000£ [*c.300,000 dollars*]' a figure which C could

'scarcely credit'

132f   Winlock: Hoving, *Untold Story*, p61f. And McCall, 'Howard Carter, Egyptologist 1874 - 1939, p22f, who suggests that Winlock's evidence might explain 'why the Metropolitan Museum was prepared to take over the concession'

134   'Decauville' track: Romer, *Valley of the Kings*, p250f

134   Gertrude Capon Thompson: see her *Mixed Memoirs* (1983), p83

134   Varying interpretations: Hoving, *Untold Story*, p72f

135   Carter's return: *Discovery*, chapter 5

135   Breasted's version: *Pioneer*, p323f

136   Carter's canary: Hoving, *Untold Story*, told by Winlock in a letter of 28 March 1923 to Edward Robinson, director of the Metropolitan Museum

136f   October. 28–Nov, 6: *Discovery*, p86f

137   Carter's movements: *ibid*, and Carter, *An Account*. Also, Alan Gardiner, forty years on, recorded 'On November 6th 1922 Carnarvon telephoned me... saying that he had just received a cable from Carter, in Luxor, saying that he had made a wonderful discovery in the Valley, a magnificent tomb with seals intact, and Carnarvon asked me whether it could possibly be the tomb of Tut'ankhamun.' *My Working Years* by Sir Alan Gardiner (published privately, 1962), p37

137   American story: Breasted, *op.cit.*

138   Woolley and Abraham: Winstone, *Woolley of Ur*, p145

139   'Tomb of the Bird', Breasted, *Pioneer*, see p178 and note

Chapter 10 *'Yes, wonderful things'*, pages 141 - 166
page
141f   Carter's movements in Egypt: *GI*, Carter rough diary (1922 - 24); and see *Discovery*, p86f, and *The Tomb*

141   Callender, *ibid*, p92f

141   Accounts, *Diary*

142   Arrival of Carnarvon and Evelyn: *Discovery*, p90f; and *Diary*

142   Seal impressions, 'past mischief, *Discovery,* p90

143   'Day of days': *Discovery,* p94

143   Engelbach and Lacau: see Drower, *Flinders Petrie,* p348, Lacau known irreverently to archaeologists as 'God the Father'. And on Lacau's professional standing, see Sir Alan Gardiner, *My Working Years,* p34f

144   26th Nov: *Diary*

145   'Yes, wonderful things', *Discovery* p95. Carter's diary entry for that day *(GI)* records, '... Lord Carnarvon said to me "Can you see anything". I replied to him Yes, it is wonderful. I then with precision made the hole sufficiently large for us both to see...'. [author's note] I record this as written. I think Carter can be forgiven the omission of a few punctuation details on such an occasion, and allowed some subsequent poetic leeway

146   Quotes, *ibid*

147   Quotes, *ibid*

147f   Lucas: Lucas, Notes on some of the Objects from the Tomb of Tutankhamun, *ASAE 41* (1942), p135f

148f   Hoving: *Untold Story,* chapter 9

149   Carter's description: *Discovery,* p101

150f   Fifty-six years on: Hoving, of course, wrote his book in 1979. When I wrote the first edition of this work I did not have the benefit of Nicholas Reeves's *Tut.ankh.amun, The Politics of Discovery,* in which he quotes on page xvi an annotated typescript by Carnarvon in the British Museum, 'and then as he [Carter] moved about with the candle, we knew that we had found something absolutely unique... between two life-sized statues of the tomb owner, evidently lay a third chamber, closed off with a plastered and sealed doorway...'. Then: 'The company returned to the Antechamber, and hid their means of access into the Burial Chamber and Treasury with the lid of a basket and some artistically arranged reeds from a decaying mat that was conveniently to hand'. The facts of the matter were now clear, and a few hours later Carnarvon was able excitedly to write to...Alan Gardiner:

'I have got Tutankamen [*sic*] (that is certain) and I believe...intact.' Dated 10 December 1922, *GI*

150 Quote, *Discovery*, 104

151f Hoving, *op.cit.*

153 Three months later: Breasted, *Pioneer*, p316f says 'preparations' made on 15 February 1923 for opening sealed doorway, as does Carter's diary; see note to page 178. On 17 February, Carter's diary recorded, 'Preparations for visitors'. On the 18th the Queen of the Belgians turned up

153 Sgt Adamson: See John Lawton, *ARAMCO World*, vol.32, No.6, 1981. [author's note]. I should perhaps add that my own efforts to persuade members of Mr Adamson's family to discuss with me their father's recollections, drew a blank

154 Official opening, 29 Nov: Carter, *diary*; and *The Times*, 30 Nov. 1922, and *ibid*, Dec. 4/11, first pictures. In fact, the official opening was performed in two parts, the first on the 27th when the local inspector, Ibrahim Effendi, was present. On the 29th, the newly appointed Resident, Lord Allenby, was unable to leave duties in Cairo to attend. The Egyptian Governor of the province attended in his stead

155 Merton and *The Times:* News International plc, *The Times* internal correspondence

156 Chronology of Eighteenth Dynasty and Tutankhamun's ancestry: See Redford's *History and Chronology of the 18th Dynasty of Egypt:* and see Baines and Malek, *Atlas of Ancient Egypt*, Dynasty 18, p44f; and more recent discussion in *Antiquity* magazine between Egyptologists H.W. Fairman and John Ray. An even more detailed debate based on the anatomical and serological examination of human remains some 3,500 years old, is to found in *Nature*, 224, p325f

158 Petrie: *The Times*, 30 November 1922

159 Differences among archaeologists: Carter, letter to Newberry, *GI*, 17 Jan. 1923, and Drower, *Flinders Petrie*, p355, Petrie 'regarded himself fortunate not to have been involved in the unseemly quarrels and petty jealousies...'

159   Reuters: Williams, *The World of Action,* p357
159   Closure of Tomb: *Discovery,* p106, and *diary*
159   In Cairo with Lady Evelyn, *diary,* 7 Dec.1922
159f   Metropolitan Museum staff: *Discovery,* p108; and Reeves, *The Complete Tutankhamun,* p56
160f   Lucas: *ibid,* p106. The evidence cited by Hoving of the opening and resealing of the hole in the door to the burial chamber, based on Lucas's published statement, is plausible, but Lucas's claim to have seen, in Carter's house, before the official opening on 29 November, 'the magnificent perfume box' which Carter had found between the first and second shrines, is less convincing. Lucas did not join Carter until early December when the latter went to Cairo. *Discovery,* p107, and Carter *diary,* 9 Dec. 1922
161   Gardiner and Breasted: Interestingly, this distinguished duo was in Cairo not to see Carter but to co-operate in the copying of texts on the painted interior walls of mastaba tombs of the immediate pre-Middle Kingdom period, in conjunction with Lacau, who had already started on the task. They were soon involved, however, in helping Carter with translations of the Tutankhamun material. See Gardiner, *My Working Years,* p34f
161   Cairo and return to Luxor: *Discovery,* p106f
161   Hoving. *Untold Story*
162f   Lacau and antiquities law: Foreign Office correspond. re. antiquities law, *FO371/8981,* Jan. 1923; 'Dr Hall of BM informs FO that M. Lacau, Maspero's successor in 1913, recently wrote to EES informing them that a new law was being drafted whereby no private excavator would be allowed to take any proportion of the finds out of the country
164   Foreign Office attitude: *FO371/8981-3.* Correspondence between High Commissioner Cairo, and Sir William Tyrrell and Sir Eyre Crowe
164   Sir Leonard Woolley: Winstone, *Woolley of Ur,* p188f
165   Historical perspective, Schliemann etc: Winstone, *Uncovering the Ancient World,* p97f, 229f, 254f

period of the powerful monarchs of the 18th – 20th dynasties

178   Bird story: *Pioneer*, p316f and Hoving, *op.cit.*, p123f

179   Clearing of Antechamber and opening of burial chamber. [author's note], I may have been a day awry in stating in the first edition that the dividing wall was taken down on 17 February. Breasted and Carter's diary are indeterminate, simply saying that 'preparations' were made on the 15th. Reeves, *op.cit.*, says 16th 'Opening of Burial Chamber'. See note to page 153

179   *The Times* agreement: Announced by *The Times* editorially on 17 Jan. News International archive, record by Lint Smith, general manager; *FO371/8982*, Feb. 9, 1923. Also, see Hoving, *Untold Story*, p150f. Hoving cites letter from Merton to Sir Campbell [?Stuart, *The Times* director] dated 24 Dec. 1922

180f   Press response: See Williams, *World of Action*, p359f. And see *Discovery*, Chapter IX, 'Visitors and the Press'

180   Equivocal attitude: Hoving *op.cit.*, p239f. As for Carter's alleged hostility to Carnarvon's arrangement, see *Discovery*, p143, 'we in Egypt were delighted when we heard Lord Carnarvon's decision…'

180   Dawson/Gardiner: Hoving, *op.cit.*, p149f. Hoving cites Professor I.E.S. Edwards, Curator Emeritus, British Museum

180f   Film rights, etc: *ibid*. Hoving cites Carter to Carnarvon (cable), 29 Dec. 1922, and letter Carnarvon to Carter 10 Jan. 1923, suggesting 'auction of press rights', both in Metropolitan Museum files. I have been unable to verify any of the New York museum's evidence. [author]

181   RGS: Gardiner, *My Working Years*, p38. 'Dawson then …added as a persuasive argument that at the time of the Everest expedition this had been given as a monopoly [to *The Times*] to the complete satisfaction and advantage of all concerned'

182   Sightseers, common touches: *The Times*, 15–18 Jan.

182   More marvels: *ibid*, 19–26 Jan.

183   To Cairo: *ibid*, 27 Jan.

183   Newberry lecture: announcement, *ibid*, 30 Jan.

183   *Illustrated London News: IL,N,* 6/13/20/27 January 1923

184   Newspaper opposition, Perry Robinson's team: News International archive, file 1. And see *Discovery,* Chapter IX

184   Williams: Hoving, *op.cit.,* p156f

184   *Daily Express*/H.V. Morton: *ibid*

184   Bradstreet: *ibid*, p109/186

185   Morton's meeting: *ibid*, p156

185   Williams: see his *World of Action*, p359f

186   Burton's pictures in press, 30 Jan: *The Times* Syndication Service

186f   Williams to Tyrrell: *FO371/8982*, telegram 9 Feb. 1923

187   Allenby, *ibid*

187   Breasted: Carter *diary,* 14 Feb. 1923

187f   Opening of burial chamber: *ibid*, 16/18 Feb.

187   Carter's list of guests in the diary is incomplete. Winlock's list in the Met. is given by Hoving, (*Untold Story,* p193): Lord and Lady Allenby, TRH the Princes Kamal ad-Din, Omar Tuson, and Yusef Kamal; the envoys of France, Belgium and the USA; their Excellencies Adly Jegen Pasha, Tufiq Nassim Pasha, Husain Rushdi Pasha, Abdal Khaleq Sarwat Pasha, Muhammad Said Pasha, Ismail Sidky Pasha, and Ismail Sirry Pasha; Lord Carnarvon, Lady Evelyn Herbert, the Hon Mervyn Herbert, Sir Charles Cust, Sir William Garstin, Sir John Maxwell, the Hon. Richard Bethell, Sir Alan Gardiner, the Governor of Q[K]ena Province, HE Abdal Halim Pasha Sule[ai]man; then the working contingent, Carter, Mace, Lythgoe, Winlock, Burton, Callender, Lucas, Merton, Lacau, Engelbach, James and Charles Breasted, and several unidentified representatives of the Government and Press Bureau. Carter also included the Antiquities Department Inspector, Ibrahim Effendi. A separate VIP list compiled by Carnarvon and the Court Chamberlain, consisted of HM King Fuad (who declined, though a personal friend of Carnarvon), HM Queen Elisabeth of the Belgians, the

Crown Prince Leopold, Lord Leigh, Lord and Lady Swaythling, Lady Somerleyton, Sir Philip Sassoon, Sir Louis Malet, Lady Juliet Trevor, the Raja of Poonah

189   Description of visit: Carter, *Discovery,* p186

189   American reactions: *The Times,* 19 Feb., quotes 'American press'

191   Petrie, jewels from Euphrates: the view was perhaps not quite so extraordinary at the time. It was Breasted who coined the phrase 'Fertile Crescent' and who postulated the idea, still held in some respectable quarters, that the Tigris-Euphrates/Nile Valleys were originally 'one cultural unit'. See Field, *The Track of Man,* p41

191   *Morning Post, The Times,* 14 March: Hoving, *Untold Story,* p181; and 'Bradstreet's despicable campaign', p182, 'wantonly malicious campaign', p210, *et al;* quotes confidential letter, Quibell to Carter (undated) from Antiquities Department, 'Both Bradstreet and Valentine Williams have been to see me…'

192   World's newspapers: *The Times* syndicated article 'Luxor 22 February'

193   Closure of tomb: Carter, *diary,* 28 Feb. 1 March, 'paid workmen'

193   Carter and Carnarvon: Breasted, *Pioneer,* p324

194   Treatment of guests: *ibid;* and McCall, *op.cit.,* notes

194   Concession agreements; *EES* 36th AGM, 1922, Report, p12f; See also *Untold Story,* p64f and *Pioneer,* p326

195f   Carnarvon and Carter, letter 23 Feb: *ibid,* p223

197   Movements Feb–March: Carter *diary* shows that while he was busy closing the tomb at this time, Lord Carnarvon and Mace left for Aswan on 28 Feb., returning on 6 March, by which time work at the tomb was resumed

197   Carter and Lady Evelyn: Queen Elisabeth remained in Luxor until 9 March and there was much social activity in Lord Carnarvon's absence. Lady Evelyn seems to have acted as hostess and companion to Carter at this time

197   Lady Evelyn's attitude: Her daughter, Mrs Patricia Leatham, in telephone conversation with me on 17 March 1990,

said: 'When I, as I grew up, asked her about Carter, she replied, "At first I was in awe of him. Later I was 'rather frightened of him.'" Letters from Evelyn to Carter were usually affectionate, however, and used the address 'Dearest Howard', and she often gives an impression of desiring his company (see Hoving, *op.cit.*)
Most of the relevant letters are in the Metropolitan Museum archive and I was denied access to them when writing this biography [author]

197f   Breasted, 12 March: *Pioneer.* It is noteworthy that Carter's diary entry for the same day simply noted the arrival of the Maxwells. On the 13th, Carter noted, 'Arranged with Lord C. for completion of season's work'

198   Evelyn to Carter: *ibid*

198   Lythgoe: *ibid*

198   Bethell: Hoving, *Untold Story,* p224

199   Carnarvon to Aubrey Herbert: Fitzherbert, *The Man Who Was Greenmantle,* p242

200   King to Carnarvon, and Hon. Membership EES: *The Times,* 22 March

200   Death of Carnarvon: French/Arabic Certificat de Décès. 'Henry George Stanhope, Earl of Carnarvon', death due to pneumonia, duration of illness, 8 days

200   Nahman, 31 March: Maurice Nahman had resigned his job as chief cashier at the bank Credite Foncière in order to become an international dealer, and one of Carter's main contacts in Cairo. *Diary,* 31 March, records money received from Lythgoe on behalf of Harkness

Chapter 12 *'Rape of the locks',* pages 202 - 230
page
202   Strange events: see Carnarvon (6th Earl), *No Regrets,* p117

202   Myth and superstition: See Reeves, *The Complete Tutankhamun,* p62f for summary

202   Last Will and Testament, General Registry No. 841, Carnarvon, Earl of, GCSM, of Highclere Castle,

Hampshire, and 1 Seamore Place, Middlesex, d.5 April 1923, at Continetal Hotel, Cairo. Probate granted in London 14 May to Rt. Hon. Sir John Grenfell Maxwell, Sir Robert Hutchinson and Mr Arthur Fitzhardinge Berkely Portman. Effects £416, 554.18.6

203   Carter, *Diary:* 9 April, Lady E. left with Porchester, P&O to Marseilles. 14th, Lady C. left Cairo 11pm with Lord C's remains & Johnnie Blumenthal [Blumenthal's father, George, was President of the Metropolitan Museum]; 16th, Lady C. left on P&O *Malwa.*

203   Bequests: See Last Will, above. And see Reeves, *op.cit.,* p47, 'the Carnarvon collection, listed by Carter in November 1924'

203f   Prosaic matters: diary, 6-14 May. On 28 April Carter noted 'Send Lacau advice re. transporting of material from tomb of Tutankhamen'

204   Cairo to London: *diary* 29 May-3 October

204   In London, *ibid*

205   Visitors, *ibid*

205   Percy White: Reeves, *op.cit.,* p67, suggests that White, a successful novelist and sometime professor of literature at Cairo, contributed significantly to the text of Vol. I of *The Discovery of the Tomb of Tut.ankh.Amen,* as it was originally titled. It is probable in my view that White edited Carter's diary notes in compiling parts 2 and 3 of that volume (Mace was the acknowledged co-author of the first part). A typescript acquired by Carter's niece Phyllis Walker and published long after Carter's death as *The Tomb of Tutankhamen,* may well have been worked on by White, whose ungrudging literary help' is acknowledged in Carter's original Preface. [author]

205f   Visitors, *diary*

206   Almina: See Reeves, *op.cit.,* p63f

206   Evelyn: diary. Her marriage and details of Beauchamp family from contemporary newspaper and 'society' magazine reports, *Who's Who,* and conversations with Mrs Leatham in the Spring of 1990 (see note to p184)

207 Editorial comment and pictures, ILN, 10 March - 13 October 1923
207 Queen Ankhesenamun [Ankhesenpaaten]: here given the name adopted under the reversion to Thebes
207f Due to appear in Nov: ILN, 10 November 1923
208 Meetings with *The Times* staff and others: *Diary*, and News International archive, file I. Quote from *Outlook, 8* Dec. 1923, 'How these archaeologists do love one another!' And see Hoving, *op.cit.*, ref Metropolitan political papers
209 Garden party: 'laconic diary entry', 26 July. 'Mace. Garden party 4pm Buckingham Palace. HM King does not want the mummy removed from there'
209 Breasted, *Pioneer*
209 Literary agent, *diary* 20 July
209f Meetings at *The Times: Diary*, and News International archive, file I
210 Meetings July-Aug: *Diary*
210f Movements and contacts, Aug-Sept: *ibid*
211 Lectures: *ibid,* and News International archive containing diary of events from Jan. 1923 to July 1924, lecture programmes, press cuttings etc. 'Charles B. Cochrane has the honour to announce two lectures on the discovery of the tomb of Tut.Ankh.Amen by Mr Howard Carter, Tuesday 25th and Friday 28th September at 3 pm. New Oxford Theatre'
211 Royal Scottish Geographical Society, *diary*
212 Newberrys: *ibid,* 29 Sept.
212 Ship to Egypt: *ibid,* 3 Oct.
212 Meetings with Egyptian leaders: *ibid*
212 Renewal of contract: Carter, *Tutankhamun, Politics of,* (ed. Reeves), p13f, corresp. with Lacau and others
212 Antiquities Department, Quibell: *ibid*
213 Press arrangements, *ibid*
213 Merton's appointment: *ibid,* p20
213f Negotiations and discussions in Cairo, October-December 1923: *ibid,* and Carter *diary,* Oct-Dec 1923
214 Carter at Luxor: *Diary,* Oct-Nov.

CHAPTER NOTES

214   James Breasted: *Pioneer,* p333

214   Charles Breasted and 'George Waller Mecham': *ibid,* and Hoving, *Untold Story,* p192

215f   Meetings with Ministry of Works, Cairo: See publication 'Statement, With Documents, as to the Events which occurred in Egypt in the Winter of 1923 - 4, leading to the ultimate break with the Egyptian Government' (for Private Circulation only), Cassell and Company Ltd., undated, headed 'The Tomb of Tut.ankh.Amen', and marked 'Confidential'. Also, for precise dates of meetings, Carter, *diary.* And see *Untold Story,* p239f

216   Arrangements with *The Times,* News International archive, diary of events

216f   Gertrude Bell: Unpublished letter, 30 August 1923, University of Newcastle upon Tyne, Department of Archaeology (Bell letters)

218   Continuing press war: *The Times* [News International] archive, 'Luxor discoveries', Jan–Dec. 1923

218f   Season's work: uncovering of shrines, *Discovery,* p150; *The Tomb,* vol 2, p51f; *Pioneer,* p337f; McCall, *op.cit.,* p30f; Carter *diary,* 18 Nov ('opened tomb')-24 Dec. 1923. For most detailed description of work and objects, see Reeves, *op.cit.,* 'The Shrines and Sarcophagus', p100f

220   Mace charted: Mace's diary, November 1923 - February 1924; see notes to Chapter 13. Carter *diary,* 14 November, 'Mace and Bethell arrived on 15th'

220f   Carter ill: By mid December Carter's diary had ceased to record any but essential matters, eg. 1st, wire Breasted, 5th Lunch Sir John Marshall (director of Antiquities Department, India), 15th, renew car license, 17th Press Preview (Shrines), and accounts showing shareholdings: Credit Finance, £710.15.3; National Bank of Egypt, £5959.5.0; Agriculture Bank of Egypt, £1153.7.0. Fortunately, Mace's meticulous record of events fills the gaps from here on

220f   Lacau: *Mace diary,* 13/14 Dec.

221   Breasted: *Pioneer*

Breasted letter for P.M.'; Wednesday 5th, 'Saw Breasted…
(had in his pocket letter I gave him yesterday)'

237f   Breasted and court action: *Pioneer,* p34f. And see *Untold Story,* p300f

Chapter 14 *The American experience,* pages 243 - 265
page
243   In London: GI, Carter diary, Tuesday 25 March, 'arrived Victoria 11 pm' – Saturday 12th April 'I leave for USA per *ss Berengaria'*

243   Mace: Lee, …*the grand piano came by camel,* p38, quotes Lacau, 'M. Mace est toujours calme'

244   Americans in London, American press reports: Hoving, *Untold Story*

244f   Carter's engagements: 'rough diary' 1924: 27 March, 'Seamore Place, 1 pm lunch with Eve; Royal Society, 6.30 pm'

246   Law suit against British Empire Exhibitions Ltd: News International file I, Luxor Discoveries. *The Times,* presumably out of consideration for Carter, did not publicise the case, but the rest of Fleet Street had a field day. See *Daily Express,* 22 April, 'Carter's Wembley Bombshell', *et al.* And correspondence in file between Carter's solicitors, Messrs Hastie's of 65 Lincoln's Inn Fields, and *Daily Express* and *The Times.* See also, Hoving, *op.cit.,* p326

246f   Intolerant attitude: Mrs Mace quoted in Lee, …*the grand piano came by camel,* p48

247f   In America: Carter, *diary,* Saturday 12 April 1924 – Tuesday 8 July 1924, first entry, Saturday 12 April, 'leave for U.S.A. per *ss Berengaria',* last entry Tuesday 8 July 'Returned from U.S.A. per *ss Mauretania.* Arrived Southampton 3 pm, London 7 pm'. And see Hoving, *op.cit.,* chapter 32, 'Carter in America'

253   Winlock: *ibid.* And see Carter, (ed. Reeves), *Tutankhamun, The Politics of Discovery,* Appendix IV, p145, April 7th

CHAPTER NOTES

266 Resumption of work: Merton: *The Times*, 16 and 26 January 1925
267 Visitors: See Wynne, *Behind the Mask*, p235
267 Hogarth at Westminster School, *ibid*, 7 Feb.
268 Lecture, *ibid*, 12 Sept.
268 New season: Carter, *diary*, 23 Sept 1925 – 21 May 1926
268 Grand Continental, Savoy hotels in Cairo amalgamated after war
268f Coffins: *diary*, 13 Oct *et seq;* and *The Tomb*, p51f, Ch.III, 'Clearing the Burial Chamber and Opening the Sarcophagus'
269 Quote: Carter, *ibid*, p51
270 Carter quote, *ibid*
270 Breasted quoted: *Pioneer*, p350
271 Breasted's estimate and observations on Egyptian 'parsimony': *ibid*, p350f
272 Removal of coffin: Carter, *diary*
272f Autopsy: *ibid*
272 Herodotus: *ibid*
277 Official communiqué: *The Times*, 20 Nov. 1925, 'The Luxor Treasure'
277f Derry's report: *The Tomb*, Appendix I, 'Report upon the examination of Tutankhamen's mummy'
278f Elliot Smith, quoted: *ibid.* Tutankhamun's age, reign and relationships: I have been guided in an on-going argument by Carter, *Discovery*, and by Fairman in *Antiquity*, XLVI, Redford, *History and Chronology of the Eighteenth Dynasty of Egypt,* Baines and Malek, *Atlas of Ancient Egypt,* and Aldred, *Akhenaten King of Egypt*. But see also, Reeves, *op.cit.,* chapter 'Chronology and Family Relationships'; and see the *Independent* newspaper, 24 Jan. 05, where Dr Michael Ridley, director of the famous Tutankhamun permanent exhibition in Dorchester, England, comments on the latest scientific tests with regard to the cause of the king's death: '...it is unlikely that they will provide much in the way of new evidence'. He asserts, however, widely accepted view among Egyptologists that he died from a

blow to the head, though it is still debatable whether from a deliberate or accidental act

302 Store Room and contents: *Egyptian Gazette,* quoted in *The Times,* 4 Dec. 6 Dec. Min. of Public Works communiqué lists objects incl., figure of Anubis, box of king's jewels, earrings, sceptres, boats, etc.

303 Allenby and Lloyd: Wavell, *Allenby,* p347

Chapter 17 *Of the living and the dead,* pages 304 - 327
page

304 New season, Sept. 1927 - April 1928: Carter, *diary*

304 Clearance of Annexe: *ibid,* and *The Tomb,* p272f. See also Desroches-Noblecourt, *Tutankhamen,* p90f, and Reeves, *Complete Tutankhamun,* p70f

304 Lady Carnarvon: Carter, *Tut.Ankh.Amen* (ed. Reeves), Appendix III, p138f

304 Rushdi Effendi, Burton and Landauer, Carter, *diary*

304 30 Nov: Burton commences the photographic records of the Annexe, *ibid*

305 Final draft: *Discovery,* p134f

305 Breasted and Gardiner: *ibid,* p109

305 Carter at pains: *diary,* notes 'Season 1927 - 28'

306 Carter's impressions: *Discovery,* Ch. VIII, 'Clearing the Antechamber'

307 British Association; *The Times,* 6 Aug. 1926

307f Historical summary: *The Tomb,* p278f

308 Visitors: *diary*

309 Jan-Feb 1928: *ibid;* and *The Times,* 4 Jan., 'More Tutankhamun Discoveries' and 6 Feb. 'Further Discoveries'. The report of the 6th (written on the 4th), stated 'As the tomb is now open to visitors, Mr. Howard Carter has been obliged to suspend his work'

309f Death of Mace, April 1928: Lee, ...*the grand piano came by camel,* p53f. Remarkably, I could find no reference to this event in his 'rough' diary for the period; probably written some time in arrears

310 'Willie lost his wife – 3 pm': Carter, *diary,* 4 Dec. 1924

311 Madrid lecture: Carter, 'Notes upon objects in Store

Room, 1925 – 27', *GI,* used in compilation of Spanish lecture notes

311   New Season, Sept. 1928 – April 1929: Carter's 'rough' *diary*

311   Burton/Lucas: *diary,* 9 Oct – 4 Dec.

312   Troubles, 15 November 1928: *diary*

312   Lint Smith, Merton/Hastie: News International file, Egypt 1912 – 30

313   Tyrell to Dawson: *FO371/14647,* File J2703, 12 August 1930

313   Nefertiti: *Sunday Times,* 6 April 1930

313   Carnarvon settlement: *diary,* ('Season 1929 – 30'); and *FO371/14647*

314   Merton: News International file, 1912 – 1930

315   Dr Mahmud: *ibid*

315   Savile Club: club secretary in correspondence with author

315   Last two seasons: Carter, *diaries,* 1929 – 30 and 1930 – 1

316   Thompson, *Mixed Memoirs,* p148, Nov/Dec. 1930

317   'Sunk in gloom': Margaret S. Drower to author, 2 March 1990

317   Gardiner: Cottrell, *The Lost Pharaohs,* p168

318   Griffith Institute: see introduction to this volume

319   Young man's story: Carter, *Notebook 16,* Sketch V, 'The Rat and the Snake'

319f The last days: I have relied to some extent on the research of Henrietta McCall, carried out in connection with her degree work at Oxford through the Griffith Institute, and on the recollections of contemporaries and their offspring

320   Lady Evelyn Beauchamp: author's conversation with Mrs Patricia Leatham; see earlier note

321   Visits to Norfolk: Mr D C Butters, Swaffham Museum, and author's correspondence with Miss Elisabeth Reeves and Mr N.G. Stafford Allen, 7/12 Feb. 1990

322   Drinkwater: notes in author's possession taken by Henrietta McCall in interview with the late Cyril Aldred

322   Axel Munthe: see *The Story of San Michele,* p257 (1937 edn), re claim to have hypnotised a cobra into state of catalepsy in Karnak temple

322   Last consignment: note from Service des Antiquités, 17 March 1931

322   Lecture, University College: *The Times,* 22 July 1931

324   Callender: Reeves, *op.cit.,* p57/63; and Consular Registry, London

324   Woolley at Ur: Winstone, *Woolley of Ur;* and see Mallowan, *Memoirs*

325   Agatha Christie and Mallowan: *ibid;* and see McCall, *Max Mallowan*

325   Egyptian view: See Sabit, *A King Betrayed,* p99

326   Alexander: Carter had almost certainly read of Belzoni's vain search for the Siwa oasis where the Macedonian King was reputed to have been buried, and he (Carter) often claimed to have found the resting place in search of which a Persian army once perished. In 1999 Michael Haag, author of several books and articles on Alexander and his city, wrote to me: '...if it [Carter's claim] was not some off the cuff remark arising out of bitterness, and if he had indeed decided that the tomb was somewhere, is there anything to suggest that that somewhere was Alexandria, or that everyone was off track and that it might have been elsewhere, eg. Saqqara?' I put the question unavailingly to several Egyptologists over the years and to Dr Jaromir Malek of the Griffith Institute, but no clue has so far emerged as to the veracity of Carter's story. Mr Haag told me in 2005 that a French team was searching an area of the Christian cemetery in Alexandria. Perhaps Carter was as good as his word to his Belgian royal guests in 1936, and took the secret to his own grave

326   Death: *The Times,* 3 March 1939

326f   Burial: *ibid,* 7 March. It should perhaps be said that each year on the anniversary of Carter's death and into the last years of the 20th century a single bouquet of flowers was laid anonymously on the grave, which otherwise showed every sign of neglect

       The authorities at Putney Vale Cemetery always claimed ignorance of the donor [author]

Chapter 18 *Aftermath,* pages 328 - 338
page

328 Carter estate: Registry London. Probate 5 July (1939). Effects £2002.19.8d. Resealed Cairo 1 September 1939. The will was witnessed by Francis Franklin, solicitor, of 28 Lincoln's Inn Fields, and P. Wilson his clerk

328f Artefacts from tomb: *FO371/23355,* 9 March 1939, re. accusations against Engelbach, and 7 December, re articles from tomb 'found among personal possessions of late Mr Howard Carter'. See article by Mary Greene in *Independent,* 3 July 1990, 'A Child Among the Pharaohs', based on interview with Mrs Margaret Orr, daughter of Arthur Mace; quotes her mother 'disapproved of Carter'

330 Involvement of HMG: *ibid*

330 Williams: see his *World of Action,* p363; Wilkinson: later curator of near Eastern Art, MMA. See *Untold Story,* p58

331 Card index: *GI*

331f Hoving: *Untold Story,* chapter, 'The Secret Division'

333f Objects from tomb of Amenophis III: List dated 17 Nov. 1924. *The Times,* 15 October. 1990. The discovery was made by Dr Reeves, curator at Highclere in 1988. And see quote by author in 'Peterborough', *Daily Telegraph,* 9 March 1988

335 Return to tomb: notes made by Henrietta McCall in interview (undated) with the late Cyril Aldred

336 Adamson: Interestingly, Adamson's career in the Palestine Police force is shown on the internet with reference to records in the Middle East Centre, St Antony's College, Oxford, but I can find no reference to his alleged work at the tomb. But Reeves, *op.cit.,* p57, accepts the evidence of interviewees and includes his signature among those of the rest of the Carter team

337 Callender: Registry, London, *entry 7a 470.* Reeves, *ibid,* p56f, gives 'd.1937?'. He was born according to the Registry at Boston (Lincs ?), March 1876, but no official record of death

337 Burton: Reeves, *ibid,* 1879 - 1940

SELECT BIBLIOGRAPHY

For abbreviations used here and elsewhere, see legend in CHAPTER NOTES

Aldred, Cyril, *The Egyptians: Ancient Peoples and Places,* London and New York, 1961
— *Egyptian Art,* London, 1961
— *Akhenaten and Nefertiti,* London, 1973
— *Akhenaten King of Egypt,* London, 1988
Allen, T.G., *The Egyptian Book of the Dead,* Chicago, 1960
Amherst, Lady of Hackney, *A Sketch of Egyptian History,* London, 1904
Andrews, Carol, *Near Eastern Art,* London, 1969
— *Catalogue of Egyptian Antiquities VI, Jewellery from Earliest Times to the End of the Seventeenth Century,* London, 1981
— *Egyptian Mummies,* London, 1984
Antrobus, George P., *King's Messenger 1918 - 1940,* London, 1941
Baikie, J, *The Amarna Age: A Study of a Crisis in the Ancient World,* London, 1926
Baines, John and Malek, Jaromir, *Atlas of Ancient Egypt,* Oxford, 1978
Belzoni, Giovanni–Battista, *Narrative of the Operations and Recent Discoveries within the Pyramids, Temples, Tombs and Excavations in Egypt and Nubia; etc.,* London, 1820
Bénédite, Georges, *Egypte,* Paris, 1900
Bierbrier, M.I., *The Tomb Builders of the Pharaohs,* London, 1982
Bissing, F.W. von (Baron), Ein thebanischer Grabfund aus dem Anfange des neuen Reichs, plates from drawings by H. Carter, Berlin, 1900
Brackman, Arnold, *The Search for the Gold of Tutankhamun,* New York, 1976
Breasted, Charles, *Pioneer to the Past,* London 1948
Breasted, J.H., *Ancient Records of Egypt: Historical Documents,* Chicago, 1906
— *History of Egypt,* New York, 1910
Brier, Bob, *The Murder of Tutankhamun, A 3000-year-old Murder Mystery,* London, 1998

Brovarski, E, and others, *Egypt's Golden Age, The Art of Living in the New Kingdom, 1558 – 1085 BC,* Boston, 1982

Brunton, Winifred (ed.), *Great Ones of Ancient Egypt. Portraits by Winifred Brunton, History of Eminent Egyptologists, Foreword by Professor J.H. Breasted,* London 1925

Budge, E.A. Wallis, *By Nile and Tigris,* 2 vols, London, 1920

— *Tutankhamen, Amenism, Atenism and Egyptian Monotheism,* London, 1923

— *The Mummy,* Cambridge, 1925

— *Amulets and Superstitions,* Oxford, 1930

— *From Fetish to God in Ancient Egypt,* Oxford, 1934

Cambridge Ancient History

Capart, Jean (ed.), *Letters of Charles Edwin Wilbour,* Brooklyn, 1936

— and others, *Tout-Ankh-Amon,* Brussels, 1943

Carnarvon, 6th Earl of, *No Regrets,* London, 1976

Carter, Howard, *The Tomb of Tut.Ankh.Amen,* 2 Vols, London, 1927/1933

— *The Discovery of the Tomb of Tutankhamen,* New York, 1977

— *The Tomb of Tutankhamen,* London, 1972; (introd. John Romer), London, 1983

— *Tut.Ankh.Amen, The Politics of Discovery,* edited and introduced by Nicholas Reeves, London, 1998

— and Mace, A.C., *The Tomb of Tut.ankh.Amen. discovered by the late Earl of Carnarvon and Howard Carter,* London, 1923

— and Newberry, Percy Edward, *The Tomb of Thoutmosis IV,* Antiquités Egyptiennes du Musée du Caire, Nos 46001-46529, London, 1904

Ceram, C.W., *Gods, Graves and Scholars,* London, 1967

Cerny, Jaroslav, *The Valley of the Kings,* Cairo, 1973

Collins, Andrew, and Ogilvie-Herald, *Tutankhamun, The Exodus Conspiracy,* London, 2002

Cone, P (ed.) *The Discovery of Tutankhamun's Tomb,* New York, 1976

Cottrell, Leonard, *The Lost Pharaohs,* London, 1950

— *Lost Cities,* London, 1957

— *Wonders of Antiquity,* London, 1960

Cooney, J.D., *Amarna Reliefs from Hermopolis in American Collections,* Brooklyn, 1965

Daniel, Glyn, *A Hundred and Fifty Years of Archaeology,* London, 1975

Daressy, Georges, *Fouilles de la Vallée des Rois* 1898 - 1899, Cairo 1902

Davies, N.M., and Gardiner, A.H., *The Tomb of Huy, Viceroy of Nubia in the Reign of Tut'ankhamun,* London, 1926

— *Ancient Egyptian Painting* (3 vols), Chicago, 1936

Davies, N de G., *The Rock Tombs of El Amarna,* I –VI, London, 1903 - 08

Davis, Theodore M., *The Tomb of Thoutmosis IV,* London, 1904

— *Biban El Moluk. Description and Excavation of the Tomb of Hatshopsitu,* London, 1906

— *Theodore M. Davis's Excavations, The Tomb of Iouiya and Touiyou,* illustrated by H. Carter, London, 1907

— and others, *The Tomb of Sipta,* London, 1908

— *The Tomb of Queen Tiyi,* London, 1910

— and others, *The Tombs of Harmharbi and Touatankhamanou,* London, 1912

Dawson, W.R., and Uphill, E.T., *Who was Who in Egyptology,* London, 1972

Desroches-Noblecourt, Christiane, *Tutankhamen: The Life and Death of a Pharaoh,* London, 1963

Deuel, Leo, *The Treasures of Time,* Ohio, 1961

Drower, Margaret S., *Flinders Petrie,* London, 1985

Edwards, Amelia B., *A Thousand Miles Up the Nile,* London, 1877

— *Pharaohs, Fellahs and Explorers,* London, 1982

Edwards, I.E.S., *The Pyramids of Egypt,* London, 1961

— *Treasures of Tutankhamun,* London, 1978

— *Tutankhamun – His Tomb and its Treasures,* London, 1979

Eliot-Smith, G., and Dawson, W.R., *Egyptian Mummies,* London, 1924

Emery, W.B., *Archaic Egypt,* London, 1961

Faulkner, Raymond O., *The Ancient Egyptian Book of the Dead,* (ed. Andrews), London, 1985

Fitzherbert, Margaret, *The Man Who Was Greenmantle,* London, 1983

Fox, Penelope, *Tutankhamun's Treasure,* Oxford, 1951

Frankfurt, Henri, *Ancient Egyptian Religion,* New York, 1961

Freud, Sigmund, *Moses and Monotheism*, London, 1940

Gardiner, Alan, *Egypt of the Pharaohs,* Oxford, 1961

— *My Working Years,* Privately Published, 1962

Giles, F.J., *Ikhnaton, Legend and History*, London, 1970

Greenwood, Sarah, *Highclere Castle,* Banbury, 1988

Herbert, George E.S.M., 5th Earl of Carnarvon, and Carter, H., *Five Years' Exploration at Thebes*, with chapters by F.Ll. Griffith, George Legrain, George Moeller, Percy E. Newberry, William Spielberg and Henry Frowde, London, 1912

Holst, Meno, *Hinter versiegelten Tueren, Unter Forschern, Pharaonen und Fellachen,* Reutlingen, 1956

Hornung, E, *Conceptions of God in Ancient Egypt,* London, 1983

Hoving, Thomas, *Tutankhamun: The Untold Story,* London, 1979

James, T.G.H., *Hieroglyphic Texts From Egyptian Stelae etc,* Part IX, London, 1970

— *Excavating in Egypt: The Egypt Exploration Society 1882 - 1982,* London, 1982

— *The British Museum and Ancient Egypt,* London, 1983

— *Howard Carter, The Path to Tutankhamun,* London 1992

— and Davies, W.V., *Egyptian Sculpture,* London, 1983

Lee, Christopher C., *...the grand piano came by camel, The Story of Arthur C. Mace,* Lochwinnoch Community Museum, Department of Arts and Libraries, Renfrew, 1989

Lucas, A, and Harris, J.R., *Ancient Egyptian Materials and Industries,* London, 1962

McCall, Henrietta, *The Life of Max Mallowan,* British Museum 2001

Mallakh, K. al, and Brackman, A.C., *The Gold of Tutankhamen,* New York, 1978

Mariette, Auguste, *The Monuments of Upper Egypt,* London, 1877

Marlowe, John, *Spoiling the Egyptians,* London, 1974

Maspero, Sir Gaston, *La Trouvaille de Deir al Bahari,* Cairo, 1881

— *Les Momies Royales de Deir al Bahari,* Paris, 1889

— *The Struggle of the Nations,* London, 1896

— *New Light on Ancient Egypt,* London, 1908

— *Egypt: Ancient Sites and Modern Scenes,* London, 1910

Mekhitarian, A., *Egyptian Painting,* Geneva, 1978

Michalowski, K., *The Art of Ancient Egypt,* London, 1969

Munthe, Axel, *The Story of San Michele,* London 1929 (Thin paper edition, 1937)

Murray, Margaret, *My First Hundred Years,* London, 1963

Nagel, G., *Egypt,* London, 1978

Peet, T. Eric, *The Great Tomb-robberies of the Twentieth Egyptian Dynasty,* Oxford, 1943

Pendlebury, J.D.S., *Tell el Amarna,* London, 1935

Perepelkin, G., *The Secrets of the Gold Coffin,* Moscow, 1978

Petrie, Sir W. Flinders, *Qurneh,* London, 1888

— *Tell el Amarna,* London, 1894

— *A History of Egypt,* Methuen, London, 1924

— *Seventy Years in Archaeology,* London, 1924

Piankoff, Alexandre, *Egyptian Religious Texts and Representations* (5 vols), Princeton, 1954-68

Redford, Donald F., *History and Chronology of the Eighteenth Dynasty of Egypt,* Toronto, 1967

Reeves, Nicholas, *The Complete Tutankhamun,* London, 1990

— (ed.) *Tut.Ankh.Amun, The Politics of Discovery* by Howard Carter, London 1998

Reisner, G., *The Development of the Egyptian Tomb,* Oxford, 1936

Romer, John, *Valley of the Kings,* Michael Joseph, London, 1981

Sabit, Adel M., *A King Betrayed: The Ill-Fated Reign of Farouk of Egypt,* London, 1989

Sayce, A.H., *Reminiscences,* London, 1923

Smith, Sir Grafton E., *Tutankhamen and the Discovery of the Tomb by the late Earl of Carnarvon and Mr H. Carter,* London, 1923

Smith, Joseph Lindon, *Tombs, Temples and Ancient Art,* Oklahoma, 1956

Smith, Sydney, *Sir Flinders Petrie,* London, 1943

Thomas, Elizabeth, *The Royal Necropoleis of Thebes,* Princeton, 1966

Wavell, Field Marshal Viscount, *Allenby: Soldier and Statesman,* London, 1946

Weigall, A., *A Guide to the Antiquities of Upper Egypt,* London, 1910

— *The Treasury of Ancient Egypt,* London, 1911

— *Tutankhamun and Other Essays,* London, 1924

— *A History of the Pharaohs,* New York, 1925

Wheeler, R.E.M., *Archaeology from the Earth,* Oxford, 1954

Wheeler-Holohan, V., *The History of the King's Messengers,* London, 1935

Wilbour, Charles Edwin, *Travels in Egypt* (ed. Capart), New York, 1936

Williams, Valentine, *The World of Action,* London, 1938

Wilson, John A., *Signs and Wonders upon Pharaoh: a History of American Archaeology,* Chicago, 1964

Winstone, H.V.F., *Gertrude Bell,* London, 1978

— *The Illicit Adventure,* London, 1982

— *Uncovering the Ancient World,* London, 1985

— *Woolley of Ur,* London, 1990

Wood, Christopher, *The Dictionary of Victorian Painters,* 2nd ed., London, 1978

Wynne, Barry, *Behind the Mask of Tutankhamun,* London, 1972

Specialist Sources

Allen, J.P., 'The Natural Philosophie of Akhenaten' in Simpson (ed.) *Religion and Philosophy in Ancient Egypt,* Yale, 1989

Beinlich, Horst, and Mohamed Saleh, *Corpus der Hieroglyphischen Inschriften aus dem Grab des Tutanchamun* (2 vols), Warminster, 1989

Bierbrier, M.I., *The Late New Kingdom in Egypt,* Warminster, 1975

— *Hieroglyphic Text from Egyptian Stelae etc,* Part X, London, 1982

British Museum, Catalogue of loan Exhibition, *Treasures of Tutankhamun,* (introd. I.E.S. Edwards), London, 1972

Brunton, Guy, 'Howard Carter' *obit., ASAE 39,* 1939

Burton, Henry (Harry), 'The Late Theodore M. Davis Excavations at Thebes, 1912 - 13', *Bulletin of Metropolitan Museum of Art,* XI, 1916

Butters, David, *In the Pedlar's Footsteps,* North Walsham, 1990

Carter, Howard, 'Report on the Tomb of Sen-nefer', *ASAE 2,* 1901

— 'Report on the robbery of the Tomb of Amenophis II', *ASAE 2,* 1902

— 'Report on General Work', *ASAE 4,* 1903

— 'Excavations at Biban el Moluk', *ASAE 4,* 1903

— 'Report on work done in Upper Egypt', *ASAE 4,* 1905

— 'Report on the Tomb of Zeser-ka-ra, Amen-hetep I, discovered by the Earl of Carnarvon in 1914', *JEA 3,* 1916

— 'A Tomb prepared for Queen Hatshepsut', *JEA 4,* 1917

—, and Gardiner, Alan, 'The Tomb of Ramesses IV and the Turin Plan', *JEA 4,* 1917

City of Akhenaten, The, (3 vols), EES, London 1923 - 51; contributions by Peet, Woolley, Gunn, Guy, Newton, Frankfurt, Pendlebury, and others

Davies, N. de Garis, *The Tomb of Nefer-Hotep at Thebes* (2 vols), Metropolitan Museum of Art, Egyptian Expedition, New York, 1933

—, and Gardiner, A.H., *The Tomb of Huy, Viceroy of Nubia in the Reign of Tutankhamun, EES,* 1926

— and Martin, G.T., *The Rock Tombs of El Amarna* (7 vols), Archaeological Survey of Egypt, London, 1903 - 8

Derry, D.E., 'Note on the skeleton hitherto believed to be that of King Akhenaten', *ASAE 31,* 1931

— 'Report upon the examination of Tutankhamen's mummy', in Carter, *The Tomb of Tutankhamen,* 1972

— 'The Dynastic Race in Egypt', *JEA 42,* 1956

Deutsche Orient-Gesellschaft, seit 1898, im *Dienste der Forschung,* Short history compiled by Museum für Vor and Frühgeschichte, Schloss Charlottenburg, Berlin

Dijk, J. van and Eaton-Krauss, M., 'Tutankhamun at Memphis', *MDAIK 42,* 1986

Eaton-Krauss, M, 'Tutankhamun at Karnak', *MDAIK 44,* 1988

Engelbach, R., 'Material for a revision of the history of the Heresy Period of the XVIIIth Dynasty', *ASAE 40,* 1940

— 'An Essay on the Advent of the Dynastic Race', *ASAE 42,* 1943

Fairman, H.W. 'Tutankhamun and the End of the 18th Dynasty', *Antiquity,* 46, 1972

Gunn, B., 'Notes on the Aten and his names', *JEA 9,* 1923

— 'Notes on two Egyptian kings, *JEA,* 1926

Gueterbock, H.G., 'The deeds of Suppiluliuma as told by his son, Mursil II', *Journal of Cuneiform Studies,* 10, 1956

Harris, James, E. and Weeks, Kent R., *X-Raying the Pharaohs,* New York, 1973

Harrison, R.G., 'The Anatomical Examination of the Pharaonic Remains Purported to be Akhenaten', *JEA 52,* 1966

Herbert, Almina Victoria Maria Alexandra, Countess of Carnarvon, *Christie's Catalogue of sale of French furniture,* Sèvres porcelain, gifts of late Alfred de Rothschild, auctioned on 19 May 1925; and drawings and pictures auctioned on 22 May 1925

Jones, Dilwyn, *Model Boats from the Tomb of Tut'ankhamun,* Warminster, 1988

Knudtzon. J., and others, *Die el-Amarna Tafeln* (2 vols), Leipzig, 1915; reprinted as *Tell el-Amarna Tablets* by S. Mercer, Toronto, 1939

Leek, F. Filce, *the Human Remains from the Tomb of Tut'ankhamun,* Warminster, 1972

Littauer, M.A. and Crouwell, J.H., *Chariots and Related Equipment from the Tomb of Tutankhamun,* Warminster, 1986

Lucas, Arthur, note on the Temperature and Humidity of Several Tombs in the Valley, *ASAE 24,* 1924

— notes on Some of the Objects from the Tomb of Tutankhamun, *ASAE 41,* 1942

Manniche, L., *Musical Instruments from the Tomb of Tut'ankhamun,* Warminster, 1976

McCall, Henrietta, 'Howard Carter, Egyptologist 1874 - 1939' (unpublished thesis), 1987

Mcleod, W., *Composite Bows from the Tomb of Tut'ankhamun,* Griffith Institute publication, Warminster, 1970

— *Self Bows and other Archery Tackle from the Tomb of Tut'ankhamun,* Warminster, 1982

Meyer, E., *Aus dem Sande Aegyptens,* Mitteilungen der DO-G 62, 1923 1 5ff, Berlin

— *Die Stadt von Echnaton und Nofretete,* Mitteilungen der DO-G 55, 1914 3ff

Murray, Helen, and Nuttall, Mary, A Handlist to Howard Carter's *Catalogue of Objects in Tutankhamun's Tomb,* Griffith Institute, Warminster, 1963

Naville, H. Edouard, *The Temple of Deir al Bahari* (6 vols), EEF, 1895 - 1908

Newberry, Percy E., 'Howard Carter' obit., *JEA 25,* 1939

— 'Report on the floral wreaths in the coffins of Tutankhamen', in Carter, *The Tomb of Tutankhamen,* 1972

Petrie, W.M. Flinders, 'Tell el Amarna' *Illustrated London News,* 22 October 1892

Piankoff, A., *The Shrines of Tut-Ankh-Amon,* Bollingen Series XL.2, New York, 1955

Tait, W.T., *Game Boxes and Accessories from the Tomb of Tut'ankhamun,* Warminster, 1982

Tutankhamen's Treasure, catalogue, American Association of Museums and Smithsonian Institute, 1961 - 2

Vergote, J., *Tutankhamon dans les archives bittites,* Historical-Archaeology Institute of the Netherlands in the Near East, Istanbul, 1961

Weigall, Arthur, 'Excavations and Explorations in Egypt', *EEF* Report, 1909 - 10

Woolley, C. Leonard, 'The Heretic Pharaoh's Prime Minister and his House', *Illustrated London News,* 16 December 1922

Other specialist sources are acknowledged in chapter notes.

INDEX

Ancient dates in text and index are generally those given in the latest available edition of the *Cambridge Ancient History*. Alternative forms and vowel renderings of ancient and Arabic words are shown in square brackets.